GHOST FLEET OF MALLOWS BAY

Other Books by the Author

GHOST FLEET OF MALLOWS BAY
And Other Tales of the
Lost Chesapeake

Donald G. Shomette

TIDEWATER PUBLISHERS
Centreville, Maryland

Library of Congress Cataloging-in-Publication Data

Shomette, Donald.
    Ghost fleet of Mallows Bay and other tales of the lost Chesapeake / Donald G. Shomette. — 1st ed.
       p.   cm.
    Includes index.
    ISBN 0-87033-480-8
    1. Chesapeake Bay (Md. and Va.)—Antiquities. 2. Shipwrecks—Chesapeake Bay (Md. and Va.) 3. Excavations (Archaeology)—Chesapeake Bay (Md. and Va.) 4. Underwater archaeology—Chesapeake Bay (Md. and Va.) 5. New Jersey (Steamship)   I. Title.
F187.C5S47   1996
975.5'18—dc20   96-30525

Manufactured in the United States of America
First edition

Contents

Preface

The history and lore of the Chesapeake Bay are as enduring and vast as that great body of water itself. Indeed, they are nothing less than the chronicle of a sprawling, boisterous, wondrous America in microcosm. Yet, they are eternally in need of a new suit of clothes, as generation after generation leave their particular imprints upon the bosom of the Chesapeake's waters. Thus, legions of historians, antiquarians, and well-meaning dabblers have continually sought to redocument and redefine the Bay's past, dressing it in the most recent and fashionable apparel. Some have succeeded with eloquence and veracity, providing new insights into the Tidewater's marvelous heritage and its relevance to who we were, and who we are. Others have merely rewritten rewrites, often as not erroneously reinventing history to suit their peculiar theories, while seeking their own sense of roots. Yet all, until recent years, have relied entirely upon the amalgam of the written record to provide the reader with parameters for their own perceptions of the past.

Sadly, the truth is that the historic record itself is often flawed, corrupted, or nonexistent. Throughout history, indeed until recent times, only a very small percentage of the population was literate, and the record of state or church (or whoever was in charge) was imbued with the official bias of the establishment. That which pertained to the daily life of Everyman or was unacceptable to the status quo of authority or society was entirely ignored or, worse, destroyed. Indeed, the deliberate or unthinking devastation of records has consigned untold acreages of the past to seeming oblivion. Our conviction that everything is documented and will survive us, carrying the memory of ourselves and our deeds forever into the future, is as erroneous as our belief in the impartiality of the historic record itself. We have only to look back a century or so, to our more recent ancestors, most of whom, unlike in earlier times, were literate and left records of a wide variety, to see how quickly we can forget. Most of us cannot even name our own great-grandparents. Unfortunately, our regard for the historic record itself exhibits a predilection for awe and reverence reserved only for the "first this," and the "biggest that," which the noted historical archaeologist Ivor Noël Hume once called the Barnum and Bailey Syndrome. Our historical selectivity of what is and what

Preface

is not important has often been as counterproductive to our under-standing of the whole picture as any destruction of records could be.

Despite the great attention given to Chesapeake Tidewater history in the last few decades, vast potential areas of study have gone untapped for a variety of reasons. The shrine complex, based upon our interest in kinship and the need to laud our heroes and more virtuous aspects of our culture, has, until recently, guided our every direction. As a people we are reluctant to embrace the common man or our darker side, our faults, or our weaknesses. Nevertheless, the products of these all-too-human characteristics have left their footprints in the archaeological record, as indelibly as any ink upon a document.

In the study of the actual physical remnants of everyday life, as well as those of the epochal events that have formed and channeled the broader course of history, the very material register of humanity itself can produce an unbiased perspective on the past or fill in the chinks of documentary records that are incomplete or no longer existent. Through the science of archaeology, by which the remains of humankind can be methodically and systematically studied, we can reinforce, challenge, endorse, or correct the written record. We can provide data for undocumented events and peoples and for preliterate times that would otherwise be impossible to scrutinize.

In presenting the trilogy of stories herein I have sought to step aside from the traditional subjects of Chesapeake history. My research into the little-known but no-less-important aspects of Tidewater events, utilizing both the written record and archaeological inquiry, addresses topics that may be unsavory or unacceptable to some. Although they challenge some of our views of our icons and selves as being without blemishes, I have sought to avoid the conventional biases that have influenced the very perception of regional history and the myriad peoples who made it. I have attempted to let both the historic and archaeological records speak for themselves whenever possible.

Yet, I am aware that not everyone will be happy with the presentations or embrace my perspective: many avocational divers will probably be embarrassed with the account of the destruction of the wreck of the steamboat *New Jersey*, a unique archaeological time capsule, for the sake of private relic collecting; traditionalists supporting the long-held notion that the Lords Baltimore represented the epitome of toleration, that St. Mary's City was the first permanent European occupation in what is now the state of Maryland, and that the Virginian "pirate" William Claiborne was evil incarnate will not take kindly to the tale of the founding of the Claiborne settlement on Kent Island; and the proponents of American "can-do" resourcefulness and the infallibility of government-at-any-cost may find the account of the Ghost Fleet of Mallows Bay, a paradigm for today, unsettling. Yet, all three stories are voyages into rich Tidewater

Preface

history, albeit launched from a different point of embarkation. In order that the reader may further investigate the historic record into which I have dipped my oars, I have provided "sailing directions and soundings," as Samuel Eliot Morison so elegantly called them, in bibliographic note form.

As few successful voyages are launched without a trusty cadre of officers and a stout crew, so it is with the publication of this book. I would like first to recognize the enormous contributions of my colleagues Dr. Fred W. Hopkins Jr., Emory Kristof, Michael Pohuski, John Kiser, and Joseph M. McNamara, for this work is as much a product of their talents and labors as of mine. Indeed, this book could not have been written without them. Without the support of Wilbur E. Garrett and William Graves, of the National Geographic Society, Edward R. Miller, of the National Oceanic and Atmospheric Administration, and Tyler Bastian, former Maryland State Archaeologist, Maryland Geological Survey, the *New Jersey* Project, which is chronicled herein, would never have happened. Without the support of Michael Humphries, Director of the St. Clement's Island–Potomac River Museum, the Mallows Bay Project, the apex of this work, would still be a mere chimera. I would also like to recognize the support provided by my colleagues in Nautical Archaeological Associates, Inc., Nicholas Freda, Kenneth Hollinghsead, Larry Pugh, Dale Shomette, and Eldon Volkmer, all of whom have worked long and hard in many of the endeavors I have documented.

Many institutions have provided support for both my field investigations and the promulgation of this book. Principal among them is the Maryland Historical Trust and its Director J. Rodney Little, Chief Archaeologist Richard Hughes, and Maryland State Underwater Archaeologist Dr. Susan Langley. Special thanks is extended to the St. Clement's Island–Potomac River Museum, for its unstinting support of the Mallows Bay Project. My gratitude is also extended to the staffs of the Calvert Marine Museum, the Library of Congress, the Maryland Geological Survey, the Maryland Historical Society, the Mariners' Museum, the National Archives and Records Service, the National Oceanic and Atmospheric Administration, the National Park Service, the Steamship Historical Society, the U.S. Army Corps of Engineers, the University of Baltimore, the U.S. Navy, and the Public Record Office, London, England, for providing a wide range of services and superb assistance, both in their archives and in the field.

Literally thousands of hours of research and field time, donated by many people, went into producing the historic and archaeological fruits presented in these narratives of events. For their efforts in the *New Jersey* Project I would like to recognize John Brewer, Michael Cather, Alvin Chandler, Dr. Jay Cooke, Capt. Jerry Cox, Lt. Comdr. Robert Gwalchmai, CN, Capt. Varice Henry, Harold Herring, Mark Jacobs, Keith Moorehead,

Preface

Theodore Morgan, Chris Nicholson, David Porta, Dr. James Qualls, Donald Scott, David Sisson, Helga Sprunk, Dr. Kenneth Stewart, Dr. Garry Wheeler Stone, Greg Strinson, Gary Walton, Dr. Kenneth Weaver, Dana Yoeger, Rick Younger, and, most especially, Martin and Peter Wilcox.

For their assistance on the Claiborne Project, I would like to thank Bobby Aaron, Bill Baxter, John Chamberlin, Dr. Ervan G. Garrison, Trudy Guthrie, Ted Lee, Darrin Lowery, Jackie Ringgold, Willie Roe, Steve Ruth, Reverdy Saddler, Betty Seifert, Fred Skove, the Archaeological Society of Maryland, and the wonderful citizens of Kent Island, Maryland, who opened their homes, hearts, and history time and again to total strangers.

The mysteries of Mallows Bay would never have been plumbed without the support of the Friends of the St. Clement's Island–Potomac River Museum. I would like to recognize, in particular, the late Garnett Arnold for according us his personal recollections of his shipbuilding days at Quantico, Virginia, and Joe Densford for his ever-ready assistance in field and courthouse. I would like to thank Capt. Reed Scott, who has become, during the course of the project, not just a local source and supporter, but a personal friend. Recognition must be accorded the Maritime Archaeological and Historical Society and, particularly, Tom Berkey, E.T. Drance, S. Carey Filling, Dave Kerr, Chris Kopac, Carl Leubsdorf, Ted Schutzbank, James Smailes, Dr. Ted Suman, and William Rutkowski for their prodigious labors in the field. There were many other volunteers who deserve thanks for many days of assistance. They include: Sylvia Enz, Dr. Ralph E. Eshelman, Charles Fithian, Chris Joe, Chuck Lancaster, Dr. Henry Miller, John Mitchell, James R. "Rick" Moreland, Bryant Pomrenke, George Savastano, Carol Shomette, Dave Van Horn, Robert Wood, and Tom Zyla. Claude E. "Pete" Petrone deserves recognition and thanks for providing his considerable technical expertise and guidance whenever and wherever needed.

Last, and most important of all, I would like to thank my father, Grady F. Shomette, an oak of a man if there ever was one, for infusing me with his own great love of history, archaeology, and life. His inspiration has, through the years, guided me well.

PART ONE

ROBOTS BENEATH THE CHESAPEAKE

Indiana Jones has turned his bullwhip in for a PC.

Emory Kristof

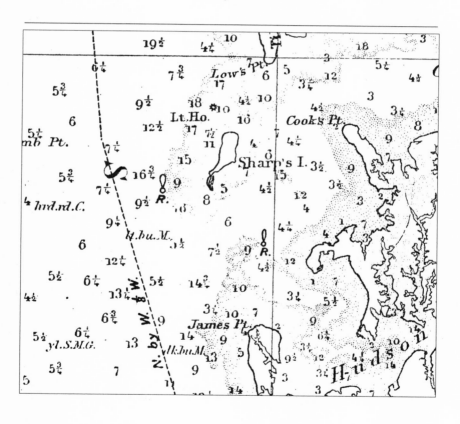

O N E

As Her Service May Require

At 4:30 A.M., April 12, 1861, a ten-inch bombshell was fired from a mortar battery on Morris Island in Charleston Harbor, South Carolina, and burst without apparent effect over the federally held bastion of Fort Sumter.1 The echo of the explosion, however, reverberated across the land, awakening a slumbering nation to the fact that civil war in America was at hand.

The events that followed in rapid succession stunned both North and South. On April 13, Fort Sumter, its walls and casements battered and collapsing from the terrible bombardment, was surrendered. Immediately afterwards, Pensacola Harbor, Florida, was blockaded by the Union Navy, even as federal officers were seized and imprisoned by Confederate authorities throughout the South. Fort Pickens, Florida, was occupied by Union troops, and Virginia secessionists attempted to obstruct passage into Norfolk Harbor. The U.S. schooner *Buchanan* was seized in the James River by Southern forces and taken to Richmond. And with each escalatory step, Maryland and Virginia, both of which had refrained from formal secession, moved ever closer to declaring for the Confederacy.2

On April 15, in response to the growing crisis, President Abraham Lincoln issued a fateful proclamation declaring seven states of the South to be in a state of insurrection against the federal government and called for seventy-five thousand militia troops to restore order and control.3 What had only weeks before been deemed a Southern conspiracy had become a full-blown rebellion, the future success or failure of which depended in large measure upon the course taken by critical border states such as Maryland and Virginia.

Two days after Lincoln's proclamation, the Virginia Convention, meeting in secret session, passed an ordinance for secession by a vote of eighty-five to fifty-five. Despite the course taken by her sister state and though strongly secessionist in sympathies herself, Maryland was narrowly prevented from following suit by the prompt and deliberate actions of her Unionist Governor Thomas H. Hicks, who immediately moved the state legislature to Frederick and jailed those members supportive of the rebellion.4 Despite Hicks's efforts to maintain order, a mob of ten thousand Confederate sympathizers in Baltimore fell upon Union troops, the Sixth Massachusetts Regiment, as the soldiers were passing through the

3

city from Pennsylvania on their way to the defense of imperiled Washington, D.C. The ensuing riot was both bloody and deadly. The fury of the mob assault obliged additional troops, then en route, to return to Philadelphia to await orders.[5] The situation for the Unionists worsened almost overnight in Maryland and the nation's capital. Defended by a handful of soldiers and surrounded on all sides by innumerable enemies, Unionists in Maryland and Washington waited fearfully for the next Confederate move. On April 19 railroad bridges north of Baltimore were burned, telegraph lines cut, mail service suspended, and all roads north torn up. Baltimore was in the hands of secessionists, disorganized though they were. Washington had become an island surrounded by a sea of rebellion.[6] The federal city was completely cut off from the North save for a single avenue of communication and rescue—the waterways.

On April 20, as the crisis increased in tempo, Captain Philip Reybold, a veteran Delaware shipowner and commander, suggested to federal authorities a plan to get troops through to the beleaguered capital. Certain steamboats, he pointed out, of dimensions suitable for traversing the Chesapeake and Delaware Canal, which connected the Chesapeake Bay and the Delaware River, might be employed to carry federal troops quickly from Philadelphia to Annapolis. From Annapolis, they could entrain for Washington, thus making an unexpected end run around the secessionists at Baltimore.[7] The canal locks, though 220 feet long, were only 24 feet wide and thus limited the size of vessels passing through to fairly narrow-beamed craft. Side-wheelers were simply too wide for the job. The task would have to be accomplished by propeller steamers. Despite the size limitations, the idea was immediately adopted, and on the same day every steamboat near Philadelphia that could pass through the locks was commandeered by federal authorities and loaded with troops and supplies. The final plan called for troops to be carried by canal steamers through the C&D Canal to Perryville at the mouth of the Susquehanna River. From there they could be ferried to Annapolis and then carried aboard railroad cars bound for the capital.

Federal authorities were not in a negotiating mood when it came to obtaining vessels.[8] According to depositions later provided by Captain Abraham Colmony of the steamboat *A. Whildin,* his ship had been loaded and ready to sail when it was seized and employed under charter by government agents at Philadelphia. The ship's cargo was then off-loaded and replaced with military goods bound for Perryville, Maryland, from which point they would be reshipped to Annapolis. The *Whildin* continued in government employ under the charter until mid-June.[9]

Sixteen propeller-driven steamers were similarly conscripted into service as transports. By the following day, much to the dismay of Maryland secessionists, federal troops were being landed in Annapolis, where they boarded trains for the capital. With the arrival of the troops at Washington that evening, the capital was narrowly saved for the Union.[10]

The use of propeller-driven steamboats capable of traversing the canal systems specifically for federal military service was thus demonstrated for the first time and at one of the most critical periods in the early days of the Civil War. The crucial lessons learned from the success of this operation were not lost on federal planners. In the course of the next few years, the C&DCanal, which crossed both Maryland and Delaware territory, and the Delaware and Raritan Canal (D&R), which traversed the waist of New Jersey, would become major conduits through which troops, guns and ammunition, equipment, food, and clothing would be funneled to feed the voracious appetite of war. The steamers that plied these canals would prove critical to Union survival.[11]

One of the so-called chartered vessels, large enough to carry several hundred soldiers and well equipped for travel on canal, river, bay, or ocean, was the modest little propeller steamer *New Jersey*.

The steamboat *New Jersey* was a product of what might be termed the "canalization" of America—that is, the national infatuation with canals as a means of commercial transportation, a concept that had begun to sweep across the new nation shortly after the close of the Revolutionary War. Among those states vigorously embracing the idea early on was New

The steamboat *New Jersey* in 1862. Courtesy Steamship Historical Society Collection, University of Baltimore Library

Jersey. In fact, William Penn had authorized a survey across that colony as early as 1676 for a canal that never came to fruition. Concepts and plans had emerged with regularity after the American War of Independence, in 1794, in 1804, and again in 1808, but not until the close of the War of 1812 did the New Jersey Legislature begin to consider canal development in earnest. Finally, on February 4, 1830, the state legislature created a private corporation to construct an artificial waterway from the Raritan River to the Delaware River, effectively dividing the state across its waist and providing direct waterborne access by canal between such major port cities as New York, Philadelphia, and Trenton. By May 1834 the Delaware and Raritan Canal was opened for through navigation.[12]

The size of the locks and channels of the D&R Canal was to prove instrumental in the design, draft, and dimensions of vessels constructed specifically to traverse its length. The seven locks between Trenton and Bordentown each measured 24 feet in width and 110 feet in length, although the length was eventually increased to 220 feet (the width remained constant) to accommodate the larger shipping and bulk carriers. The main channel of the canal varied from 60 to 80 feet wide and was 8 feet deep, while feeder channels were 50 feet wide and 6 feet deep.[13] Hence, vessels specifically built to ply these waters could be no wider or longer than the lock dimensions or of greater draft than a feeder channel.

The outbreak of the Civil War had proved a boon to the company that managed the canal as well as to the commercial shipping firms owning vessels that traversed its waters. Total tonnage carried on the canal began to increase rapidly owing to wartime demands, and many freighting companies rushed to have new ships built to accommodate the bonanza in freight hauling. One such company was the Commercial Transportation Company of Trenton, New Jersey. In late 1861 or early 1862, the CTC had placed an order with the shipyard of Fardy and Auld, located in the Federal Hill area of Baltimore, for a round-sterned wooden propeller steamer for use as a freight hauler both on canals and in adjacent waterways. She was to be 166 feet 9 inches in length, 23 feet in width, 8 feet 9 inches deep in hold, and would draw only a few feet of water. Her size would be quite adequate to permit passage through both the D&R Canal and the C&D Canal, as well as to provide service on the waters of the Chesapeake, Delaware, Raritan, and Hudson. Her tonnage capacity was given at 224 28/100 under tonnage deck, 234 between decks and above tonnage deck, and 35 on the upper deck. Her engines were to be produced by the foundry firm of Reany and Archibald of Chester, Pennsylvania, and, when delivered, she would have a displacement of 324 10/95 tons.[14]

Of singular interest, however, was that *New Jersey* not only was propeller-driven, but also carried three masts, schooner-rigged fore and aft. As one of the end products of a veritable revolution in maritime development that had taken hold in the industrial world between 1807 and 1860, the little steamer was a hybrid of many unique components, illustrative of the rapidly evolving technology of the era—a technology specifically attempting to address the environment in which she was to serve.

By the outbreak of the Civil War, steam power had been an acceptable means of propulsion for more than half a century. Yet, even then, American and European shipbuilders hosted certain misgivings about its reliability as a means of propulsion on water. By 1860 it had come to be accepted that "the principal propeller of a steam vessel, generally is her engines," yet "it is . . . necessary that the vessel should be supplied with sails, in order to have recourse to in case of need." Leading authorities on ship design waxed endlessly on the virtues and faults of the marriage of sail to the propeller steamer. Steam vessels, it was said, "being generally of small beam in proportion to their length [are] therefore not practicable to have . . . as heavily masted sailing vessel."[15] In designing and building such vessels, shipwrights had to address many technological considerations that, during the age of sail, had not existed. The position of the engines frequently influenced the situation of the masts. The overall lengths of the masts and spars, some experts stated, could not be too great, for too large a spread of sail might cause the vessel to incline "more than is consistent with the proper working of the machinery." The length of a vessel's masts had to be proportional to her beam and depth of hold, as well as her diminishing stiffness or stability as she consumed her fuel.[16]

By the onset of the Civil War era, the fore and aft schooner rig had been determined to be the most suitable for most coastal and river steamers. Yet the nature of the rig depended upon the service for which the vessel was intended. If the characteristic speed of a packet boat was desired, and the saving of fuel a minor consideration, then short, light masts were best and were carried only as auxiliary backups to the engine, though with enough canvas to steady the vessel in a seaway. For transatlantic travel, heavy spars were a must. By lifting the screw or dismantling it, the vessel could become a fully rigged sailing ship.

The design and position of the propeller, the angle of the shaft, the boiler and engine design, and myriad other engineering considerations were also subjects of endless debate in professional journals and engineering societies and among shipbuilders and foundry operators across the country. There was, for instance, no determined rule for the number of masts a steamer might mount. Some had as many as four or six, though most averaged only two or three. Not infrequently, the mainmast in steam vessels had to be placed in the space allotted to the engines and boilers. When the mainmast thus came too near the fires, "an iron leg [had] to be introduced to support the mast; and, at other times, the mast [was] leaded in front, facing the heat."[17] The problem was sometimes alleviated by placing the boiler-engine complex in the stern of the vessel. Such

7

design considerations were undoubtedly debated and taken into account by *New Jersey*'s constructors and employed or ignored as their expertise saw fit, for ships were still largely built by "wrack of eye."

Finally, on December 23, 1862, the completed steamer was surveyed, certified, and temporarily registered at Baltimore by her new master, Michael Garrett (or Jarrett), in behalf of the Commercial Transportation Company of Trenton. She was officially registered and enrolled as No. 18336 and entered into the service for which she was designed. Her intended career, however, was destined to be relatively short-lived.[18]

By the late fall of 1863 the Civil War was well into its second year, and the U.S. War Department found itself increasingly obliged to rely upon commercial charter vessels to haul war material, troops, and provisions to the various theaters of battle. With the Union Navy largely committed to enforcing Lincoln's blockade of Southern ports and the Atlantic sea lanes constantly menaced by Confederate commerce raiders, such as the CSS *Alabama,* the inland waterway between New York, a major hub for federal shipping and supply, and the Virginia theater of operations took on a strategic significance far beyond its prewar import. Vessels that met dimensional criteria and could traverse the D&R and the C&D Canals, as well as negotiate the open waters of the Chesapeake Bay and its various shallow tributaries, were in ever-increasing demand by the War Department.

The owners of the Commercial Transportation Company, Stephen and James M. Flanagan of Philadelphia, each of whom held one-quarter of the corporation's stock, and William G. Cook of Trenton, who controlled the remaining half and served as president, were from the beginning undoubtedly under considerable pressure to charter their new ship to the military.[19] At the outset of the war, with the federal government's desperate need for suitable watercraft to transport troops and supplies to the front, such charters were almost always involuntary and not particularly fair or beneficial to the owners. Outright seizures were not unheard of. But by 1863, the situation had been modified somewhat and the burden of loss or damage was guaranteed by the federal government.

Thus, on December 20, 1863, the U.S. Army chartered *New Jersey,* then at New York, from Stephen Flanagan, at a rate of $175 per day for "a Trip to Washington D.C. and Back to New York, and as much longer as her service may be required." Beginning on the day of the charter agreement, whenever *New Jersey* was tendered alongside by the quartermaster of the U.S. Army, his factors or assigns, the vessel was to be ready to receive on board any troops, animals, supplies, or other cargo the army deemed necessary and that the vessel could conveniently stow and carry. Thus laden, she was ordered to proceed without delay, at the "first good opportunity," to Washington to deliver her cargo, in good order and condition, to the quartermaster there, with the dangers of sea, fire, navigation, "and the restraints of Princes and Rulers always being excepted." The normal marine risks were to be borne by the owner, but all war risks, fuel costs, pilotage fees, and port charges after leaving New York would be borne by the United States.[20]

If the government elected to purchase the ship during the period of the charter, it reserved the right to take her at the appraised value, $58,000, at the date of charter, and all money then already paid and due on the charter (minus the cost of running and keeping the vessel in repair during the charter), together with a net profit of 33 percent per annum of the original appraised value, was to be paid to the company. The contract was signed on January 1, 1864, by Flanagan and Captain J. T. Crilly of the Quartermaster's Department. In the meantime, the Commercial Transportation Company had appointed P. F. Hoxie of Rhode Island to the command of the vessel. Hoxie was destined to remain as captain of *New Jersey* throughout her Civil War career.[21]

That the U.S. Army employed *New Jersey* well beyond the initial voyage from New York to Washington and back is not surprising, considering her ability to carry large amounts of cargo through the canal systems and into the shallow tributaries of the Chesapeake. That she was to see service in combat areas is also not surprising, for the entire southern section of the Tidewater had become a battleground. By mid-May 1864, massive numbers of Union and Confederate troops were beginning to square off near Drewrys Bluff on the James River between Petersburg and Richmond, Virginia. In early May, federal forces under General Benjamin F. Butler moved aggressively to secure a major toehold at a point called Bermuda Hundred in preparation for what was hoped to be the final march on Richmond. On the evening of May 15, four or five steamers arrived at the Union base at Belle Plain on the James, somewhat below Bermuda Hundred, and began taking on board recently captured Confederate prisoners. The following day, two of the vessels, *New Jersey* and *S.R. Spaulding,* departed with prisoners bound for Camp Hoffman, Maryland, the big prisoner-of-war camp on the tip of the Point Lookout peninsula, at the confluence of the Potomac and the Chesapeake.[22]

In early May, when Butler's campaign against Drewrys Bluff began, there were already 5,741 prisoners of war confined to Point Lookout. As a consequence of the battles that followed, however, the camp population more than doubled with the influx of an additional 6,876 prisoners, most of them brought in by steamboats such as *New Jersey.* The diary of one Confederate prisoner, Sergeant Bartlett Yancey Malone of Company H, Sixth North Carolina Infantry, regularly recorded the comings and goings of the steamers. On May 17, at about the time *New Jersey* and *Spaulding* would have reached the point, Malone reported that "about one thousin Prisonors arived at this plaice was captured at the wilderness The 17th about 1000 was brought in from General Leas armey." The following day, he recorded, an additional four hundred men were brought into camp.[23]

Robots Beneath the Chesapeake

Exactly how many runs *New Jersey* made from the James River to Point Lookout is unknown, but it is likely that she made at least several. By November, however, the army had found other work for her: hauling military cargo and troops from New York to Hampton Roads, Virginia. With federal naval control again firmly asserted over the middle Atlantic seaboard and Confederate commerce raiders no longer a serious threat to the region, the little steamer began to utilize the more direct Atlantic passage between New York and the Virginia theater.[24]

In November, *New Jersey* was again in Hampton Roads. She did not tarry long, for she had been directed to ascend the James to Bermuda Hundred. Here, on December 8, she took aboard 329 enlisted men and 16 officers of the Sixth U.S. Colored Troops, as well as six horses and food and forage for five days, and headed for Hampton Roads. There, the troops, which had been intended for a landing at Beaufort, North Carolina, and afterward a grand assault on the Confederate fortifications guarding the Cape Fear River, were transferred to seagoing troop transports. Such was the typical wartime service of *New Jersey*.[25]

New Jersey continued in service under her original charter to the United States until May 11, 1865, almost a month after Robert E. Lee's historic surrender to Ulysses S. Grant at Appomattox Court House. Anticipating a return to peacetime commerce, on June 2, 1865, her owners were granted a permanent enrollment and entered the ship as home ported at Philadelphia. Escape from military service, however, would be delayed for nearly another full year.

Upon the conclusion of the war in the Virginia theater, there remained an urgent need for transport vessels to carry the thousands of Union troops, supplies, and equipment home. On June 10, *New Jersey* was again chartered for transport duty. The ship, then moored at the large federal military base at City Point on the James, would receive forty-five cents per ton per day, or $222.30, for additional service. Not until April 12, 1866, would the vessel finally be returned to the discretionary use of her owners. Despite the wear and tear on her from the undoubtedly arduous military service, *New Jersey* had been profitable for her owners, earning at least $160,000 for raw tonnage alone, plus a healthy sum for the carriage of troops and freight.[26] She had emerged unscathed. And, in the doing, she had provided the Union Army important logistical support for some of the most historic and pivotal military episodes of the Civil War. Now it was time to test her commercial wings in the uncertain postwar economy.

T W O

Burned to the Water's Edge

Following *New Jersey*'s military service, the Commercial Transportation Company of Trenton returned the steamboat to her former, if short-lived, occupation as freight hauler on the New York-Delaware-Chesapeake route. But the world had been irrevocably changed by the Civil War, and the CTC was evolving to accommodate the times. Thus, in 1867, *New Jersey*, perhaps a bit worn and frayed by her military service, was traded to the Baltimore Steam Packet Company for the iron side-wheel passenger steamer *Thomas A. Morgan* and two thousand dollars.[1]

When *New Jersey* entered the service of the Baltimore Steam Packet Company, affectionately known by those who traversed the Chesapeake as the Old Bay Line, she became a member of the fleet of the then-second-oldest steamer line in the Tidewater. The company was an institution incorporated by an act of the General Assembly of Maryland in 1839.

That the Old Bay Line had sought and acquired a vessel such as *New Jersey* in 1867 is of some import. During that year, the company had begun to experience a drastic change in administration, which would significantly alter the course of its corporate history. And it was an evolutionary chapter in the history of company management objectives and policy that the acquisition of *New Jersey* directly reflected. During the year, one John Moncure Robinson succeeded Moor N. Falls to the presidency of the corporation. The son of Moncure Robinson, the first chief engineer of the Richmond, Fredericksburg, and Potomac Railroad, John Robinson had served during the Civil War as a Confederate Army officer.[2] Under Robinson's able hand and command, wrote noted maritime historian Alexander Crosby Brown in 1940,

the Line was to witness many important changes bringing its ships and services to the state of perfection and efficiency which are associated with modern times. The ships of the [Old Bay] Line gradually changed from wooden side-wheelers to iron hulled craft. The screw propeller replaced the cumbersome paddle wheel and, at the last, iron hulls gave way to ships of steel. Steam steering gear replaced the cranky, manually operated wheels; gas light was abandoned for electricity; pot-bellied stoves gave way to steam-heated radiators. Likewise the high silk hats

11

and frock coats of captains and pursers were discarded for uniforms, first resplendent and gaudy, later more utilitarian and conservative.[3]

And the wooden-hulled *New Jersey,* the first propeller-driven steamboat to be acquired by the line, led the way.

The history of *New Jersey*'s employment by the Old Bay Line is far from well documented, and little mention of the vessel appears in the marine reports of the day. That she sailed from Baltimore far more frequently than the published record indicates, however, is suggested by the fact that clearance for her final voyage, on February 25, 1870, was not published at all.[4]

New Jersey served under three commanders during her short tenure with the Old Bay Line. Captain L. B. Eddens (or Eddins), her first known commander, was destined to command other Old Bay Line steamers, such as *Adelaide,* well into the 1870s. Her second commander, reported only as Captain Kirwan, may have been either John H. Kirwan, who would later hold command in both the Maryland Steamboat Company and the Tolchester Steamboat Company (as captain of *Susquehanna*), or Jacob Kirwan, who had held command of the Potomac River steamer *St. Nicholas* in 1861. Her last commander, A. K. Cralle, employed by the Old Bay Line since his youth, had served as captain of the company steamer *Thomas Kelso* and was in command of *Kelso* on December 8, 1866, when her steam drums exploded off Wolf Trap Light, scalding her engineers and firemen and injuring several passengers. In January or February 1870, he was given the command of *New Jersey,* in which capacity he would serve until her own unfortunate demise.[5]

❏   ❏   ❏

By the beginning of the last week of February 1870, *New Jersey* had begun to take on freight at the Old Bay Line's big Union Dock in Baltimore Harbor. As city newspapers later reported, by departure time, a large cargo consisting of 1,500 bushels of corn; 60 tons of guano, meat, bacon, and pork in barrels; petroleum; "and numerous other items" totaling approximately 750 tons of freight overall, bound for Norfolk, had been loaded aboard. The cargo was said to be worth "not less than $40,000." There would be, as was usual for a freighter such as this, no passengers on the run, only Captain Cralle and his ten officers and crew.[6]

The voyage between Baltimore and Norfolk was short, fewer than two hundred miles overall and one that most of the steamboats in the Old Bay Line fleet could make with speed. Company executives, however, were often concerned by an overly fast voyage, for "ware and tare" on machinery could be expensive. Hence, Bay Line masters and engineers were "strictly enjoined that they do not make their trips between Baltimore and Norfolk in less than 15 hours," though the record was held by the company's fast steamer *Herald*, which had made the trip on January 25, 1853, in ten hours and forty-five minutes.[7] A typical freight run for a vessel such as *New Jersey* might take from seventeen to twenty hours. It was a voyage expected to be conducted with a minimum of duress or danger for both ship and crew.

By the afternoon of Friday, February 25, *New Jersey* was finally ready for departure. In the late afternoon, the Washington Monument could be seen in the distance as the ship pulled away down the harbor. As evening came on, the navigational beacons on the Patapsco River, familiar to all veteran steamboaters such as Cralle, began to blink on one by one— the Lazaretto Point Light, the Fort Carroll Light, then the Upper and Lower North Point Lights. As *New Jersey* entered the Chesapeake Bay, Cralle could see the bright Seven Foot Knoll Light and then the Bodkin Tower.

The progress of *New Jersey* was apparently normal, though notable landmarks seen in the daylight, such as the steeple of the Annapolis State House, could not be discerned in the dark. There were many other guides, though, to shepherd the vessel down the channel and away from the numerous shoals that pepper the Chesapeake. Thomas Point Light, a fixed screw-pile lighthouse, standing sixty-three feet above the sea, was one of the most formidable and provided a distinct warning of a shoal lying to the southeast of the point. But veteran steamboaters like Cralle were, for the most part, well aware of the hazards to navigation and knew the Bay like the veins in their hands.[8]

At about midnight, *New Jersey* approached the dangerous flats off Poplar Island. The island was then about two miles in length, with a stand of timber on its northern and southeastern portions. The danger here lay in the sandy spit projecting from the southern tip of the island. Not only was it shallow, but the shelter afforded by the island from northerly winds provided smaller vessels seeking to anchor on the southwest side a welcomed sanctuary. It also made the section a particularly dangerous area for steamboats to traverse at night, and collisions here were numerous. Wisely, Cralle kept his ship well out in the main Bay channel.

If necessary, the commander of *New Jersey* would have been easily able to determine his position on the Chesapeake at night by triangulating his bearings from the pattern of lights and beacons. As he approached Poplar Island, the Thomas Point and Greenbury Point lights would be on his starboard stern and the Sharps Island light ahead on his port bow. The Sharps Island Lighthouse of 1870 was a red brick and stone affair standing forty-one feet above the sea and erected on the north end of tiny, two-mile-long Sharps Island, an eroding islet just off the mouth of the Choptank River. Southbound ships would have to maintain the light on their port side, and if they stayed in the channel, they were assured of ten to eighteen fathoms of water beneath them. If they strayed from their course, however, there was the grim probability of running onto the Sharps Island Flats, a spit extending off the southern end of the island.[9]

Everything seemed in order, as Cralle undoubtedly paid the obligatory heed to the navigation of his ship down Chesapeake Bay, until shortly after midnight. At about 12:30 A.M., February 26, after passing Poplar Island and while approaching to within three miles of Sharps Island, Cralle and his mate smelled smoke. Quick investigation revealed catastrophe of the worst sort: the ship was on fire amidships, midway between decks in the freight room. The crew was instantly mobilized to fight an apparently already substantial blaze: "The hatch was raised to allow of water being thrown from the hose [sic], connecting with the fire apparatus so as to extinguish the fire, but the flames gained such rapid headway, reaching even up the masts and burning the sails, as to compel them to retire. The propeller was then rounded or turned to enable the officers and crew—eleven in number—to reach the stern where the two quarter boats were secured, and which being lowered in the water, all embarked in them."[10]

Captain Cralle and his men lay by the burning ship in the quarter boats and watched helplessly, praying for assistance, as the flames licked the midnight sky. They were unaware that potential help was in the area but would not be forthcoming. At 3:00 A.M. the steamer *Kennebec*, Captain Reybold commanding, bound from York River to Baltimore, passed the blazing ship but pressed on with her voyage, apparently unwilling to divert from her schedule to lend assistance. It was later claimed that "as the latter [*New Jersey*] was already burned to the water's edge, no assistance could be rendered." Captain Cralle and his men, shivering in the freezing February darkness, might have thought otherwise.[11]

An hour after *Kennebec* had sighted and ignored the burning ship, another Baltimore-bound steamboat, the Old Bay Line's own *Louisiana*, also sighted her. Captain Darius J. Hill, commander of the ship, observed the disaster from a distance of six miles but also failed to render assistance. Exactly why neither Reybold nor Hill came to the aid of their fellow mariners is unknown. It is possible, however, that by the time they had sighted *New Jersey*, she had drifted dangerously close to the Sharps Island Flats, waters too shoal for large-draft vessels such as *Louisiana* and *Kennebec* to venture into in the dark. Captain Cralle and his men hung doggedly by the burning ship. Then, at 4:00 A.M., a small oyster pungy hove in sight, undoubtedly drawn by the fire, and rescued the beleaguered mariners. Yet Cralle refused to abandon his ship and continued to sail the pungy around her for the balance of the night. Slowly, with wind and tide, the doomed steamer drifted ever closer to the perilous flats. Slightly before daybreak, another vessel, the steam tug *Pacific*, hove onto the scene, and *New Jersey*'s captain made one last-ditch effort to save whatever he could.[12]

Cralle and his crew immediately boarded *Pacific* and "endeavored to pull the *New Jersey* on to a bar or ashore, in order to save any portion of the cargo not burned." His efforts were not without precedent or logic. Had he abandoned the vessel entirely, and had the ship eventually drifted ashore, by time-honored tradition codified in the admiralty courts of the Western World, the right of salvage belonged to the party that first touched the ship after its abandonment. Cralle did his best, but his boldest efforts were doomed to failure. The ship continued to burn, even as *Pacific* labored to haul her toward the shoals. Then, at 10:00 A.M., she sank in ten to eleven fathoms, less than half a mile from the objective.[13]

There was little left for Cralle and his weary crew to do but return to Baltimore. En route, *Pacific* encountered another Old Bay Line steam freighter, *Transit*, steaming hell-bent down the Bay, bound for the disaster site. On board the ship was the company's superintendent, William C. Smith, who had learned of the catastrophe only hours earlier, undoubtedly from either Captain Reybold or Captain Hill. He had immediately organized a relief expedition but, sadly, was too late to be of assistance. Thus *New Jersey*'s despondent officers and crew were again transferred, this time to *Transit*, and continued their voyage to Baltimore.[14]

On Monday morning, February 28, 1870, the directors of the Baltimore Steam Packet Company convened in melancholy council to decide the fate of *New Jersey*. The vessel, it was noted in the press, was said to be valued at between thirty thousand and thirty-five thousand dollars. The Baltimore *Sun* stated that she was insured. The *American and Commercial Daily Advertiser* noted that she was covered for only half of her value, but that it "was not ascertained whether any portion of the freight was insured." Whatever the facts may have been, the company directors, assessing the cost of a possible salvage operation against the potential returns, decided not to institute an effort to raise the ship. *New Jersey*'s fire-scarred remains would be left on the bottom of Chesapeake Bay. But there were more important reasons dictating her abandonment than the simple expense necessary to salvage her.[15]

As with the loss of any steamboat, an investigation into the cause of the ship's destruction was, by federal law, mandatory. Such investigations were normally carried out by the office of the district inspector of steamboats, a member of the U.S. Board of Supervising Inspectors of Steam Vessels. Both Baltimore and Norfolk fell within the jurisdiction of the Third Supervising District, which included other ports such as Savannah and Charleston. It was a vast administration area for a single inspector to manage. In 1870 alone, the Third District Inspector was responsible for inspecting 286 steam vessels of every type, totalling 56,051.40 tons, and the annual licensing of 467 pilots and 454 engineers. The most dire authority, however, required the investigation, through boards of local inspection, into the loss of any steam vessel occurring within his jurisdiction.[16]

The investigation into the loss of *New Jersey* followed hot on the heels of the disaster, and the officers of the steamer were obliged to provide testimony at a board of review of the incident. Then the whole truth of the disaster was revealed. The official verdict regarding the tragedy was published in January 1871 in the *Proceedings of the Nineteenth Annual Meeting of the Board of Supervising Inspectors of Steam Vessels*: "From the testimony obtained from the officers of the steamer [*New Jersey*], it is quite evident that the fire originated from the ignition of some dangerous freight shipped on board, and marked, contrary to law, as ordinary merchandise; this opinion is further confirmed by the subsequent discovery of shipments of freight of a dangerous character on the same line of steamers marked merchandise." [17]

Despite the nefarious shipping methods that had brought about the loss of *New Jersey* and jeopardized the lives of her crew, the entire affair failed to surface publically. Neither the Old Bay Line, which knew of, but failed to prohibit, the illegal shipment of dangerous combustibles, nor those who had shipped the incorrectly marked freight would suffer any consequences. The Old Bay Line and its influential directors were able to bury the entire episode without duress. Indeed, within the year, *New Jersey* had been replaced by a new freighter called *Roanoke*, built along much the same lines as her predecessor and carrying three fore-and-aft sails. But the trim, black-painted hull of *Roanoke* bore one revolutionary, distinctive feature differing from *New Jersey*: she was constructed entirely of iron.[18]

As for *New Jersey*, she would slip from memory for the next 105 years, her wounded hulk sleeping undisturbed at the bottom of Chesapeake Bay.

T H R E E

Captain Henry's Mystery Wreck

Captain Varice Henry was delighted with the new fathometer he had installed aboard his fishing boat *Bammy II* in the fall of 1973. As a busy communications engineer at the National Aeronautics and Space Administration's Goddard Spaceflight Center at Beltsville, Maryland, he had enjoyed precious little time of late on the medium he loved best—the Chesapeake Bay. Yet he, like most boaters at the little marina on Fishing Creek where *Bammy II* was moored, took particular delight in mucking about the water whenever possible. Any excuse to put out would do. And with his new "fish finder" in hand, the excuse seemed ready-made. A weekend fishing trip on the Bay was just the thing. And, like most seasoned fishermen, he knew that some of the best fishing spots to be found on the Chesapeake were frequently in the vicinity of old wrecks.

Over the years, Captain Henry had made it a hobby of sorts to search for forgotten shipwrecks lying on the bottom of the Bay and its tributaries. He had long since developed the habit, when a new site was located with his depth sounder, of taking compass bearings on prominent landmarks and navigational markers, triangulating the position of the site, and committing it to memory. He would mentally log the running time from various points on the Bay to his personal preserves and file them away for later use. The record-keeping, he liked to say, was all in his head. It was a technique he had learned from watermen who knew the Bay bottom better than their own backyard. Some sites had not only proved to be good fishing grounds, but also provided the grist for endless conversation with his fellow scientists and engineers at NASA who shared his love for the Bay. To one such longtime colleague and friend, an engineer named Eldon Volkmer, the interest was in more than the art of angling.

Not long after leaving the shelter of the Fishing Creek marina, Captain Henry proceeded alone for the fishing grounds along the east side of the main channel of the Chesapeake along the western lip of Sharps Island Shoals. The shoals, he knew, were now all that remained of a sizable island, once nine hundred acres in extent, which had totally succumbed to erosion in 1963.[1] As he motored in a southeasterly direction, he could see the last physical vestige of the island, the second Sharps Island Lighthouse, built in 1882, protruding from the northern end of the shoals.[2]

17

Robots Beneath the Chesapeake

Using the lighthouse and several navigational buoys as range markers, he cruised slowly southward in search of the savage sharp-toothed bluefish that tended to linger about the edge of the channel drop-off. The needle arm of his strip-chart recorder whirred quietly, displaying in its own marvelous mechanical way the acoustically generated graphic representation of the Bay's bottom. For the most part, the imagery revealed a bottom both flat and featureless.

Then, suddenly, while running in seventy to eighty feet of water, the penciled needle of the recorder began to display the presence of a large object on the bottom. Whatever it was, he thought, it certainly was as big as anything he had seen in the Bay. In fact, one of the features of the site rose nearly twenty-five feet off the sea floor!

Captain Henry stroked his chin and grinned. That he had run over a large shipwreck was almost certain. He knew there were, indeed, a number of fair-sized wrecks in the vicinity. But none was even near the dimensions of the wreck he had just encountered. In fact, there was no indication of any such site on his nautical charts at all. He had, he realized, just discovered another unchartered shipwreck—and a sizable one at that. Its position on the lip of the main shipping channel, over which passed the giant tankers and freighters bound to and from Baltimore, made it unsafe to anchor over or fish on, even though it was not directly in the shipping lane itself. But somehow it didn't seem to matter. Captain Varice Henry's curiosity had been piqued. What, indeed, was the identity of the big hulk lying in deep water off Sharps Island Shoals, and how had it met its fate? Two years were destined to pass before he would have his answer.

❏ ❏ ❏

I first learned of Varice Henry's mystery wreck in late 1974 through my friend and colleague Eldon Volkmer. Volkmer was a senior communications engineer with NASA and also served on the board of directors of a recently formed nonprofit historical and archaeological research corporation chartered in the state of Maryland called Nautical Archaeological Associates, Inc. (NAA). The organization comprised a multidisciplinary group of scientists, historians, and professionals in numerous fields who had worked on many early underwater research projects in the Americas. I had the honor of serving as the company's president and director. Henry, Volkmer noted with some excitement, was anxious to have NAA examine an unchartered wreck site off Sharps Island Shoals. We had, I noted with some skepticism, examined over the years several sites Henry had "discovered." But for the most part, they had usually turned out to be modern barges, plywood pleasure boats, or workboats. None had proved to be of historical or archaeological importance.

18

Captain Henry's Mystery Wreck

Having been diving on and studying Tidewater shipwrecks for nearly a decade, I viewed the prospect of yet another deep blackwater dive on a sunken skipjack or steel barge with the same enthusiasm I usually devoted to working on my taxes. Eldon prodded mercilessly, pointing out to me the general location of the site on a chart. I extracted from my files the lists and locations of vessels that my research had determined were in the area. There was the old *Brunswick*, a barge sunk only eight years before in rather shallower water,[3] and another called *Bright*, lost in 1940 in over ninety feet.[4] Up on the flats were the rotting remains of a number of workboats such as *M.E. Dennis*, lost in 1928,[5] and *Gladys Melba*, sunk in 1952.[6] Off nearby Blackwalnut Point were several bugeyes such as *Nelly Bly*.[7] For each of these I had exact coordinates and had even visited several of the sites. And then there was the steamboat *New Jersey*, the only wreck on my list in the vicinity that had not been found.

A hands-on investigation was scheduled for the spring of 1975. Despite the best of intentions, however, conflicting schedules, the demands of other projects, and myriad delays contrived to postpone the expedition until the following fall. Not until October 4, 1975, in fact, would the first in-depth examination take place of what would become, a decade later, one of the most controversial archaeological sites in Maryland, and one of national significance.

❑ ❑ ❑

As we left Fishing Creek aboard *Bammy II*, I counted heads. There were three NAA divers aboard: Eldon Volkmer, Ken Hollingshead, a professional marine biologist, and me; three volunteers—Dr. Jay Cooke of the National Institutes of Health, Harold Herring of the U.S. Navy Applied Physics Laboratory, and Charles Camp; and, of course, Captain Varice Henry.

Having drawn the short straws en route to the site, Jay Cook and I were scheduled to make the first exploratory dive. As we made our entry and began to descend the anchor line, which Varice had planted outside the wreck upon our arrival, visibility dropped almost immediately to mere inches. We had planned our dive for slack tide, when the high energy currents would be minimal. There was roughly fifteen minutes to locate the site and plant a marker buoy. As we descended, the few inches of visibility all but evaporated as the particulates in the water made even our dive lights useless. Varice's fathometer indicated that he had anchored in eighty feet, but it might as well have been eighty miles.

After what seemed an endless descent, we gently touched bottom, unleashing billows of black silt, which instantly engulfed us in total darkness. I have been told that there are no absolutes in the universe, but that day I witnessed absolute black.

Robots Beneath the Chesapeake

I would later write about the first encounter with Captain Henry's mystery wreck:

> Allowing the silt to settle, we began to inspect our find closely. Eighteen-inch-thick framing ribs projected five or six feet above the mudbank, sweeping ominously out over our heads. After backing up, ascending these obstacles, and attaching an underwater cave reel line to one of the more sturdy members, we clambered over and began a slow descent into the bowels of the hulk. Visibility inside the hull had increased to approximately a foot, and we both felt more at ease now that we could "see." As we inched downward, I could feel giant iron bolts [actually drift pins] protruding from rotten wood disintegrating at the merest touch. This wreck was old, and we would have to proceed with utmost caution. [8]

Given the hostility of the environment, the first exploration of the wreck was admittedly limited. From the moment of our initial contact with the site, it was readily apparent that massive debris of every kind, including machinery, copper pipes, and fallen or burned timbers, lay dangerously spread about the bottom, often jutting up from the black sediments like the teeth of some giant sea monster. As we began our investigation, we could feel the turn of the tide begin to assert its force against our bodies. Instinctively, Jay lunged for some purchase in the darkness, inadvertently causing a large timber to collapse, again engulfing us in a submarine midnight. This was certainly not the place for a claustrophobe. Moreover, the site was quite frail, and we had already jeopardized its integrity. Physical contact would have to be avoided whenever possible.

For the most part, we discovered the hull was almost completely filled with sediments, presenting a terrain both flat and featureless. A single natural scour pit, swept clear by regular tidal action, was encountered along what would later be determined to be the port side. At the base of the scour, which ran perhaps twenty-five feet in length and up to eight to ten feet in depth, were revealed the heads of crates and barrels. Some bore stencil marks too faint to be read in the eternal dusk of the bottom. Several, however, had apparently become disarticulated during the wrecking episode itself, exposing their intact contents: glassware and ceramics of various sizes and shapes. Carefully, we collected several samples of glass and stenciled wood from two different crates, noting the position on a rough site map I had begun, and then continued our explorations.

As we proceeded slowly along the inner lip of the hull, reeling out our safety line and stopping every few minutes to take compass bearings, we encountered a large pipelike cylinder. Possibly a fallen smokestack, I thought to myself. Soon after, we were confronted by what appeared to be a sheer wall of iron. Close examination, however, revealed the structure to be a large iron boiler. Directly adjacent to it was a large, primitive-looking, simple-reciprocating engine. I had seen models of the like in museums and in elegant engineering drawings of the mid-nineteenth century, but never face-to-face on board a shipwreck. I was awed, for it appeared to be largely intact. But, more important, it was now suddenly apparent that Captain Henry's mystery wreck was indeed some long-forgotten steamboat.[9]

After we had surfaced, an examination of the artifact samples revealed that we had recovered two types of whiteware commonly referred to as milk glass. Both samples were severly discolored by stains later determined to be petroleum. One of the pieces was eventually identified by Paul Gardner, curator of ceramics at the Smithsonian Institution, as the base of either a common domestic oil lamp or a pitcher for liquids, both of which were prevalent typologies dating from the 1850s to the 1890s. A rather plain item, its most prominent feature was a bulbous seamed body that tapered to a rough, narrow, spoutless top. A simple appliqué handle graced one side. The entirety of the surface of the body was covered by a stippled blister pattern known as hobnail. The second sample, a featureless pitcher, however, was far more revealing. Of the same dimensions as the hobnail

Crates of cheap milk glass molasses pitchers, such as that pictured above, were among the 750 tons of cargo carried by the steamboat *New Jersey* on her final voyage in 1870. One intact pitcher bore the inscription "J.H. Hobbs & Co. Pat. May 11, 1869" in its britannia lid.

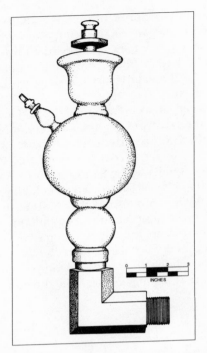

A steam release valve recovered during archaeological survey work on the steamboat *New Jersey* and housed in the collections of the Calvert Marine Museum. When recovered, the valve still contained fresh water generated from the last steam produced by the engines of the ship on her final voyage in 1870.

lamp base and featuring an identical handle, this sample was topped by a britannia lid which bore the inscription "J.H. Hobbs & Co. Pat. May 11, 1869." The stenciled wood bore the faint fire-scarred letters "BALT."[10]

To say that we were excited would have been an understatement. On the first dive, we had been able to ascertain that the mystery ship was a steam-powered vessel of substantial size, which could not have been lost prior to May 11, 1869, the date noted on the pitcher lid—but slightly less than a year before the loss of the steamboat *New Jersey*. The letters undoubtedly referred to the city of Baltimore. There seemed to be no field of candidates but one to chose from. I was convinced from the limited evidence we had gathered that we had, in fact, discovered *New Jersey*.

Throughout the remainder of the day, data assemblage, despite the near-zero visibility and high-energy currents, continued unabated. The orientation and condition of the main hull as well as a rough evaluation of the terrain within and surrounding the immediate site were undertaken. The wreck, lying on the slope of the main channel, was determined to be wooden hulled and carvel planked and bore considerable signs of fire damage, such as melted glass, lending further credence to the ship's suspected identity. One significant clue to the degree of site survival encountered by sheer luck on the first dive was examined more intensively by Eldon Volkmer, who had discovered the ship's remarkably intact steam whistle. Though most of the hull had been filled with sediments, the single eight- to ten-foot-deep natural scour amidships on the interior of the port side suggested that only the upper sections of the ship may have succumbed to the flames. The remainder lay buried in the extremely porous, soft silts of the Chesapeake.

I was delighted, because the prospects for the preservation of whatever lay beneath the sediments, quite probably in an anaerobic environment, free of oxygen and destructive marine biota, were considerable. It was possible that here lay the proverbial time capsule, a gigantic cultural and technological warehouse of nineteenth-century Maryland technology and culture buried and preserved beneath the black muds of the Chesapeake by some forgotten catastrophe more than one hundred years ago. Although it had been resolved early on that the vessel was a steamboat, there were no visible indicators from exposed components of her machinery to suggest that she had been a side-wheeler. And, owing to the burial of her stern, it was impossible to confirm or deny her identity as a propeller steamer.

Between the end of October and the middle of December, we made several additional forays to the wreck to carry out a limited evaluation of the site. At the same time, NAA board member Nicholas Freda and I set out to research, evaluate, and identify the few artifacts recovered.

On October 26, having completed several days of reconnaissance work, we returned to the wreck prepared to conduct a limited, nonintrusive survey and to develop a preliminary site plan. Our first objective was to erect a permanent datum. A prominent frame protruding from the forward third of the vessel was selected as a primary datum point. From here, a baseline was established along the inside of the port hull. Owing to poor visibility and frequently treacherous currents that swept over the site at flood tide, reducing the safe areas of investigation to a few yards at a time, subdatums were erected along both port and starboard sides at five-foot intervals. Both the datum and subdatum markers were made of luminescent plastic tags with numbers cut out to facilitate tactile identification. Hand-held compass bearings along the taut lines run from the datum point to the subdatums were taken to establish horizontal realities. Elevations were plotted from depth ranges from the surface of the water at low water. Although admittedly crude, the effort, utilizing the simplest and most inexpensive tools at hand, was designed to acquire as rapidly as possible only parametric data on the extent and lie of the hull and on those major features that were exposed above the silts.[11]

23

Robots Beneath the Chesapeake

Our initial objective, once the datums and baselines were erected, was to conduct a series of systematic radial surveys on measured lines from the subdatum points of both port and starboard sides. This was undertaken to plot the interior components of the site that stood above the silt. Gentle, systematic probing beneath the soft sediments with calibrated iron rods during the radial surveys would, we hoped, provide us with the contours of the subsediment areas without disturbing site integrity. Owing to a total lack of conservation capabilities in the state of Maryland to stabilize and preserve waterlogged materials, very limited sampling of diagnostic artifacts would be carried out, if any. Acting without a sponsor or any financial support, with extremely limited funds in the NAA coffers, and the need to maintain site integrity, the survey was intentionally low-key and limited in scope—and, as it turned out, only partially successful.

Throughout the late fall and early winter, as opportunity, weather, and funding permitted, the survey continued in fits and starts. Nevertheless, we continued to obtain reasonably good data. The exposed hull was found to be well over 150 feet long, and was unquestionably longer. The ship's extant beam of 20 feet amidships suggested a slightly wider deck beam of 23 feet or so. Several immense iron anchors were found protruding from the silt in the forward 25-foot section of the hull and draping over both the port and starboard sides. Near the bow, the remains of a single fragile bulkhead were encountered barely projecting above the bottom, and those of a second one a dozen feet aft. Between the two bulkheads lay an area of mixed debris such as copper pipes, disarticulated wooden features, crate fragments, and miscellaneous detritus. Abaft the second bulkhead lay a substantial complex of copper and iron pipes, twisted mechanical debris, a large iron flywheel, and more timber fragments. Additional bulkheads were noted abaft this complex.[12]

In several areas the possible presence of crates, barrels, and other solid objects of both wood and metal composition were noted. Abaft a fourth bulkhead, a scatter of coal, the ship's boiler, machinery, and engine, all fairly well preserved and standing proud above the bottom, were examined. The stern section abaft the big cylinder and boiler complex, however, was totally covered by sediments, with only the top portion of what was either a capstan or bollard barely discernible.[13]

As winter finally began to set in with all of its fury, fieldwork was becoming more difficult and hazardous with each trip out. Despite a consensus among NAA members to continue, it was finally decided to break off operations until the spring. In the interim, with state support, we hoped that additional funds could be raised and a more intensive, organized survey program launched. I had little idea that I would not return to the site for another decade. Nor could I have envisioned the furor its rediscovery by an agency of the U.S. government, three years after our preliminary investigations, would eventually engender.

F O U R

A Cargo of Pottery Vessels

The wreck of the steamboat *New Jersey* was archaeologically and historically significant in many ways. She had been typical of a distinct breed of canal boat common to many of America's inland waterways but capable of duty on the coastal seas as well. Yet her species was short-lived, thriving only during that fleeting moment in time when canal transportation still vied with the young titan of American commerce, the railroad. Built by Marylanders, fielded by one of the oldest steamboat companies on the Chesapeake, and carrying—we later learned—commodities of virtually every description when she sank, *New Jersey*, in her present state, offered the rare opportunity to examine a physical slice of regional maritime history of the mid- to late-nineteenth century in one self-contained package.

The first of many propeller-driven freighters of the Baltimore Steam Packet Company, her largely intact boiler-engine complex presented unparalleled potential for the documentation and study of once-working components of nineteenth-century maritime steam technology during a singularly important transitional phase in history. Her hull design and propulsion system were hybridizations of several prevalent typologies of the era, each reflecting the parameters of the many environments in which she was to be employed and the services she was to perform. Her maximum draft, length, and beam were dictated by the limitations imposed by the canal systems she would traverse. Yet she had to be sturdy enough to withstand the rigors of open sea duty. Her propulsion system, employing the propeller in lieu of the wider side-wheel paddle, had also been selected because of the limitations of canal lock size.

In addition to the physical and dimensional limitations of canal commerce, *New Jersey*'s intended usage on the waters of the Chesapeake, Delaware, and Raritan required that she be capable of operating in wide estuarine environments, in high-energy riverine systems, and, as events proved, even occasionally on the open ocean. Her incorporation of a three-masted fore-and-aft schooner rig as a means of auxiliary or emergency propulsion, a trait in common but declining usage aboard steamboats of the era, was indicative of the distrust many ship designers and builders still held for steam power and propeller propulsion. She was, in short, a superb example of how the influences of function (or mission), environment, and societal considerations directly affected vessel design and operation. She was an archaeological gem of the Age of Steam.

As the carrier of 750 tons of cargo on her final voyage, *New Jersey* offered the tantalizing prospect of being the greatest single, self-contained "time capsule" of her era found to that date in the Chesapeake. Yet her actual contents remained an enigma. In 1977, an extensive search for her shipping records and final cargo manifest led to the unhappy discovery that they had probably been destroyed in the great Baltimore fire of 1904. Indeed, all that could be gleaned concerning her lading were data noted in contemporary newspaper accounts of the catastrophe, a few official government reports of the tragedy, and comparison with information derived from archaeological investigations of similar shipwreck sites. The absence of precise archival documentation, in fact, made the archaeological record contained within *New Jersey* more important than ever. Yet comparison to similar finds elsewhere caused me to shudder in awe at the archaeological potentials. One such discovery, which has since become a benchmark in steamboat archaeology, offered a unique parallel.

In 1864 the stern-wheel river steamer *Bertrand* was built for service as a commercial freight hauler on the western rivers of the United States. After barely five months' service, the steamer sailed north from St. Louis, on the Missouri River, bound for Fort Benton, Montana Territory, with a lading of over 250 tons of mining equipment, foodstuffs, and general cargo. On April 1, 1865, the ill-fated ship snagged and sank twenty-five miles above Omaha, Nebraska, and became a total loss. A little over a century later, treasure hunters discovered her bones on federal lands in the Desoto National Wildlife Refuge buried beneath the earth in the now-filled, nineteenth-century river channel. In 1968-69, the site was fully excavated by the National Park Service.[1]

Though one was found beneath the earth and the other beneath between forty and seventy feet of water, comparison between *Bertrand* and *New Jersey* was inevitable. Both were steamboats, built within two years of each other during the Civil War. Both were commercial freight haulers designed for service in a specific environment and employing the product of then-modern technology in both design and motive power. Upon being excavated, *Bertrand* yielded nearly two million artifacts, three hundred thousand of which, buried in an anaerobic environment, were of museum-display quality. The artifacts recovered required over three years of concerted effort by a full staff of conservators to catalog, stabilize, mend, and preserve.[2]

The figures were sobering, to say the least. Using *Bertrand* as a rough benchmark, I calculated that *New Jersey*, buried for the most part beneath Chesapeake muds in an anaerobic environment, could conceivably carry more than six million artifacts! Even assuming that most of the perishables were destroyed by the fire, the potentials were still awesome.

To carry out a comprehensive and responsible archaeological survey in relatively deep water on the open Chesapeake would require major financial resources, at least several years of field work, sophisticated shore support and conservation facilities, and an institutional or state program willing and competent enough to manage the resources and their ultimate disposition and protection. Sadly, none of these requirements existed. Worse, there were no clearly defined state or federal antiquities codes suitable or strong enough to protect the site from relic hunting, treasure salvage, or damage from other stress factors should its location become public knowledge.

With its precise position known to only a few individuals in NAA and the Maryland Geological Survey (MGS) Division of Archaeology, there appeared to be no immediate danger from wholesale looting by pot hunters. And with the wreck's burial deep in the preservative sediments of the Bay bottom, it was in little danger of further natural deterioration for many years to come. Thus it was decided to leave the site in the condition we had discovered it until such time as an appropriate avenue of further investigation could be found. *New Jersey* had lain untouched for over a century. She could, we reasoned, wait a few more years.

We could not have been more wrong.

❏   ❏   ❏

One of the principal missions of the Hydrographic Survey Branch of the National Oceanic and Atmospheric Administration is to survey, record, and map the topography of the ever-evolving submarine environment of American waters and to provide accurate charts and information on all navigable waters therein. One corollary mission of this program is the location and removal or destruction of hazardous obstructions to navigation, including shipwrecks, in and adjacent to navigable channels. In 1978 one such operation was carried out by the NOAA hydrographic survey and wire-drag ships *Rude* and *Heck* in the central Chesapeake Bay channel approaches to Baltimore. It was during this operation that *New Jersey* was rediscovered. And it was then that the future of this unique time capsule was unintentionally, yet irrevocably, placed in jeopardy.

The heavy, weighted dragline that snagged *New Jersey* on that fateful day in 1978 apparently caught in the ship's still-standing smokestack at a depth of 41.5 feet, ripping it from its foundations. Though diver investigation had ascertained that she was at least fifty years old, there was little apparent concern for her historical value. That was not the business of NOAA.[3] The duty of *Rude* and *Heck* was simply to clear the sea lanes of potential hazards to navigation.

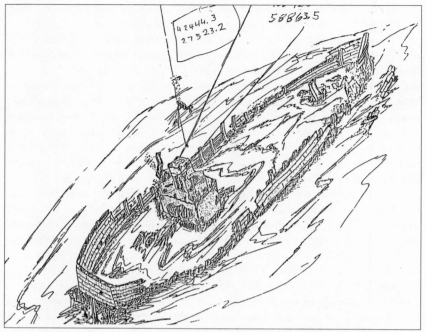

Sketch of the *New Jersey* wreck site accompanying the NOAA AWOIS report.

NOAA diver investigation of the site had been limited and the accuracy of the findings somewhat off the mark. A rough plan of the site had been sketched and submitted along with a site report. The exact Loran-C radio position coordinates were plotted and recorded. Then, following standard procedure, the data were entered into NOAA's automated wreck and obstruction information system (AWOIS), a sophisticated computerized index of shipwreck and obstruction information.[4] The following year, 1979, the new data were published on no fewer than three NOAA navigational charts. The exact location of a major unsurveyed archaeological resource was thus efficiently and systematically made public for the first time.[5] The consequences were devastating.

Soon after NOAA's publication of the site location in both chart form and in the publicly accessible AWOIS, dive shop operations headquartered in Washington, D.C., among the first to learn of the wreck, began running charter dives to the new site. Divers from one shop, discovering a "cargo of pottery vessels," correctly concluded the ship to be *New Jersey* and dutifully reported their findings to NOAA. The new data were methodically added to the AWOIS computerized files. The site's potential as a grab bag for relic collecting expanded almost geometrically as word of the wreck and its inviting cargo of pottery spread about the diving community. Here was a "virgin wreck" with a seemingly limitless supply of souvenirs for the taking.

By 1982, when I published an account of our discovery of the ship (sans specific locational data), *New Jersey* had already become the object of frequent visits by wreck divers, sport diving clubs, and dive shop charter operations. Evidence of looting, however, was as yet unproved, and Maryland State Archaeologist Tyler Bastian, under whose jurisdiction the site fell, decided upon a wait-and-see strategy. It was, unhappily, management strategy, born of necessity since Maryland possessed neither program, personnel, nor monitoring capabilities to do otherwise. Pandora's box had been opened, and no one, it appeared, knew how to close it. There was no management policy within the state's Department of Natural Resources to address such issues, other than those governing state actions in matters pertaining to littoral sites under state jurisdiction, nor was there any high-level interest in doing so. Indeed, Bastian's own resources to manage the programs under his purview had been stretched to the limit. And with Baltimore City bus drivers then making more salary per year than Ph.D. archaeologists in the state's employ, there was little incentive among many in the bureauracy to take on the thankless additional burdens inherent in managing underwater sites.

To his credit, Tyler Bastian attacked the problem as best he could. That the site was clearly important in archaeological terms was without question. "It seems to me," he wrote on January 12, 1983, "that the 'Pitcher Wreck' is sufficiently important from the standpoint of age, condition, and cargo to warrant protection."[6] But without Department of Natural Resources' ability or willingness to assist or monitor the site, there was little recourse along those lines. Bastian decided to take another tack. Setting out upon a campaign of friendly persuasion, public information, and consultation, he personally engaged the diving public in open forums on the value and fragility of the state's submerged cultural resources, and shipwrecks in particular. His was both a thankless and unrewarding task, undertaken in less-than-hospitable settings, addressing a public that neither understood the value of, nor cared for, archaeology, especially when it concerned shipwrecks. He quietly sought to organize and support the establishment of an amateur underwater archaeological society and to involve them directly in underwater projects. The Underwater Archaeological Society of Maryland (UASM) was soon in operation, with membership reaching over two hundred in its first year afloat. It wasn't much, but it was a start, and many were deeply influenced.[7]

By the late summer of 1985, through information quietly provided to Bastian and his staff by concerned members of the diving community and UASM, it was becoming painfully clear that organized efforts to recover artifacts from the wreck by some individuals and groups were increasing dramatically. Hundreds, perhaps thousands, of artifacts had been brought up by divers who were totally ignorant of the damage they were inflicting upon a major archaeological resource.

The gravity and intensity of relic collecting on the site became even more apparent as detailed descriptions of artifacts recovered began to filter into Bastian's office at the MGS. Some were later voluntarily loaned to the Division of Archaeology, regional maritime museums, or to authorities on maritime collections by well-intentioned divers for the purpose of identification or recording. Most, however, went unreported or undocumented and were learned of through third parties.

It was becoming increasingly evident from the variety of those artifacts examined or reported, as well as from descriptions of the wreck itself, that fairly deep penetration of the silts within the hull was probably taking place. A wide assortment of items relating to the cargo, such as wagon wheel hubs, crate loads of ceramics and glass, music boxes, pharmaceuticals, kegs of bird shot, barrels of corn and animal bones, as well as numerous components of the ship and its machinery, had been recovered.[8]

By late August 1985 reports began to reach the MGS that at least one group had begun planning concerted salvage operations to "mine" the hull of artifacts through the use of an airlift. Another party had the temerity to call me for information on just how the propeller and ship's anchors might be recovered. Some regular visitors to the site expressed concern for its condition and reported that they had discovered large craters in the silts that were not there before, suggesting that airlifting had already begun. Others stated that the ship's fallen smokestack had been removed.[9]

As a consequence of the increasing stream of data and rumors concerning the relic hunting and possible ongoing site destruction, Bastian moved with alacrity. On August 22, 1985, he secured a resolution of support from the MGS Advisory Committee on Archaeology confirming state jurisdiction over the site.[10] Armed with that body's support, he requested a voluntary meeting with members of the Maryland diving community, the press, and concerned parties from various state agencies and educational and private institutions to address the issue publically for the first time.

The meeting was convened on September 10, 1986, in the Tawes Office Building in Annapolis.[11] From the outset of the conference, it was apparent that intensive visitation and artifact collecting at the wreck had been going on for years. One charter captain arrived with crates of artifacts recovered from the site, proudly noting that divers utilizing his charterboat had spent over nine hundred manhours on *New Jersey* in the last four years alone. Many who had managed to recover only broken pottery had discarded the pieces in the water beside the charter boats' anchorage at Chesapeake Beach, a site that was to become known as "the *New Jersey* Dump." For the most part, however, it was clear that the bulk of diver activity was neither malicious nor intentionally detrimental. But damage was being done, and much of it was serious. One visitor reported evidence of extensive deep dredging that had exposed ornate but fragile cast-iron and wood detailing, which would scarcely last a year in its present state of exposure.[12] As the discussion progressed, I began to ask myself which was worse, the unintentional damage to the site by the sport diving community, or the large-scale destruction caused by NOAA's wire drag operation?

Despite the initial tensions of the meeting between archaeologists and divers, Bastian and staff archaeologist Joseph McNamara, a diver of no small accomplishment himself, slowly and with candor outlined the importance of the site, state codes governing the ownership of the wreck, and current antiquities regulations. They noted that by virtue of the Wetlands Act of 1965, anything lying on or beneath the bottoms of navigable waters within the territorial jurisdiction of the state of Maryland belonged to the state. And as such, all archaeological or historical re-sources therein were to be administered and protected by the Office of the State Archaeologist. Fortunately, little note was made of recent court decisions in other states regarding the upholding of the tenets of English Admiralty Law and the rights of salvage over state antiquities and archae-ological codes. They were decisions that could well reverse Maryland's assertion of ownership. Bastian, nevertheless, pointed out that airlifting or other forms of dredging, without benefit of a permit, were also violations of the Maryland Water Resources Act.[13]

He stressed that the state neither sought confrontation nor wished to restrict diver access to the site. Rather, he hoped to elicit a group consensus regarding divers' willingness to comply with state codes. There would be no prohibition of diving on the site as long as destruction was halted.

Though the majority of divers present expressed a concern that any prohibition on diving or collecting on *New Jersey* might set a precedent that could lead to prohibitions on wreck diving in general, most agreed to cooperate with the state, thanks to Bastian's firm stance. Yet, it was a symbolic gesture at best, for those present were but a few of the growing multitude of divers visiting the site.[14] And recent federal court decisions in states such as Florida, which had upheld the rights of salvors over modern state antiquities codes, offered no consolation for those of us concerned about the archaeological integrity of *New Jersey*.[15]

On September 30, at my suggestion and through the auspices of State Administrator of Archaeology Richard Hughes of the Maryland Historical Trust, a conference of concerned agencies, institutions, and archaeolo-gists was convened at the Trust office in Annapolis. At issue was not merely the need to address an archaeological catastrophe in progress—everyone was in agreement that something had to be done—but just who would do it and, more importantly to many in attendance, who would pick up the tab. It was finally resolved that the Division of Archaeology would initiate an effort to inventory artifacts already recovered from the wreck which had been voluntarily loaned by sport divers. Though provenance would be nonexistant, at least typological data could be recorded, and the basis for a small study collection established. NAA would organize and carry out, at no cost, a remote-sensing survey and follow-up ground truthing of the site and would conduct limited systematic surface sampling. Upon conclusion of the investigation and with a more reliable arsenal of current environmental and actual site data in hand, a strategy for future actions, possibly including site reburial, could be developed.[16]

A prompt response to the situation was almost mandatory. Deliberate state-mandated action by the archaeological community would visibly demonstrate, for the first time, Maryland's official concern for its endangered submerged cultural resources and a willingness to promulgate adequate efforts to evaluate them. Such actions might well serve as a benchmark against which all future efforts under similar stress situations might be measured and, thus, had to be as thorough and scientific as feasible. Finally, and most importantly, it would provide a database concerning the realities of the *New Jersey* sites and, indeed, similar shipwreck sites in like environments throughout the state. Without a standing program to address the crisis, it was, in fact, about all that could be done.

Unfortunately, immediate funding for such an undertaking was practically out of the question. The Maryland Historical Trust could allocate barely two thousand dollars to the project,[17] NAA had less than seven hundred dollars in its account, and the MGS was at the end of its fiscal tether for the year. Securing state or federal funding through normal channels would take months. We had an objective and a plan, but what was really needed was a white knight—and quickly.

FIVE

The Glass Pit

When I first met him at an underwater archaeology conference in Baltimore in 1981, I found Edward R. Miller an unassuming fellow whose quiet demeanor belied a formidable portfolio of experience in underwater research. A 1974 graduate of the U.S. Naval Academy with degrees in both engineering and history, he had earned his fins in the field of naval salvage, deep submergence work, and saturation diving. While at the academy he had developed strong interests along many lines, foremost among them in the then-ongoing search for the remains of the famed Civil War ironclad *Monitor*, lost in a storm off Cape Hatteras, North Carolina, on December 31, 1862.

Unlike many then competing to locate *Monitor*, Miller had developed a comprehensive research design, incorporating both a historical study and a systematic high-tech remote-survey program, aimed at the documentation and location of the wreck site. Utilizing the expertise of the Naval Ship Research and Development Center, he organized an aerial magnetometer survey of the coastal region in which the ship had been lost and soon found himself a centerpiece in the thick of the *Monitor* hunt. Soon after the ironclad was finally discovered in 1973 by a team from Duke University, Miller, quite naturally, was among those who participated in the dramatic verification of the site, quickly becoming the quasi-official U.S. Navy liaison with the various institutions and agencies competing for dominion over the wreck. In 1984, when jurisdiction over the administration of the wreck finally fell to the National Oceanic and Atmospheric Administration, Miller was a natural choice as project manager for the *Monitor* Marine Sanctuary Program, the first national historic shipwreck sanctuary program in America.

In August 1985 I had received a query from Ed regarding a shipwreck near Annapolis. From the side-scan imagery and locational data he provided, I readily determined the vessel to be the remains of the four-masted schooner *Herbert D. Maxwell*, built at Bath, Maine, in 1905 and sunk with a cargo of guano after a collision in 1911.[1] But, more important, the side-scan printout Ed had sent me was absolutely the best I had ever seen. Cavalierly, he had volunteered to return the favor I had rendered in identifying the wreck. He could not have guessed how soon I would

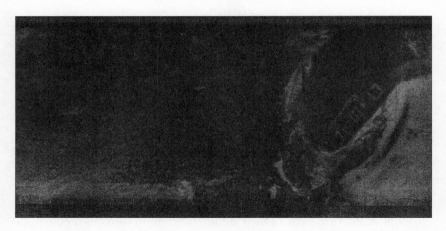

NOAA's side-scan sonar image of the four-masted schooner *Herbert D. Maxwell*
was acquired in 1985 during preliminary field testing of equipment intended
for use at the USS *Monitor* Marine Sanctuary. The wreck is still largely intact
and lies in a huge scour area in eighty feet of water off Kent Island.
Courtesy National Oceanic and Atmospheric Administration

take him up on the offer, for if anyone could help get things moving on
the *New Jersey* investigation, it was Ed Miller. After all, I reasoned, NOAA
owed the old steamboat a favor or two.

The timing could not have been better. Soon after the conference at
the Maryland Historical Trust, I contacted Ed and explained the situation.
He was quite sympathetic to our efforts, particularly since his agency had
been partially responsible for the publicizing of the site location. Miller
responded in the positive. NOAA was preparing to mobilize for another
remote survey of *Monitor*, he said, and it just might be possible to dovetail
our projects.

By October 2, NOAA had officially agreed to provide a survey vessel, a
side-scan sonar unit, a tracker-plotter system, technicians, and related
support personnel and material for the side-scan survey.[2] Ed noted, however, that, owing to a restricted operational budget, he would be obliged
to attach the work to an already funded exercise, probably during an
equipment-testing phase prior to a deep-sea performance. *New Jersey* had
been deemed a suitable pre-test site for the fall side-scan survey of *Monitor*.
We would, however, have the benefit of NOAA's equipment, services,
and talent for only one day—whatever the results might be.

Our white knight had come through.

❑   ❑   ❑

The morning of November 14, 1985, was crisp and clear as we boarded
the big ocean survey vessel *Peter W. Anderson* at her berth at the Naval

Research Laboratory wharf near Annapolis. The ship had been temporarily placed at NOAA's disposal by the U.S. Environmental Protection Agency for the equipment shakedown operations on the Chesapeake before actual work on *Monitor* was carried out.[3]

At 165 feet in length and 24 feet abeam, the survey vessel was very nearly the same dimensions as the ship that we hoped to document later that same day.[4] Her on-board scientific capabilities were indeed formidable, but the only systems I was truly concerned with were the EG&G side-reading sonar units and the Mini-Ranger II data positioning system, both of which were central to our investigation. One would provide a comprehensive sonar-generated image of *New Jersey,* and the other would tell us exactly where we were, to within a foot of accuracy on the globe at any given second. Fixed-point shore transponder stations had been erected at Annapolis and at Cooks Point at the mouth of the Choptank River to provide signals from which the Mini-Ranger system would instantly calculate and record our position far more accurately than Loran-C. Technical expertise for both systems was provided by the big ocean research firm of Eastport International, under the personal direction of company president Craig Mullins.[5] As Richard Hughes, Joe McNamara, and NAA's historian, Dr. Fred Hopkins of the University of Baltimore, and I boarded *Anderson,* it was like Christmas with all the trimmings.

By noon we had arrived in the target area, and as in all such shakedown or debugging operations, glitches popped up immediately. Malfunctions in both the track plotter and the sonar systems appeared. Finally, the sonar "fish" was deployed and a trial run initiated. The gremlins reappeared, this time on the side-scan recorder. More tinkering, cursing, and sweat. Again we deployed. Again glitches. Then the fish was run into an unchartered mudbank, but fortunately emerged unscathed. A new fish, deployed to a depth of fifty feet, changed our luck. By now, just as all systems had begun to hum along gracefully, it was late afternoon, and our day of high-tech time was almost at an end. Another hour and we would have to head back.

Even though sea conditions had begun to kick up, I requested one more shot. A fourth sprint over the site was ordered. As we turned for a south-north run on the wreck, the side-scan strip chart hummed along, picturing a stark, featureless plain, interrupted only occasionally by large anchor scars in the mud. Then, the captain announced over the intercom that we were approaching the wreck. "Five hundred, four hundred, three hundred, two hundred, one hundred. We should be right on her."

The image on the strip chart was clean and clear. A cheer went up. Another pass was ordered. Again the imagery was crisp, but exposing a different range of details on the wreck. A third pass was requested, from north to south. And then another from southwest to northeast. Suddenly, there was a scurry, and a set of orders broadcast in staccato style by

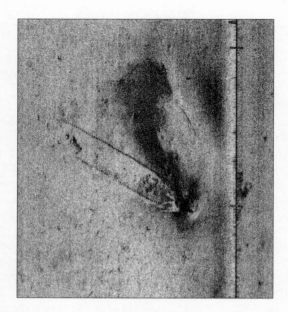

Side-scan sonar image of the *New Jersey* site made during the November 1985 survey. Note the dark area adjacent to the wreck, the first indication of the formation of a major scour area.

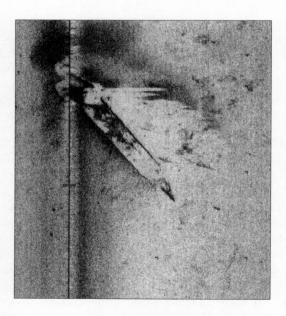

A second side-scan sonar image of the *New Jersey* site suggests that the scour extends not only along its port side but around its stern as well. The bow appears to have been bent slightly toward the starboard side, possibly a result of going down bow first and impacting against the bottom.

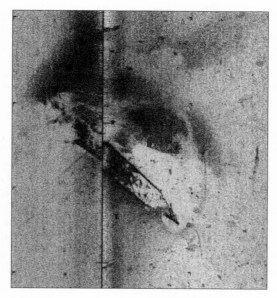

A sonar image produced during the near-collision of the side-scan "fish"
with the wreck clearly portrays not only the extent of the scour surrounding the
port and stern areas of the ship, but also the debris field within the forward
confines of the hull itself. The white area off the port bow is an acoustic
shadow produced by the hull.

A pair of buoys is deployed from the fantail of *Peter W. Anderson*
to mark the position of the *New Jersey* wreck site in preparation for
a hands-on survey in November 1985.

Robots Beneath the Chesapeake

Eastport's technical officer: "Haul her up to forty." I could see the two men on the monitor move quickly and with an economy of motion, one to a large winch and the other to manage the cable. The strip chart readout had recorded the entire event in frightening detail, for the fish had narrowly missed by a few feet being dragged into the boiler-engine complex of the wreck.

At a cost of thirty thousand dollars for the fish alone, the consequences would have been more than an embarrassment. Thus, with darkness setting in, it was resolved that we had pushed our good fortune as far as possible and, after dropping marker buoys adjacent to the site, we called it a day.[6]

That evening, I began to evaluate the imagery produced by the survey, the first actual site data, other than artifacts collected by sport divers, that I had examined in a decade. I was both impressed and disturbed. As much as three-quarters of the upper hull area of the wreck was now exposed enough to provide a clearly delineated acoustic shadow—far more area than had been exposed in 1975. Outward collapse of a five-foot section of the hull was apparent on the starboard midships. The bow sections seemed to be slightly bent toward the starboard side, possibly a consequence of the ship's collision with the bottom as she sank. The anchor complex, which had been partially buried in 1975, was now totally exposed, with arms and shafts protruding over both port and starboard hulls. One bulkhead could clearly be discerned in the forward section. A heavy rubble area appeared abaft the anchor complex and could have been the remains of the collapsed pilothouse and forward cabins.[7]

Amidships, a very deep depression, corresponding to the area where we had encountered the cargo of whiteware and other crated goods, was quite distinct. The boiler and cylinder were also clearly defined, apparently disjoined from the bracings that had once held them in place, lying diagonally across the aft end of the wreck. The port hull was quite pronounced and appeared to be in a substantial state of preservation, as its linear integrity seemed still to be in good order. Indeed, on one of the readouts, the individual frames of the hull were clearly discernible.[8]

The extreme stern end of the site was obscured, a condition I attributed to still being buried in the silt. The rudder assemblage, propeller, fenders, stern decking, and other features were still undetectable. From the fathometer readouts and the side-scan shadows, it was evident that the scour pit on the port side of the wreck was approximately seven feet deep. The peak elevation on the site was still the boiler-engine complex, which, judging from the acoustic shadow, stood between ten and fifteen feet off the bottom. It appeared that an enormous amount of the wreck was extant and exposed.[9]

The assembled data were invaluable, for on the following day, we were scheduled to begin systematic ground truthing, that is, a hands-on examination of the site. When I finally turned in at 4:00 A.M., I did so with the

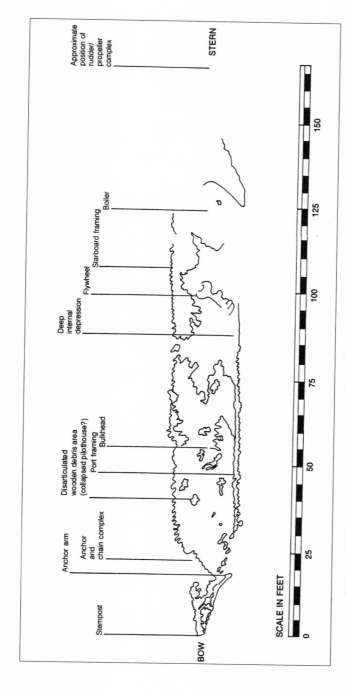

This profile interpretation is drawn from composite data provided by several side-scan sonar images obtained during the November 1985 survey of *New Jersey*.

39

confidence that at last we had hard evidence that the site was, as feared, exposed to the elements and the destructive biota of the Chesapeake. Whether such exposure was natural, induced by human hands, or a combination of both remained to be seen.

Several days of hands-on survey of the site had been scheduled, beginning on November 15 aboard a borrowed survey boat named *Option*, commanded by Captain David Sisson. Our objectives were the following: (1) to evaluate systematically the exposed extent of the site, identifying those features revealed by the side-scan survey; (2) to note areas where extensive alterations of the bottom had occurred since 1975; (3) to conduct a limited surface collection of artifacts for diagnostic evaluation by the Division of Archaeology; (4) to conduct, if possible, a limited photographic foray to record imperiled key features while *in situ;* and (5) to probe systematically those sectors of the interior hull still covered by sediments.[10]

In order to accomplish the aforementioned goals, a nylon baseline was to be run along the entire length of the ship, from bow to the sternmost exposure. The baseline was divided into four sectors and thirty-four discrete subsections of five-foot intervals per section. At each subsection mark, a clip was affixed to the line. Each major sector, or study area, was based upon the complexity of the site as revealed by the data from the side-scan survey and the depth of the area to be examined (which determined bottom time). Each survey team was assigned a twenty-foot-long clip line, a six-foot steel probe, and record-keeping gear. The teams were instructed to evaluate their assigned sectors by attaching their clip lines to the baseline at each five-foot interval to be investigated and then by swimming at right angles from the baseline to port and then to starboard hulls, systematically probing the sediments and recording data as they proceeded. Thus, it was hoped, features on the surface and solid anomalies below the sediments might be plotted. Based upon this assemblage of data, with key features plotted, both controlled surface collecting and photographic documentation could be carried out. As our objective was simply to conduct a systematic in-depth reconnaissance, no effort at excavation or precision mapping would be attempted.[11]

Although the site had been marked by two buoys during the side-scan survey the day before, heavy weather during the night had swept one from its line and sunk the other. Compounding our difficulty, a malfunction of *Option*'s Loran-C obliged us to relocate the wreck with a fathometer and by landmark bearings. No sooner had we anchored off the site than several dive boats arrived on the scene; the captain of one of them was one of the people present at the September meeting. Both McNamara and Richard Hughes, who again joined the operation as an observer the following day, resolved to adhere to Bastian's proclamation that no one would be prohibited from diving on the site provided they did no major damage to it, even if they got in our way.[12]

The Glass Pit

Making the first dive with McNamara, I was surprised at bottom conditions, with visibility ranging up to fifteen feet. Then, as our uninvited guests arrived on the scene, furiously fanning the bottom in search of buried artifacts, visibility rapidly deteriorated to mere inches. On at least several occasions, we literally bumped head-on into a relic hunter scooping up glass fragments from the the old steamer's bones.[13]

I was appalled, for not only were they mucking up the site, they were pushing to the limit the willingness of state agents to observe Bastian's desire for compromise. With the flood tide coming on and visibility having all but evaporated thanks to our unwanted guests, the speedy establishment of a baseline was out of the question. Systematic surface survey or collecting would prove impossible, as would any effort at photography. The situation was duplicated during each of the following days on the site. It was thus resolved to conduct a general sectored survey based upon site landmark features, assigning specific areas of investigation to each diver—no small task in near-zero-visibility waters.

Still, the investigation proved extremely fruitful. Though the stern section had not been clearly defined by the side-scan, it was soon discovered that portions of it were now almost entirely exposed, except for a thin dusting of sediment. The propeller was three-quarters cleared, and measurement of the blades and shaft were taken. Although the rudder assembly was not examined, the remains of what may have been the stern fender, and a portion of the rounded stern itself, were documented, and the framing configuration along the port stern section was measured and recorded.[14]

Amidships, the starboard hull, with several feet partially cleared, was not surprisingly found substantially intact. There had been some collapse in the forward midships area, confirming interpretation of the side-scan record. Internally, bulkheads and partitions were found exposed. Beneath the center of one such bulkhead, the top of a passage, possibly a doorway, had been revealed.[15]

In the forward portion of the wreck, a large amount of wooden debris, possibly the remains of the collapsed pilothouse and cabins, as indicated on the sonar, littered the area. This sector, like the stern, had been deeply buried in 1975, although some structural features had even then protruded somewhat from the silts.[16]

The entire anchor complex in the bow was now almost entirely exposed, with gigantic iron arms, shafts, and flukes hanging over both sides of the hull, apparently thrown there when the ship collided with the bottom. In 1975 they, too, had been largely buried. Now rotting anchor chains ran downward into largely accreted conglomerates of iron and muck. Forward of the anchor complex, the bowstem stood entirely exposed, rising at least six to eight feet off the bottom.[17]

As Joe and I explored along the port side scour, we noted it to be still well defined and deep, revealing the hull almost to the turn of the bilge.

A possible release valve was recovered from *New Jersey* by a sport diver following our survey in 1987. The piece was later turned over to State Archaeologist Tyler Bastian in a spirit of cooperation between the diving community and Maryland. Conservation measures were immediately taken and the crumbling artifact was eventually stabilized and saved by archaeological conservator Katherine Singley. The artifact is pictured *in situ* prior to recovery (top); following recovery and donation (bottom left); and after months of conservation and stabilization treatment (bottom right). Photograph (top) by Richard Carey; (bottom) by Katherine Singley

42

The Glass Pit

Any more, I thought to myself, and the ship itself might well be undercut. The exposed wooden frames and planking were quite fragile, sometimes crumbling at the merest touch. Following along the inner hull line to a distance approximately eighty feet abaft the bow, a deep depression extending more than halfway across the ship was encountered. This pit was, at one point, approximately eight feet deep, and its bottom was covered by a blanket of broken glass. Later analysis of samples of the glass indicated that the breaks were almost all new. Here, we encountered relic hunters eagerly probing and fanning for intact treasures beneath those broken by their predecessors, who had also been in search of souvenirs.[18]

Immediately abaft the "glass pit," a name that the pot hunters had dubbed the area, a large six-spoked flywheel, with both wheels estimated at four feet in diameter, was discovered. Immediately abaft the wheels, we found a large complex of pipes, several of which were connected to the main condenser unit of the boiler. Iron bands, apparently recently broken and believed to have been associated with the funnel assemblage, were noted lying at the base of the engine. There was no evidence of the smokestack itself.[19]

The forward and central starboard side of the ship appeared to be still heavily smothered by the silts. Pot hunting had apparently not yet ravaged this area. But to our dismay, we soon noted numerous small, medium, and large pits, some of which could only have been caused by airlifting, with broken artifacts at the base of many, along the port side from the forward locker areas to a section immediately forward of the boiler-engine complex. Although the sediment depressions along the starboard side now ranged between two and four feet below the hull, the massive digging efforts primarily on the port side threatened not only the local integrity of the hull, but that of the entire ship. The removal of sediments, both manually and by dredging, especially in the central port region, had resulted in the collapse of adjacent silt beds into the pits, reducing both the support for and protection of the starboard hull.[20]

It soon became apparent that our principal concern had become a reality: the alteration of the silt beds within the confines of the hull was inducing a revision of the natural hydraulic flow over the site to one producing an eddying and scouring action within the wreck. As a consequence the wreck was rapidly becoming exposed to the destructive biota of the Bay, both microscopic and macroscopic.[21]

Under current conditions, I predicted, the site as it lay would be substantially altered within the space of a few years. Given the current benchmarks of biotic destruction of wood in the Chesapeake system and unbridled relic hunting at the site, *New Jersey* would cease to exist as a shipwreck with any integrity within the next two decades. A time capsule, illustrative of every aspect of Maryland and Tidewater life, commerce, and marine technology in the year 1870, would be lost forever.

Flying Eyeballs

The steamship *New Jersey*'s prospects for survival were discouraging. The situation promised to set a catastrophic precedent for other still-to-be-discovered underwater archaeological sites in Maryland waters. Yet there seemed to be no positive solution short of a full-scale underwater site survey, for which money and expertise were in short supply. The Maryland archaeological community appeared powerless to act, although advice was plentiful. Suggestions were offered up by the Maryland Geological Survey's Advisory Committee on Archaeology, which served as a consultative body for the state archaeologist. A few proposals had merit but simply cost too much. Others were impractical or politically unfeasible.

One scheme that was seriously considered was that the entire site be covered by a plastic tarpaulin and wire mesh and then be reburied beneath a mantle of sediment and oyster shells, returning it to the state in which it had been when discovered. The sediments and shells might either be borrowed from the immediate terrain or brought in by barges from borrow areas up the Bay. The anaerobic status of the wreck might thus be restored, site stability at least temporarily insured, and illegal excavation frustrated. But at a projected cost of over two hundred thousand dollars, the idea was scuttled almost as soon as the estimate was in.[1] Indeed, without financial resources, prospects for immediate action of any kind seemed hopeless. Without the ability or will to enforce existing state statutes (which would undoubtedly be overturned in federal court if challenged), *New Jersey* was likely to end up as the first well-documented underwater historical and archaeological site to be lost in Maryland waters. NOAA and the MGS had come through to assess the situation. But what was needed was either a miracle or an act of Congress. Although no one could have forseen it, both were soon to become a reality.

❏ ❏ ❏

On an otherwise ordinary day in mid-June 1986, I had little inkling of what good fortune was about to descend on the old *New Jersey* when I received a phone call from Emory Kristof of *National Geographic*. Although I had never met him, I was well acquainted, as a reader of the magazine, with Kristof's remarkable pioneering work in underwater photography and his recent forays into the field of deep-water robotics. His dramatic undersea expeditions were the stuff of childhood dreams and swashbuckling adventure, from the lochs of Scotland to the polar seas. He had been a leading light in the search for the famed *Titanic* and had plumbed the depths of the great Galápagos Rift in the far Pacific. He had directed the photography of the wreck of *Breadelbane*, one of the lost ships of the famed Franklin Expedition, beneath the Arctic icepack. More recently, he had orchestrated the spectacular robotic photography of *Hamilton* and *Scourge*, two intact War of 1812 American warships lying at the bottom of Lake Erie. Emory Kristof was certainly the last person in the world I expected to hear from. He wanted, he said, to have lunch with me to discuss my participation in an upcoming project. I instantly agreed.

The luncheon, at a Chinese restaurant near my office at the Library of Congress, was forgettable, but my first encounter with *Geographic*'s premier photographer was anything but. Emory Kristof is an imposing fellow, with a long, coal-colored explorer's beard tinctured with gray and the stature of a tall man, although he is only of moderate height. If he had been outfitted with a bandolier of pistols, a cutlass, and blazing matches in his hatband, he would easily pass for Blackbeard the Pirate. A graduate of the University of Maryland, he was the youngest photographer ever hired by *Geographic* and, after nearly twenty-five years' service, was also one of the widest traveled and longest tenured. With a booming voice that dominates every conversation, he is at once imperious and inquisitive, extremely gregarious, entirely likeable, and always seeking answers to questions that have never been answered, and on occasion never even asked.

When I asked him why he wanted to meet with me, he replied that he was here at the direction of the magazine's editor in chief, Bill Garrett, to invite me along as a consultant on an expedition to a remote piece of rock in Lake Superior called Isle Royale. All I knew about the island was that it was famous for its timberwolf and moose populations, and that its coast was lined with scores of deep-water shipwrecks.

Why I was chosen to participate in the Isle Royale Expedition was at first a mystery to me. The objective of the project, I was soon told, was to field-test the use of remotely operated vehicles (ROVs), or underwater robots, to document and record for the National Park Service the exceptionally deep shipwrecks surrounding the island. Somehow, the executives at the National Geographic Society had gotten the impression that I knew something about ROVs and would be good to have along. Though anything but an expert, I had, in fact, studied the industrial applications of several prototype ROVs being deployed in the Louisiana "oil patch" in the Gulf of Mexico as early as 1982 and soon afterward had begun to consider their possible applications for deep-water archaeology. But, like many others who studied them from afar, I had been obliged to dismiss their use outright as simply too expensive and the technology too young to be practical. After all, archaeology is a pauper's science, and deep-water archaeology is the stuff of dreamers.

Kristof's work on the *Hamilton* and *Scourge* project, wherein two well-preserved warships had been photographically documented by an ROV, or "flying eyeball" as he liked to call it, in nearly three hundred feet of water, had changed the whole scenario in underwater archaeology overnight. And now I was being offered a chance to participate in another such undertaking. I accepted immediately.

❏ ❏ ❏

Getting to Isle Royale was not a simple matter. To say that the town that Emory, the National Geographic Society's ROV pilot Michael Cole, and I were leaving from was isolated would be an understatement. As we drove along in our rented car, I knew we were close when we passed a sign saying, "End of the Earth 2 miles. Houghton 4 miles." At our hotel in Houghton, Michigan, I was introduced to the rest of the field team: Keith Moorehead, a genial, wise-cracking engineer and ROV technician; Wayne J. Bywater, a mustachioed, redheaded graduate of the Florida Institute of Technology, president of a company called Northeastern Underwater Services, and one of the most experienced ROV pilots in New England; and Don Moore, a U.S. naval officer and expert in robotics who had been invited along as an official observer for the Navy.

The following morning, with six great cartloads filled with cameras, video gear, two ROVs, cable, food, camping equipment, luggage, and miscellaneous "stuff," we embarked aboard the National Park Service (NPS) Ship *Ranger III* for a nearly seven-hour voyage across Lake Superior to Isle Royale.

The waters of Lake Superior were deep blue-black, and there was a continuous wind out of the southwest that heaped up waves of oceanic proportions. With depths in some places exceeding thirteen hundred feet, the lake seemed more like the Atlantic than a docile inland waterway. Embraced by frequently rocky shorelines, it was not surprising that Superior's waters covered the bones of innumerable ships. Indeed, the coast and deep waters surrounding our destination, Isle Royale, were famous the world over as the Great Lakes Graveyard of Ships. The island was a national park, and, as such, wrecks lying within three miles of her coast were considered property of the federal government, and many of them were considered to be submerged historic and archaeological resources. It was our mission to assist the Park Service's highly regarded Submerged Cultural Resources Unit (SCRU), already on the island, by conducting a video inventory of the deeper, more inaccessible sites with the Geo's "flying eyeballs." We would be sending, for the first time, ROVs to dive and record deep sites around the island that were considered too dangerous or difficult for the SCRU divers to explore and survey in the traditional manner.[2]

Geologically, Isle Royale is a relative infant still being formed. It is a rocky, rugged, and often precipitous piece of land, forty-five miles long, perforated by many small, natural harbors, with high ridges running along its length. There are only four ranger stations on the island, all of which are abandoned during the two worst months of every winter to its famous population of wolves and moose. The apex of human occupation, strictly regulated by the NPS, comes during the summer months when campers, naturalists, and a spate of hard-core divers make the long boat trip from the Upper Peninsula to Royale's beautiful and dangerous shores.[3]

As soon as we arrived, we were met by the SCRU chief, Dan Lenihan, one of the most respected marine archaeologists in the country. Little time was lost in setting up housekeeping in several log cabins on the island. Kristof and Bywater set off at once to examine our vessel support, while Cole and Moorehead began checking out the *Geographic*'s ROV. The machine, dubbed "Goober" by Moorehead, was long, yellow, and tubular. A third-generation robot called Sea Rover, the vehicle had been the brainchild of Chris Nicholson, a young, blond-haired, bespectacled engineering genius who had quit high school to build robots. He had early on made a name for himself in the field of deep sea systems development, and it was his vehicle, the RG-247, which had served as the vehicle that had carried Kristof's cameras to record *Hamilton* and *Scourge*. Sea Rover was awkward looking, with runners on either side and a dome in its snout in which a pan-tilt Vivitar UMC Skylight lA video camera was mounted to serve as the unit's eyes. A thirty-five-millimeter Nikonos camera could also be mounted in the dome and triggered by remote control. Propelled by four thrusters (two aft on port and starboard, and one on top and bottom), for forward, reverse, vertical, and lateral translation and yaw rotation, the ROV was connected to the surface, from which it was navigated and managed by a complex of oil-insulated, fiber-optic cables. The cables were outfitted with a dozen or so detachable ball floats to insure that they always floated clear of the ROV and kept the vehicle from dragging its tail in the bottom. The cables were managed by a topside tender whose primary mission was to feed them out and take them in as necessary and to insure that they were always clear of obstructions on the surface.

The pilot of the ROV, while usually ensconced within the comfort of a ship's cabin, and propped up in front of the robot's television monitor, virtually "flew" his craft through the water with the aid of attitudinal and directional sensors. His attention rarely left the screen, while his fingers deftly managed the vehicle's movements with a pair of joysticks in manual control modes. Simple switches were used for the imaging system, tilt mechanism, remote focus, and remote iris control. The pilot's eyes were always on the attitude data, such as trim, course, and depth, which flicked down one side of the monitor at incredibly rapid speeds, along with whatever happened to be passing in front of the ROV's eye at the moment. In many ways, flying an ROV was akin to flying a model airplane, except that the ROV was no model. Indeed, flying an undersea "eyeball" could be a hair-raising experience.

The dangers to the machine itself were considerable. A descent of several hundred feet into the black murk in which a twisted carcass of a wreck lay, perhaps amid sprawling, jagged boulders, always offered the chance of snagging a cable, perhaps at a depth that divers could not penetrate to effect a rescue. Landing in a field of silt offered the prospect of indefinitely obscured visibility and the possibility of crashing into some unseen obstruction. A cracked dome could prove fatal to the vehicle and its bank of cameras. Although Sea Rover was outfitted with a clawlike mandible, or arm, strong enough to cut a small iron cable in half, and dextrous enough to hold and carry small solid objects, it was as yet awkward and incapable of conducting the simplest work with any delicacy. Yet, powered only by a small five-kilowatt generator, it had given humans the ability to dive deeper (up to 550 feet when fielded from the surface), stay longer (as long as one could keep a topside generator fueled), and with minimal danger (the ROV took the plunge and did not suffer from the bends, narcosis, or any other human hazards of diving). As a tool for undersea exploration, its possibilities were self-evident, but more significantly, as a tool for deep-water archaeology, its potential applications seemed endless.

Despite its prospects, there was much to be cautious about. We had two ROVs with us. One belonged to *Geographic*. The other was a second-generation system, much smaller and considerably less complex than Sea Rover, called Mini-Rover, which belonged to Deep Sea Systems International (Nicholson's new company). Together, the two vehicles were valued at over one hundred thousand dollars. To lose one would mean a major financial embarrassment for either institution and an end to the project, and neither group was eager to jeopardize its equipment. It was one thing to be on the cutting edge of technology, but another to be bloodied by it.

❑   ❑   ❑

On August 30, with National Park marine archaeologists Dan Lenihan, Ken Vrana, and Anne Belleman and the Director of the Canal Park Marine Museum in Duluth, Minnesota, Patrick Labadie, we set off from Rock Harbor, on Isle Royale's southeast coast, in an NPS thirty-one-foot Bertram named *Lorelei* and a twenty-five-foot steel-hulled boat called *Beaver* for what was to prove to be the first of many shipwreck sites investigated. Our primary target was a wreck called *Kamloops*, a single-screw canal boat designed for operations through the Welland Canal and built in 1924.[4]

As we pressed northward around the rocky east end of Isle Royale through Amygdolin Sound, then southwest along the north coast of the island toward a remote outcrop of boulders called Twelve O'Clock Point, I had plenty of time to bone up on the ship's history by reading a study entitled "The Shipwrecks of Isle Royale: The Historic Record," being prepared for publication by the NPS. For a Great Lakes canal boat, *Kamloops* was impressive: 250 feet between perpendiculars and 256 feet deck length, nearly 42 feet abeam, 26.5 feet molded depth, with a 14-foot draft and 2,400-deadweight-tons capacity.

Kamloops's loss with all hands during one of the worst blizzards in Lake Superior's history, on or about December 7, 1927, was a Great Lakes tragedy that had become a classic shipwreck legend—a great ship that had simply disappeared without a trace. Her bones had long remained undiscovered, and her whereabouts had acquired the russet hue of an insoluable mystery. That is until 1975, when Captain Roy Oberg, in his boat *Voyageur II*, located a strange anomaly with his fathometer in the dangerously rocky stretch of isolated and turbulent waters near Twelve O'Clock Point. On August 21, 1977, a sport diver named Ken Engelbrecht dived on the anomaly and landed on the stern of *Kamloops*, in nearly 190 feet of water. The following year, a party led by one John Steele explored the site further, discovering the engine telegraph and engine room. Steele claimed that the starboard side of the ship had been smashed and the pilothouse sheered off. Her bow lay in over 270 feet of black, treacherous water. *Kamloops*, it was readily discerned, was one of the most remote and deepest shipwreck sites discovered in Isle Royale's waters—and certainly one of the most dangerous to dive on.[6] To the sport divers of the Great Lakes, she had become the Mount Everest of shipwreck sites. To the National Park Service, she was an important maritime cultural resource and a substantial tile in the complex mosaic of Great Lakes history.

When we arrived on site, Lenihan and NPS diver Ken Vrana moved with quiet efficiency in preparation for a 175-foot descent to attach a downline and a buoy to the fantail of the wreck. The mission was completed in less than fifteen minutes but required a twenty-minute decompression stop at thirty feet on pure oxygen to avoid the deadly "bends," or decompression sickness. As soon as the dive had been completed, *Beaver* arrived on the scene and dropped anchor. Within minutes Kristof and Moorehead had unlimbered and deployed the two ROVs by hand, Mini-Rover over the starboard side and Sea Rover over the port. Both pilots, Cole flying Sea Rover, and Bywater flying Mini-Rover, were soon navigating their vehicles entirely by video monitor in the tiny cabin of *Beaver*. Ever so slowly, they pressed their robots deeper, never leaving sight of the yellow polypropylene downline until the wreck loomed large. Within *Beaver*'s cabin, cluttered with video gear, recorders, and cameras, our entire team crowded about on bunks, deck, ladders, and in the hatchways, watching intently as one vehicle and then the other casually probed the wreck, relaying video records of every image encountered for later evaluation. The exploration, in the hands of the two able pilots, proceeded as if it were little more than a video game being played by a pair of intent teenagers. From time to time Emory would shoot a sequence of thirty-five-millimeter pictures from the single-lens reflex camera mounted in Sea Rover. Aside from the irascible generator on the deck that supplied the power for the ROVS, which would sputter occasionally, causing their halogen lights to dim momentarily and their thrusters to slow, the investigation proceeded smoothly. Almost too smoothly.

Ken Englebrecht, who knew as much about the wreck as anyone, had been invited along to offer his valuable input and had provided a sketch plan of the site to assist the ROV exploration. With Englebrecht's plan, navigating around the hazardous hulk was made far simpler. *Kamloops* was clearly lying tilted on her starboard side and owing to the extreme, cold, freshwater environment was in a remarkable state of preservation. The starboard coal bunkers were visited at a depth of 225 feet, and coal was found still in abundance. The vessel had obviously not become powerless during her final hours from a lack of fuel as some historians had hypothesized. Her fire control system had not been touched, nor were there signs of a fire, ruling out another oft-cited cause for her destruction. A pass was made along a set of transoms atop the engine room, several of which were open, and then along the remains of the officers' quarters. With both

Mini-Rover examines the propeller of the ill-fated *Kamloops*.
Photograph by Emory Kristof

vehicles within sight of each other, the ship's boat davits were discovered still in place. Upon close inspection, it was soon discerned that one of the lifeboats had been forcefully released from the starboard davit, as the chocks were down. Another davit, on the port side, had not intentionally deployed any vessel, as the chocks were still up. A lifeboat was found virtually intact, waiting to perform a service that would never be asked of it. A legend long accepted by many as fact, that at least four of the crew had made it ashore in a boat only to freeze to death before rescue could be effected, was now given new life. Further investigation along the stern revealed that the rudder, rudder shoe, and propeller had escaped unscathed from the catastrophe that had befallen *Kamloops*, suggesting that she was capable of steerage at the moment of her loss.

How had she come to her final grief? When rubber hoses were observed in the scuppers, the first evidence that the ship had been frozen in the ice was offered up. It was common habit on the lake freight haulers that whenever a vessel was laid up, the hoses were thus stowed, a practice never employed while under way. The evidence began to mount. Hull damage on her stern suggested either collision with the nearby rocks or potential debilitation as a result of ice. A debris field running from the rocky outcrop of the point to the stern of the boat seemed to indicate that either before or during the sinking process, she had struck the rocks and slid down the steep slope bow first.

But what of her crew? Had they frozen to death ashore or on board? Sport divers had circulated rumors of a body lying deep in the engine room, at 250 feet, and that the telegraph had been set at "Finished with engines," suggesting that the engines were out. Lenihan decided that an inspection might determine the answer. Mini-Rover, the smaller of the two vehicles, was selected for the task. It would enter the engine room through an open transom above the room.

Ever so carefully, Bywater steered the little ROV into the ship, turning it from time to time to make certain its cables were free and clear. At this great depth there could be, after all, no simple diver rescue if the vehicle ran into trouble. The room was black, and Bywater took more than half an hour merely inspecting the entrance before committing his robot to the entry. As we watched the monitor, the tension among us was palpable.

As the ROV finally passed through the transom, constantly turning to make certain that its cables were free, the room was suddenly brightly lit for the first time in more than half a century. Slowly, the engine heads came into view. The head bolts, Lenihan quickly observed, had been removed. The engines had apparently been under repair at the time of loss.

Bywater pressed on. Down the steps of an iron gangway, untrod for nearly 59 years, the robot flew. A tiny white object could be made out in the murk, lying on the floor ahead. Cautiously, the robot moved on, skirting an iron ladder as it pressed deeper into the engine room. As the camera lens focused on the white object ahead, a hush fell over the spellbound group of observers in the cabin of *Beaver* as they peered into the past. Almost simultaneously, we realized that the object that we were staring at through the cold lens of a machine was the body of a man, dressed in white overalls and rubber boots. The body was that of *Kamloops's* engineer, lying in the agonizing repose of his final moment of life, his remains preserved in death for nearly six decades by the freezing waters of Lake Superior. No one said a word, except for a quietly mumbled prayer for his soul.

The investigation took on a distinctly personal hue now, for unlike the vessel that had become his coffin, the engineer had been a living, breathing being, not merely another artifact to be studied *in situ*. Yet his presence added new questions to the mystery of *Kamloops*. Had he died attempting to fend off the cold in the last place where residual heat might remain aboard ship? Had the ship's engines malfunctioned or been damaged (as was suggested by the removal of bolts on the heads), causing a loss of power and permitting the entrapment of the hull in the ice as he struggled desperately to get power back? No one spoke as the video continued to roll, until the sad investigation was brought to a close.

In the hold of *Kamloops* we had seen first-hand what a shipwreck really was. It was indeed more than merely a vessel's remains, random pieces of architecture or cargo to be meticulously sorted out and placed in neat categories for historians and social scientists to evaluate and argue endlessly about. A shipwreck was nothing less than a devastating human tragedy, filled with death and ruin, in the most awful fashion possible. It is unspeakable terror and suffering, often without hope of redemption or salvation. For me, the meaning of archaeology had taken on a deeper perspective. We kept on, however, for there was still much work to do.

Finally freed from its sad mission below decks, Mini-Rover approached the extreme stern, passing along a deck littered with rolls of bailing wire, lard in wooden boxes, and a tangle of debris that could snare an ROV cable at any minute. Soon the wheel and binnacle came into focus—intact and lacking only a skeleton to complete the scene. It was certainly a more prosaic, classic picture of a shipwreck than the one we had just witnessed.

Suddenly, Mini-Rover, now being flown by Cole, came to a halt. Its lines had snagged in the aft boom assembly of the ship. The robot seemed to be hopelessly hung up and couldn't be freed. Then came even more chilling news over the ship's radio: a strong squall line was moving in from Thunder Bay to the north and would be over us by 6:00 P.M. With sea conditions even now picking up, a diver rescue was entirely out of the question. If we had to up anchor and run before the storm, the captain of *Beaver* said rather matter-of-factly, we would have to cut the ROV loose.

Flying Eyeballs

Yet as long as we had generator fuel, our robots could remain under power and were capable of limited movement. Bywater immediately suggested that a robotic rescue of the snared vehicle be tried with Sea Rover. For the next hour and fifteen minutes, the veteran pilot worked to loosen the devil's grip on the little robot. At 5:45 P.M., as large swells began beating us about, we watched the Sea Rover free its partner. Cheers arose for what was probably the first time in history that one ROV had rescued another.

❏ ❏ ❏

Many questions had been answered about the loss of *Kamloops*. Moreover, a remarkable video inventory of the site had been collected for the National Park Service to study and to assist in the development of its resource management policy and programs for the shipwrecks of the Isle Royale sanctuary and in other national park areas. We would visit at least four more shipwreck sites before the survey was over. Though none of them was of the legendary stature of such vessels as *Titanic* or *Monitor*, or as dramatic as *Kamloops*, each was just as significant in its own unique way.

As the work with the two robots continued, I became more convinced than ever that their use in systematic archaeological survey (as opposed to their use as a set of flying underwater eyeballs) was entirely feasible. Given the right set of tools, it seemed possible that ROVs could not only record and inventory sites *in situ*, as we were doing at Isle Royale, but could also excavate them, survey them, and recover artifacts from them in a controlled fashion entirely within the accepted doctrines of traditional archaeological methodology.

One evening, about midway through the project, still full of the most recent day's excitement, Emory and I talked well into the early morning hours about the potential for robotics in archaeology. If a short baseline sonar unit could be mounted aboard an ROV or on a tripod adjacent to a site and hard-wired to the surface, Emory suggested, it might be possible not only to track a robot and calculate and record the course of its flight, but also to determine the provenance of the object it was viewing at any given time. Feeding its on-board navigational data into a computer in real time and integrating it with the sonar data could prove invaluable. Actually mounting a sonar unit on board while tracking the vehicle with a second system might expand accuracy even more. If the mandible on the Sea Rover could be provided with or replaced with an auxiliary set of tools, I chimed in, such as clamps, shovels or spoons, suction cups, and so forth, we might even be able to do limited, small-scale excavation and recovery.

"All we need," said Emory, "is a site close enough to home to experiment on, shallow enough for divers to effect a rescue if necessary, yet deep and inhospitable enough to challenge the technology and teach us something." "How about *New Jersey*?" I asked.

53

After more than three hours of discussion, Emory Kristof was sold. He would be willing to employ *Geographic*'s ROV and influence to promulgate a robotic survey of *New Jersey*. All we needed was a plan, a ship to serve as operations platform, another ROV, a few short-baseline sonar units, and some of the most advanced technology available.

"You get the ship and divers," said Blackbeard the Photographer as the first light of dawn crept into our cabin, "and I'll handle the rest."[7]

❏ ❏ ❏

In late September 1986, soon after my return from Isle Royale, I presented a formal plan for the robotic survey of the steamship *New Jersey* to State Archaeologist Tyler Bastian and the Maryland Geological Survey's Advisory Committee on Archaeology. The project's objective, addressed in the oral presentation, was "to evaluate an impacted archaeological site that will be nominated to the National Register of Historic Places." To achieve our objective, it would be necessary to develop robotic survey and sampling procedures and to devise appropriate techniques for systematic robotic underwater archaeological survey utilizing at least two ROVs, sector scanning sonar, and other survey and recording systems, integrated with ROV and shipboard computer systems. If the Maryland Geological Survey could provide a research vessel for three weeks, the National Geographic Society would provide or secure the robots and all necessary technical support. After a short video presentation on the ROV work at Isle Royale and with strong support by committee member Dr. Gary Wheeler Stone, director of archaeology at St. Mary's City, the committee unanimously recommended approval of the scope of work, albeit on conditional grounds: a full field demonstration of an ROV on the *New Jersey* site would be necessary to prove the validity of our project design.

The field test date was set for November 10. We would be demonstrating not only the ROV, but also a short-baseline sector scanning sonar unit being loaned to *Geographic* by the Department of Defense. The state of Maryland, with the approval of Dr. Kenneth Weaver, head of the MGS, would provide the sleek, forty-nine-foot research vessel *Discovery* to serve as our ROV operations platform. With a considerable laboratory outfit in her main cabin and state-of-the-art navigational and electronics array, the boat was well suited for the task ahead. Moreover, she carried both a bow and an aft winch and two adjustable mast booms that could prove useful for heavy at-sea lift work. *Discovery*'s career had been impressive. She had been employed in a wide range of research projects and her master and crew were longtime Bay hands of the first order. The *New Jersey* Project would prove to be a first for both ship and her crew.[8] State regulations, however, forbade non-state personnel from diving from the vessel, which caused a temporary glitch. Fortunately, Dave Sisson, who had provided logistical support for the 1985 work, again volunteered *Option* as a dive platform.

The stakes were high. If this field demonstration proved successful, Emory vowed he could rope in additional technological support from the commercial sector that, he claimed, would be all too eager to show off their gear in a high-visibility "field lab environment." In the end, if the project took off, we would be conducting a $350,000 investigation on borrowed everything.

But our initial demonstration scenario was simple. A prefabricated eight-foot-tall, specially designed iron tripod would be lowered to the site and guided by divers into a preselected position adjacent to the stern of the wreck. The sonar unit, hard-wired to a screen console aboard *Discovery*, would be mounted atop the tripod. The ROV would then be deployed to conduct a brief recon of the stern and boiler-engine complex while the vehicle's every move was tracked by sonar.

Construction of the tripod and outfitting of the ROV was undertaken in the Geographic Society's spotless machine shop by their chief engineer, Al Chandler, an ex-submariner, sometime sheriff, electrical and camera whiz, and expert in anything that needed to be designed, fabricated, mended, or repaired. Al had witnessed more than one man's fair share of adventure in service to *Geographic*. With a full mane of white hair, a Gay Nineties mustache, the demeanor of a southern gentleman, a sharp-shooter's eye, and the ability to outdrink or charm the socks off anyone, he was definitely "an original" who would prove his worth during the more trying days of the project. To facilitate and complement Al's work, I had signed on my old NAA colleague, Eldon Volkmer, an engineer and inventor in his own right. If that team couldn't design it, build it, repair it (no matter what "it" might be), then no one could.

For the first time in my archaeological career, I had decided that, owing to the nature of the project, which focused on robotic survey, I would for once learn more by administering the project from the surface than from the water. Thus, I decided to turn over the underwater operations management to a pro. Our new dive master, John Kiser, was a tall, lanky, no-nonsense professional diver, licensed charter-boat captain, diving instructor for the U.S. Naval Academy, and businessman with more than twenty years of underwater experience under his belt, much of it in blackwater environments.

❑ ❑ ❑

When *Discovery* set off from her temporary anchorage at Sandy Point State Park near Annapolis on the morning of November 10 to rendezvous with *Option* on site, sea conditions could not have been better. The initial stages of the operation proceeded flawlessly. Kiser and his divers, Joe McNamara

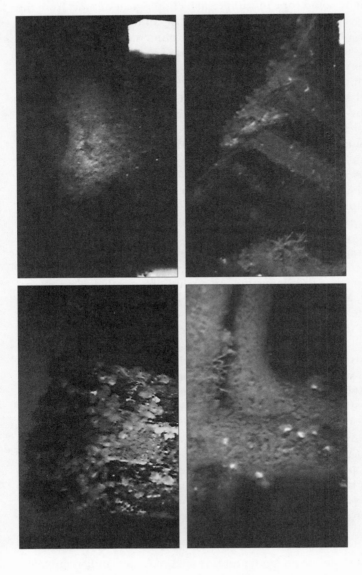

The first ROV images of the steamboat *New Jersey* taken during field demonstrations of equipment for state officials in late 1986. (Top left) The starboard stern, heavily covered by marine growth, still contains the vestige of iron fittings that held hull planks in place. (Top right) A six-inch outlet for an upper exhaust valve on the ship's simple reciprocating engine. The sled runners of the ROV are visible at bottom left and right. (Bottom left) Reinforced iron cross member of the "A frame" supporting the engine complex. (Bottom right) A cross section of a heavily corroded section of the condenser. Photographs by Emory Kristof

and Douglas Campbell, planted the tripod and attached the sonar assembly without a hitch less than twenty feet from the wreck and moved it about with ease to different positions as needed. The ROV was fielded immediately after the sonar hookup, and within minutes the boiler, condensers, and engines of *New Jersey* came into view on the monitor in *Discovery*'s cabin. It was the clearest and longest continuous examination I had ever experienced on the old steamer. The sonar unit not only provided a comprehensive track of the ROV and divers as they scurried about the site, but actually produced the first intensive sonar study of a historic shipwreck in Chesapeake Bay history. Tyler Bastian was sold. The Maryland Geological Survey was sold. The National Geographic Society was sold. I was stunned. We had a project.

❏   ❏   ❏

There was an enormous amount of organizational work to be done before the *New Jersey* Project could be launched. Within hours after our return to shore, the juggling act had begun. The second week in February 1987 had been picked as a start-up date, which was without question the very worst time of the year to be on the open Chesapeake, yet the only time that the disparate schedules of all project participants were open.

With downtime caused by foul winter weather almost a certainty, both Emory and I agreed that a minimum of three weeks would be necessary to complete the work we hoped to do. But to insure that a ship was available for at least twenty-one days, I would still have to secure another research boat—or at least a suitable ROV operations platform—for the balance of the field operations as quickly as possible, and for free. Once again, I appealed to Ed Miller and the good offices of the NOAA Marine Sanctuary Program. It was anything but a hollow appeal, because NOAA had been studying the Chesapeake for some time as a potential field laboratory for research work in marine archaeology, and Ed Miller, as manager of the USS *Monitor* Marine Sanctuary, had been the front man. If a small research vessel could be loaned to the project, it might be possible to secure the necessary boat time to complete the three-week period. Miller agreed, but noted there would have to be a major stipulation. According to NOAA Directive 64-23, issued in 1983, only NOAA-trained and NOAA-certified divers could dive from a NOAA vessel—a training process that could take weeks for our yet-to-be-formed dive team. Nevertheless, I jumped at Ed's offer.[9] All I needed now was another vessel, at no charge, to serve for three weeks as a dive boat. No problem. Sure!

With over four hundred thousand registered vessels in the Tidewater, there had to be boats out there to be had. After all, who could resist the chance of a lifetime to see diving robots in action on the Chesapeake for (almost) the first time? Who could resist the opportunity of working with

Robots Beneath the Chesapeake

a famous *National Geographic* undersea explorer attempting to conduct the first-ever systematic robotic archaeological survey in history? Everybody, I quickly learned, especially if it was in the dead of winter on the open Bay.

Persistence often pays off, especially when it has help. By early January it was decided that operations would be headquartered at Solomons Island. Though the harbor was some distance from the site, there were considerable critical winter service and fueling facilities, both military and commercial, to be had there. Moreover, Dr. Ralph Eshelman, the director of the Calvert Marine Museum at Solomons Island, had generously agreed to permit at least one vessel to tie up at the museum wharf on Back Creek and to provide whatever backup services the museum could offer. But his aid did not stop there. With his help, lodging for up to ten project personnel was secured at the Chesapeake Biological Laboratory dormitory if needed, and private lodging for others was found elsewhere. The National Geographic Society would cover the balance by housing their staff at a local inn in Solomons. But of singular importance, through a contact with key naval personnel at the Patuxent Naval Air Station and with Pentagon approval, Eshelman was able to secure the loan of a U.S. Navy search-and-rescue vessel and a crew to man her for as long as necessary. We had our dive boat.

❑ ❑ ❑

On January 6 I flew to Nashville to attend the Council on Underwater Archaeology conference at the annual meeting of the Society for Historical Archaeology. I was to present a paper on the *New Jersey* "crisis," and hoped to formally seal the deal on the NOAA boat with Ed Miller, who would be in attendance. I ran into Ed almost immediately. He nonchalantly informed me that a research boat called *Laidly* would be available for the project for ten days. Now we had our ship time. All that was left was the refitting and testing of the ROV.

That night, when I phoned Kristof to tell him the good news, he informed me that the outfitting of the ROV was scheduled to be carried out in the test pool of the Benthos Corporation, in Falmouth, Massachusetts, in late January. I was delighted, for Benthos was the birthplace of some of the most important advances in ROV technology in the nation. Of equal importance, he said, he had invited along both Chris Nicholson and a scientist named Marty Wilcox, founder and president of a company called Applied Sonics. But Wilcox was more, much more. He was, in fact, the "father" of medical ultrasound, and the famous sonogram used in every hospital in the Western world.

Marty and his brother Pete, Emory informed me, had been working for some time on the development of a revolutionary new technology specifically designed to facilitate the rapid mapping of underwater archaeological sites ultrasonically and would be testing their own systems with ours during the work at the Benthos labs. Although a first generation of their gear had been tested with promising results in an enclosed coffer-dam environment around the remains of a wreck (44-YO-88) which once belonged to Lord Cornwallis's ill-fated fleet at Yorktown, the system had never been successfully employed in the open sea or in conjunction with robotic survey. Emory had invited the Wilcoxes to join us on the Chesapeake and they had accepted. All I had to come up with now was some personal computers to facilitate their work!

❏   ❏   ❏

As January pressed on, the expansion of the project to incorporate even more technologies, corporate support, and widened objectives continued unabated. Although I was the designated principal investigator, the project was obviously a multidisciplinary effort. Through the influence of Dr. Fred W. Hopkins Jr., an NAA board member and a historian of considerable note who had already carried out an impressive body of research on *New Jersey*, the University of Baltimore had provided the computer systems for some of the on-board needs at sea, and Dr. James Qualls, a soft-spoken expert in quantum physics, had been brought in to oversee their installation and management. Kristof, a veritable wheeler-dealer who traded at-sea ship time in return for the use and testing of the latest subsea technologies and diving equipment for the operation, worked tirelessly to bring in additional corporate support and hardware. And all of our sponsors were more than eager to jump on the bandwagon. The name *National Geographic*, I quickly learned, was worth its weight in gold. One corporate participant later told me that one product photo in the magazine, with ten million subscribers and twenty million readers, would provide enormous merchandising value. With promotion like that, who could resist?

Near the end of the month, Qualls and I drove to Falmouth with the university computers to participate in the lab and water testing of the new Wilcox ultrasonic mapping system and refitting of the ROV. For the first time ever, the possibility of linking the latest in ultrasonic mapping technology with robotics would be attempted, albeit in a laboratory setting. When we arrived at Benthos, many who would play key roles in the project were already there: Kristof, Chandler, the Wilcox brothers, Nicholson, and others. The *Geographic*'s ROV had already been stripped of its shell and was undergoing "massive surgery," even as Nicholson was putting his own vehicle through its paces in the deep testing pool in the lab. The personnel present represented truly an impressive array of talent. But the most impressive was the president of the Applied Sonics Corp.

Marty Wilcox is a tall man with a Captain Ahab beard, an easy laugh, and one of the most inquisitive minds I have ever encountered. He had become an electronics addict at the age of twelve and majored in electronics engineering at the University of Pennsylvania. His early career had been spent building missile ground support equipment, after which he made the leap into the field of medical ultrasonics. It was a momentous decision both for himself and for medical science. In 1967 he joined forces with a heart surgeon and formed his own company, developed the first successful ultrasonics system for medical applications, the sonogram, sold the company in 1982 for a fortune, and formed the Applied Sonics Corporation to extend state-of-the-art medical ultrasonic imaging technology to the oceanographic world. As a student of Dr. George Bass, the "father" of marine archaeology, and later as a member of the board of directors of the prestigious Institute of Nautical Archaeology, founded by Bass, one of Wilcox's first fields of endeavor had been the application of ultrasonics to underwater archaeology.

Marty Wilcox was well aware that scientific archaeological techniques on land or under water required that the size and location of structures, features, and artifacts on a site be accurately measured and recorded if a complete database were to be provided for subsequent study and analysis. Difficult enough on a land site, accurate and repeatable measurements underwater had been an enormous problem, particularly on deep sites where nitrogen narcosis could rob divers of their normal faculties and where bottom time was precious. Strong currents, poor visibility, surface winds and waves, and hypothermia provided additional torments for the underwater investigator. Unless a site was in shallow water, each diver was limited in the amount of time he or she might spend on the bottom, and bottom time decreased with the increasing depths of sites. Thus, he had reasoned, if a device could be developed for speeding up mapping and data-recording processes, it would prove invaluable to marine archaeology, and to many other subsea disciplines.[10]

One of Marty's colleagues, Dr. Donald Frey of the Insititute of Nautical Archaeology at Texas A&M University, had faced all of these problems on ancient shipwreck sites under excavation in the eastern Mediterranean. In January 1984 Frey suggested to the Wilcox brothers that the problem of accurate measurement might be solved using some type of ultrasonic measuring device similar to existing underwater navigation systems, but with improved accuracy. Navigation systems, Marty knew, operate at low ultrasonic frequencies over long distances and are accurate to within a meter or two. Measurement for mapping purposes, however, required improving that accuracy by a factor of one hundred.[11]

From first-hand experience, Marty was aware that under the pressure of intense international competition, medical ultrasonic equipment had become very good at producing highly detailed, real-time images of internal organs using the principle of "pulse-echo reflection," or what the navy refers to as "active sonar." Medical imaging systems create their images with extremely short, high-frequency pulses, the same technique used to locate submarines. The difference lies in the length and frequency of the pulse and the range to the target. When the Wilcoxes formed Applied Sonics in 1983, though they had a strong background in medical ultrasonics, they had very little experience in underwater technology. "This inexperience," Marty recalled,

> proved invaluable. We didn't know that almost every sonic navigation system uses the transponder principle to measure range. This means that the ship being navigated over the bottom sends a narrow-band-width (long-duration) sonic pulse to a group of transponders installed around the operating area. Each transponder detects this signal and replies with a narrow-bandwidth, coded sonic pulse on a frequency unique to itself. The equipment on the ship times the return of these responses and triangulates the location of the ship in the net. Given Frey's original suggestion about improving the accuracy of navigation systems, knowledgeable underwater sound engineers would have started with the transponding approach. Although this technique is elegant, perfect for its intended task, and permits the use of isolated, "wireless" transponders, our ignorance of it later proved to be fortunate.[12]

Wilcox soon learned that most underwater archaeological sites rarely exceed one hundred meters in diameter. He thus decided to try a simple approach. After discovering experimentally that he could send very short, high-frequency ultrasonic pulses over surprising distances underwater, he reasoned that he could set up a group or "net" of ultrasonic transceivers around a site connected by cables to a workboat anchored above. A diver or an ROV would carry a portable transceiver that could be used as if it were an electronic "pen." As the diver or ROV outlined objects on the site, the pen would emit short ultrasonic pulses. The pulses would be received at the other transceivers at times proportional to their distances from the pen. Each transceiver would send a "pulse received" message up the cable to a computer on the boat, which would gather the resulting data, make the necessary triangulation calculations, and display the resulting position points on its screen.[13]

Dubbed SHARPS, an acronym for sonic high-accuracy ranging and positioning system, the system in its production form consisted of at least four stainless-steel-covered transceivers, each nine inches long and weighing approximately two pounds, connected by underwater-grade coaxial cables to a junction box. The box was connected by a three-foot multiple-conductor cable to a control card that plugged into an input/output channel of a computer. A small power supply was connected to the control board to provide power for the transceivers. The control board could operate up to six transceivers, and up to four control boards could be

operated together to construct a net with as many as twenty-four transceivers. Software could set this maximum count to represent from 14 to
1,750 meters. The diver transceiver "gun" could be triggered by the diver
in either a single-point or continuously running mode. A software package created by Dana Yoerger and Don Scott of MIT included an automatic
net calibration feature, a graphics editor, pop-up window menus, EGA
(enhanced graphics adapter) graphics, quick-test functions, and data
filters.[14] It was, Marty said, even theoretically possible to draw a wreck site
on a computer by literally tracing it with a SHARPS pen!

But there were problems. Cables, always a hazard in underwater work,
might snag and thereby hinder freedom of movement for both ROV and
diver. Sonic interference by marine creatures such as pistol shrimp, which
emit loud, sharp snaps underwater, might dilute the record. And it would
be necessary to avoid placing transceivers where objects might get in the
way of transmitting and receiving. All of these difficulties, he assured us,
could be overcome with practice, field testing, and hardware and software
refinements.[15]

It all sounded wonderful but was as yet largely theoretical. A net was
first erected around the sides of the Benthos pool, after which a pen was
mounted on the manipulator arm of Nicholson's ROV. All systems were
switched on, and the ROV began to pirouette and fly through the water.
As I sat in the control room watching little green dots come up on Dana
Yoerger's computer screen, I could hardly believe what I was seeing. It was
nothing less than a comprehensive record of the precise position of every
second of the ROV's flight within the ultrasonic net. I was a believer. Now
all we had to do was prove it in a real-world survey situation on the open
Chesapeake in the middle of winter.

S E V E N

A Hurricane on the Bottom

The morning of February 8 was numbingly cold as *AVR-1*, the search-and-rescue vessel assigned by the U.S. Navy to assist the *New Jersey* Project, cast off lines from Boat House Number 3 at the Patuxent Naval Air Station. At 65.5 feet long, 17.25 feet abeam, and drawing 5.5 feet of water, the boat seemed, at first glance, to be the perfect platform for the initial diving operations ahead. Her twin five-hundred-horsepower diesel engines were capable of providing a top speed of twenty-four knots (thereby causing little time loss in getting on site), while her eight-hundred-gallon fuel tank permitted a cruising range of over 250 miles. Moreover, her crew of six seemed quite adequate to perform all necessary tasks.[1]

Our objectives for this first day of field work were quite simple. Working in concert with *Laidly*, we would first relocate the wreck and bracket the site by dropping weighted buoys. Divers would then be deployed from *AVR-1* to place permanent markers on *New Jersey*'s bow and stern and conduct a limited recon of the wreck. Finally, two nine-hundred-pound surplus locomotive wheels would be deposited adjacent to the site to serve as permanent moorings for project vessels for the next three weeks. John Kiser had secured a pair of experienced blackwater diving instructors, Ted Morgan and Michael Pohuski, as well as a cadre of equally qualified divers as needed, to work with him and Joe McNamara in the initial underwater work.

By 7:15 A.M. *AVR-1* was under way. Within the hour, we had completed the operations briefing. The dive team, all of whom were from Baltimore and had been up since 3 A.M., began to suit up in their bulky Parkways dry suits and then attempted to steal a little sleep before hitting the site. Nearly two hours had passed, however, before *Laidly*, which had been slowed considerably in coming up by the nearly two tons of locomotive wheels carried on her fantail, was in view. Sea conditions were now far from ideal as choppy whitecaps began to fleck the Bay's gray surface. Winds had also picked up, with gusting from fifteen to twenty knots. Worse, flood tide would be coming on within the hour, after which getting a diver down at all would be difficult and retrieving him nearly impossible. Our window of opportunity was less than an hour, and immediacy of action was imperative.

AVR-1, a U.S. Navy search-and-rescue vessel, provided critical logistical support to the *New Jersey* Project during the 1987 archaeological campaign.

The NOAA research vessel *Laidly,* employed as an operations platform during the opening days of the 1987 *New Jersey* Project, was already a veteran of several NOAA archaeological expeditions to the wreck of the famed USS *Monitor.*

Laidly, which possessed the better Loran unit and bottom sounder of the two vessels, was quickly instructed to find the wreck and drop buoys adjacent to each of its extremities. On the first try, the site was located. A second run was made to plant the buoys, but the attempt failed. Then a third also failed, as each of the lightly weighted markers was immediately swept off the site by rough surface conditions. Instructions to the NOAA commander to increase the weights and line length on the buoys were to no avail. Kiser suggested that a small grapple be deployed to drag into the wreck, a method I had hoped to avoid, fearing possible injury to the site, but it was a risk that I now felt was necessary.

Laidly was repeatedly radioed instructions to commence grappling operations but each time failed to respond. Her captain, we soon concluded, was either deaf, ignorant, or simply wanted to do it his own way. When the request was finally acknowledged, the good captain vociferously disagreed with the plan and continued attempting to plant lightly weighted markers—with predictable results. In the meantime, Pohuski and McNamara had positioned themselves on a platform below the fantail of *AVR-1* to be ready to drop off at a moment's notice. As the minutes ticked away, the seas continued to swell and the tide began to return. *Laidly* made yet another attempt to plant the site markers. Two large, gray plastic cans were dropped, but both were too poorly weighted to remain in position for long and were soon seen moving slowly along with the currents.

Both Kiser and I were growning irritated at the delay and increasingly worried about the current flow. Few invectives were spared in the name of the NOAA captain. With flood coming on, a firmly planted direct downline was absolutely necessary for our divers to descend. Still, *Laidly's* commander continued to obstruct our progress. The frustration was maddening. If he wouldn't acquiesce, I belatedly decided, then *AVR-1*, though a bigger, less maneuverable boat with a wide turning radius, would have to do the grappling herself.

At 10:25 A.M. we began to drag for the wreck, with instant success. Unfortunately, our only grapple proved too small to hold our boat against the flood, which was now setting in with full force. Worse, *AVR-1's* radioman interrupted the effort long enough—shades of Isle Royale—to inform me that a major storm front was rapidly moving in and would be in the area by 2 P.M. Now an air of critical urgency seemed all-pervasive.

A second grappling effort duplicated the first. Again *New Jersey* slipped from our grasp. Then, as we maneuvered to thread between *Laidly's* slowly moving markers for a third attempt, *AVR-1's* engines suddenly cut off at the worst possible moment. Carried by rough seas, the boat immediately became fouled in the marker lines. There was little choice but to drift off the site and regroup.

A half hour later we prepared for the final assault. *Laidly* was again instructed to pick up her markers and add another twenty-five pounds of weight to each line (making each seventy-five pounds) and then to redeploy them on the site. We crossed our fingers that the independent-minded NOAA captain would follow directions. This time the obstreperous officer complied, although three more runs were necessary for *Laidly* to accomplish her mission. The delay, unfortunately, caused myriad unforseen problems. The dive team, which had been uncomfortably ensconced on the open fantail platform for nearly an hour, exposed to the cold, the ship's exhaust fumes, and rolling with every sea, were becoming nauseated. Yet both McNamara and Pohuski gamely refused to be replaced. Armed with inflatible buoys and a small hand grapple to be manually placed in the wreck, they awaited the signal to dive.

At 11:14 A.M. *AVR-1* approached to within ten feet of one of the markers, and the two divers splashed into the water. The seas immediately proved far more powerful than anyone had anticipated. Though landing within mere inches of the buoy line, the two divers were quickly swept away by the full flood. Both men were powerful swimmers and struggled heroically for the next ten minutes to reach the downline, but it was apparent their strength would soon ebb. A line was cast to tow them to the downline, but in the now-turbulent seas they could not hold on. Each time they tried, the towline was literally stripped from their hands and their regulators from their mouths by the violence of the sea. *AVR-1* was simply incapable of running slowly enough to tow the weakening divers safely and at the same time make headway against the current. Worse, each time the two men released the line, the considerable turning radius required for *AVR-1* to double back and engage them again, combined with the current, took us farther and farther from the site, making the next effort to bring them up even longer and more dangerous.[2]

By 11:45 it was decided to retrieve the two exhausted men. When both were finally brought aboard, it was discovered that Pohuski's pony tank and backup regulator had been torn from his back pack. The two divers' gloves were in shreds. I had made an extremely bad call, indeed, a potentially fatal one, by even permitting the operation to go forward. Pohuski later recalled of his ordeal: "I swallowed most of the lower Bay and was jerked around like a trolling line."[3] Yet both he and McNamara voiced their readiness to try again as soon as they were rested. Kiser suggested that *AVR-1* anchor upcurrent from the wreck and that he and Morgan be permitted to drift back on a line over the site. It was then that the coxswain sheepishly informed us that the windlass generator was down and we would be unable to get the anchor up if it stuck in the mud.

"Why," I fumed, "hadn't we been informed of the problem before we sailed?" "Nobody asked," replied the sailor with a simple shrug.

Indeed, we could not have anchored the boat if we had wanted to! Frustrated and angry at the navy, NOAA, Mother Nature, and most of all myself, I ordered the day's operation scrubbed.

For the next thirty-six hours the Chesapeake Bay was unsailable. High winds, with gusts of up to sixty-eight miles per hour and waves of six to ten feet, enforced our stay in port. The time, however, was put to good use at the Naval Surface Weapons Test Center, working on the SHARPS tripods and on fine-tuning Sea Rover. Helga Sprunk, a young ROV pilot hired by *National Geographic* specifically for the expedition, and Keith Moorehead and Larry Kinny, *Geographic*'s technicians, had discovered serious problems with the vehicle's fiber-optic system, apparently stemming from alterations made at Woods Hole, Massachusetts, in adding the mandible, and considerable repair work was necessary.

By the morning of February 10, sea conditions were again deemed favorable enough to permit another shot at marking the site. Again the dive team assembled at the Naval Air Station to board *AVR-1*. Across the river, in Second Creek, the NOAA captain and his first officer readied *Laidly* with the assistance of a much-welcomed addition to their small crew, one Rick Younger, an enterprising mate from the Maryland Geological Survey's research vessel *Discovery,* which was to replace the NOAA vessel later in the project.

The winter scene on the Patuxent was what one might term "marine bucolic," as the little NOAA research boat gingerly cut her way through a skim of ice on the creek before reaching the open river. Along the shores one could see the detritus of years of military usage of the area, typified by scores of empty casings of World War II magnetic mines. As we passed beneath the Thomas Johnson Bridge, two doughty skipjacks, among the last of their breed, could be seen working the waters off Drum Point.

By the time *Laidly* arrived at the wreck site two hours later, Kiser's team had already deployed a pair of preliminary marker buoys. In contrast to the violence of our last visit, surface conditions were almost placid, and slack water offered the option of a hands-on recon. Aware that the *AVR-1* bottom recorder was inferior to *Laidly*'s sophisticated Raytheon DSF-6000F strip-chart unit, I ordered a run over the wreck to confirm the buoys' positions relative to the site, only to find them to be well off the mark. Kiser suggested that a dive be made to hand-plant a marker immediately adjacent to the wreck, but this time from his Zodiac inflatable, which we had brought along to serve as a chase boat. I radioed back my concurrence, with the proviso that the chase boat remain over the divers until their return. There would be no repeat of the debacle of February 8 this time. By 1:00 P.M. the work had been successfully completed. Though visibility was a disappointing two inches over the site, a buoy had been rooted by hand in a scour on the port side of the wreck. *Laidly* could now systematically determine what the orientation and general parameters of the site were, and the business of deploying the train-wheel moors at both ends of the wreck could be carried out with accuracy.

By late afternoon, the giant iron wheels had been placed and the mission completed to everyone's satisfaction. Yet, three precious days had been consumed in merely marking the site and providing a pair of permanent moors. Winter work did indeed have its drawbacks!

One of the difficulties with erecting a SHARPS electronic network is that each net transceiver must have a reception field open to the remainder of the transceivers. Any obstruction in the path of the sound pulse emitted from the pen gun will obscure the record. To survey a shipwreck or even a portion of a site the likes of *New Jersey* thus required that the transceivers be mounted on stations above the wreck site. In a pool, such as at the Benthos Lab, or within the cofferdam environment of 44-YO-88 at Yorktown, elevation had been no problem. The open seas, however, were different.

Given the problems already encountered and the valuable experience gained from the on-site ROV testing the previous November, Al Chandler had designed and constructed in the National Geographic Society's machine shop in Washington, D.C., three prefabricated metal tripods, each eight feet in elevation. A neck projecting from each unit's summit would serve as a mount for one SHARPS transceiver. The tripods could be marked by buoys to permit ready relocation each day, in theory allowing the expensive transceivers to be easily and rapidly deployed and retrieved daily by divers. In reality, there were more than enough problems to compensate for high-tech marvels.

On February 11 we prepared to deploy the tripods. By midmorning, Kiser's divers (McNamara and a young volunteer named Mike Cather) had already conducted a site reconnaissance, located the old steamer's now-exposed propeller shaft, and attached a permanent marker buoy to it. A second buoy was attached amidships. Again, *Laidly* ran an orientation survey over the site, calculated the approximate location of the bow, and dropped a third, heavily weighted marker. At last, *New Jersey* was effectively boxed in by markers, an absolute necessity if we were to field the three SHARPS tripods successfully.

As the survey was being run, Al Chandler and Eldon Volkmer, with the assistance of State Archaeologist Tyler Bastian, worked diligently on the fantail of *Laidly* to complete the construction of the prefabricated mounts. To each completed tripod they attached a seventy-five-foot line with a red buoy at its end to facilitate relocation at any time. Iron-weighted feet were riveted to the legs of the tripods to maintain vertical stability. Using the Zodiac to haul the structures to their designated positions around the wreck, Kiser was able to position them on the bottom within an hour and a half. Great pains were taken to arrange all three units so that the ultrasonic pulse from each transceiver would not be obstructed by the engine, boiler, or other possible elevations near the stern of the wreck. Each unit had been deployed in 48 to 51 feet of water, from 50 to 175 feet from the wreck on both port and starboard sides. Despite the apparent success of the effort, the stability of the tripods had yet to be proved, and the first actual deployment of the SHARPS system would be a task requiring considerable effort.

❏　❏　❏

That evening, the heavy hitters began to arrive. Chris Nicholson, president of Deep Sea Systems International, caused little notice when he checked in at the Comfort Inn in Solomons with his assistant, Will Sellers, and his high-tech gear hidden snugly in a cluster of big aluminum carrying cases. But the equipment was, to say the least, impressive. As Chris carefully, indeed fastidiously, unpacked one item, a Deep Sea Mini-Rover, from one of the cases, I was reminded of the ritual the famed ventriloquist Edgar Bergen always went through when taking his equally famous dummy, Charlie McCarthy, from his own carrying case. And there were some similarities.

Nicholson's robot was, after all, nothing more than a very sophisticated dummy that was obliged to respond to its master's every command.

The vehicle, a duplicate of the unit employed by Wayne Bywater at Isle Royale, was light and fast, a veritable undersea hummingbird. Weighing between 45 and 50 pounds, it could be easily launched by hand. While operating in currents of up to 1.5 knots, it was capable of speeds of 2.2 knots and operational depths of up to 850 feet. Its on-board television camera featured a 4.8 millimeter f 1.8 lens, with a resolution of 350 lines per inch. To help its big video eye see in the dark it carried two 150-watt, long-life quartz-halogen lamps.

Nicholson had also brought along Mini-Rover's big brother, a Mark II Sea Rover, a 140-pound machine capable of carrying a payload of up to 22 pounds and, when rigged for deployment from a submersible, operational to depths of up to 20,000 feet. It was, however, hard to tell that the Mark II was Goober's twin brother, for it was decorated with a vicious-looking set of shark teeth and eyes painted on its orange hull that gave it a fearsome appearance—at least to the fish.

With Nicholson's and *Geographic's* vehicles together, the expedition was capable of fielding a veritable flotilla of robots. Remote deployment of the various instrument packages that we hoped to test during our survey of *New Jersey* was now possible. And the toys were there in abundance, courtesy of our numerous sponsors. The University of Baltimore, through the efforts of Fred Hopkins, had supplied the project with AT computers, under the direction of Jim Qualls, capable of managing the enormous stream of data expected to be generated by the various tracking, plotting, and navigation systems we would be using. Additional computers, provided by the Woods Hole Oceanographic Institute (WHOI) and the Applied Sonics Corporation, were also on hand for use both on land and aboard the survey ships.

One of the most intriguing pieces of equipment we were to use had been loaned to us by the Sony Corporation. The gear was a unique, high-resolution electronic imaging and recording system called the MVR 5500, whose prototype we had tested at Isle Royale the previous fall. Its uniqueness lay in its ability to store computer- or video-generated images on three-inch floppy disks. Dr. Kenneth Stewart of MIT, who had joined the project in hopes of testing some of his own concepts, had developed a "library" software program for us, which interfaced the various sonic data, computer, and ROV images with the MVR. This library software both interfaced the display and coordinated the MVR image with in-water positioning systems, thereby allowing full recording of the provenance of each image. Up to fifty individual frame images per disk could be stored for later retrieval and print generation, in either Polaroid or 35-mm slide formats. Not surprisingly, though it was the first unit of its kind to be marketed in America, like many of the technologies employed during the *New Jersey* Project, it would soon become commonplace.

Another piece of equipment, provided by the Ferranti Corporation, along with a team of technicians to install it, was a sophisticated sonar tracking and positioning system called the ORE Trackpoint II. This unit was capable of providing real-time tracking of up to six or more targets underwater on an electronic grid on user-determined scales. Its utility was in its ability to track sonically and plot underwater vehicle courses, diver movements, or other mobile objects—a must for the navigation of ROVs in dark water.

The abundance and variety of high-tech equipment awaiting field testing seemed, at first, almost unending. By the evening of February 11, when Dave Porta of the Datasonics Corporation arrived with an assistant to install, deploy, and demonstrate his company's new Aquanav acoustic navigation system, I began to wonder if we hadn't reached the saturation point. Porta's equipment included a multichannel command unit for the recovery and control of subsea instrumentation; Aquafish and interrogator transceivers, used for interrogation of transponders; and a data-processor unit utilizing an off-the-shelf computer, printer, and plotter for easy-to-use calibration and navigation software. This system, it was hoped, might be utilized for long-baseline operations, surface-to-bottom positioning, and ROV, diver, or equipment tracking.

The two principal mapping tools to be tested during the project, of course, were the SHARPS and a sophisticated new navigation system, the Mesotech Model 671 color sector-scanning sonar display processor. The latter was a short-baseline sonar unit that we hoped to deploy aboard the most powerful of our robot fleet, Nicholson's Mark II Sea Rover. The Mesotech had a unique "split head" transponder, that is, one with the sonar scanning head separate from the electronics. By mounting only the scanning head directly on the Mark II and hard-wiring it along with the ROV's fiber-optic cable system to an electronics and video package topside, it would enable the ROV pilot to navigate and record sonar imagery in virtually zero-visibility conditions, even with a strong tide running. The sonar package produced a multicolored image, with all colors being relative to distances from the transponder. An electronic measurement cursor in the processor, which could be moved about at will by the sonar manager, would permit the remote gathering of measurements accurate within four inches between any two select points on the site within scanning range. We hoped that the unit might be used not only for ROV navigation but to provide usable, measurable depictions of the wreck, terrain, and debris field that lay above the seabed surface. The sonar imagery and data acquired would be displayed on the topside and recorded on video tape with the MVR 5500. These, in turn, would be used to provide a comprehensive map of the *New Jersey* wreck site that might then be synthesized into any number of usable electronic computer graphics formats for analysis and manipulation.

One of the main experiments that we wanted to carry out had been proposed by Ken Stewart. A quiet, droll, bearded scientist who looked like a kempt Grizzly Adams, Stewart had developed a software program for displaying and manipulating high-resolution sonic imagery. His program smoothed and filtered the data, utilizing multiple colors to represent different depths below an ROV-deployed sonar transducer. His data were to be collected over the wreck via the Mark II, outfitted with a 1½-degree sonar transducer and the Trackpoint sonic positioning system. The sonic imagery had the capability of producing up to ten-centimeter resolution. Ideally, after all of the data were synthesized and processed, we would have yet another totally electronically generated, computerized, three-dimensional model of the site to help us analyze the condition of *New Jersey*.

And there would be more. It was, indeed, a veritable cornucopia of experimental as well as tried-and-true technologies that would be applied for the first time in the name of marine archaeology. Some, as a result of the project, were destined to become the underwater archaeologist's stock-in-trade within but a few years. Others would be obsolete before the year was out.

❏   ❏   ❏

For the next several days, weather conditions on the Chesapeake were atrocious. Yet, the field teams were kept busy ashore, checking and rechecking, testing and retesting the equipment. A snowstorm aborted one effort to get to sea, and high seas the next. Mother Nature, however, failed to discourage the continuous flow of visitors, most of whom were marine archaeologists from around the nation invited to participate or observe the testing of the new technologies.

But delays, what with the expensive equipment, scientists, technicians, and boats fitfully awaiting the green light, were becoming frustrating. Indeed, it was downright wasteful. By midmonth, I had resolved that unless we could get back to the *New Jersey* site, weather or no weather, I would have to begin equipment testing elsewhere or risk losing many of the project's corporate sponsors and participants. Unfortunately, it would have to be conducted beneath the omnipresent glare of the press, for myriad journalists had been drawn to the project from the very outset.

Yet there was hope. With the arrival of Marty and Pete Wilcox in the Applied Sonics Corporation's *Sonic Boom,* a fast thirty-six-foot Hatteras, on the evening of February 12, we at last had a well-outfitted diving platform of workable size, capable of operating in shoally waters and comfortable enough to field four to six divers at a time. Perhaps, I reasoned, if we experimented with only some of the equipment in calm, protected, shallow waters, we might be able to refine and streamline our field methodology enough to handle *New Jersey* more efficiently when placid weather finally returned. *AVR-1* was released from service and replaced with *Sonic Boom*. I decided to use as a test subject the wreck of a vessel that I had already investigated during an archaeological research project in the Patuxent River in the late 1970s. The wreck was that of a 66.5-foot, 32-ton schooner called *Henrietta Bach*, which had been built at Cambridge, Maryland, in 1888 and abandoned in the late 1920s in a quiet, shoally indent of St. Leonard's Creek, some miles north of the mouth of the Patuxent. For years the site had been frequented by curiosity seekers and relic hunters and, in 1978, by an archaeological survey team fielded by NAA. Now, the bones of the decrepit old schooner were again to be visited, but this time to make archaeological history in a fashion that none of us would have dreamed of only a few years earlier.

When *Sonic Boom* and *Laidly* rendezvoused in St. Leonard's on the morning of February 13, the outdoor temperature was twelve degrees Fahrenheit. But the water was clear and the sheltered, ice-fringed cove in which the wreck lay was tranquil. Our primary objective was to attempt the first-ever field test of the SHARPS in open waters using both diver-held and ROV-managed transceivers.

By noon, Kiser's divers, McNamara, Pohuski, and volunteer Mark Jacobs, had deployed the Zodiac and were awaiting orders. But delay followed delay. It was readily apparent that Goober was having trim and communications problems as Helga Sprunk labored to maintain control of the ungainly craft. The SHARPS cables had been hopelessly snarled during an unreeling and required nearly an hour to untangle.

Fortunately, by midday everything began to hum in sync. Several divers were soon at work driving iron poles into the muck around the wreck to serve as SHARPS transceiver stations, while others swam the cables and hardware from boat to shore to connect on-board computers with the transceivers. Below deck on *Laidly,* the first video pictures of *Henrietta Bach,* transmitted from an ROV cruising along her keelson, were received with a communal cheer. The great experiment was about to begin.

With the ultrasonic transceivers in place, John Kiser was instructed to first make a single test run with the SHARPS gun along the hull of *Henrietta Bach*. Below deck on *Laidly,* green pinpricks of light began to course along the computer screen, as the electronic plot of his track was recorded within a millimeter of accuracy, six pinpricks per second. Suddenly, random spots dubbed "flyers" began to appear. The ROV and two divers tending cables in the water had unknowingly moved into the survey field within the electronic net, interfering with the signals bouncing from transceiver to transceiver and thereby creating the haphazard spots. The obstructors were promptly moved from the grid area. Another test run was made, then another, and another, until all the "bugs" were exterminated.

A Hurricane on the Bottom

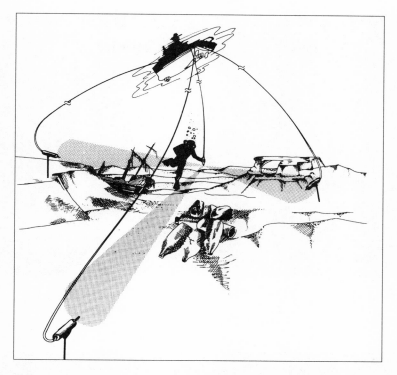

Originally intended for use in archaeological survey of shipwreck sites of
early antiquity in the Mediterranean, the SHARPS' first truly successful open
water use was on the wreck of the schooner *Henrietta Bach* during the
New Jersey Project. This diagram illustrates a typical SHARPS setup.
Courtesy Marine Telepresence Inc.

At 2:00 P.M. I decided to go for a complex mapping exercise. Pohuski,
who had never seen the wreck site before this day, was handed the
SHARPS gun and instructed to trace the outlines of the keelson and every
frame member attached to it. We all watched in silence as the site's jagged
outline began to take form on the computer screen. Fifty-five minutes
later, the wreck had been electronically surveyed. The electronic pen had
worked flawlessly. Exactly 1,038 points of reference with precise XYZ
coordinates had been recorded on our computer by a man who had never
seen the site, using a revolutionary underwater survey technology that had
never been deployed in an actual controlled, open-water field exercise
before. To have acquired the same data in the traditional fashion would
have taken weeks.

We had just witnessed a revolution in the field of underwater archaeological mapping. The first thing anyone said was, "Hey! Is that not sexy?"
Minutes later, amidst the round of self-congratulations, a NOAA lieuten-

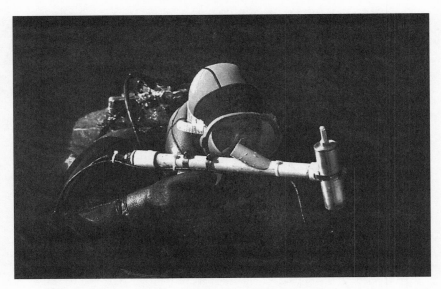

Diver Mike Cather fields the prototype SHARPS "gun" used for the first time in an open sea underwater archaeological survey. Photograph by Emory Kristof

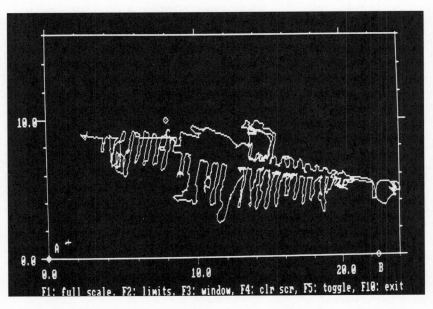

The SHARPS map of the keelson and frames of the schooner *Henrietta Bach*, the first ultrasonic electronic mapping of an underwater archaeological site in open water ever produced. Photograph by Emory Kristof

ant quipped in mock derision, "What's so great about that? You spend a quarter of a million [in fielding the expedition] and you end up doing what a guy with a pad and pencil could do." The lieutenant narrowly missed being hung from a boom for such seditious talk.

There was no letup now as test after test was conducted on the site with the SHARPS, each providing varying degrees of new information or techniques about the deployment or capabilities of the equipment. Below deck, Don Scott, the Applied Sonics resident computer technician, began to play with the imagery, connecting the dots on the screen to form a lined profile of the hull. He was soon rotating the computerized schematic to view the site from either side, upside down, and at various angles in between. The day had been a triumph unexpected by all. That night, after a complete debriefing, it was steak and beer all around. And for the next several days, owing to foul weather on the Chesapeake, we would return to the *Bach* for even further testing and refinements of our methodology.

❏   ❏   ❏

On February 17, the Maryland Geological Survey research vessel *Discovery* came on line as a replacement for *Laidly* as the principal operations platform. To everyone's relief, the Maryland captain, Jerry Cox, possessed the invaluable traits of ship savvy, a cooperative nature, and a knowledge of the fickle Chesapeake Tidewater. Yet, conditions on the open Bay continued to frustrate every effort to survey our primary target, *New Jersey*, despite Cox's willingness to try anything vaguely within reason. Work, however, went on.

At the Patuxent Naval Air Station, Volkmer and Chandler had begun building another SHARPS tripod, this time a twenty-foot-tall piece which we hoped to deploy at the *New Jersey* site to ensure that when work finally began there, our transceiver signals would not be obstructed by vertical projections such as the boiler and engines. The tripod was enormous and vaguely reminiscent of the Martians' machines in H. G. Wells's *War of the Worlds*. When asked what he proposed to do with the structure after the project was over, Volkmer replied, "Lease it to an oil company."

Aboard *Discovery*, Nicholson had taken command of the central operations cabin to rig his Sea Rover, while a small army of technicians worked about him installing pieces of sophisticated equipment, much of which would be tested on an archaeological site for the first time. The room was quickly dubbed "Star Wars Central." With all of the hatches and doors open to the weather to permit ready passage for the riggers and technicians, and the transfer of cables and equipment, there was no warmth to be found anywhere aboard ship. Everyone was covered from head to toe in full Arctic gear.

Somewhere on board a radio played an old Gary Lewis and the Playboys tune, "This Diamond Ring." And from beyond, the almost chimelike sounds of Solomons Harbor, caused by winds whipping lines and rigging against the myriad aluminum masts of hundreds of sailboats moored for the winter, provided a surreal ambiance to the scene.

Yet the cold alone could not frustrate our objectives, for still another visit to St. Leonard's was in the offing. This time, both State Administrator of Archaeology Richard Hughes and State Archaeologist Tyler Bastian would be going along as observers. They arrived at 9:00 A.M. to what must have seemed a chaotic scene. The decks were still cluttered with innumer-

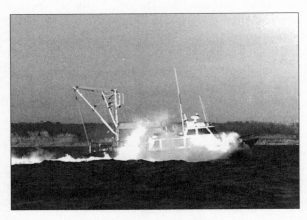

The Maryland Geological Survey's R/V *Discovery* en route to the *New Jersey* site.
Photograph by Emory Kristof

"Star Wars Central" in the cabin of *Discovery*. Photograph by Emory Kristof

able large gray boxes with foam plastic innards, half-filled with sonabuoys, ROV components, cameras, and miscellaneous pieces of electronic equipment still awaiting assembly. On the fantail, a Datasonics engineer was rigging a small piece of gear that looked like a white plastic bat with wings extended, while a computer "tekkie" sat nearby in the cold with a notepad on his lap and worked out arcane computations. A sonar technician, Lieutenant Robert Gwalchmai of the Canadian Navy, our newly arrived Mesotech expert (and a professional ship-carver on the side), was wearing Dayglo orange "total immersion" sea gear and sitting calmly amidst the chaos as he casually chiseled a model ship hull from a block of wood.

By late morning *Discovery* and *Sonic Boom* had returned to the *Henrietta Bach* site. Our objective this time was to attempt to survey the wreck using two separate techniques simultaneously. The first was to mount the split head of the Mesotech on an ROV and test its efficiency as both a navigation and survey tool; the second was to use the Trackpoint system to track and record the route of the ROV in real time. We hoped that this would permit a millimeter-correct correlation between acoustic data acquired during the ROV survey voyage over the wreck site and precise positioning. Moreover, for the first time, we would be loading the ROV with enough equipment to monitor, record, and synchronize navigation, angle, depth, course, pitch, range to target, video imagery, and ultrasonic and standard sonar data. With enough data, an electronically generated rotatable computer image of the wreck site might be constructed. We

A SHARPS transceiver is mounted on the bow of Sea Rover for the first attempt at a systematic robotic archaeological survey of a shipwreck site.

Robots Beneath the Chesapeake

The author fielding Goober in St. Leonard's Creek.
Photograph by Emory Kristof

would also field-test the accuracy of the SHARPS data by taking precise measurements of the hull and comparing it with a traditional hand-held tape measure.

By 1:30 P.M. all systems had been set in place. Sea Rover, with Nicholson at the controls and running through a final test, was blowing, sinking, and surfacing like a frolicking baby whale at play. With its handpainted shark's face, bright orange lights glowing like bulbous eyes, and dorsal rail and cables festooned with green floats for trim, the craft might have just slipped from a Jules Verne novel.

In Star Wars Central, the technical team monitored an array of screens filled with ever-changing numbers, sonar images, computer data, and navigational coordinates as Sea Rover began its underwater swim toward the wreck. Behind the technicians, off-duty divers, clothed in their bulky red and blue dry suits, watched the video and Mesotech monitors intently.

On the video, the worm-eaten frames of the old schooner slowly marched into view. At the bottom of the screen, the Mesotech head, mounted below the ROV's protective video bubble, was clearly visible, turning slowly from left to right and then back again. Visibility was perfect. The sonar imagery was spectacular.

To the right of the Mesotech screen, the Datasonics imagery seemed less dramatic and colorful yet was no less impressive as it tracked the course of the ROV, the Zodiac circling the area, each of the divers in the nearby waters, and numerous other objects. And so it went throughout the remainder of the day, trial after trial. As the early February evening set in, one last test, a comparison of measurements of the keel length of the wreck carried out with the SHARPS with that of an actual tape measure and the Mesotech, was undertaken by Kiser's shivering divers to determine the degree of precision of the SHARPS system versus the Mesotech.

"He's on the bow," shouted Kiser from the shore at precisely 5:29 P.M. as a diver armed with the SHARPS gun arrived at his appointed position. "OK, move him out," I ordered. At exactly 5:32 P.M., Kiser shouted again, "He's on the stern now."

The SHARPS work had taken three minutes. The tape measurement took eight minutes. The Mesotech took less than three seconds for a complete sweep of the site, and another five to place two measurement cursors that allowed a distance to be calculated between any two selected points on the screen. The difference was less than an inch.

A twenty-foot-tall iron tripod, one of three upon which SHARPS transceivers were to be mounted, is secured aboard the R/V *Discovery* at Patuxent Naval Air Station. Photograph by Emory Kristof.

Robots Beneath the Chesapeake

The following day, the Chesapeake Bay decided to cooperate with our efforts. A return to *New Jersey* was at last to be afforded us by Mother Nature. We hoped to make the most of it. The giant SHARPS tower would finally be fielded, and the first serious effort to survey the wreck with the new ultrasonic technology attempted. At the same time, three sonabuoys would be deployed several hundred yards from the site to track a robotic effort to document the wreck using both the Mesotech and the Trackpoint mounted on the Sea Rover.

By midmorning, *Discovery* had temporarily moored at the Patuxent Naval Air Station wharf to take aboard the twenty-foot-tall SHARPS tower. With some effort, the structure was carefully lifted by crane and hoisted aboard, and its spindly legs were tied to the stern of *Discovery* with brace lines. Two hours later both *Sonic Boom* and *Discovery* were on site, deploying the tower, as Kiser and his divers prepared to rig the SHARPS transceivers and then to drop the Datasonics sonabuoys in position around the wreck site. For once, the Chesapeake was absolutely mirror calm. The air was actually warm.

At 2:30 P.M. John Kiser set out with his dive team to rig three hard-wired transceivers onto the tops of the towers surrounding the wreck. Visibility was less than two inches; the well-rehearsed mission had to be completed almost entirely by feel. In the meantime, Nicholson and Stewart worked relentlessly to reconfigure the ROV with a Mesotech mounted below the camera dome on the bow and a transponder beneath the hull. On deck, Gwalchmai and Marty Wilcox had begun to spool out two hundred feet of cable, affixing small green floats at strategic intervals as they went. Within a short time, the ROV was being unlimbered in the frigid Chesapeake waters, its pilot flying entirely by radar. Suddenly, a commotion and shouts on deck alerted the control cabin that something was amiss off the port side of *Discovery*. The ROV, it was immediately perceived, had somehow entangled its cable with the coaxial lines running down to the SHARPS transceivers being placed around the site by Kiser and Cather. The thin cables on the starboard side of the ship had been too fine a target for the sonar to pick up, and with a tide again running, the ROV had been pushed off course without its pilot being any the wiser.

The danger of cutting expensive coax cables and losing ten thousand dollars in equipment was more than unnerving. But it was soon discovered that more was at stake than the loss of cables. Both Cather and Kiser, holding the transceivers at the ends of the cables, had been whipped around mercilessly in the dark as the ROV continued to entangle itself in the assortment of lines and cables (six in all). They soon found themselves trapped fifty feet beneath the Chesapeake, in near-zero visibility, with little more than ten minutes of air left. No one topside was even aware of their desperate situation. For either of the divers to have panicked would have

A Hurricane on the Bottom

Diver Mike Cather and the *National Geographic*'s ROV Goober.
Photograph by Emory Kristof

proved fatal. It was now that Kiser's years of training and experience paid off. With considerable dexterity, presence of mind, and no small amount of will, the two men managed to extract themselves and surface uninjured. The thunder of imprecations heaped upon the pilot of the ROV by the two frazzled and enraged divers (who climbed aboard *Sonic Boom* in total exhaustion with empty air tanks) would have made the most profane seadog blush. A revolt of the dive team seemed imminent.

Aboard *Discovery*, Nicholson had sprung into action almost instantly. Upon the first indication of the mishap he had rushed topside before fully recognizing the gravity of the situation, controls in hand, to attempt to visually manage the unsnarling. Carefully, he began to maneuver his craft to untangle its fragile lines from the even more fragile SHARPS coaxials. When the divers surfaced, he momentarily ignored their imprecations. The unravelling of six intertwined lines by the 140-pound robot, he said, would take the remainder of the day and then some. It was clearly a situation fraught with problems and hazard, and it looked like we might be on site well into the night. Finally, the embarrassed pilot was forced to seek the help of the divers he had almost killed by accident. The ROV was retrieved, and the cables and lines unsnarled. That evening, Marty Wilcox drove to his laboratory in Gloucester, Virginia, to fetch a replacement for the special coax, while Emory and I attempted to negotiate a truce between the irate dive team and the ROV engineer. By dawn the next morning, Wilcox had returned, replacement in hand, to a fragile peace.

We had learned our lesson. There were simply too many cables, lines, machines, and divers in the water at one time! Henceforth, navigation and tracking systems would always be on-line anytime the ROV was deployed—and no diver and ROV operations would be carried out simultaneously in black water.

Robots Beneath the Chesapeake

❏ ❏ ❏

There were two big red buoys, one large gray one, and two white ones marking the wreck on the morning of February 19 as *Sonic Boom* arrived on site well in advance of *Discovery*. Within minutes of anchoring, our divers were already at work. As usual, their job was complex. In an effort to facilitate and streamline the rigging and unrigging process for the SHARPS system, it had been decided that the topside ends of each SHARPS coaxial would be pigtailed with the others and then tied as a single unit to the big gray buoy each night after the completion of our underwater work. In this way, all that would be required was the retrieval of the cable ends and hookup to the computer system each morning.

The following day, we were again actually ready to begin the SHARPS survey. It was the same day already scheduled for the retrieval of the Datasonics sonabuoys, our testing with that particular equipment having ended. The recovery was supposed to have been a simple thing requiring less than an hour. All that was necessary was for Dave Porta of Datasonics to send a radio signal to the three sonabuoys to release them from their anchorages around the wreck site and then to have a boat team pick them up. The water was somewhat choppy at 10:30 A.M. when the signal was sent out, and John Kiser and a diver named John Brewer set off in the Zodiac to retrieve the giant white, oblong cylinders. Within a short time, two of the units had been recovered, but the third, a $25,000 item, either had not responded to its release signal, was stuck in the mud, or had been somehow prematurely released and was floating somewhere down the Chesapeake Bay. As no response signal was forthcoming from its homing device, Porta determined that the instrument had probably been free-floating for at least twenty-four hours (when he had last tested the signal). Calculating drift rate, current flow, and myriad other considerations, he quickly came to the conclusion that it could be anywhere within a thirty-mile range to the south of *New Jersey*. Homing in on its signal would be seeking the proverbial needle in a haystack. But we had to try. I immediately instructed *Sonic Boom* to set off in search of the lost sonabuoy. Miraculously, at precisely 2:49 P.M., the buoy was sighted bobbing about in the water seven miles due south of the wreck and was picked up a few minutes later. "Son of a bitch," yelled Porta's assistant in utter delight as he hove the big instrument aboard. "We couldn't have gotten luckier." But the day, with the dive boat unable to return to the wreck site for another hour, had already been largely wasted.

❏ ❏ ❏

Many guests had been invited to participate in or observe the *New Jersey* Project, from state administrative types, archaeologists, technicians, and scientists to the ever-inquisitive agents of the media. For many, it was their first contact with the Chesapeake, and one of the most common questions asked was, "What on earth is so important about an old steamboat that you have to go out in the worst possible weather in the dead of winter to study it?" My reply was a tongue-in-cheek little fiction, which became more refined with each telling.

"Have you ever heard of the Fabergé eggs?" I would ask in mock seriousness.[4]

"Certainly," most interviewers would answer, "but what do they have to do with *New Jersey*?"

"Well, when the noted Russian Le Roi Fabergé, Czar Nicholas's famed creator of the world-renowned diamond-and-gold-covered Fabergé eggs, fled Russia at the onset of the Russian Revolution, he brought with him a carton of his most valuable creations. Upon his arrival at Norfolk, Fabergé took passage for Baltimore on *New Jersey*. When the ship sank, Fabergé went down with it. Somewhere down there, in that old hulk, lay a carton of his most marvelous treasures, guarded by the spirit of the old Russian himself. And we are here to find them both."

The mere hint of "treasure" protected by a Russian ghost was enough to send most reporters into euphoric conniptions before they were brought down to earth. Gradually, the false tale of the Fabergé eggs, which changed with every telling, became a standing joke, understood by every expedition member and used to initiate every new visitor to the project. Indeed, no event was spared a role in the Fabergé saga. When an unsuspecting reporter watched a rare moment when the ROV could actually get a video of the wreck, marine growth sprouting from *New Jersey*'s hull was determined to be the "hair of the Fabergé eggs." Technical glitches were chalked up to old Le Roi's ghost, and the foul weather was attributed to the Fabergé Curse. It was amazing to see how many otherwise intelligent people believed the tales until told otherwise! It was indeed a wonderful diversion on very cold afternoons.

❏   ❏   ❏

On February 21, the weather was again unseasonably warm, and the Chesapeake was a glass pond. By noon, the SHARPS system was on line, ready for the dive team to begin mapping a select sector of the forward starboard hull. Once the diver's bottom time had been used up, Nicholson's Sea Rover, carrying the Mesotech and tracked by the Trackpoint, would attempt a comprehensive short-baseline sonar survey of the same area. The sonar data to be recorded as measurements from discrete points in the wreck would be acquired using the Mesotech processor cursor capacity. It would be the first comprehensive, systematic archaeological survey of its kind to be conducted robotically.

"We're not going to get too many days like this," quipped Marty Wilcox prophetically. "I can feel it in my bones."

Robots Beneath the Chesapeake

Divers Kiser, Cather, Brewer, and McNamara were given instructions on exactly what areas we hoped to survey with the SHARPS. They were to trace literally every board, frame, seam, treenail, and other feature encountered along the forward starboard hull with the SHARPS "pen." The electronic grid and the computers would do the rest. Or so we believed.

From the outset, it was apparent that something wasn't working. "Flyers" and obstructions prevented our getting an accurate signal. The current made it even more diffficult for the divers to conduct their work in the near darkness of the bottom. The SHARPS gun cable kept getting snagged. Lack of direct communications between Star Wars Central and the divers caused even more wasted time as the divers needed to surface continually to relay information. But more significantly, the flat "filleted" skeleton of *Henrietta Bach* had been a far simpler survey target than the complex three-dimensional hull of a 165-foot-long steamboat. In short, what we were finding out was that the system worked, but that our primitive survey methodology needed a lot of improvement.

By late afternoon, the divers' bottom times had been fully expended, although little usable data had been acquired despite the team's best efforts. The system, we sadly resolved, was too complex for use on moderately deep-water and convoluted three-dimensional sites such as *New Jersey*. Tracing a wreck was not the way a SHARPS should be employed. Moreover, with its complex of cables and deployment difficulties in deep water, it had become apparent that the system was more suitable for shallow marine environments.

We decided to spend the remainder of the day with the Mesotech sonar survey. This time, the plan was more comprehensive. The ROV would fly down and come to rest on the bottom at various predetermined points along the outside perimeter of the starboard hull. With the Mesotech turned on, we could systematically take measurements from any given point within the scan range to any other point within the scan using the built-in cursor measurement capacity. By establishing a single arbitrary datum point at the bow (or any other place, for that matter), it would be possible to leapfrog along the hull from bow to stern, taking measurements of any features we chose, while maintaining total provenance.

The ROV's descent was flawless. Its landing, twenty feet off the starboard side of the hull and thirty feet abaft the bow, was perfect. The Mesotech was soon scanning the bones of the old steamer as if it were an everyday occurrence. And with each scan the secrets of *New Jersey*, hitherto masked by mud and murk, took colorful form. By early evening, as the flood tide was about to begin, the salient features of the entire starboard side, stern end, and boiler-engine complex had been robotically and sonically measured and recorded. The port side, with the huge declivity undercutting the hull and extending nearly fifty feet or more from the

Chris Nicholson, inventor of the Sea Rover, lowers his ROV from the stern of *Discovery* to conduct the first systematic robotic archaeological sonar survey of a shipwreck. Photograph by Emory Kristof

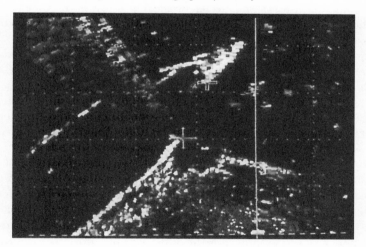

Sector scanning sonar imagery of the bow of the steamboat *New Jersey*. Note the two cursors measuring a gap in the starboard side. Photograph by Emory Kristof

ship, would prove more of a challenge, as would a survey of the complex interior components of the vessel.

Our confidence knew no bounds. We had successfully conducted the first entirely systematic robotic underwater archaeological survey of a historic shipwreck site, in zero visibility and with a current flow approaching two knots; after that, anything seemed possible. We had little notion, as we slogged home on that cold winter evening, that the day's efforts were to be nearly the last of our successes.

The weather forecast for the next day was, in fact, dismaying: twelve to eighteen inches of snow and winds of up to thirty knots on the Bay. It was an unfortunate time for poor weather to strike, for there were only four days left in the project, and an observer from the National Park Service, veteran underwater archaeologist Larry Murphy, was due to join us for the wrapup.

The day was not wasted, however, as we paid a visit to Dr. Garry Wheeler Stone at St. Mary's City to discuss the proceedings of the project and to invite his critical and valued comments on our effort. But there were equally significant matters to be discussed. Stone is considered by his peers to be one of the leading historical archaeologists in the United States and a formidable champion of both state and federal legislation to protect the nation's submerged cultural resource base. As chairman of the Legislative Committee of the Society for Historical Archaeology (and later president of the society), and as a leading member of the Maryland State Advisory Committee on Archaeology, he had fought long and hard on behalf of historic and archaeological preservation. An extremely erudite, soft-spoken, and gentle man by nature, he was seldom bested in debate.

New Jersey had found a friend in Dr. Stone. It had been Stone who first drew the stunning parallel between *New Jersey* and the famed *Bertrand*.[5] It was a comparison that had influenced the thinking of many in state and federal antiquities circles regarding the importance of the site. He had early on taken the *New Jersey* Project under his wing and had provided the pivotal support on the Advisory Committee necessary to secure Maryland state assistance for the effort.

Garry Stone had quickly realized that the sad old wreck might well serve as a cause célèbre in the decade-long national campaign for federal legislation to preserve historic shipwreck sites in American waters. If enough attention could be drawn to the wreck and its desperate condition, it just might serve as a catalyst in rallying significant and influential state and federal support for the most recent efforts for antiquities legislation in Congress, the proposed Abandoned Shipwreck Act of 1987.[6]

I had served with Garry on both the Society for Historical Archaeology's Legislative Committee and the Advisory Committee on Archaeology, but until the September 1986 Maryland Advisory Committee meeting, neither of us had seen an opportunity with so much positive potential as *New Jersey*. He suggested that publicizing the degenerating disposition of the site would promote both the need for federal legislation and the creation of a unified state program in underwater archaeology. We were both aware that without a state regulatory program there would never be a means to protect and evaluate Maryland's submerged cultural resources. And without federal legislation to override the tenets of Admiralty Law and the Law of Finds (which had repeatedly supported the commercial salvage of historic resources for profit), a state program for the preservation of such historic sites would never happen.

The moment for action was upon us. In late January, Stone had successfully lobbied for key support from Senator Bill Bradley of New Jersey to sponsor the proposed Abandoned Shipwreck Act of 1987 in the Senate by citing, among other examples, the sad tale of *New Jersey*. In his own moving written testimony in support of the bill, Bradley became one of the principal sponsors of the act. Not long afterward, Stone and I agreed to employ the example of *New Jersey* aggressively to secure the support of our state's congressional delegation through a personal presentation to the governor of Maryland. There could be no better opportunity to promote marine archaeology in our state than having the governor visit the *New Jersey* Project.

The prospect for a gubernatorial visit was quickly raised with J. Rodney Little, director of the Maryland Historical Trust, and Tyler Bastian, the state archaeologist. Both were enthusiastic, and Little immediately invited the newly elected governor and his entourage down. The governor's

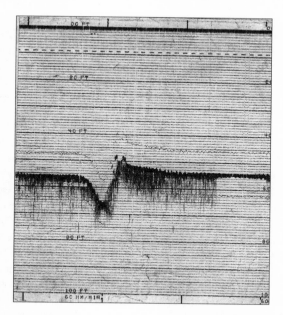

Bottom contour of the scour on the port side of *New Jersey*. The scour at this point is 11 feet in depth and nearly 19 feet below the topmost portion of the wreck, which was already beginning to collapse into the ravine. Along other sectors, the scour was found to be nearly 22 feet deep and undercutting the hull. Courtesy Applied Sonics Corporation

office accepted, and the morning of February 27, the last day of scheduled field operations, was chosen for the visit.

Garry Stone was delighted. J. Rodney Little was delighted. I was terrified. But the die had been cast.

❏   ❏   ❏

On February 24, the seas, although still running high after the recent blizzard, had subsided enough to permit a return to *New Jersey*. Our objective for the day was to conduct an experiment for ultrasonic survey, data assemblage, and computer mapping of the site. The latest storm, however, had wrought its havoc. The bow marker on the site had been swept away, and one of the SHARPS transceivers and its mount had been lost when a coaxial cable snapped during the blow. A replacement transceiver (our last) was deployed, but noise from the system quickly indicated that damage had been done to one of the other transceivers or coaxes. With the impending gubernatorial visit swifty approaching, each new delay took on a considerably more ominous visage. Either a quick location of the problem would have to be accomplished or the entire system would have to be yanked, repaired, and redeployed. Considering our previous deployment difficulties, our options were indeed limited. Late in the afternoon, a decision was made. We would again field the ROV and Mesotech, not for archaeological survey, but to examine each component of the system close up and then to send divers down to repair it, even though visibility was near zero. Misfortune, however, continued to hound us. Within minutes of the ROV deployment, the vehicle had again become ensnared in the cables. Once again, Kiser's dive team was dispatched to free the helpless robot.

On February 26, the last foray by *Sonic Boom* was dispatched to *New Jersey,* even as *Discovery* continued her work in St. Leonard's Creek. The specific objective of *Boom*'s mission was to recover wood samples from various parts of the wreck's architecture—specifically from the port side ceiling planking, the hornpost, and the strakes—for speciation study. It would also be our last chance to locate the lost transceiver. The investigation resulted in a dramatic though sad discovery. Hitherto, survey work, by both ROV and divers, had concentrated on the starboard side of the wreck because of the scour pit that had been etched out along and beneath the port hull. From our various sonar records acquired during the survey, we had deduced that there was a substantial portion of the wreck suspended over the scour pit (which had expanded threefold to a depth of twenty-two feet below the hull in a single year). Thus, survey in this specific area had been avoided because of the hazard of snagging an ROV cable or of potential collapse of the overhang on an unsuspecting diver. This time, however, I had instructed the dive team to circumnavigate the wreck in search of the transceiver and cable and to investigate the scour area fully.

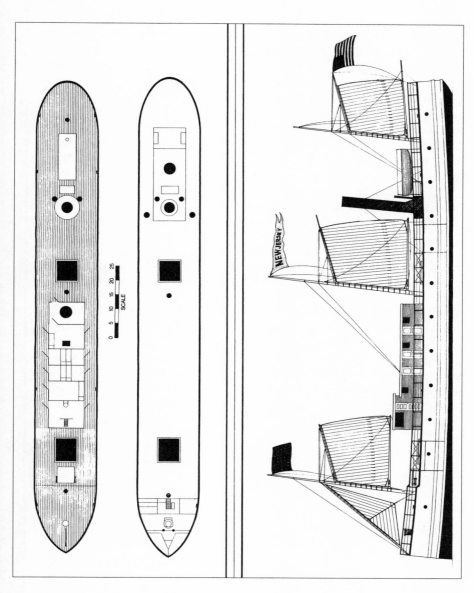

A conjectural plan of *New Jersey* based upon the historic and archaeologic record.

Robots Beneath the Chesapeake

When John Kiser and Mike Cather surfaced, sans transceiver but with plastic zip-lock bags filled with wood fragments in hand, they were exhausted.[7] "The current is blowing like a hurricane down on that bottom," reported Kiser, rolling his eyes in disbelief. "We were flapping on the side of that wreck like a flag in the wind." Looking over the *Boom*'s gunnels into the frothy seas, Cather quipped matter-of-factly, "That stuff is naaaaasty."

Their evaluation of the site's preservation, however, was even worse. Kiser morosely observed that from the excessive timber debris at the base of the scour, it was his opinion that the ship had begun to collapse into the abyss as undercutting continued to make inroads beneath the hull. It wouldn't be long, he grimaced, before the entire ship had collapsed into the pit like a heap of twigs. *New Jersey* was doomed, and there wasn't a thing anyone could do about it.

After weeks of roller-coaster science, the entire *New Jersey* Project team was nearing emotional and physical exhaustion. We had accomplished much of what we had hoped, namely, to evaluate more thoroughly the old steamboat's remains before they were totally destroyed by humans and nature. We had successfully employed technologies never before applied to the science of archaeology, and under the worst possible conditions, at the most inhospitable time of year, on a body of water noted for its dangerously fickle nature. And we had gained invaluable data in a manner that would have otherwise been impossible. Now all that remained of the project was to deal with the impending visit of a man noted to be one of the most active, hands-on governors in Maryland's long history.

EIGHT

Fabergé Eggs

The impending visit of the new governor of Maryland, William Donald Schaefer, to the *New Jersey* Project had produced an air of organized frenzy among the project team. The morning of the visit, February 27, was raw, gray, and cold, with winds ranging from ten to twelve knots on the open Chesapeake. Having anticipated just such a problem and the difficult logistics required to get the chief executive and his entire retinue into midbay, I chose instead to return to St. Leonard's Creek, a historical waterway that was smooth, shallow, protected, and filled with worthy targets suitable for demonstration purposes. I had decided to use the wreck of either *Henrietta Bach* or *Dashaway*, an 1883 schooner I had discovered in 1984 in nearby Mackall's Cove, as subjects for the ROV and SHARPS demo, since the visibility over both sites was usually good and both were lying in coves relatively sheltered from wind and weather. Although the wreck, at 51.6 feet in length, was in a far inferior state of preservation than the *Bach*, *Dashaway* was finally selected as the primary target since she lay adjacent to the nearby Jefferson Patterson Archaeological Park and the bluffs on which American gun batteries had been mounted during the War of 1812. The idea, of course, was to immerse the governor in as much history and technology as necessary to promote underwater archaeology as quickly and efficiently as possible.

My thoughts on how to conduct a demonstration and the particulars of site selection were not universally popular. When I had called my colleague Fred Hopkins (who had been laid up for the duration of the project with a crippling leg injury, but who had done most of the research on *Dashaway*), his views were candid and to the point. He felt that the timing of the demonstration was ill conceived, owing to quirky weather and site conditions, and that the visit stood a good chance of failure, which would embarrass the Maryland Geological Survey, the National Geographic Society, and me in the process. His opinions were shared by Tyler Bastian, who was growing increasingly negative over the plan. On February 26, Tyler telephoned Richard Hughes, the state administrator of archaeology, and beseeched him to call the whole thing off. But the ball was already in motion. The governor was excited about the visit and simply wasn't about to cancel it, come rain or shine. The most Hughes could promise was to delay a press conference scheduled for the day following the demonstration.

In any event, the final details had already been worked out, at least on paper. The plan was that I would meet the governor at Mackall's Wharf and escort him and his immediate party aboard *Sonic Boom*. I had picked Mackall's over the more accessible White Sands Marina farther up the creek, because of the former's symbolic nature. The wharf was located at the site of a tract of land called the Brewhouse, or Johnsons Fresh, which had been settled in the mid-seventeenth century by Captain Peter Johnson. It had been the birthplace of Maryland's first elected governor, Thomas Johnson, a member of the Continental Congress, the Maryland Provincial Congress, and the U.S. Supreme Court. So, after all, where could it be more fitting for the new governor of Maryland to step into a historic endeavor than at the birthplace of the first elected governor of Maryland. Indeed, the wharf area itself was a site where we had also conducted an archaeological survey in 1980!

From Mackall's, I planned to conduct a brief water tour of the historic locations on the creek, rounded out with a visit to the *Henrietta Bach* wreck site, which, if conditions were right, we might even catch a glimpse of from the boat. After this warmup, we could rejoin *Discovery*, conduct our demonstrations, present a case for a state program in underwater archaeology, and solicit the governor's support for the Abandoned Shipwreck Act. The thirty to forty members of the press would be provided controlled access to the proceedings by several Department of Natural Resources police boats and would be given a statement by the governor after the demonstration. The plan *seemed* simple enough!

I had not slept at all the night before the governor's visit, fearing that I might overlook some critical point as myriad details of the coming affair rushed through my brain. Still, with the dawn, eveything seemed in order. Emory Kristof and Al Chandler had spent the whole day of February 26 in the photo lab at *National Geographic* in Washington, piecing together a wonderful fifteen-minute video overview of the project to present to the governor while he was aboard *Discovery* and for later distribution to the media. And, as is normal with Emory and Al, the end product had indeed been a miracle. In the meantime, everyone had been briefed on his or her individual mission for the grand finale of the *New Jersey* Project, and all were keyed to the moment. This was Graduation Day, the American League Pennant, and the Superbowl, all wrapped up in one.

Skipping breakfast, I telephoned Ralph Eshelman to request the loan of artifacts recovered in 1975 from *New Jersey* to show the governor. I packed away several books I had written as well as a report on *New Jersey* to present to our illustrious guest as a personal gift. In the meantime, the Wilcoxes prepared *Sonic Boom* for the executive visit, hosing her down and scrubbing her clean, while John Kiser organized last-minute equipment checks with his divers. Nothing was left to chance. Or so I thought.

Although I had hoped to have both vessels on site by 9:00 A.M., since the first contingent of the press was scheduled to arrive at Mackall's shortly thereafter, the details of getting *under way* kept getting *in the way*. Two key team members, Helga Sprunk and Keith Moorehead, who operated Goober, had seemingly vanished, and a full hour was lost before they were located in a local hardware store, filling their pockets with knickknacks.

Soon afterward, Pete Wilcox informed me with a smirk that the *Boom*'s head was completely full and there wouldn't be any room to flush if the chief executive of Maryland or any of his coterie required the facilities. "Why now? Why not two days ago, or tomorrow? " I asked the heavens. There was, unfortunately, no answer, and less time to spare in such queries to the Fates. I immediately rushed down to Zahniser's Marina to see if we could get a rush pump job for the holding tank, only to find that the station had closed down for the winter. Fortunately, after I explained the situation to the good folks at the marina, an emergency exception was made for the visit of the governor of Maryland, and the tanks were pumped. So far so good.

When I boarded the *Boom* to bring her down to the gas dock, I conducted a once-over inspection of the boat. Upon peeking into the forward cubby I was stunned to discover a fully operational assault gun, replete with clip, lying casually in the corner. Was there some plot to do in the popular governor? Was there a kidnap scheme afoot? The answer proved to be far more mundane. Pete Wilcox, I knew, was an ardent gun collector, a military history buff, and a regular participant in Civil War reenactments. The gun, I soon discovered, was his, and I was certain his intentions were innocent enough, for I knew he frequently carried side arms. Nevertheless, I cringed. Hobbies were one thing, but explaining a loose machine gun belonging to a man with a penchant for army camouflage flack jackets, fatigues, and combat boots, and who wore a black beret with the insignia of a professional mercenary unit, was something else. It was a delicate task, ridding the *Boom* of the insidious gun. After some gentle persuasion, however, Pete finally agreed. To this day, I think he brought it aboard just to get my goat.

When we finally reached Mackall's Wharf, both vessels in company, Richard Hughes and Dennis Pogue, the archaeologist from Jefferson Patterson, were there waiting for us, along with a few reporters from the Associated Press, who were visibly distressed by the cold and by the early arrival they had been told to adhere to.

The next group to arrive at Mackall's was the governor's advance man and security personnel. The advance man, an efficient, pushy fellow obviously puffed up with his own self-importance, demanded that I run through the whole exercise with him as if I were taking the chief executive himself around. The governor's security agent, a portly, tubby little police corporal, closely surveyed the shoreline as we cruised up the creek. When I asked her why all the close scrutiny, she replied seriously: "Snipers." I muffled a groan and tried not to roll my eyes heavenward.

I had already decided to greet the governor ashore, snipers or no snipers, and to bring only his immediate party aboard *Sonic Boom*. The remainder were to be transported to *Discovery* aboard two police boats that had just arrived. But the advance man wanted his due, and right away. Dutifully, I ran through the paces, up St. Leonard's to the *Bach* site, down to the cove, and then aboard *Discovery*. The governor's man strongly "suggested" that when the governor arrived, we do a bit of deck display, introduce the key players, and then sequester ourselves below in Star Wars Central where the area could be closed off to reporters, and where we could press upon Governor Schaefer whatever it was we wanted to say. As a staff member of the Library of Congress, exposed to the instantaneous demands of Congress and anyone else of importance on Capitol Hill who had to be coddled, I thought I had grown inured to such imperious security types, who constantly screened the institution and the civil servants who labored therein to clear the way for the visits of the high and mighty. I had witnessed many such necessary but self-important people, whose mere proximity to power made them all the more obnoxious. It was, unfortunately, an unpleasantness to be borne with the job. However, I could not help but resent both the bossy advance man and the "little corporal." After all, whose party was it, anyway? Still, the show had to go on, and I consoled myself by repeating that they were only doing their jobs.

Even before we arrived with the advance man and security types to run through our paces, Emory had already got operations under way aboard *Discovery*. Helga and Keith were actively unlimbering Goober while Marty Wilcox directed several divers in setting up the SHARPS transponders around the wreck. Al Chandler busied himself, after checking out our survey gear, by manufacturing peanut butter and jelly sandwiches in the off chance the gubernatorial palate required sustinence.

As I conducted a final once-over of *Discovery*, I picked up the tied-to-gether bundle of my books, which I had prepared to give to Mr. Schaefer as a personal gift, to toss them into a readily accessible nook. It was then that I discovered the *Hustler* magazine slipped between two of the copies. Lieutenant Commander Robert "G. W." Gwalchmai, of the Canadian Navy, who had been serving as our project sector-scanning sonar expert and resident comedian, had narrowly missed pulling off the "gotcha" of the decade. It wasn't the only trick to be foiled at the last minute. Don Scott, our ace "hacker" from MIT, had prepared titles for the SHARPS computer display welcoming our illustrious guest with a barrage of off-color kickers. Fortunately, formality and propriety prevailed and neither the magazine nor the modest computer headlines made the evening news. My reputation among the survey team as a genuine prig was assured.

Shortly before 10:30 A.M., a bus arrived, filled with scores of Schaefer's staff, aides, reporters, and state personnel of all stripes. With Richard Hughes in company, I walked up the road to welcome Maryland's new chief executive but failed to pick him out from the crowd filing off the bus and moving en masse down the hill. I spied Tyler Bastian and the director of the Maryland Geological Survey, Dr. Kenneth Weaver, in the horde, and thought of Fred Hopkins's dire warnings not to attempt a "dog and pony show" under winter conditions and at the site selected. But it was already too late to backpeddle. Suddenly, I was standing in front of J. Rodney Little, the state historic preservation officer and director of the Maryland Historical Trust, being introduced to the governor of Maryland.

William Donald Schaefer is an average-looking man. It is, however, an appearance that belies his famous ability to get things done, his occasionally outrageous opinions, candid speeches, and short, violent temper. He had a reputation for never countenancing failure, whatever the excuse —at least according to the press, which eternally dogged him. In person, however, he was unlike anything I had expected. On this occasion, one of the first field excursions of his administration, he was like a kid at Christmas. He walked quickly and for a short, older man, seemed to have a vitality in his step that outstripped all of his staff and the entourage behind. I liked him instantly.

From the moment we boarded the *Boom,* I enjoyed the undivided attention of my guest. It was obvious from the start that he was here to see what we had accomplished, and, moreover, what was in it for the state of Maryland. As I spoke of the historic events that had transpired on this beautiful, tranquil body of water, such as the erection of the once-important, but now extinct, riverport of St. Leonard's Town, the Battle of St. Leonard's Creek during the War of 1812, and the rich maritime heritage of the waterway as evidenced by the remains of vessels such as the *Bach,* I felt more like a tour guide than a project director. The governor, however, appeared rapt, expressing amazement that with so many events occurring on the little creek, no one had heard about them. When the comptroller of Maryland and Calvert County's most prominent native, Louis L. Goldstein, who had come down with the governor, attempted to insert a comment or two about the local wonders, Schaefer commanded him, "Be quiet and let the man talk."

As we cruised up the creek, I pointed out many historic sites, such as the scenes of the 1814 battles on the creek, the sites of the American gun batteries, and the location of Jefferson Patterson Park. When we arrived at the *Bach* site, the water had unfortunately grown murky with the change of tide and the wreck was obscured from view, so I rolled into a briefing on the history of the vessel and our investigations of her remains. Again

Goldstein sought to interrupt, this time about the wreck. "Please be quiet, sir," said the governor again, even more firmly. "The man is talking." The comptroller of Maryland said nothing more. Months later, during a reception in the chambers of the Maryland State Senate, Goldstein informed me that what he had been attempting to say was that as a youth he had actually served as a crew member aboard the *Bach*, and later as an attorney for her captain, Jim Breeden!

As we approached Mackall's Cove half an hour later, I was stunned to see large crowds of people aboard a little flotilla of boats anchored about the *Dashaway* site. The two police boats and the *Discovery* appeared to be awash with reporters and cameramen. In the water, Goober was swimming erratically about the wreck with three green flotation balls tied to her body, while Helga Sprunk stood on the stern of the survey boat, ROV controls in shaking hands and a desperate look upon her face. Two divers were already in the water, swimming toward Goober, and others were preparing to enter. Something was wrong, but I could not discern what.

As we boarded *Discovery*, which was brightly festooned with the national and state flags, as well as that of the National Geographic Society, I was surprised by the multitude of faces already crowded aboard. It was obvious that no one was concerned with the Coast Guard regs on this one. There was a melange of officials and reporters, notables and not-so-notables. I immediately introduced the governor and comptroller to Kristof and our field team and then invited Schaefer's senior entourage below to Star Wars Central for a demonstration.

It was my intention to provide the governor's party with a synopsis of our project using Emory's video, then to provide a live demonstration on the use of the ROV, SHARPS, and Mesotech systems. The governor would then ceremoniously be given the controls to Goober and, hopefully, attempt to fly her. Afterward, I would make my pitch for the establishment of a state program in marine archaeology and lobby for his support for the proposed Abandoned Shipwreck Act of 1987. Unfortunately, Murphy's Law had, without my knowledge, already been liberally applied.

Unbeknownst to me, disaster had struck. During my absence, the ROV had blown a thruster, and the computer system had briefly crashed. Fortunately, Emory had cooly flown into action, even as we were coming aboard, by dispatching a pair of divers to swim over and manhandle Goober into a position adjacent to the wreck. We could at least get some video of the site and then physically manhandle the ROV around to different positions underwater with divers. Don Scott gimmicked up some computer imagery that looked amazingly like a SHARPS computer track to the uninitiated. Another diver, bearing the SHARPS gun, had been ordered to swim back and forth over the wreck site as if taking data. Incredibly, it looked for all the world like an actual survey was in progress. Emory quickly turned on the VCR and began to offer narration to accompany his short video production and computer demonstration of the SHARPS. The governor was enthralled.

As Emory boomed on with increasing gusto to our captive audience, I went topside and brought down some artifacts recovered from *New Jersey*, including the ship's steam whistle and several milk-glass molasses pitchers. The governor stroked these mundane artifacts of a past era as if they were the Holy Grail. No one said a word. The moment was pregnant with potential. I clicked on the video screen, where the wreck of *Dashaway* was being slowly scanned by Goober's television eye. I had the governor and comptroller of Maryland, the director of the Historical Trust, the director of the Maryland Geological Survey, the Maryland state archaeologist, and the state administrator for archaeology to myself for the next forty-five minutes. It was an opportunity of a lifetime.

William Donald Schaefer was a most inquisitive man, roiling with questions about the history we were probing, about underwater archaeology and historic preservation. What exactly did the state's submerged cultural resource base consist of? How many shipwrecks were there? What was needed to protect them? How could underwater sites be studied and culturally exploited for the benefit of Maryland's citizens? What would it cost? I did my best to answer his unending barrage of questions while working in my own agenda. I addressed the acute need for state support of the federal Abandoned Shipwreck Act and beseeched him to utilize his enormous influence with Maryland's representatives in the U.S. House and Senate to support the bill. I promoted the necessity of a state program in underwater archaeology and a conservation facility to preserve the

Maryland Governor William Donald Schaefer (left) discusses the future of underwater archaeology in Maryland aboard *Discovery*, as State Comptroller Louis Goldstein (center), John Kiser (center rear), J. Rodney Little, and the author look on. Photograph by Tyler Bastian

fruits of such a program. I also discussed the benefits the program might reap for education, tourism, and cultural awareness. The inventory of topics seemed unending. It was, indeed, a heady and fertile conversation, in which many seeds were planted.

We adjourned to the deck to address the waiting press—first Governor Schaefer, then Comptroller Goldstein, then Rodney Little, and, finally, me. Surprisingly, the largest single sponsor of the project, the Maryland Geological Survey, remained mute. Still, I was both stunned and elated as I listened to the governor present a cogent, impassioned speech on the need for and potential benefits of an underwater archaeology program and a major conservation facility to handle archaeological materials in Maryland. He spoke excitedly and with an air of incredulity of his "sudden revelations" regarding Maryland's maritime heritage and seemed to support everything we had addressed. The governor was sold on underwater archaeology. It was now his show.

"Do you realize what has happened here?" said Rod Little, pulling me aside in excitement as the governor continued to speak, almost as if I had been a perfect stranger to the events that had transpired. Of course I did. A program in underwater archaeology for Maryland had been given birth.

❑ ❑ ❑

Shortly after 1:30 P.M., Governor Schaefer, his entourage, and the mob of reporters departed aboard *Sonic Boom* and the Natural Resources police boats, leavinng behind a handful of television newsmen to eke out the last few interviews before we closed the project down. As I was attempting to field questions from a Washington television news reporter below deck, I was suddenly summoned by frantic shouts from the fantail. Helga had apparently been attempting to fly the crippled ROV back to *Discovery* and had just managed, with the aid of a diver, to bring it alongside, but with a mysterious object clutched in its claw. As I stumbled over the reporter, half killing him and myself to get on deck, I saw both the pilot and Keith bending over the stern and reaching toward the bobbing robot—more precisely, reaching for its outstretched claw. Goober, they were yelling loudly, had recovered something from the wreck!

Held in the claw was a diver's collection bag, filled with brightly colored oblong objects. "My God," laughed Helga. "It's picked up the Fabergé eggs!" Indeed, the bag was filled with six gaudily painted plastic hosiery eggs, each filled with nuts and bolts, miniature plastic animals, and odds and ends of junk and fake jewelry, which could be readily viewed through holes cut in the shells. On each eggshell were enscribed names such as "Lee Roy Fabroget" and "Carlos Fabroget." Thus was revealed the cause for Helga and Keith's tardiness. They had been rounding up the long-lost Fabergé eggs as an end-of-the-project gift for me!

Fabergé Eggs

That night, as we all watched ourselves on the evening news in the lobby of the Comfort Inn, I received a call from Richard Hughes. He enthusiastically informed me that the governor had been absolutely elated over his visit. The governor's aide, Mark Wasserman, said Schaefer hadn't been so excited in a decade, even on the night of his election to the state's highest office.[1] He had vowed on the trip back to Annapolis to select a committee immediately to formulate guidelines for a program in underwater archaeology for Maryland, and would support a state archaeological conservation facility. Furthermore, he intended to lobby Maryland's U.S. House and Senate delegations personally to support the Abandoned Shipwreck Act. And, finally, he vowed to support the foundation of a maritime complex in Baltimore that would house the greatest underwater archaeology center in the nation! His word was almost as good as gold.[2]

On March 4 Governor Schaefer formally met with the Maryland congressional delegation to outline his priorities and to encourage their support in Congress, placing great emphasis on the need to pass the Abandoned Shipwreck Act. He also encouraged the delegation to support the funding of the Federal Historic Preservation Fund (this is the money that goes to state programs) at $60 million, rather than the $20 million which had been received in the past years.[3]

Moreover, the Maryland Historical Trust, which had long sought full control over all of Maryland's state-managed archaeological endeavors (including the functions and jurisdiction of the office of the state archaeologist), already had a plan ready for the creation of an underwater archaeology program. The Trust had moved with rapidity on all fronts.[4] As early as March 2, J. Rodney Little had dispatched to the governor's office a succinct but comprehensive review of the status of the reintroduction of the Abandoned Shipwreck Act (H.R. 74) in the U.S. Congress and the need for Maryland's total support of the bill.

The following day, Little circulated a memorandum to Schaefer through the governor's aides, Mark Wasserman and Paul Schurick, recommending the creation of a special Advisory Committee on Maritime Archaeology to advise the governor and Historical Trust on the establishment of a state program. The committee, Little proposed, would include recognized leading experts on maritime archaeology, representatives from involved state agencies, experts in conservation and curation, and representatives from affected interests groups such as sport divers, dive shop owners, and the like, from both around the nation and Maryland. Its mission was to prepare written recommendations for the establishment of a state maritime archaeology program under the auspices of the Maryland Historical Trust. The recommendations, formulated over a period of a year, would provide the basis for a legislative package for submission to and action by the 1988 General Assembly. The office of a State Underwater Archaeologist would be created, under whose administration the committee's recommendations would be implemented. The plan was immediately approved by Wasserman and Schurick and forwarded to the governor.[5]

On March 17, a second action plan was submitted. It called for a state conservation and curation laboratory suitable to handle archaeological materials, both large-scale and waterlogged, to be erected at Jefferson Patterson Archaeological Park and Museum.[6] The plan, replete with copies of key segments of the final reports on the 1986 investigations of *New Jersey*, and of projects I had directed at Point Lookout, Maryland, and on the Patuxent River, as evidence of need, would require $286,000 in funding for design alone but was already being successfully pressed through the Maryland Senate Budget and Taxation Committee and the House Appropriations Committee.[7]

On April 29, Governor Schaefer dispatched seventeen invitations to prospective members of the newly mandated Advisory Committees on Archaeology and Conservation and Curation.[8] On July 20, the committees convened in the Maryland State House in joint session for the first time.[9] Within a year of this conference the Maryland Maritime Archaeology Program was created and the first state underwater archaeologist, Paul Hundley, a native Minnesotan working in Australia, had been hired.[10]

Governor Schaefer's ardent sponsorship of underwater archaeology continued unabated. He pressed Maryland's congressional delegation to support passage of the revised Abandoned Shipwreck Act of 1987 (S.858). He emphasized his own support by paying a dramatic, unannounced personal visit to the U.S. Senate committee debating the bill to press home Maryland's avowed interest in its passage. By this time, the *New Jersey* Project had drawn national attention. Dr. Garry Wheeler Stone, president of the Society for Historical Archaeology, actively lobbying for support of the shipwreck bill in the Senate and House, cited the devastation done to the old steamboat by relic hunters as an example of what lay in store for all historic shipwreck sites if the act were not passed. "We are tired of weeping," he wrote to one legislator. "We want new legislation."[11] His pleas did not fall upon deaf ears. On the floor of the Senate, senators like Bill Bradley of New Jersey began to cite the case of *New Jersey* in laying the groundwork for passage. Their efforts were not in vain.

On December 19, 1987, the U.S. Senate passed the bill in its entirety. On April 13, 1988, the House of Representatives followed suit. Fifteen days later, President Ronald Reagan signed the bill into law as Pub. L. No. 100-298.[12] The battered and beaten *New Jersey* had contributed to a legacy of immutable merit.

PART TWO

MELTED BEADS

*There remaine dyvers places and partes of this
Kindome of Virginia not yett discovered since the
beginning of this Colony, by the search and discovery
whereof the bounds and limitte of this plantation
may be far augmented and such other commodities
found out as may be for the benefit and good of the
people inhabiting the same.*

John Pott, *Governor of Virginia*

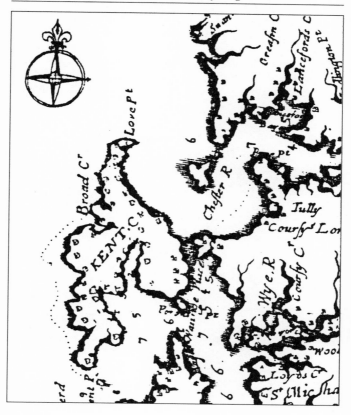

A Commission to Goe

In Chesapeake Bay, less than 10 miles from the city of Annapolis and approximately 180 miles north of the Virginia capes, lies Kent Island. Until recently, this low-lying, all-but-ignored body of land was, for most travelers, little more than the eastern anchor of the Chesapeake Bay Bridge, suitable only for short rest stops made on weekend jaunts to the Atlantic coastal resorts of the Delmarva Peninsula. As islands go, it is a modest piece of real estate, barely 14½ miles long from Love Point on its north end to Kent Point on its south, scarcely 5 miles across at its widest, and several hundred feet at its narrowest. Its northeast side, abutting the Chester River, and its western face, on Chesapeake Bay, are largely unbroken by major streams, and present elevations above high water are only 18 feet or less. Its low southeastern fingers are frayed with salt marshes and eroded wooded sections that claw into the shallows of Eastern Bay. Although the island is generally encompassed by a shoally belt of water less than 10 feet in depth, near Bloody Point on its southwestern extremity, within a distance of 350 yards from the shore, the bottom drops off precipitously from a mere 13 feet into the 174-foot-deep remnants of the ancient paleochannel of the Chesapeake.[1]

Today, the "Sunny Isle of Kent" (as some real estate promoters like to call it) is under siege, with 30 percent of its coastline developed and 39 percent more slated for development or under cultivation. Once heavily forested, its waterfrontage has lost all but 6 percent of its native growth. Shopping malls, housing developments, marinas, recreational areas, and highways increasingly threaten its bucolic inlands and dappled shoreline. Like much of the Eastern Shore (indeed, much of rural America) faced with the cancer of uncontrolled urban expansion, great swaths of this pastoral Eden seem fated to a future of concrete and asphalt. Ironically, Kent Island, where city-bred immigrants flee to escape the unforgiving lifestyles of nearby Washington, Baltimore, Annapolis, and the dull, indistinguishable suburban satellites that surround them, appears doomed to becoming another gigantic bedroom community for megalopolis.

Despite such "progress," Kent has successfully managed to conceal well her treasures and her colonial heritage and history. She has held jealously close to her bosom secrets that have for at least two centuries challenged and frustrated gentrified antiquarians, historians, and archaeologists alike. For here beneath the same fields, marshes, and estuaries beseiged by urban development are hidden the remains and relics of the earliest permanent European settlement in Maryland and the artifacts of the first armed conflict between English-speaking peoples in the New World.

❏ ❏ ❏

William Claiborne was an implacable, complex, ambitious man. The most accepted biographical account of this prince of destiny suggests that he was born in the year 1600, the second of five children of Sara and Thomas Claiborne, the latter a successful merchant and government official of Crayford, Kent, England.[2] Others claim that Will was the son of Edmund and Grace Cleborne of Cleborne Hall, in Westmoreland, whose noble family line extended back to Saxon times. Little is known of his youth until May 31, 1617, when his admission was certified as a pensioner at Pembroke College, Cambridge.[3] Although the record of his collegiate career is minimal, his later life suggests that he must have been an aggressive student, quick to learn and more than eager to accept a challenge or, when necessary, a fight. He was swift to recognize and seize upon an opportunity when it suited him. And for Claiborne, opportunity had been clearly identified early on, and its name was Virginia.

By the summer of 1621, although barely twenty-one years of age, Will Claiborne had become enamored of the prospects offered by the Virginia

William Claiborne of Virginia, founder of the Kent Island settlement in 1631.
Courtesy Library of Congress

colony, where, it was said, a well-connected entrepreneur could make his fortune and earn his fame. Just how his infatuation with Virginia was given birth is questionable, although some historians have suggested that it was through some personal contact with the famous Captain John Smith.[4] How he then managed to bring himself to the attention of the directors of the Virginia Company of London, under whose charter and auspices the infant settlement on the James River in far-off America was being managed, is equally questionable. Some have asserted that it was through the influence of William's persuasive mother, and others claimed that it was through the intercession of the influential Countess of Pembroke.[5] In any event, on June 13, Will Claiborne was recommended to the company directors "as very fitt in ye art of surveying"; he secured from them a three-year appointment as surveyor for the Virginia colony. His salary, modest for the task ahead, was thirty pounds per annum, with an initial allowance of twenty pounds for the necessary instruments, equipment, and books. In addition, he was to be given two hundred acres of land and an allowance for free transport to the colony for himself, his servant, and a third person of his choice.[6] Though certain members of the board of directors complained of this expenditure for one so young and unproven, given the monumental task allotted him and the services he would ultimately render, they had struck more than a fair deal. On July 24, Claiborne's mission was outlined in full to the new thirty-four-year-old governor-to-be of the colony, Sir Francis Wyatt, and his council.

Clairborne was to map the metes and bounds of an entire frontier colony, most of which had not even been explored, and the properties and patents therein. This would be no small endeavor, for the Virginia Company's 1609 Charter was, in fact, unrealistically grandiose: it encompassed all territory ranging from two hundred miles north of Old Point Comfort on the Chesapeake to two hundred miles south of that point; that is, all territory on the seaboard side between the thirty-fourth and forty-first degrees of latitude, and stretching "up into the land from sea to sea," from Atlantic to Pacific. Early in April, the company had chartered the 140-ton ship *George* and the 80-ton *Charles*, specifically to convey Wyatt and his official family, including Claiborne, to Virginia. By the end of July, the two vessels had come to anchor at the port of Cowes at Isle of Wight, to complete final provisioning and boarding of passengers before commencing the long Atlantic voyage. It was here that Claiborne embarked to begin his American adventure.[7]

Unlike many resupply ships that had sailed annually to the Virginia colony, *George* and *Charles* made their voyage without incident or the loss of a single life. By October 1621, laden with new immigrants and provisions for the colony, both vessels safely hove to off James Fort, the palisaded defense work on "James Citty" Island, in the James River, which had, since the colony's founding, served as its nucleus and refuge.[8]

Melted Beads

Within a short time, Claiborne was furiously engaged in unsnarling overlapping land claims, laying out large plots of public lands, and recording patents. Somehow, the energetic young surveyor found time to travel widely, exploring forests and fields, and crops and crofts of ambitious Englishmen busily planting roots in the Virginia soil and industry upon her shores. Nor was his curiosity expended entirely upon the colonists, for it extended to those who had been there when the white man first arrived. He visited the long huts of the local native werowance and his men, with whom he smoked the long-stemmed calumet, or peace pipe. And Claiborne listened intently through an interpreter as they told him of their people, prowess, customs, and, most interesting of all, the limitless supply of otter and beaver pelts to be had in trade for the Europeans' goods.

Claiborne's rise to power was almost meteoric, despite (or possibly because of) a catastrophic sequence of events that exploded soon after his arrival. On Good Friday, 1622, the Powhatan Confederacy, under the leadership of the canny chief Opechancanough, had risen up in a desperate attempt to exterminate every English settler in Virginia. As a result of the surprise attack, more than 350 men, women, and children were butchered outright, many as they slept in their beds or worked in the fields. Jamestown, fortunately, had been forewarned, and the colony survived. Governor Wyatt's reprisals against the Powhatans were as swift and brutal as had been the natives' initial surprise assaults. Throughout the bloody war that ensued, William Claiborne appears to have been an active participant. In a 1624 campaign against Opechancanough's principal seat of power at Candayak, or West Point, where the York and Pamunkey Rivers converge, he commanded the attack. During the grim encounter that followed, the youthful soldier/surveyor is thought to have received a severe arrow wound in the thigh that would cause him pain for the rest of his life.[9] But it failed to slow him down, for soon afterward he would actively participate in an effort to erect a safe permanent settlement on the Eastern Shore at Accomac, where he would establish his own plantation.[10] It would seem that the interests of William Claiborne and of Virginia, even at this early date, were one and the same.

Despite his frequent involvement in military affairs, Will Claiborne's survey work was not ignored. Soon after the Opechancanough uprising, he was busily employed in laying out a fifty-acre "New Towne" tract adjacent to the palisaded works on James City Island, a site that would soon see the erection of the finest houses in the colony by its most important citizens.[11] He also found time to settle land owed him by the Virginia Company and to establish another plantation near the Indian village of Kecoughtan (where the city of Hampton would one day take root). On June 21, 1624, Claiborne's first patent, which covered several neighborhood parcels and totaled 150 acres, owed him for transporting three servants from England, was granted.[12]

Though now only twenty-four, Claiborne had, through hard work, dedication to duty, blood, and no small amount of pluck, earned the respect and admiration of his peers and elders. When the charter of the Virginia Company was rescinded in June 1624, after years of company failure to produce a profit, King James appointed a commission of Lords of the Privy Council and certain others to draw up his own royal charter for the colony.[13] Henceforth, Virginia would be a royal colony subject only to the prerogatives of the sovereign and his appointed officials, and with only restricted rights to regulate or self-govern as it had during the company's administration.[14] On August 26, the crown appointed Wyatt as the first royal governor of Virginia and eleven prominent men to constitute his council. Among them was William Claiborne.[15]

Unlike many members of the council, young Will was conscientious to a fault and, never missing that body's thrice-monthly meetings, addressed his duties seriously. As his political star ascended, his personal holdings increased commensurately. By 1626 he possessed more than nine hundred acres of land and a reputation for good judgment and political acumen.[16] On March 4, 1626, less than two years after his appointment, Wyatt was replaced by Sir George Yeardley as governor by King James's successor, King Charles I. Yeardley's commission also announced the appointment of the first secretary of state of Virginia. The candidate had been personally recommended by Yeardley, nominated by the commissioners for Virginia, and approved by King Charles. The nominee was none other than young William Claiborne.[17]

On May 14, 1626, at the age of twenty-five, William Claiborne, in receiving the appointment as colonial secretary of Virginia, had been elevated to the second-highest office in the land. The benefits and remunerations of his position were many. Land and the manpower to work it was an inherited privilege of all officeholders. Social prestige, commercial preferment, and special opportunities for monopolies were among the more lucrative advantages of his position.

Despite the heady velocity of his rise, Claiborne's ambitions had only been tickled. He was well aware that among the king's instructions to Sir George Yeardley was a specific order authorizing the governor and his council to bestow commissions or licenses for exploration and discovery between the thirty-fourth and forty-first parallels of northern latitude so that "the limits of the said plantation may be augmented." Such latitude meant many things to many people, but for Claiborne, the specifics meant only one thing—a golden opportunity to truck with the natives for furs (already the major commodity of trade among the French along the St. Lawrence, the Dutch on the Hudson, and the Puritans in New England)

and the colony's staple of survival, corn.[18] The secretary of state was not slow to test the waters. By 1626 he had already begun to make short trips into the Chesapeake. The following year, confident of his own ability and with Governor Yeardley's blessing for the "preservation and happie success of soe good an action," he prepared to conduct his first serious exploratory foray northward up the Bay.[19] Having learned through his friendly native contacts, servants, and other traders that the most propitious time of year to conduct trade with the natives were the months of March, April, May, and June, he sought, on April 3, 1627, "a Commission to goe with a boate and a sufficient Company of men into the Bay And to discover any rivers or Creekes within the Bay up to the heads of the same and trade with the Indians for Corne Skins or any other Commoditie whatsoever."[20]

On April 27 the commission was granted.[21] Almost immediately, Claiborne set sail in a shallop with over half a dozen armed men bound first across the Chesapeake for his new Accomac plantation on the Eastern Shore. There, he diplomatically attended to a recent failure of his tenants to pay their moiety of tobacco and to the issue of illegal settlement by a number of squatters on his lands. Turning northward, following in the footsteps of Captain John Smith and spurred onward by his own boundless curiosity, he began to probe and explore the intricate network of creeks, nooks, and crannies indenting the Eastern Shore of the Chesapeake.[22]

Very probably, on this, his first major exploratory voyage up the Bay, William Claiborne first laid eyes on the large, unspoiled island that so reminded him of his pastoral homeland in Kent, England. With its forests and fertile soils, placid waters and sheltered anchorages, the place gracefully but strategically corsetted the upper Bay. Known to early mapmakers as Monoponson Island, after a nearby tribe, it offered proximity to another tribe, the docile and friendly Matapeakes, with whom a profitable trade in corn and furs might easily be established.[23] If a trading base or, indeed, even a self-supporting plantation settlement could be erected on this island, it was possible that the wealth of the upper Bay and the still-unexplored regions beyond could be tapped and, if managed correctly, even controlled by anyone with the organization and will to do so.

The visit to the island, which he would soon dub Kent, had undoubtedly been exhilarating beyond measure for William Claiborne. Even a successful stop on his return down the Bay to truck on the western shore with the Patuxent Indians failed to dull his ardor.[24] His mind was bursting with ideas and plans of how such an enterprise as founding a frontier trading settlement on the placid shores of Kent Island might be accomplished. That he must establish ties with the natives, earn their trust, learn their ways, and continue to expand trade with them was a given. It was also immediately obvious that a second expedition up the Bay in 1628 to forward these objectives was imperative.

A Commission to Goe

In the fall of 1627 Governor Yeardley died. He was temporarily succeeded by Captain Francis West until his designated successor, Captain John Harvey, arrived in the colony to take command. West, however, was soon replaced by Dr. John Pott, who had sailed over with Wyatt and Claiborne. Pott was a man of little political ability and less diplomatic talent. The changes of governors, the ebb and flow of politics, and the onerous duties of Claiborne's own offices, however, failed to dissuade the young Will from pursuing his grand scheme.[25]

In 1628 Claiborne again ascended the Chesapeake on a second trading and exploring voyage, possibly as high as the uppermost extremity of the Bay. Here, he knew, was the land of the fearless and stately Susquehannock Indians, whose access to the northern regions teeming with fur-bearing animals offered the keys to untold wealth: their river, the mighty Susquehanna, the prehistoric trunk and headwaters of the Chesapeake itself, was the portal through which that wealth would flow. Claiborne moved with measured resolution and foresight. In 1629 he requested a commission from the governor and council to make "discoveries" in the country of the Susquehannocks. His efforts, he suggested, would not only improve the government's knowledge of Virginia's resources, but would help check the potential for incursions in those areas by the Dutch. On January 31, 1629, exercising one of the emoluments of office (in this case the right to a monopoly), the governor and council granted Claiborne, one of their own, a commission "to goe to the Susquehanas." To insure that competition from other trading interests would not intrude, no one but Claiborne would be allowed to visit them until the termination of his commission.[26] On March 13, 1629, Governor Pott formally issued Claiborne's commission:

Whereas there remaine dyvers places and partes of this Kingdome of Virginia not yett discovered since the beginning of this Colony, by the search and discovery whereof the bounds and limitte of this plantation may be far augmented and such other commodities found out in the same. Now know you that I the said John Pott out of the good opinion I conceive of the sufficiency and experience of William Clayborne Esquire who intendeth this sommer to emply himself with sufficient Company of men a shipp and other necessary provisions requisite for such a voyage to discover the parts and territories of this Colony situate and lying to the Southwards of this place as also of some particular places to the northward and in the Bay of Chesepeiacke and greatly favoring the prosecution of such enterprises tendeth so much to the enlargement and welfare of this Colony doe by these presents give full power and authority unto him the said William Clayborne to goe and make his voyage and saile into any the Ryvers Creekes portes and havens within the said Bay of Chesepeiacke or into any other part or parts of this Country within the degrees of 34 and 41 and there to trade and trucke with the Indians for furres Corne or any other Commodities of what nature or quality soever they bee.[27]

William Claiborne's third voyage up the Chesapeake would take him into the very mouth of the Susquehanna River, where he hoped to meet and trade with the great chief of the Susquehannocks. About midway between the thirty-ninth and fortieth parallels, barely a mile from the river's mouth, he landed on a small island, "halfe meade, halfe wood," of which he had heard. The place lay within the precincts of a patent granted by the Virginia Company in 1622 to Edward Palmer, an art critic, a gentleman, and an adventurer in the company, who had died in 1624 before taking up his claim.[28] Situated barely thirty-five miles downriver from the palisaded community of the Susquehannocks, it was a perfect place to powwow and truck for trade. Appropriately enough, the place was dubbed Palmers Island. Claiborne could not fail to be impressed by, and perhaps a little fearful of, his hosts, whose descriptions had been so ably recorded by Captain John Smith, who had visited these parts in 1608:

> Such great and well proportioned men are seldome seene for they seemed like Giants to the English, yea and to the neighbours, yet seemed of an honest and simple disposition. . . . Their language it may well beseeme their proportions, sounding from them as a voyce in a vault. Their attire is the skinnes of Beares, and Wolves, some have Cassacks made of Beares heads and skinnes, that a mans head goes through the skinnes neck, and the eares of the Beare fastened to his shoulders, the nose and teeth hanging downe his breast, another Beares face split behind him, and at the end of the nose hung a Pawe, the halfe sleeves comming to the elbowes where the neckes of Beares, and the armes through the mouth with pawes hanging at their noses. One had the head of a Woolfe hanging in a chaine for a Jewell, his Tobacco pipe three quarters of a yard long, prettily carved with a Bird, a Deere, or some such devise at the great end, sufficient to beat out ones braines: with Bowes, Arrowes, and clubs, suitable to their greatnesse.[29]

The long summer days and evenings of powwow and trade between the white men and the majestic, if frightening-looking, natives undoubtedly began cautiously on both sides but proceeded profitably, as beaver and otter pelts were exchanged for iron axes, hoes, beads, and trinkets. For the Susquehannocks the event would prove to be one of their better moments of contact with the Europeans. For William Claiborne, it was the long-hoped-for beginning of a trading empire. Palmers Island would be its forward outpost, and Kent Island was to be its foundation.

T E N

Unplanted by Any Man

Sir George Calvert, baron of Baltimore and lord proprietor of the recently failed colony of Avalon in Newfoundland, cautiously stepped ashore at James City Island, en route home with his family and a handful of retainers, about the first of October 1629. His arrival, totally unexpected by the Virginians, marked for himself the end of a particularly unhappy odyssey and for many of his hosts the beginning of another. Yet his travails were those that Virginians could easily relate to. Between 1620 and 1624, with the full approbation of the crown, Sir George had worked hard to establish a colony of his own on the barren shores of Newfoundland, but the privately funded effort had failed to prosper. By 1627, when all appeared lost, he had sailed for Avalon to attend to matters personally and to resuscitate the colony. He had maintained the struggle for another two years, but to no avail. Avalon was doomed to failure.[1]

Defeated but undismayed, Calvert turned south on his way home, resolved to search for a more hospitable clime and land. Although he was a court favorite in England, particularly of the king's Catholic consort Henrietta Marie, as a Roman Catholic himself, he was coolly welcomed by the staunch Protestant population of Virginia, who were deeply wedded to the stern doctrines of the Reformation. Unswerving in his faith and with remarkable courage, Baltimore outright refused to take the oath of supremacy, as required by Virginia's laws providing for strict Protestant conformity. Within a short period, both he and his party were made to suffer from the derision and hostility of their hosts. Had the Virginians known that their univited "papist" guest had, as early as August 19, 1629, already requested that the crown grant him a precinct of land in Virginia "with such privileges as the king your father, my most gracious master, was pleased to grant me [in Avalon]," it is doubtful he would even have been permitted to land.[2]

Calvert had, in fact, come to the Chesapeake to evaluate the region of the "Bay of Virginia" as a place in which he might attempt to establish yet another colony. When the Virginians belatedly discovered the nature of his visit, they were outraged and ordered him to leave immediately. On November 30, a letter signed by Governor Pott, Secretary Claiborne, Councilmen Samuel Mathews, and Roger Smyth was sent to His Majesty's

Privy Council, detailing Calvert's failure to take the oath of supremacy and imploring that he not be suffered to settle in the colony. To reinforce their pleas, the governor and council determined to dispatch Claiborne to England to present their objections personally to the Privy Council to thwart the influential "papist" lord's designs.[3]

Like his colleagues, William Claiborne, who had only recently returned from another punitive expedition against hostile natives, viewed Calvert as a potentially dangerous Roman Catholic interloper on Protestant Virginia territory and one quite willing and capable of slicing off a whole piece of it for himself. Unfortunately for Virginia, the territorial limits and integrity of the colony, as set forth by the recently rescinded Virginia Company charter, had already been seriously compromised and were a prime target for future interlopers. As recently as February 10, 1629, Sir Robert Heath, formerly recorder of London and now attorney general of England, had requested that territory between the thirty-sixth and thirty-first parallels, fully two degrees of latitude hitherto considered part of the Virginia Colony, and known as Carolana, be granted to himself and his associates. Moreover, if Baltimore were successful in securing territory of his own, he was surely to become a serious personal rival to the secretary of Virginia over the potentially lucrative fur trade of the upper Chesapeake.[4]

Upon his arrival in England, his first visit in more than eight years, Claiborne busied himself with personal matters as well as affairs of state, visiting friends, relatives, and government officials alike. One of those relatives he called on was his cousin, Reverend Richard James. The reverend was captivated by the Virginian's adventures and, no doubt, by his tales of the godless state of the settlers in America and their need for spiritual support. Like many impressed by the enterprising Claiborne (and possibly because James's former patron was deceased), the minister quietly resolved to soon cast his lot with the Virginia secretary of state.[5]

While visiting the home of Thomas Butler, a relative of Captain Nathaniel Butler, former governor of Bermuda and a member of the king's Board of Commissioners on Virginia, Will was introduced to Butler's niece, Elizabeth.[6] The relationship between Claiborne and Elizabeth Butler apparently warmed quickly—so quickly that she would one day become Mrs. William Claiborne.

It is unknown exactly when William Claiborne first visited William Cloberry, a well-connected Puritan and London merchant, at his office on Coleman Street at Buttolph Lane. Cloberry was a canny financial adventurer and no stranger to the Virginia trade. In 1627 he had invested heavily in the Chesapeake fur traffic by supporting the operations of the famous Captain Henry Fleet. Thus, it is not surprising that he found Claiborne's concepts and entreaties regarding the advantages of further investment in the Tidewater more than engaging. For a shrewd, experienced merchant like Cloberry, the secretary's descriptions of the potentials for the upper Chesapeake, based upon first-hand knowledge, were more than the usual claptrap published by get-rich-quick promoters.

Here was no catch-as-catch-can grizzled frontiersman, but a man of power, influence, and vision, offering an opportunity to systematically siphon off the rich trade in beaver and otter pelts of the Great Lakes country, the Hudson River valley, New England, French Canada, and Quebec through the backdoor access of the Susquehanna. If, as the secretary suggested, a settlement could be established on the strategically situated Isle of Kent, and stocked with hogs and even cattle from his own plantations, a permanent base from which to assert control over all of the trade with the natives of the north might be established. Claiborne even suggested that corn, acquired through trade with the natives, could be successfully marketed in New England and Nova Scotia to further increase the profit margin. Cloberry was sold.

Within a short time an agreement was drawn up. Claiborne agreed to put up one-sixth of the money necessary for the projected cost of the venture, the actual field effort of which he would personally command and manage. But there was more than money involved. In light of the potential challenge by Lord Baltimore, the secretary had lost confidence in the value of a simple commission from Virginia's new governor and council. In order to cement his right to establish a trading monopoly, settlement, and trading stations on the upper Chesapeake, a much higher and inviolable authority must be found. Thus, with his purported close ties to the Privy Council, it was Cloberry's job to obtain a patent from King Charles, both to override any opposition that might be forthcoming from Governor Harvey (whose disposition toward such matters was an unknown factor) and to avert any interference from Lord Baltimore.

Claiborne undoubtedly smiled inwardly. Once the settlement and trade were established, with or without Cloberry, he might even erect a Virginia Hundred, with full representation in the Virginia Burgesses. Control of the region would then be guaranteed—a control that would cement Virginia authority over the upper Chesapeake despite the best efforts of the Calverts and their Catholic coterie.

Cloberry quickly subscribed to two-sixths of the venture. Claiborne brought in Maurice Thomson, another London entrepreneur once termed England's "greatest merchant of his day," for one-sixth, while two other investors, John Delabarr and Simon Turgis, took up the remainder of the partnership for one-sixth each. The Virginia secretary, it was agreed, would personally "undertake a trade discoverye and plantacon" in the "joint stock" venture. Although he would be obliged to keep his partners apprised of his actions by promising that a "true and juste" account of his trade with the natives be rendered, and the "transportation of corne and of all profitts and benefitts any wayes made" be documented, he was to be given full control over the project.[7]

Cloberry and Company promptly hired, manned, and victualled the good ship *Africa*, of London, and loaded her with a cargo "of goods wares merchandizes and other necessaries" valued at £1,318.19s.8d., all of which were to be committed to Claiborne's care. Expenses—for accounting purposes, of course—were to be divided into sixths. Seventeen "servants" were to be taken on (although twenty were initially agreed upon) to be employed "in traffique and trade with Indians and others in buildinge of houses Mills and other such things as were fitting usefull and necessary for the foresaid trade discoverye and Plantation and in planteinge of Tobaccoes and other necessaries fit and convenient for those parts."[8]

Within a short time, the necessary manpower was being assembled. There was Lieutenant Arthur Figes, hired at a salary of thirty pounds per annum as Claiborne's assistant, to oversee the day-to-day operations of the trade; John Bagwell, a professional trader; laborers; three men and a boy to tend the kitchen, dress victuals, bake bread from corn, and carry out other domestic chores; John Belson, a carpenter; John Parr, a hog keeper; and Henry Pincke, a "reader of prayers," who unfortunately broke his leg and proved unserviceable. There was even a "mayd servant to wash our linnen" by the name of Joane Young.[9] Claiborne was diligent in ensuring maximum utilization of the resources at hand, including the full use of the vessel allotted him. Soon after chartering *Africa*, he entered into a contract with John Winthrop Jr., son of the governor of Massachusetts, to ship forty tons of "Indian wheat" and corn from the Chesapeake to the new town of Boston aboard the ship in exchange for a cargo of fish. The corn, Winthrop had been informed, could be readily acquired from the natives inhabiting many places to the south of the Massachusetts Bay Colony, indeed as far south as Florida, in exchange of "toyes, beads, copper, tooless, knives, glasses and the like."[10]

Although Claiborne had addressed his end of the agreement with zealous proficiency, William Cloberry was less than successful in promulgating his own part of the bargain. Despite his connections, he was unable to obtain a royal patent as he had promised: the best he could do was to secure a trading commission drawn up by Sir William Alexander, Viscount Sterling, the secretary of Scotland, and then only with the stipulation that the company would provide corn for Sir William's own intended colony in Nova Scotia.[11] It was definitely not a land or jurisdictional patent or even a grant of trade in Virginia, which would have held possible rivals such as Baltimore at legal bay, but it would have to do.

As *Africa* lay at anchor in the Thames, off Gravesend, fully laden and ready to sail, Claiborne was obliged to accept this deficient second-best offering with diplomacy. He rushed to Greenwich, where King Charles personally confirmed the commission. The document was still impressive in its sweep. "Charles by the Grace of God," it began,

> King of England, Scotland Fraunce and Ireland Defender of the faith etc. Whereas as our trustie and welbeloved William Clayborne one of the Councell and Secretary of State for our Colony of Virginia and some other adventurers with him have condescended with our trustie and welbeloved Councellor of both the kingdomes Sir William Alexander Knight or principal secretary for our kingdome of Scotland and others of our loving subjects who have charge over our colonies of New England and New Scotland to keep a course for interchange of trade among them as they shall have occasion as allso to make discovery for increase of trade in these parts. And because wee doe very approve of all such worthie intentions and are desireous to give good incouragement to their proceedings therein being for the releeife and comfort of those our subjects and enlargement of our dominions. These are to license and authorize the said William Clayborne his associates and Company freely without interruption from time to time to trade and traffique for corne furres and any other commodities whatsoever with their shipps men boates and merchaundize in all seas, coasts, rivers, creeks, harbours lands and territories in neere or about these partes of America for which there is not already a patent graunted to others for the sole trade and to that effect wee require and command you and every one of you and particularly our trusty and welbeloved Sir John Harvey Knight Governor and the rest of our councell of and for our Colonie of Virginia to permitt and suffer him and them with their said shipps boats and merchaundizes cattell marriners servaunts and such as shall willingly accompany or be eimployed by them from time to time freely to repaire and trade to and agen in all the aforesaid partes and places as they shall thinke fitt and their occasions shall require, without any stopp, arrest, search hinderance or molestation whatsoever as you and every one of you will answer the contrary at your perrills. Giveing and by these presents graunting unto the said William Claybourne full power to direct and governe correct and punish such of our subjects as shall be under his command in his voyages and discoveries and for his soe doing these presents shall be a sufficient warrant. Given at our Mannor in East Greenwich the 16th day of May in the seaventh yeare of Our Raigne 1631.[12]

With commission finally in hand, William Claiborne made his way to Deal, to which place *Africa* had moved, completed all necessary accounting, finalized his agreement with Cloberry and Company, and took on last-minute provisions of sheep, butter, and beer for the Atlantic voyage.

Unlike the crossings of *George* and *Charles*, *Africa*'s voyage was more than eventful. Six of Claiborne's servants perished en route or soon after arrival, and others became so ill that their services would prove of little value for months to come. Nevertheless, on July 20, *Africa* arrived at Kecoughtan, the secretary's Virginia plantation, where "for the discharge of our shipp we staied till the 11th of August." Here hogs and sows, ducks, hens, and a breeding cock were brought aboard for the last leg of the voyage to Kent Island. Provisions were purchased to supply the adventurers until they reached their destination. Bricks for an oven to be built on the island were loaded, as were corn pestles, wheelbarrows, stools, chairs, a malt mill, and other necessities. At Elizabeth City, Claiborne procured a pair of rudder irons and fir and pine deal boards for the immediate construction of two trading shallops, one of which was to be built at his plantation at Accomac and the other at Kent. Wisely, he also purchased "2 murtherers and 2 chambers . . . for our defence" against hostile natives, that is, small antipersonnel guns and large cannons, intended for mounting on a fortification for the protection of the settlement.[13]

Departing from Kecoughtan, Claiborne sailed first for Accomac to pick up an interpreter, Ensign Thomas Savage, to secure a quantity of salt, and to take aboard ten freemen willing to join the enterprise as replacements for those servants who had died or were too ill to work. Although hired for less than the wages commonly being paid in Virginia for the same work, the new recruits had joined, they later testified, because of the love and goodwill they felt toward their leader.

On August 17, as he later reported, Claiborne again set foot upon the Isle of Kent, a place hitherto "unplanted by any man." This time he had come to stay. Fortunately for the little party of settlers, the local population of approximately one hundred Matapeake Indians proved friendly and tractable. He contracted with them for twelve pounds sterling in trade goods and bought their right to "hould of the Crowne of England to him and his Company and their heires and by force or virtue thereof William Claiborne and his Company stood seized of the said Island."[14]

It was sheer good fortune that he had encountered the docile Matapeakes on his landing, for had he been obliged to engage the warlike Wicomesse, Ozinies, Monoponsons, or Choptanks to the south, or the hostile natives that had recently massacred the entire Dutch settlement at Zwaanendael, on the Delaware River, the outcome might have been radically different. The site chosen for the settlement, situated on the south end of the island, was eminently suitable for a substantial defense work. There was plentiful game and fowl in the forests, while the waters of the Bay were endowed with fish and waterfowl of an infinite variety.

Although the trading season, which normally ran from March to June, was well behind him, Claiborne was eager to press on in an attempt to make his presence known to the Indians—and to prove himself to

Cloberry and Company. Once *Africa* had been unloaded and construction of a fort, warehouses, and a number of thatched houses for habitation was well under way, he set out for Palmers Island. If he were fortunate enough, he might yet be able to truck for corn and pelts. He could then send *Africa* home with a healthy cargo of furs, via New England, of course, where they could be exchanged for fish or sold outright according to his contract with Winthrop. It would, Claiborne knew, be but a token demonstration, for both the Indians and his partners, of what lay in store, but it was of great symbolic importance. Claiborne had confidence that next spring, with the settlement firmly entrenched, crops planted, and a flotilla of shallops at his behest, the real trading could begin.[15]

Yet misfortune, which had trailed him from England, would not be denied its due, even before the new settlement was fully under way. By October 18, 1631, Claiborne and his traders were already bound northward up the Bay aboard *Africa,* and most of the servants left behind in the settlement were "abroad" from the open, unfinished palisaded fort. It was then, about noon, that a "lamentable and fearfull fire," that would impede the settlement's very future and 360 years later provide clues to its location, began. The consequences were devastating. The conflagration was thought to have been started by an incendiary servant named Richard Haulsey, later described by Claiborne as "a very untoward youth." Although no lives were lost, the event was catastrophic in its extent, for it destroyed not only the recently constructed warehouses, but practically all of the company's trade goods stored within.[16]

The disaster had wide-ranging implications. For Cloberry and Company, it had wiped out more than 90 percent of the trade goods in storage. Knives and scissors were ruined, axes and hoes were spoiled, the sides and bottoms of kettles all but dissolved, copper was rendered useless, soft goods went up in smoke, and the ever-popular glass trade beads were melted into worthless lumps. Aside from those goods being carried by Claiborne on his trading foray, barely £53 sterling worth of truck survived from the total warehouse stock valued at £593. Of domestic items, only a few pieces of ironware, several axes, thirteen guns, and a few miscellaneous items, valued at £150, could be saved.[17] Worse, the settlement's entire stock of gunpowder and all of the servants' clothing save that on their backs had been destroyed. With winter coming on, prospects seemed bleak indeed.

Upon his return, Claiborne stoically addressed the disaster. The indenture time of Haulsey, who was accused by fellow servants of having "fyred the houses willingly" and whom they "would not indure," was sold. A letter was then dispatched to Cloberry and Company informing them of the calamity and urging that a replacement stock be sent immediately. In view of the serious financial loss to the investors, however, Claiborne was discreet enough to leave it to them whether they wished to continue in the venture, vowing to carry on the plantation at his own expense until their wishes were known.[18]

The difficulties in maintaining the settlement through the winter of 1631–32 were considerable for both the settlers and their leader. Claiborne was destined to endure great personal suffering. Constantly obliged to travel between Kent and the settlements to the south to secure the necessities for the company servants and freemen, his life was frequently in peril. On one occasion, during a particularly long, cold voyage to Accomac, he was shipwrecked, castaway, and forced to trek the remainder of the way on foot through hostile Indian territory.[19] He lost the use of his right arm in the process. Once he was taken prisoner by natives "whoe, hee conceaveth, if hee had not bine presently rescued from them would have kild him, as they have done many others heretofore."[20]

Work on the fort continued; the storehouses were rebuilt, and additional houses and fences were erected. Claiborne persevered in his frequent trips to Accomac, Kecoughtan, and Jamestown, despite the hazards, to obtain supplies and livestock. A pair of "greate hinges for the forte gate" was brought up in November, and twenty-eight to thirty "neat" milk cows were shipped from his plantation at Kecoughtan and reserved for the nourishment of the sick servants who had come over on *Africa*. A dozen head of cattle had been secured from the hearty stocks of Sir Thomas Gates, governor of Virginia during the "starving time" in 1609–10, when the colony almost failed. Claiborne did his best to restore the provisions and supplies lost by the fire and brought up a quantity of powder, half a dozen powder horns, several guns, and even an ancient matchlock harquebus for the fort's defense.[21]

That the plantation was at risk and needed every weapon at its disposal was quickly proved when the settlers, during one of Claiborne's absences, discovered the approach of a party of sixty to eighty hostile Wicomesse Indians. The Europeans had already learned from friendly Matapeakes of the annihilation of the Dutch settlement at Zwaanendael in July, and the Kent Islanders were not about to let the same thing happen to them. Feigning friendship, the Wicomesse approached the fort but were held at bay by a ruse conceived by a freeman named William Coxe. By firing a few warning shots, parading the few able-bodied men in the fort with guns, and making a show of cutting holes in the works from which to fire, Coxe managed to impress the marauders with the apparent impregnability of the defenses. The attack was aborted.[22] Had the Indians known of the short powder supplies and of the sick and weakened state of many of the defenders within, the outcome might have been different. But the Kent Islanders held on.

Faced with the Herculean task of keeping his island enterprise afloat until spring, William Claiborne proceeded to assure its survival, despite the odds. He was obliged to placate the increasingly hostile new governor of Virginia, Sir John Harvey, who had alienated himself to his council, the assembly, and every planter in the colony. Yet stability and continuity in the government were an absolute necessity if the secretary of state were to continue in power and reap the emoluments and fees necessary for him to keep the Kent settlement operative, at least until he had heard from Cloberry. At the same time, Claiborne continued to pursue his long-cherished scheme of having the plantation recognized as a Virginia Hundred, as an additional hedge against possible encroachment by Baltimore. He began to govern the island in accordance with the laws of the colony and England. "As a planter of Virginia," he had legally taken possession of Kent by planting crops. Kent Island, no longer "unplanted," was now qualified to be considered as a Virginia Hundred.[23]

On February 21, 1632, Captain Nicholas Martiau, Claiborne's friend and colleague (and ancestor of George Washington) who had earlier participated with the secretary in a venture to establish a settlement at Kiskyack (the present site of Yorktown, Virginia), registered at the General Assembly in Jamestown as a burgess representing "Kiskyacke and the Isle of Kent." The plantation was thus officially recognized as a Virginia Hundred by the royal government of Charles I.[24]

When a monthly court was established at Accomac, it was specifically for the benefit of the settlers there as well as those on Kent Island, who would no longer be obliged to travel the inordinately difficult distances to Jamestown or Elizabeth City to settle legal disputes. Claiborne had helped implement the creation of the court and would, as a commander of a Hundred, preside as one of its first commissioners, with powers equivalent to a justice of the peace. Thus, further credibility was added to the Kent Island establishment as a permanent Virginia plantation.[25]

In March, Claiborne sought and secured from Governor Harvey a commission to visit and truck with the Dutch on the Hudson or anywhere else he might find them. The mission had, of course, a double purpose. By visiting the Netherlanders in their newly established settlements, he might determine whether they planned any encroachment on English territory. But, more important, because Dutch trade goods were more highly prized by the natives than the poorer-quality English products and brought a greater return in pelts, and as his own stocks had been all but destroyed in the fire, the trip offered him the opportunity to restock and carry on trading until the long-expected Cloberry goods arrived. Claiborne's little flotilla of barques, led by his own pinnace under the command of Captain Tom Butler, sailed soon afterward. In early May, flush with success and in plenty of time for the trading season, they turned their prows homeward, bearing Dutch broadcloths and "red cotton bayes." The return, however, was not without incident.

En route home, at the Virginia capes, Claiborne fell in with the renowned Captain Henry Fleet's ship *Warwick*, fresh from a trading voyage of her own to New England. Fleet was bound for the Potomac with a quantity of trade goods to truck for furs but had failed to secure a commission from the Virginia government to do so. Claiborne was keen to investigate the possibilities of the Potomac tribes and strongly requested that he be allowed to accompany Fleet. Recognizing the secretary as a competitor, but moreover as a high official with authority to arrest him and seize his goods if he failed to cooperate, the captain assented. The visit to the village of the Yowaccomocos on the Potomac proved profitable for both traders. After parting with Claiborne, Captain Fleet was nevertheless arrested on the upper Potomac by another of Governor Harvey's councilmen, Captain John Utie, for failure to secure a commission. Though later freed, with his beaver pelts returned after a quiet agreement struck with the governor, Fleet did not forget Claiborne's implied blackmail.

Throughout the summer of 1632, the Kent Island plantation continued to grow as additional freemen, artificers, coopers, sawyers, smiths, millwrights, laborers, and traders were brought in to erect houses, mills, and boats, cultivate the land, tend the growing stock of hogs and cattle, and conduct the all-important business of trading with the natives. A wherry, built at Accomac, was brought up for service in the trade, even as small trading shallops continued to slide off the ways at the little boatyard on the island. Paving tiles and bricks were laid down for the hall of the commander's house in the fort, and "pewter dishes for the house of Jesus Christ" and "bibles and bookes of prayers for the howse and boates . . . and a black velvett cushion and a black cloth for the pulpit" were imported at the request of the plantation's new parson, the Reverend Richard James.[26] Having arrived in Virginia shortly after *Africa* in the fall of 1631, the minister had awaited the spring before coming up to the settlement to tend to the spiritual needs of the plantation. He brought with him his sister Gertrude, who was to minister to the more practical requirements of the Claiborne household.[27]

Claiborne had by now become one of the most proficient traders on the Chesapeake. His ability to deal with the natives was almost legendary, particularly among his own men, who were loud in their praise of him. One claimed that he had succeeded in winning "the sole trade & love of the Indians more than any other Englishman had."[28] Indeed, said another who had worked closely with him, no trader who dealt with the natives between 1631 and 1637 "made soe good voyages, or gott soe much Beaver, with soe little Trucke & soe little supplies, as Claiborne did in ye aforesaid yeares."[29] He "was soe well beloved of the Indians that in case hee had had goodes sufficient to have trucked with them hee would have got a greate deal more than hee did, and more than any other whatsoever in that country."[30]

As the early summer slipped by, Claiborne's Dutch stocks and the "burnt truck" salvaged from the ashes of the warehouses dwindled, and he took to bartering in roanoke and peag, standard shell money among the Indians. Increasingly hamstrung by the paucity of trade goods but relying upon capable traders such as Henry Eubank and a faithful native interpreter he had dubbed "Constantine" (who proudly called himself "Captain Claiborne's Covenant Servant"), the commander of Kent Island Hundred gamely persevered.[31] He awoke each day in expectation of a ship laden with a great cargo of trading goods from Cloberry. But in vain. Time and again, lacking a sufficient quantity of truck, Claiborne was forced to retreat from a lucrative deal. In letters home, he begged his friends and associates to send something, anything, but with few results.

Finally, in January 1633, Cloberry's resupply arrived aboard the ship *Defense* of London. To Claiborne's disappointment, it was a middling cargo at best. His partners had sent only £112 worth of truck for trade and £43 worth of clothing for the servants of the company.[32] A supply of Spanish and French wines and vinegar, sent over separately by John Delabarr, however, was more warmly welcome.[33] Even the most modest of donations was accepted heartily. When an additional ten pieces of coarse woolen duffel were brought up by Captain Peter Andrewes in the recently arrived ship *Mayflower*, the supply was immediately put to use by the cold settlers.[34] It wasn't much, but it was something. Although the trucking merchandise was mostly of inferior quality when compared to the highly prized Dutch goods, Claiborne took heart in his partner's promises of more trade stuff and, in particular, Cloberry's pledge to continue pressing the king for a patent.

Such promises were of small consolation in light of the arrival of the most distressing news possible for the commander of Kent. Lord Baltimore had succeeded in securing his own patent, under the broad seal of England, giving him a grant of land on both sides of the Chesapeake north of the Potomac. It now seemed certain: conflict of some kind could not be avoided.[35]

Despite it all, Claiborne continued to ship great hogsheads of furs regularly to London, and Kent Fort and its growing environs continued to flourish. The first black slaves were hired from their owners in Accomac and brought up to the island to tend to the two thousand tobacco plants in the fields and the meaner tasks of the plantation.[36] Aside from the freemen who also worked the fields, served as artificers, and helped in the trade, twenty-two persons were now employed as company servants, including a new indenture and another maid named Joan Qually.[37] A shallop, which had been previously rented, was purchased and dubbed *Cockatrice*. The small fleet of trading vessels was also growing. Barter with the natives could not be conducted safely without the small flotilla, for "when they goe a tradeinge with the Indians," noted one Kent Islander, "it is moste necessary that they goe at leaste 7 or 8 togeather for feare they bee sett uppon and taken by the Indians."[38] In the meantime, Claiborne began to tend, for the first time, to his personal comforts. He purchased a set of andirons for his house in the fort, in which he, his brother Tom (who had recently arrived to throw his lot into the trading business), the Reverend James, and James's sister Gertrude all lived.[39]

Kent Island was no longer merely a trading post on the edge of survival. With its fort, houses, gardens, tobacco fields, church, mill, and boatyard, as well as its representation as a Hundred in the House of Burgesses and thriving trade with the Indians, the island had become a plantation of significance and a legal, political, economic, and social establishment, recognized as a settled and planted component of the Virginia colony.

ELEVEN

The Kent Island War

George Calvert had been financially and physically weakened by the failed Avalon project. He had grown even more melancholy after learning of the tragic loss of his wife and young child, who had briefly remained behind in Virginia only to be lost at sea while returning to England. Ill health had sapped his strength but not his vitality or resolve.[1] Though by now mortally ailing, he nevertheless labored tirelessly against powerful pro-Virginia advocates to secure another grant on the Chesapeake, which, in a stroke of political acumen, he suggested be named "Mariland" in honor of Queen Henrietta Maria, Charles I's Catholic consort.[2]

Despite opposition, on June 30, 1632, the Charter of Maryland was finally issued, though George Calvert did not live to see it. His estates and plans devolved to his eldest son, Cecil Calvert, Second Lord Baltimore, in whose name the actual charter was finally confirmed, thanks to his father's ironclad legacy. Through clever address to the chancery procedures that created the instrument of patent and grant, George Calvert had passed on to his son all the rights bestowed upon himself and his palatinate in Newfoundland and now applicable to Maryland. Cecil, in effect, was to become absolute lord proprietor of the new lands. All writs, courts, and appeals would be subject to his authority only, and not even the king himself could legally interfere.[3]

The new colony was to be bounded on the north by the fortieth parallel and on the south by the Potomac River. A line eastward from the river mouth to Watkins Point on the Atlantic Ocean completed the southern boundary. The eastern border extended along the coastline northward from Watkins Point to Delaware Bay. The western boundary was to be the meridian at the headwater of the Potomac.[4] Within these bounds, the lands "and all its apurtenances, doe remaine intirely excepted to us, our heires, and Successors for ever." Further, the grant bequested total jurisdiction over

all Ilands, and Iletts within the limits aforesaid, and all and singular and Ilands and Iletts, which are, or shall be in the Ocean, within 10. Leagues from the Easterne shoare of the said Countrey, towards the East, with all and singular Ports, Harbors, Bayes, Rivers, and Inletts, belonging unto the Countrey, or Islands aforesaid: And all the Soile, lands, Fields, Woods, Mountaines, Fennes, Lakes, Rivers Bayes, and Inletts, situate, or being within the bounds and limits aforesaid, with the fishing of all sorts of fish, Whales, Sturgeons, and all other royal fishes in the Seas, Bays, Inletts, or Rivers, within the premises: and the fish therein taken: and moreover all Veins, Mines, and Quarries, as well discovered, as not discovered, of Gold, Silver, Gemmes, and pretious stones, and all other whatsoever, found, or to be found within the Countrey, Isles, and limits aforesaid.[5]

The charter also granted Baltimore the right to defend the colony aggressively against the incursions "of Salvages [savages], or other enemies, Pyrates and Robbers" and "to Leavy, Muster and Traine, all sorts of men . . . to make warre, and to pursue the Enemies and Robbers aforesaid, as well by sea as by land, yea, even without the limits of the said Province, and (by God's assistance) to vanquish and take them, and being taken, to put them to death by the Law of warre, or to save tham at their pleasure."[6]

The Virginians, of course, had not been subdued easily and had marshalled all of their influence to petition against the charter. As late as November 1633, after the Maryland settlement expedition had already been fitted out, "Sir John Wolstenholme and other planters with Captain William Claiborne of Virginia" petitioned that Kent Island not be taken from them and that they be permitted freedom to trade without interruption. They beseeched Baltimore to settle in some other place, but to no avail.[7] The king and privy council remained resolute. Baltimore was not moved; the charter would remain inviolate.[8] To the supporters of Protestant Virginia, catastrophe loomed large. Not only had Cecil been given absolute power in Maryland (which was to be carved out of hitherto acknowledged Virginia territory), but to the Virginians he was a papist eager to secure the fur trade for himself. Indeed, Baltimore had instructed his brother Leonard, governor-designate of the new colony, to select a place on the Chesapeake convenient for trade with both the English and the natives.

Baltimore sought to confront the problem of Kent Island head-on. He instructed Leonard Calvert, upon reaching the Chesapeake, to inform Claiborne of his arrival and inform him "of the Authority and charge committed to them" by the charter, while cordially inviting him to discuss their differences—as if it mattered. Calvert was then to inform Claiborne that he was aware that the secretary "hath settled a plantacion there wthin the precincts of his Lo[rdshi]pps Pattent" and wished to encourage him in his endeavor. Baltimore, it seemed, was holding out the hand of peace. But there were stipulations, not the least of which was a demand the secretary of state of Virginia agree to Baltimore's jurisdiction over the affairs of Kent Island. And there was more. Much, much more.[10]

The Kent Island War

❏ ❏ ❏

Leonard Calvert set sail from Cowes, England, on November 22, 1633, with the three-hundred-ton ship *Ark* and the fifty-ton pinnace *Dove*, eight pieces of artillery, a set of instructions for the management of the colony, 128 colonists, several Roman Catholic laymen, two Jesuit priests, and, most important, a letter from King Charles instructing the Virginians to provide every assistance to his settlers. On February 27, 1634, the Marylanders entered the gaping maw of the Virginia capes and had soon come to anchor in the James.[11] Although Baltimore's two ships were first suspected of being Spaniards, their identity was soon ascertained. Governor John Harvey, accompanied by Secretary Claiborne, who was then at Jamestown, immediately set off to greet the visitors at a new fort then under construction at Point Comfort. The meeting between Calvert and the Virginians was strained. Sir John, dutifully following the king's instructions to the letter, was most conciliatory; Claiborne, however, bristled, especially when told that Kent Island Hundred now fell within the jurisdiction of Baltimore's patent, under the dictates of which he would henceforth be obliged to regulate his plantation and business. The most dramatic and devastating blow, however, was delivered when he was informed that his own partners, Cloberry and Company, hedging their bets, had also begun to undermine him by offering to collaborate with the very agent that threatened his control of Kent Island. Calvert informed the secretary that Baltimore "hath some propositions made unto him by certaine mrchants in London who pretend to be partners wth him in that plantation, [viz], Mr. Delabarr, Mr. Tompson, Mr Cloberry, Mr. Collins, and some others, and that they desired to have a grant from his Lo[rdshi]pp of that Iland where he is."[12]

Claiborne was undoubtedly stunned, especially when informed that his partners had some differences with him over the partnership and that in their conversations with Baltimore "made somewhat slight of Cap. Clayborne's interest." Indeed, Calvert said, it was for this reason that his brother had refused to come to an agreement with Cloberry and Company, lest, in his own ignorance of the true state of the company's business and of the plantation, he might "prejudice" Claiborne.[13] Thus, Baltimore had decided to delay a final decision regarding Kent Island until Calvert and Claiborne had arrived at an understanding of their own, which, both brothers knew, was a prospect as likely to happen as the discovery of the fabled Northwest Passage. Then Calvert lowered the boom.

The commander of Kent Island Hundred was given one year to conform to Baltimore's patent or suffer the consequences. Although Calvert wisely did not inform him of the remainder of his instructions, which had been to gather, during that same year, as much intelligence as he could regarding Kent Island, Claiborne's strengths, his designs, and what communications he maintained with Virginia, it was apparent to all three leaders present that Maryland and Kent were on a collision course.[14]

To further pique Claiborne's choler at his betrayal, Governor Harvey graciously offered to provide the Marylanders with some of his own cattle. The Council of Virginia was enraged and vowed to kill their own cattle rather than sell them to Baltimore's Catholics.[15]

Claiborne seized the moment and on March 14, less than two weeks after the Marylanders had set off from Point Comfort for the upper Bay, laid the Kent Island situation before his colleagues. Nothing less than Virginia's sovereignty over the island, a recognized Virginia Hundred with voting representation in the House of Burgesses, was at stake. Reviewing Baltimore's patent in its entirety, he pointed out that Calvert was authorized to settle only "in parts of America, not yet civilized and planted, though in some parts thereof inhabited by certain barbarous people having no knowledge of Almighty God." Everyone present was well aware that Kent Island had been settled and cultivated since 1631, well before Baltimore's patent had been issued![16]

Claiborne entreated the Council of Virginia to address the problem of "how he should demean himself in respect of the Baltimore's patent."[17] They responded that they saw no reason why Virginia—and, by extension, Claiborne—should give up rights to Kent Island, and wondered why there should even be any question at all, since "the right of my Lord's grant [was] yet undetermined in England." Correspondence would be maintained with the Marylanders, but Kent would remain part of Virginia.[18]

Although fortified by the council's support, the feisty commander of Kent resolved to prepare himself and his island plantation for the worst. While enlisting the support of a pair of colleagues and friends to further stabilize his hold on Kent by having them settle there with their families and servants, he proceeded to gather more recruits for the enterprise.[19] Several of his people would attempt to occupy nearby Popeley's Island (now Poplar Island), located to the south of Kent, while a second settlement, replete with fort and a manor house for himself, would be erected on the west side of Kent about midway up and adjacent to a small waterway called Craney Creek. The settlement would be called Crayford, after his childhood home in England.[20] In the meantime, additional vessels suitable for both trucking and defense would be rushed to completion.

While William Claiborne girded himself for the contest ahead, Leonard Calvert was busily engaged in establishing the seat of the new Maryland colony on the banks of the St. Mary's River. He was equally diligent in securing the friendship of the local Yeocomacos and Patuxents, without whose support, or at least neutrality, the infant colony might not survive.

When Governor Harvey paid a state visit to the Marylanders, giving the appearance of unity among the English, the cement of friendly relations between natives and settlers at first appeared strong. Soon afterward, however, the Marylanders began to perceive certain signs of hostility among the Indians, particularly among the neighboring Patuxents. Calvert turned to Captain Henry Fleet to investigate the cause.[21]

When Fleet returned from the Patuxent, he informed the Marylanders that the cause of the problem was none other than William Claiborne. The secretary of Virginia, he claimed, had personally been inciting the natives against the St. Mary's settlement by claiming that Calvert's colonists were Spaniards come "to destroy them and take their Country from them."[22] For the Marylanders, the horrors of an Indian uprising, the likes of which had not been seen since the infamous Good Friday Massacre of 1622, loomed large in everyone's mind.

Terrified by the threat of a native attack, the Marylanders officially conveyed the charges against Claiborne to Governor Harvey, even as Calvert dispatched a letter to his brother in England describing the secretary's purported chicanery.[23] Claiborne was promptly arrested for "animating practicing and Conspiring with the Indians to supplant" the Marylanders.[24] At Harvey's direction, a joint commission of Virginians and Marylanders was hastily appointed to investigate the matter.[25] On June 20, 1634, the commissioners and the accused met at the village of Patuxent to interview the chief. When pointedly asked whether he or his people had ever heard Claiborne report that the English were "Waspaines" (Spaniards), the king of the Patuxents replied "noe, that Captain Clayborne did never speak any thing to him of them." The king of the Piscattaways and others confirmed the Patuxent's story. The charge against Claiborne proved to have been created by Captain Henry Fleet himself. The relieved commissioners then signed a document exonerating Claiborne of the charge and laying the blame squarely upon Fleet, against whom "all the lyes would redound upon him . . . and lye uppon him . . . as high as his necke, and at last breake his necke."[26]

Despite the findings, pressure for confrontation between St. Mary's and Kent continued to build. Upon his return to the island, Claiborne grimaced at the discovery that Calvert's men had not only recently fired upon and harassed his traders on the Bay, but had also expelled his settlers from Popeley's Island.[27] On another occasion, several of his men, with seven hundred pelts aboard their boat at Palmers Island, had been outright threatened and captured by traders from St. Mary's, but after warning their captors of the probable intercession of their Susquehannock friends, had been released along with their goods.[28] Trading was becoming increasingly difficult and dangerous. And with the apparent abandonment by Cloberry, the commander of Kent was obliged to barter in lower Virginia for items with which to truck.[29]

Nevertheless, Claiborne proceeded with his plan to expand and strengthen his island dominion by erecting the planned plantation at Crayford on the high ground fronting Craney Creek. Here, assisted by Alexander Mountney and John Smyth, he built his manse (a work so substantial that it became known as Craney Fort), as well as buildings for the settlers, their families, and servants. Gardens and orchards were planted. Work at the island boatyard, under the direction of master carpenter William Paine, continued. The pinnace *Long Tayle* was nearing completion, a large shallop, dubbed *Start*, had just come off the ways, while the great shallop *Cockatrice*, purchased in 1633, was being refitted and made suitable to carry from six to fourteen men. Then there was the big wherry *Firefly*, which had been in service for more than a year, as well as a number of small shallops, which could be seen constantly flitting about the Bay like so many waterbugs. Most were armed with guns and pistols for defense. If there was to be a confrontation with Calvert, it was certain that Claiborne wanted Kent Island and its substantial flotilla to be as strong and self-sufficient as possible.[30]

But Calvert was not the only problem. With the exception of the Susquehannocks, a number of tribes were becoming more menacing than ever, particularly the Wicomesse and Choptanks. The farm of one Kent Island planter had been isolated, a man and child murdered, and two servants injured by native marauders.[31] Even trucking with the locals was becoming more difficult and dangerous. On one occasion, the Kent traders were set upon while in their boats by two hundred to three hundred Indians but had escaped. More than once Claiborne himself, leading a trading party, had been taken prisoner, but he always managed to elude his captors.[32] Still, trucking was carried on with success, despite the hazards, particularly with the friendly Susquehannocks at Palmers Island station. Despite the questionable state of Cloberry's continued support and the paucity of trucking goods available, Claiborne managed to send off half a dozen more great casks of pelts.[33]

Finally, near the end of December, the commander of Kent had reason to rejoice, for two ships, *James* and *Revenge*, were sighted entering the Virginia capes. When they came to anchor after a most difficult and costly voyage, it was learned that they had aboard twenty-seven new servants and twelve hundred pounds sterling worth of truck from Cloberry. The cost, however, had been high, for ten servants had died en route, and of those who arrived alive, three more were destined to perish before spring.[34] Cloberry was apparently unaware that Calvert had revealed his secret entreaties to Baltimore regarding a patent of his own. But having learned that the Virginia Council had upheld the commander's claim to Kent Island, and having also been rejected by Lord Baltimore in his secret advances, Cloberry blithely informed the secretary of Virginia that the company was doing everything it could to combat the efforts of the Calverts and recommended that Claiborne do the same. Claiborne, for the moment, chose to overlook his partner's indiscretion, because the trade goods, though of poor quality, were badly needed. Moreover, Cloberry's support in England was imperative.[35]

James and *Revenge* may also have brought something else of great value to William Claiborne, in the person of one Elizabeth Butler to whom he would soon be married. The commander of Kent, it seemed, had finished his new home at Crayford none too soon.[36]

❏ ❏ ❏

Leonard Calvert and his agents, bolstered by letters of encouragement from Lord Baltimore and his powerful ally, Secretary Windebank, a confidant of the king, did not cease in their efforts to undermine Claiborne and the Kent Island establishment. Without the full backing of the autocratic Governor Harvey, who was a second time instructed by the king to offer every assistance to the Marylanders, prospects for Virginia's continued sovereignty over Kent Island at first seemed dim. Through the belated efforts of William Cloberry, however, who had petitioned the crown in behalf of Claiborne, a ray of hope could soon be discerned. Indeed, a complete reversal of the situation seemed at hand.[37]

Compelled by Cloberry's lobbying and petition, on October 8, King Charles issued a royal sign manual ordering a cessation of Baltimore's attacks upon Claiborne and prohibiting any interference of his trade or any disturbance of the establishment on Kent. The commander of Kent was reconfirmed in his commission and was to be permitted to "peaceablie enjoy the said Ilands, and trade and such other places, as shall there first settle upon before others freelie without any interruption or molestation, either by the said Lord Baltimore, or any other person, or persons whatsoever." Should there be any objections, the king and Privy Council would decide the issue. Furthermore, Governor Harvey was instructed to assist the Kent Islanders in enjoying the fruits of their endeavors.[38]

Harvey's immediate reaction to the order, which he later scoffed at as not authentic, is not recorded. Apparently, however, he failed to communicate it to his council, much less to all "Lieutenants of Provinces and Countries in America," as well as "Governors and others having charge of Colonies" (presumably including Maryland) as ordered. Nevertheless, Claiborne now possessed the means to continue unharried in his grand scheme. His hold on power was something else.[39]

The relationship between Harvey and his secretary of state, never on a firm footing, had grown bitter since the arrival of the Marylanders, and as a consequence Claiborne had been spending more time at Kent attending to the plantations than at Jamestown attending to the duties of state. As the weeks slipped by, the governor of Virginia began to perceive his secretary as a powerful foe who must be neutralized. Thus, he instigated in England an effort to have him supplanted. In late December 1634, with the arrival of Richard Kemp, bearing an appointment as colony secretary, the deed was accomplished.[40] Claiborne, however, continued to retain his council status and, reinforced by the king's decree regarding Kent, proceeded with expansion of his plantations there.

Response to the stunning change of situation brought about by the king's decree was immediate. One of the first to take action was John Butler, now Claiborne's brother-in-law, who had apparently come over from England with the commander's new wife, Elizabeth. Butler and Claiborne's able lieutenant, Captain Thomas Smith, had been diligent in reinforcing their leader's hold on Palmers Island, which now, according to the king's edict, clearly fell within the Kent Islanders' jurisdiction. When two Marylanders, Sergeant Robert Vaughan and John Tomkins, arrived there in a pinnace laden with a "great quantitie of trucking commodities," they, their men, boat, and goods were seized and carried to Kent Island. Claiborne was lenient and released the trespassers with a warning. But the gauntlet had been tossed down, and escalation of hostilities seemed unavoidable.[41]

When Captain Smith, armed with copies of the king's commission and letter to Claiborne, set sail on March 26, 1635, in *Long Tayle* bound for the native settlement of Mattapany at the mouth of the Patuxent River, he did so confident that he could now trade there as freely as ever. With Mattapany located less than six miles from the Maryland settlement of St. Mary's, however, he was certain to be tempting fate.[42]

Smith arrived at the Indian settlement on April 5 eager to begin trading. The following day he was surprised by a company of armed men from St. Mary's led by Captains Humber and Fleet, Claiborne's old rival who had found favor with Calvert. Cavalierly displaying the copies of Claiborne's commission and letter, Smith assumed that the Marylanders would depart. Instead, they scorned the papers, claiming the documents permitted trade no further than Kent Island and were, in any event, little more than false copies "grounded upon false informacion." *Long Tayle* was boarded, and on the following day Fleet escorted Smith in a small boat to St. Mary's. Smith was met by Captain Cornwaleys (as Calvert was away), to whom he protested bitterly. Cornwaleys retorted that Humber and Fleet were only following orders, namely, to stop all unauthorized vessels found trading in Maryland. Again Smith's papers were examined. Cornwaleys also refused to accept their validity. After several days' incarceration and an interview with Calvert himself, the Kent Islanders were released, without food and only one gun, to make the best of their way home afoot. *Long Tayle*, the company goods, and pelts were confiscated.[43]

Claiborne determined to meet force with force. Without waiting to hear the tale of the embarrassed Captain Smith, he dispatched Lieutenant Radcliffe Warren and thirteen men in *Cockatrice* to recapture *Long Tayle*.

Failing in that, they were ordered to seize any boats belonging to Maryland as fair prize in retaliation. Warren did not find *Long Tayle* but managed to take a St. Mary's boat laden with "trucking stuffe," which was carried back to Kent. While cruising off the Patuxent and the lower Potomac, he had also learned that Calvert had dispatched one of his own pinnaces to the Pocomoke River, on the Eastern Shore, on a trading voyage.[44]

Claiborne was undoubtedly intrigued and angered. He first sent word back to Calvert via an Indian courier that the Marylander might come to Kent to fetch his boat—if he dared. He then dispatched Warren and his energetic crew in *Cockatrice* to intercept and capture the Marylanders on the Pocomoke. On April 23, 1637, *Cockatrice* sighted her prey: the pinnace *St. Helen*, an apparently easy prize and a fair trade for the *Long Tayle*. Steering directly for her, Warren undoubtedly intended to force a boarding. Suddenly, from a nearby cove, a second Maryland pinnace, *St. Margaret*, under the command of Captain Thomas Cornwaleys himself, appeared, well manned, armed, and ready for battle.[45]

As the three pinnaces maneuvered for advantage on the quiet waters of the Pocomoke, it was apparent to all that the issue would now be resolved only in blood. Suddenly, the stillness exploded in a volley of gunfire, and the din of battle echoed across the river and surrounding marshes. When the fighting stopped, Lieutenant Warren and two of his men (John Belson, who had come over aboard *Africa* four years before, and William Dawson, who had arrived in 1634) were dead while three more of their mates were badly wounded. Cornwaleys, seconded by his chief aide, Cuthbert Fenwick, had won the day, losing only one man, William Ashmore. Badly mauled, *Cockatrice* withdrew from the field of combat. The first sea battle between English-speaking peoples in the New World had ended. For the Kent Islanders it had been a humiliating defeat.[46]

In Virginia, the fight on the Pocomoke was the climax to a long series of stormy events that now threatened to topple the government. Governor Harvey's administration, despised by most in the colony, was growing increasingly autocratic. Four days after the battle but prior to news of it reaching Virginia, a public meeting had been held to express outrage at Harvey's conduct and protest against his support of the Marylanders.[47]

A petition of grievances was circulated. The following day, at a council meeting called by the governor, Harvey demanded the arrest of the petitioners, including Captain Nicholas Martiau who represented Kent Island, and menaced them with a threat of the gallows. When members of the council were threatened with arrest on the charge of treason for questioning the governor's measures, the Council of Virginia angrily responded in kind.[48] The last straw had been drawn. On April 28, 1635, after Captain John Utie and Samuel Mathews ordered the governor's residence surrounded by forty musketeers, the council arrested Harvey for treason, for failure to deliver to it the royal letters regarding Kent

Island as ordered by the king. Harvey was sent under arrest to England (along with threats that if he ever returned he would be shot), accompanied by commissioners who were to plead Virginia's charges against him before the king. In the meantime, Utie and Captain William Pierce were sent to Maryland with letters demanding that Calvert and his council "desist from violent proceedings" against Kent Island, promising "all fair correspondency on behalf of the isle of Kent" until the king's pleasure was known. It was clear to Calvert that the more powerful Virginians, no longer shackled by Harvey, wished to impose a truce and had the legal means to back it.[49]

Unfortunately, the tripwire of hostilities had been sprung and the forces of Kent and St. Mary's were already moving toward yet another engagement. Claiborne had been stung by the defeat of *Cockatrice* and the deaths of three of his men, but when he learned that *St. Margaret* was now cruising with impunity in the Pocomoke again, he dispatched *Cockatrice* to the scene, this time under Captain Tom Smith, accompanied by another pinnace from Accomac under the command of Captain Philip Taylor. On May 10, the Virginians overhauled the Marylander in Pocomoke Sound, then known as Great Wighcomoco Bay. *St. Margaret* was again commanded by Cornwaleys and seconded by Cuthbert Fenwick, but this time she was alone. Little is known of the engagement that followed, except that the Marylanders apparently got the worst of it, probably losing their furs, corn, and trade goods in the process.[50]

The following day, emboldened by his victory, Claiborne commissioned Taylor to make yet another attempt to recover *Long Tayle* and to secure corn for the Kent Island settlements. The captain was instructed to set sail for the Patuxent, the Potomac, or anywhere else the captured pinnace might be held. Failing in its recovery, he was to seize upon any of "such boates of theirs as you can light on." He was warned, however, to proceed without violence unless defence was absolutely necessary, and advised to avoid any bloodshed and to refrain from any outright assaults.[51]

Taylor's fortunes proved elusive. He soon encountered Calvert's forces in the Potomac, where the Marylanders "did severall tymes vyolently with armed men gonnes and Indyans assault this deponent in his said Pynnace and boate and tooke this deponent and the said Pynnace with all the goods therein. . . ." Possibly as a result of the Utie-Pierce delegation then at St. Mary's, Taylor "escaped" with his pinnace and all of the goods therein, including the corn for Kent Island.[52]

Despite the Taylor episode, the Marylanders had little choice but to acquiesce to the truce. A pro-Claiborne administration under protem Governor John West was in command at Jamestown, while Baltimore's staunchest ally, Sir John Harvey, was a prisoner en route to England. The Virginians controlled the entrance to the Bay, through which all succor and support for Maryland must pass. Claiborne had repeatedly exhibited his willingness to fight and fight again to hold his own after the crown had formally reconfirmed his rights to Kent Island and free trade. For the moment, the Kent issue would have to be set aside.[53]

Although Kent Island had suffered through enormous travails and experienced many dangers during 1635, the settlement had continued to grow and prosper. Two new windmills were erected, and 236 ells of French canvas had been purchased for their sails. Millstones were procured in Accomac at twenty pounds sterling a pair and "laid uppon the mills." The manufacture of pipe staves was begun. Crops and tobacco were planted. The hogs and cattle increased rapidly. A new pinnace (dubbed *Elizabeth*, after Claiborne's wife) and a shallop were purchased. Trading voyages by the island's small flotilla continued to Palmers Island and elsewhere on behalf of Cloberry and Company. At the end of the first four years of trade, more than five thousand pounds of furs had been sent to England, which were sold for thirty-five hundred pounds sterling. The new arrivals brought talents hitherto lacking. There were now smiths, carpenters, a sawyer, a tailor, woodcutters, dairy farmers, kitchen hands, laborers, traders, boatbuilders, ministers, gardeners, planters, millwrights, maid-servants, sailors, and a variety of other artificers to make the Kent Island settlements hum with industry. In early 1636 William Claiborne and his young wife welcomed the newest arrival of all to their island, a son named William Claiborne Junior.

And for the next year, an uneasy truce would reign over the Chesa-peake.

We Clearly Claime Right

William Cloberry, though continuing to support the Kent Island establish-ment, was far from delighted with its commander and, given the recent chain of events, began to view him as a liability. William Claiborne's record-keeping, which tended to lump his own private efforts and needs with those of the company, was inadequate for the London trader. Claiborne himself was well aware of his shortcomings in this area, and on at least one occasion he had requested that an accountant be sent over to keep proper records, but his appeal had gone unheeded. Still, the unsettled state of affairs on the Chesapeake, although temporarily peaceful, was not encouraging for those obliged to provide the monetary support for trading ventures in the region. Cloberry had begun to view his partner's personal enterprises elsewhere, in Accomac, Kecoughtan, and even Cray-ford, with suspicion. Had they been supported in part by Cloberry without his knowledge? Perhaps a full accounting was in order after all!

Cloberry's first move was to send orders to Claiborne to return to England to provide a full account of "certaine complaints and directions that were laied against him by the Governors of Virginia and Maryland" regarding the capture of Lord Baltimore's boats, as well as a complete report on all of his financial activities taken on behalf of Cloberry and Company.[1] He then took into the organization, as a one-sixth partner, a certain George Evelin, who had, at Cloberry's invitation, bought out the share of John Delabarr. Cloberry himself and one David Moorhead had already purchased the two-sixths shares of Simon Turgis and Maurice Thomson, giving Cloberry and his allies a controlling interest in the company.[2]

Although Evelin had been brought in without Claiborne's knowledge, the commander of Kent now had no choice but to return to England and defend his actions and accounts in person. In the meantime, Cloberry determined to send out Evelin as his "factor and agent" to take charge of and manage the Kent Island plantations in Claiborne's place.[3]

For once the resupply of Kent Island would be on a substantial scale. George Evelin sailed from England with eighteen servants for the com-pany and trade goods valued at three thousand pounds aboard the ships *Sarah and Elizabeth* and *John and Barbara* and arrived on the Chesapeake in February 1637. The first meetings between Claiborne and his new partner, who landed without mishap at Kecoughtan, seemed amicable enough. Evelin, playing the role of humble, uninformed newcomer, entreated the Virginian to "advize and assist him . . . in the employment of the said servants and goods as being better experienced in the said trade and Plantation then he was." Claiborne obligingly agreed to offer him every assistance. Evelin's eagerness to begin trading, even before he was acquainted with the local situation, seemed overwhelming. No sooner had he unloaded the servants and cargo (which had been consigned to him instead of to Claiborne) at Kent Island, than he immediately set off in *Sarah and Elizabeth* for the Potomac with a parcel of axes and trading cloth to truck with the Indians.[4]

Claiborne, understandably, had certain misgivings about Evelin. Although the new partner in Cloberry and Company (now Cloberry and Moorhead) spoke out frequently against the Marylanders and their patent, calling George and Cecil Calvert "grasiers" and Leonard Calvert a dunce and a blockhead, the man who had come to stand in for the founder of the Kent plantation seemed somehow less than trustworthy.[5] His true colors were not easily—or long—concealed. When Sir John Harvey, with the complete support of the king, returned to Virginia as her reinstated governor, he promptly proceeded to arrest the "mutineers" and enemies in his former council that had sent him to England and a loyal council was appointed. Although William Claiborne had not assisted in Harvey's arrest, he was not included in the new council.[6] Even his post as surveyor was forfeit when a new surveyor for the colony was appointed. For the first time in sixteen years, the commander of Kent found himself without major power. Surrounding himself with his supporters, Harvey immediately resumed his autocratic rule and friendly relations with Maryland. Evelin's anti-Maryland rhetoric and cordiality toward the commander of Kent evaporated overnight. Not surprisingly, in light of Governor Harvey's return to Virginia and Claiborne's impending departure, the St. Mary's Court felt emboldened enough to issue on 12 February 1637 an indictment against the latter as a pirate and robber for having attacked Thomas Cornwaleys; on 14 March 1637 a bill of attainder was issued in the Maryland House of the General Assembly for Claiborne's arrest.[7] Undaunted by the dramatic change of affairs, Claiborne proceeded with his grand scheme as if nothing had happened, seizing every opportunity for advancing his plans in the remaining time left to him.

In the spring of 1637, while preparing for his return to England, the commander of Kent was invited to powwow at Palmers Island by the king of the Susquehannocks and his "Councellors and great Men." The Susquehannocks, no doubt apprised of the arrival of Evelin's two large shiploads of trucking goods, were eager to begin the trading season as early as possible. Claiborne was equally eager to oblige them. After all, if he returned to England with a healthy cargo of pelts, and possibly even concessions on a permanent trading station at Palmers Island, his position regarding the probable censure by Cloberry and Moorhead would be inordinately strengthened. Assisted by a trusty interpreter named John Fullwood, he seized the moment. With the trust of the Susquehannocks, he pressed for the right to establish a permanent trading station on the island. The Indians consented and presented him with a gift of the island, and "a great deal of Land more of each side, the river and the Bay," the specifics of which were duly committed to a written document and signed by all.[8] Claiborne immediately ordered his servants to erect houses and a fort "for their better security" on the island (more with an eye on Calvert than on the natives), despite Evelin's whining objections to the use of company supplies for the undertaking.[9] Claiborne seemed intent on erecting not only a trading post, but another plantation. After six years as a seasonal bartering site and the key to the northern trade, Palmers Island had finally been occupied by white settlers. The importance of this event was not lost on Leonard Calvert.

As Claiborne's departure time approached, he readied himself and his family for the voyage ahead, while simultaneously attending to the erection of the Palmers Island station and working with Evelin to inventory the company's goods, servants, and properties. As the days passed, however, Claiborne grew apprehensive over the avowed loyalties of his replacement. On May 18, he informed his substitute that before the "goods, servants or whatsoever [that] belonged to the said Cloberry and Company in the said joint stocke account" could be officially turned over to his care, Evelin must provide a bond of three thousand pounds, made out to the company as an assurance that "he should not sell nor make away the said Plantation or Ilands or any part thereof unto the Marylanders or any other and not remove or carry away any of the servants from the said Iland."[10] Evelin rejected the ultimatum outright. Claiborne then angrily refused to turn over authority to him, whereupon Evelin confidently scoffed that he would have them by right of law. Soon afterward, having little real alternative but to accept the situation, Claiborne embarked with his family aboard the ship *Thomas* for England—but not before having one last meeting at Accomac to try for an accommodation with his replacement. For the former lord of Kent, the encounter was distasteful at best, because Evelin chose this moment to reveal his long-held secret: he had been given full power of attorney by Cloberry and Moorhead, authorizing him to do as he liked with company property—the plantation, its servants, and its goods—with or without Claiborne's approval. For the first time, Kent Island would not be in the hands of her founder and commander.[11] Outflanked and powerless to protest, Claiborne set sail for England, now resolved to do battle with his enemies at the very seat of power.

Evelin wasted little time in establishing his suzerainty over the island. His first act, on June 1, over the protest of Claiborne's friends and allies and with Governor Harvey's cooperation, was to secure warrants to confiscate all goods, houses, mills, servants, and vessels, including the great pinnace *Elizabeth*, belonging to (or claimed by Evelin to belong to) Cloberry and Moorhead, as well as Claiborne's personal vessels, on the grounds that Claiborne was deeply indebted to the company.[11]

Evelin's true loyalties, already suspected by Claiborne, now became apparent. He traveled to St. Mary's, where he was feted by Governor Calvert, and began to trade openly with the Marylanders, selling them Kent's stocks of corn, to the great detriment of the islanders' food supply. Consequently, the Cloberry company servants were soon reduced to subsisting almost entirely on oysters. Evelin soon set up his son, Mountjoy, as a trader, not on the upper Bay as might have been supposed, but on the Potomac, close to St. Mary's. The son's practices were so poor that he eventually frittered away the greatest part of the company's trucking goods in poor trading deals. Calvert now began to court openly Evelin's favor and friendship and soon swayed him to Baltimore's side by appointing him Maryland's commander of Kent.[13]

His ego inflated by his new title, George Evelin returned to Kent and convened the island's population, which had swollen during Claiborne's administration to 120 men able to bear arms, and their women and children. He announced that they now owed their allegiance to Maryland and must surrender themselves to the lord proprietor's authority. The Kent Islanders, led by Claiborne loyalists Thomas Smith, John Butler, and others, refused. Evelin, embarrassed, returned to St. Mary's. With Claiborne gone, Calvert was not to be put off and again dispatched his new lieutenant to the island, this time to arrest Smith and Butler. And again, faced with an island citizenry united in its support of Claiborne and opposition to Baltimore, George Evelin was unable to carry out the order.[14]

Calvert, incensed and frustrated by the rebuff as well as the islanders' continued loyalties to his archnemesis, determined to resolve the situation by force of arms. Near the end of November, he assembled twenty musketeers under the command of Captain Cornwaleys and set sail from St. Mary's to apprehend Smith and Butler and to reduce, once and for all, Claiborne's settlements to humble obedience to the lord proprietor of Maryland. The Chesapeake winter, however, chilled his ardor. After a week on the water, hindered by contrary winds, foul weather, and ice, he was unable to cross the Bay and returned in humiliation to St. Mary's.[15]

While the governor of Maryland simultaneously cooled his heels and smoldered, news arrived that the Susquehannocks intended to wage war on the Marylanders in the spring. Calvert seethed with anger, certain the natives were being inflamed by Claiborne's lieutenant, Tom Smith, who, he learned, had recently transplanted himself and others to Palmers Island to fortify the place and live independent of Baltimore's colony.[16]

This time, Calvert would not be deterred. At the beginning of February 1639, he assembled thirty musketeers under Captain Cornwaleys and, with Evelin along to provide intelligence on the island's defenses, once again set sail for Kent. "I landed wth my company a little before sunne rise," he later reported to Baltimore,

> at the southermost end thereof where Capt. Cleybornes howse is seated wthin a small ffort of Pallysadoes, but findeing the gate towards the sea at my comeing fast barred in the inside one of my company beeing acquainted wth the place quickly fownd passage in at an other gate and commeing to the gate wch. I was at opened vnto me, so that I was arriued an entered the fort wthout notice taken by any of the Ileand wch. I did desire, the easilier to apprehend Boteler and Smith the chief incendiaries of the former seditions and mutinies vpon the Ileand, before they should be able to make head against me.[17]

Neither Butler nor Smith was in the fort. Calvert, undismayed, rounded up all inhabitants within the works to prevent the spread of news of his invasion. He then set out on foot with his small force for Butler's plantation, called the Great Thicket, five miles distant from the fort, while ordering his pinnace on to Crayford. Half a mile from Butler's, he dispatched ten musketeers to "acquaint him that I was come vpon the Ileand to settle the gouernement" and escort him to Crayford, two miles away. Then he dispatched Sergeant Robert Vaughan and six musketeers to Smith's plantation, called Beaver Neck, which lay adjacent to Butler's, for the same purpose. Smith and Butler were arrested after being brought to Crayford and carried aboard the pinnace as common criminals.[18]

With their leadership captured, Calvert could afford to be lenient with the inhabitants of Kent. After appointing several loyal Marylanders to the posts of sheriff and commissioners for the court that would govern the island, he pardoned all inhabitants who submitted to him within twenty-four hours. Claiborne's plantation at Crayford was confiscated (under guise of a suit by Evelin on behalf of Cloberry and Moorhead). The former Virginia secretary of state was himself charged, in absentia, by an act of attainder "of grevious crimes of pyracie and murther," declared an outlaw in Maryland, and all of his "lands and tenements, goods and chattels" forfeited to the lord proprietor. All of Cloberry's joint stock property, including plantation, vessels, mills, goods, thirty-six servants, and thirty-five thousand pipe staves manufactured by company stave makers, were assigned to Maryland Secretary John Lewger and his personal overseer on the island, John Walker. Evelin himself carried off nine servants to erect for himself a manor house in Maryland and then dug up and transplanted many of Claiborne's fruit trees to his new estate.[19]

Calvert did not overlook Palmers Island, which was captured without incident and the spoils divided between the governor of Maryland and Secretary of State Lewger. In June, Calvert himself visited Palmers Island to supervise its transformation to an appendage of Maryland. He renamed the works Fort Conquest, but the metamorphosis miscarried at the outset. The plantation was utterly ruined in the process, and the great frontier trading base envisioned by William Claiborne was laid forever void.[20]

The consequences for the Marylanders were serious. The Susquehannocks, whose friendship Claiborne had courted so diligently, now refused to supply St. Mary's with pelts, electing instead to deal with the Swedish settlement recently established at Fort Christina, in Delaware.[21] Calvert was not dissuaded from his efforts, however. Methodically, he did his best to seduce Claiborne's lieutenants to Baltimore's side, even as Kent Island's plantations were systematically stripped of their cattle, corn, and other goods for the benefit of St. Mary's. Smith was sentenced to death by a St. Mary's court, in a trial that can only be termed a travesty of justice, for his role in the Second Battle of the Pocomoke. But Calvert, in a burst of moderation, gave him a reprieve and permitted him to return on some form of bail to Kent Island. Butler, however, was held as a prisoner in Calvert's home. The governor of Maryland, though censuring his unwilling guest for alleged piracy at Palmers Island against Sergeant Vaughan and John Tomkins, delayed bringing him to trial "because I am in hopes by shewing fauor vnto him to make him a good member" and to win him into Baltimore's service. He even toyed with the idea of making him commander of Kent.[22] Other of Claiborne's leading supporters, such as Richard Thompson, Edward Beckler, Henry Crawley, and Thomas Broadnax, biding their time until Claiborne's hoped-for return, grudgingly began to join the Maryland government.[23]

Despite Calvert's best efforts to placate the leaders and inhabitants of Maryland's new dominion, the majority of Kent Islanders stoutly refused to acquiesce. With adamant Claiborne supporters like Tom Smith again free to lead them, it wasn't long before a full-scale armed revolt erupted, albeit with predictable consequences. On June 16, Calvert and Cornwaleys again descended on the island with fifty musketeers and easily crushed the rebellion. This time, mercy was abandoned. Tom Smith and Edward Beckler, leaders of the insurrection, were captured and executed by hanging without benefit of trial. The settlers' forts, houses, and all else of value were brutally "displanted." Claiborne's property at Crayford and all of his servants that had yet to be confiscated, to the value of one thousand pounds, were seized. The island, thanks to the betrayal and chicanery of George Evelin, was now firmly in Maryland hands.[24]

William Claiborne, unaware of the events that had recently transpired on the Chesapeake, persisted in the contest for Kent in the court of the king. On February 26, 1638, he petitioned the crown for a reexamination of his alleged wrongdoings and for confirmation of his right to Kent Island under the Great Seal of England.[25] On April 4, the Lords Commissioners for Foreign Plantations, presided over by Archbishop Laud of Canterbury, convened to address the latter question. The commissioners, to Claiborne's chagrin, determined that as his license had been given under the Scotch signet and the Maryland Charter was under the seal of England, his permit was a license only to trade with the Indians. The permit provided no authority to plant a settlement or trade within Baltimore's patent (an area in which, as a palatinate, even the king was not authorized to approve courts, officers, licenses, or grants). As for the wrongdoings against him, he was told that the only recourse was the ordinary course of justice, which now, of course, meant in Maryland and not in Virginia.[26] On April 16, he was summoned before the High Court of the Admiralty to respond to Baltimore's charges of piracy and murder related to the Battle of Pocomoke. This time, the verdict was in his favor.[27]

Although cleared of criminal charges, Claiborne was undoubtedly distraught over the plantation commission's decision regarding the Maryland Charter and later angered over the news of the armed reduction of Kent and Palmers Islands in his absence. He drafted another petition to the king. At the same time, Cloberry vigorously renewed his own complaints concerning the invasions of the islands and the summary executions of Claiborne's lieutenants. The matter was again referred to the commissioners. This time, the king instructed Baltimore to desist in his actions against the Kent Islanders until the matter could be resolved. The crown, however, did not press the matter, and Baltimore diplomatically stonewalled the royal directive by ignoring it, because the issue of ownership, as far as he was concerned, had already been determined. All that Claiborne could hope for now, it seemed, was to recover whatever confiscated property he could. And even that, given that the courts in Maryland were still closed to him as a rebel and pirate, seemed out of the question.[28] The final humiliation came on October 4, 1638, when, confirming the commission's findings of April 4, Governor Harvey, Secretary Kemp, and the Council of Virginia formally proclaimed that Kent Island and other places in question belonged to Maryland and that there could be no trade in Maryland without a specific license from Baltimore.[29]

Claiborne's problems regarding the Kent Island enterprise were far from over. He was deeply angered by Cloberry's secret negotiations with Baltimore, and a breach between the partners was soon manifest. Both parties had lost substantial monies in the venture, and each blamed the other. On January 28, 1639, Cloberry brought a libel suit against Claiborne in the High Court of the Admiralty, claiming that he had skimmed company funds for his own purposes.[30] Claiborne responded with a counter-suit on February 15 charging that the merchant had not supported the venture as agreed upon. The former commander of Kent claimed that he had been obliged to pay for much of the venture out of his own pocket to put the company's trading base in operating condition.[31]

In the spring of 1640, refusing to admit defeat, Claiborne returned to the Chesapeake with his family to gather further depositions for his claims to Kent and to try again to cut his losses. He petitioned Calvert, through a friend and an attorney named George Scovell, to be permitted to recover his property and estates left at Kent, but to no avail.[32] Undismayed, he consoled himself by expanding his Virginia holdings by acquiring three thousand acres on the south side of the Potomac. Fortified with new depositions, new territory, and a renewed will to regain his lost island, Claiborne again sailed for England.[33]

The England that William Claiborne returned to was on the verge of a civil war about to be fought between the royalists of Charles I and the Puritan-led Parliament. Back on the Chesapeake, an Indian war was erupting as the Susquehannocks began to attack Baltimore's allies, the Piscataways, endangering the power of the Calverts and jeopardizing the safety of the colony. In Ireland, a rebellion, begun in 1641, had also endangered Baltimore's land revenues from his holdings in that troubled land.[34] For Claiborne, the moment was propitious, and his appeals for justice to a besieged crown did not go entirely unrewarded. Although the king did not rescind the decision regarding Kent Island, he did bestow upon its founder, on April 6, 1642, the title of Treasurer of Virginia, for life.[35] The title was undoubtedly granted in an effort to secure Claiborne's frayed loyalty (for he was a suspected supporter of the Puritan Party, and a possible Parliamentarian sympathizer), as well as a genuine gesture to compensate him for the loss of the island.

Claiborne returned to a colony that was itself on the edge of military and political chaos. In the spring of 1644, Virginia's implacable foe, the aged and wily Opechancanough, had again incited the Powhatan Confederacy to a fierce uprising. The new governor of Virginia, William Berkeley, after directing a successful but limited counterstrike, failed to quell the upheaval and ordered all Virginians to withdraw to palisaded camps. He then sailed for England to muster whatever help he could. The colony was left in a state of martial law, and William Claiborne, one of its ablest leaders, was chosen general and chief commander—the first general officer ever to be so selected by the Virginia legislature.[36] He took swift action against the enemy: after leading a bloody but successful three-week campaign into the Pamunkey country, he all but quelled the uprising. It was the beginning of the end for Opechancanough. By 1646, the Powhatan Confederacy would be completely destroyed.[37]

Although his efforts to renew his claim to Kent, by force if not by law, had been sidetracked, Claiborne resumed his interest in the prospects during the fall of 1644. With civil war now raging across the English countryside, his loyalties to Parliament's cause were finally evinced. Catholic Maryland was in disarray, confused, weakened, and unable to distinguish friend from foe. Calvert, leaving Giles Brent as acting governor, had sailed for Virginia to secure aid for the Royalist cause which had, after all, supported his colony. Kent Island was now the least of Calvert's worries and had been left to its own tender devices, under the command of Richard Thompson, Claiborne's cousin. Thompson had been appointed by Calvert as one of the island's commissioners in an effort to conciliate the island population. Thompson's sympathies, predictably, lay entirely with the Virginians and were soon apparent. Indecision at St. Mary's was now the rule, and Kent was vulnerable. Even Sir Edmund Plowden (living on the Eastern Shore, who had sought his own grant of territory ranging from Long Island to Maryland) was now laying claim to the disputed island. But Claiborne was aware that, unlike Governor Harvey, Governor Berkeley favored Virginia's sovereignty over Kent; Claiborne again took action before either Plowden or Calvert could move.[38]

In the autumn of 1644 the new treasurer of Virginia set sail for Kent with Thompson and nearly a dozen men aboard two pinnaces. Upon landing, they were met by seven or eight of Claiborne's most ardent supporters and convened in council at the home of one Edward Cummins. Claiborne wanted to bestir the inhabitants to take up arms against the government and seize the estate of Giles Brent, who had moved into Claiborne's former home on the lower end of the island. A move against Brent would have been particularly delicious and an appropriate symbolic gesture, for as recently as June 3, the acting governor of Maryland had ordered the confiscation of all of Claiborne's remaining property in the colony and on the island, which had resulted in the seizure of twenty-seven cattle by the Maryland-appointed sheriff of Kent, Simon Richardson. A proclamation had then been issued preventing vessels from trading with Kent without clearance from St. Mary's, to prevent local correspondence or intelligence from either Claiborne or Thompson.[39]

Claiborne's attempt to cajole the inhabitants to arms, despite his persuasive oratory and a parchment alleged to be his commission from the king, failed to incite the islanders. They were now too settled and too skeptical of authority to act. The treasurer of Virginia, having sounded the waters and found them not to his liking, withdrew in disappointment. Despite his failures, however, his surreptitious visit to the island had the effect of creating a flurry of excitement and apprehension in Maryland.[40]

Upon his return to St. Mary's, and undoubtedly aware of Claiborne's visit to Kent, the governor of Maryland issued a commission to two of his men, Mark Pheypo and John Genalles, "to take the command of 8 men

& a shallop & to presse to fill up that number" and to repair to "popelirs Island in such secret maner as you may to keep your shallop from being discerned at Kent . . . discovering forehad if any vessel be riding against the Southern pt of Kent . . . & not to go on shore at Kent point or thereabouts" until they had obtained as much intelligence as possible. The two were to land during the night at the home of one of the weaker plantations and to kidnap one of the inhabitants "to enquire whether Captain Clayborne or any other have made any disturbance of the peace or committed any outrage upon the Iland" and to learn his force, strength on land and sea, his intentions, and how long he planned to stay.[41]

Pheypo's and Genalles's reconnaissance, if it was ever carried out, may well have been the cause of Calvert's subsequent actions: he removed his newly appointed but weak-willed commander of Kent, John Wyatt, and replaced him with Captain William Braithwaite, a strong-handed officer who had even served for a brief time as acting governor at St. Mary's.[42] Claiborne and Thompson were promptly declared enemies of the province; all intelligence and communication with them was prohibited. Ships were again forbidden to trade with the island without securing permission to do so at St. Mary's. And William Claiborne was formally addressed as a "pretender to the said Lands."[43]

At about this time, Calvert's fortunes were to ebb to their lowest point since the trying days of the founding of St. Mary's. The difficulties began when Captain Richard Ingle, commanding the ship *Reformation* and bearing a letter of marque from Parliament, descended upon the Maryland colony like a destructive whirlwind. Only the year before, in February 1644, this one-time merchant trader, who had served as a factor for one of Claiborne's former partners, Maurice Thomson, had been arrested at St. Mary's because his ship belonged to London, seat of the Parliament forces in England. He had escaped, returned to London, secured a commission, and was now back to wreak his vengeance.[44]

Claiborne and Ingle, brothers in arms and in allegiance, were soon drawn together and conspired to invade Maryland. On February 24, 1645, *Reformation* dropped anchor in the St. Mary's River, captured the visiting eleven-gun Dutch merchantman *Speagle*, and forced the fort at St. Inigoes, immediately below the town, to surrender. For Lord Baltimore's colony, the future seemed bleak indeed, for it was at this juncture that the Susquehannocks and all of the tribes of the eastern Bay regions rose up against the Marylanders. Maryland succumbed easily, and for nearly two years, rebellion, revolution, and chaos would reign. Leonard Calvert, at the direction of Baltimore, was forced to flee to Virginia for sanctuary, and his Catholic colonists were themselves now to become victims of Protestant prejudice and destruction.[45]

Calvert, however, like his archrival, refused to admit defeat. In December 1646, with a force of fugitive Marylanders and Virginia troops provided by Sir William Berkeley (who had recently returned from England), he reinvaded Maryland and successfully reestablished his authority. A coalition government of Catholics and Protestants was formed and quickly offered allegiance to Baltimore.[46]

In the meantime, Claiborne, whose actual role in Ingle's invasion and in the resulting spoilation of the colony is uncertain, had once more landed on Kent Island with Richard Thompson and nearly twenty Virginians in an effort to keep the sputtering rebellion alive. Near Christmas 1645, he seized the Brent manor house and established headquarters in his former home. The place had most recently been occupied by Brent's sister Margaret but was in great upheaval, as it had already been attacked and looted by Edward Cummins during one of the uprisings.[47]

Soon after Claiborne's arrival, the islanders were assembled and urged by Claiborne to accept Thompson as their captain and follow him in making an attack on St. Mary's and in capturing the papist Calvert. To aid in the endeavor, the treasurer of Virginia had brought powder, shot, and several pinnaces for the expedition and had promised the aid of additional forces located at Chicacone, on the Virginia side of the Potomac River. Though the venture seemed tempting, the islanders demanded to see Claiborne's commission from Berkeley, a document that he had claimed to possess but refused to display. The islanders then asked him to take command of the expedition personally. But again, he demurred (probably on the grounds that he was a Virginia official). At that, the inhabitants declared that they must refuse to follow. The onetime commander of Kent, it was now clear, had lost his grip on the islanders.[48]

Unaware of Claiborne's rebuff, Calvert resolved to prevent the spark of revolt from bursting into open flame again. He sailed for Kent to reestablish his authority. The rebel faction, now commanded by Peter Knight, was forced to flee. Knight determined to leave little of value for the Marylanders. The great Brent estates, the island's mills, and the fort were stripped of anything of value.[49]

After securing control again, but wary of the Protestant inclinations among the islanders, Calvert permitted one of their own religion, Robert Vaughan, to assume the post of commander of Kent and instituted a lenient policy toward the rebels. Then, in June 1647, shortly after his return to St. Mary's, Leonard Calvert died. The consequences for Kent were disastrous. Despite Calvert's policy of pacification, revolt again broke out the following year. Vaughan became a captive of the insurgents, and Protestant rebels under Thomas Broadnax again attempted to seize control. In the chaos that ensued, the end of William Claiborne's grand and glorious scheme was played out amidst fire and destruction. The mills were burned, the fort destroyed, the cattle killed, and the island population scattered to the neighboring countryside. The first European settlement in Maryland lay in utter ruin.[50]

William Claiborne, though he could not have known it, would never visit his beloved islands again, although he would never give up his quest to regain them. In 1649, while attempting to take the fullest advantage of political turmoil in Maryland, he prepared a declaration on the illegality of the Maryland patent:

> Wee clearly claime right by possession haveing planted the Ile of Kent almost three yeares before even the name of Maryland was heard of, and Burgesses for that place setting in the Assemblyes of Virginia whereby it is evident that the Lord of Baltimore's suggestion to the king that those parts were uncultivated and unplanted, unless by barbarous people not haveing knowledge of God, was a misinformation, and by it that Patent appears illegally gotten. And if the Lord Baltimore takes awaie those lands (who have also purchased the interest of the Natives a right not inconsiderable) and seize theire goods and that in an hostile manner as hee hath done, How can it be sayd, those men rights and interests are preserved, they being the first discovered of that Ilan by vertue of the King's Commission, and planted there under the Government of Virginia, on the confidence they apprehended from the former asshurances, and there begann in greate part the trade of Furrs, which is now usurped by the Duch and Sweeds, the Lord Baltimore not being able to manage it himself.[51]

In his effort to conciliate the Puritan-led Parliamentarians, Baltimore had appointed a Protestant, Captain William Stone, as governor of Maryland (replacing Calvert's deathbed appointment of Catholic Thomas Greene). Claiborne immediately entered into a correspondence with Stone concerning the Virginian's claims over Kent. Again, he was rejected. In 1650 the Maryland Assembly passed an act decreeing that anyone assisting, abetting, or countenancing any effort that Claiborne might make on Kent would be punished by death and the confiscation of all his lands, goods, and chattels.[52]

Despite Lord Baltimore's efforts at conciliation with Protestantism and the institution of a bipartisan government in Maryland, Parliament ordered that the colony as well as Berkeley's Virginia be brought to total obedience to the commonwealth. Claiborne, Captain Edmund Curtis, and Richard Bennett (Virginia's new governor) were instructed to use their best efforts to reduce the "plantations within the Bay of Chesopiock" to obedience to Parliament and the commonwealth. Virginia was quickly humbled after agreeing to allow Virginians the right to "enjoy the antient bounds and lymitts granted by . . . former Kings," and soon afterward, the new executive agents of the commonwealth were landed at St. Mary's with little resistance.[53] On March 24, 1652, the three commissioners disembarked from the warship *Guinea* and demanded that the government of Maryland, under the "Catholic Tyrant" at St. Mary's, be turned over to a council of leading Protestants.

Although Stone was restored soon afterward, the ascendancy of Claiborne—and his dominion over Kent—again seemed assured.[54] But it was not to be. Upon his return from Maryland, Claiborne was again appointed Secretary of State for Virginia. He continued in authority as a commissioner for the Chesapeake (which oversaw the administration of the governments of Maryland and Virginia) until 1657 and remained as secretary of state until 1660, when the restoration of the Stuart monarchy forced his retirement. In 1658 Lord Baltimore's authority over his Maryland dominion was entirely restored, insuring that the one-time commander of Kent would never again set foot on the island that had become the obsession of his life and that of two great colonies. But Claiborne never gave up.[55]

On March 13, 1677, William Claiborne, in his seventy-seventh year of life and comfortably ensconced at his vast five-thousand-acre estate of Romancoke on the Pamunkey River, which he had acquired by patent in 1653, submitted to His Majesty's Commissioners for the Settlement of Virginia his last claim to Kent Island.[56] He entitled his work (which may have been dictated or even written in his behalf by his son William) "The Humble Petition of Coll: William Claiborne a Poor Old Servant of your Majesty's father and grandfather."[57]

The Virginia Assembly wholeheartedly supported the petition since the island had been granted to, settled, and planted by the petitioner, and because Kent had sent delegates to the Assembly, as well as other evidence of record. Claiborne reinforced his case by providing certified documents, copies of his commissions, his examination on the scurrilous charges of trying to incite the natives in 1634, records of the acts of Maryland's agents against him, many depositions taken by him in his own defense in 1640, and a brief survey of his own charges against Maryland and Lord Baltimore. A petition to King Charles II came next.

The petition was favorably noted by the king's commissioners and then, like the subject of William Claiborne's valiant but futile life-long obsession, the seat of a vast trading empire, the first English settlement in what would one day become the state of Maryland, was conveniently ignored and then forgotten.

THIRTEEN

Blowout

December 2, 1989. Michael Pohuski stared across the ice-flecked waters of Maryland's West River with certain misgivings. Although the morning sky was cloudless, a stiff breeze was blowing in from the north, and the Bay weather reports had warned that by evening, perhaps even earlier, small-craft warnings would probably be issued for the central Chesapeake. For Pohuski, a thirty-seven-year-old professional photographer and amateur underwater archaeologist from Baltimore, the conditions under which he was to begin directing the first major archaeological survey of his career were less than ideal. Only two years earlier, he had participated as a volunteer diver and photographer on the *New Jersey* Project and was well aware of the negative impact of winter conditions on marine operations.

The blustery weather did not seem to affect the buoyant spirits of either of his coinvestigators, Joe McNamara or myself, or the four midshipmen from the U.S. Naval Academy and others who had volunteered to dive in the frigid Chesapeake. Captain John Kiser, the tall, outgoing owner and master of *Thunderhorse*, the forty-two-foot steel-hulled dive boat that had been loaned to the project, *had* promised, after all, that he could get us to our target within an hour and return to Pirates Cove Marina, whence we were to sail, well before conditions might become dangerous.

Pohuski mulled over the situation as the heavy dive and survey gear was being loaded aboard the boat and as several volunteers pumped up a pair of Zodiac inflatable boats. It was imperative that everything proceed according to plan if we were to make a positive impression on the new Maryland state underwater archaeologist and his assistant, who had been invited along as observers. After all, with the recent institution of Maryland's new rules and regulations governing the administration of all submerged cultural resources in state waters, little research work could be undertaken without the archaeologist's endorsement. Indeed, his formal approbation was essential if the project were to proceed beyond the reconnaissance phase, for now permission to excavate any submerged archaeological site in Maryland waters required not only the approval of the U.S. Army Corps of Engineers, but also that of the Maryland Historical Trust (the newly authorized administrator of the state's underwater archaeological resources).

Melted Beads

By 9:30 A.M., two hours after the appointed departure time, *Thunder-horse* was still at her moorings awaiting the archaeologist and his assistant. But winds were kicking up, and a noticeable chop was making mincemeat of the river's surface. Pohuski was aware that it would probably be even worse on the open Bay. To delay further could mean the possible loss of the only weather window in weeks, the volunteer manpower and loaned equipment assembled, and the use of *Thunderhorse* for the reconnaissance. The expedition, he decided, would sail without the state observers.

Thus began the Claiborne Project, the first major project to search for the remnants of the earliest European settlement in the state of Maryland—not on land, where all efforts before had concentrated, but beneath the waters of Chesapeake Bay.

❏ ❏ ❏

Michael Pohuski is an intense fellow, serious looking, grave in demeanor, efficient and businesslike in accomplishing tasks, but ready to laugh at the slightest excuse when it doesn't interfere with the business at hand. A native Baltimorean and a graduate of the University of Maryland, he has operated his own commercial photography business since 1980, regularly serving such nationally recognized clients as McDonald's, McCormick, and Marriott. In fact, his diving career had been given birth by one of his first commercial photography jobs in 1980, when he was hired to photograph yacht hulls in the Caribbean for a recreational boat manufacturer. He had readily accepted the task, brazenly assuring his client that he was an experienced underwater photographer—and then learned to dive to do the job. By 1986 he had become a certified dive master, running charters on the side to the wreck-strewn coast of North Carolina for his friend and diving mentor, John Kiser. Pohuski's interest in the underwater universe mushroomed. In the process, he began to research every wreck and ruin he visited, consuming volumes of historic documents. Moreover, he began to view such sites as far more than great warehouses of souvenirs to be plundered at will. Here, he realized, was the very stuff of history, material that needed to be treated accordingly.

I met Michael during a series of seminars I was conducting on underwater archaeology in the fall of 1986. Later, he had volunteered to serve as a diver on the *New Jersey* Project, and thereafter he enlisted in every archaeological endeavor I undertook. He was always the first to tackle the most difficult problems and always the last to complain. He was as at home in an archive as he was in a dry suit working in zero-visibility water at eighty feet. Michael had methodically become one of the most proficient amateur underwater archaeologists I had ever met. And the hunt for William Claiborne's settlement was about to test his mettle.

The Claiborne Project was born in Michael Pohuski's head while on the homeward-bound leg of a diving trip out of Ocean City, Maryland, in the summer of 1989. Snarled in the usual summer traffic tie-up on the Kent Narrows Bridge with friend and diving companion Joe McNamara, their subject of conversation had turned to Kent Island. Only days before, Joe had heard of the recovery of a piece of pottery dredged up from the Bay by clammers and salvaged from a spoils pile by an anthropology student from the University of Delaware who was working as a mate aboard the boat. The student, Darrin Lowery, had been toiling in a summer job for a waterman named Willie Roe when the piece was dredged up from the west side of the island near Craney Creek, less than a mile from shore. The unique thing about the sherd, a Bellarmine stoneware fragment, was the date that appeared in raised letters on the medallion motif: "1593." Wood recovered from the site suggested the clam dredge may have struck the remains of a wooden well. No less an authority than Ivor Noël Hume, the director of archaeology at Colonial Williamsburg, had declared the sherd to be the earliest dated piece of European pottery found in North America.

Pohuski was captivated as his companion casually discussed the possible origins of the sherd and its potential connection to the long-lost Claiborne settlement on Kent Island. Had anyone ever attempted to locate the settlement? And if so, why hadn't it been discovered by now? Could the 1593 sherd have belonged to the settlement, or had it merely been discarded from some early passing ship? Was it possible that Kent Fort had not been located because its eroded ruins were now guarding the bottom of the Chesapeake rather than some cornfield on the island? The questions were unending, but there were no answers, only more speculation.

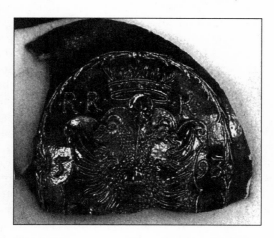

The Kent Island "Medallion" has been called the
oldest piece of dated pottery of European manufacture ever found in North America and became the catalyst for the hunt for the Claiborne settlement.
Photograph by Michael Pohuski

Melted Beads

Michael Pohuski was drawn deeper into the mystery of Kent Island by his own curiosity. He began to read every published account available on the history of the island, Claiborne, and the founding of Maryland. His research began to consume great chunks of his spare time and was soon intruding into his business hours. The corners of his home began to fill with stacks of files, notes, maps, microfilms and photocopies of documents, dissertations, and scientific papers. What had begun as a curiosity was emerging as an obsession. He gradually began to consider what it might take to locate the earliest European settlement in Maryland. Moreover, he became increasingly convinced that its remains lay not beneath dry land, but beneath the waters that had reclaimed the island's eroding coastline.

If a systematic hunt for Kent Fort was to get off the ground, he realized, it could not be undertaken without a comprehensive project design, financial backing, and adequate manpower and assistance. As an amateur archaeologist, he was aware that his own credentials would not be enough to secure economic support or to insure that state approval (almost mandatory for such an endeavor) would be possible. Thus, his first move was to consult with McNamara, then-president of the Archaeological Society of Maryland and a member of the board of the Maryland Historical Trust. McNamara supported the idea wholeheartedly and suggested that he speak with me about how to organize such an effort.

By the early winter of 1989, Pohuski had resolved to go for it and asked if I would serve as project coinvestigator with him and Joe. As one who had undertaken major archaeological projects while trying to hold down a regular job, I cautioned him to think the project through before actually committing himself to such an effort. If, by some longshot, he was successful, the discovery would be tantamount to finding the ruins of Jamestown or St. Mary's City for the first time. The personal toll could be significant. At the very least, his wife would become an "archaeological widow" for the duration of the project. And, as I had long before discovered, one's personal financial contributions to such efforts could be substantial, even with significant external monetary support. Nevertheless, I was intrigued by the prospect. Having already surveyed the remains of several inundated colonial and nineteenth-century sites, I was in full agreement with his hypothesis that at least some of the archaeological remains of the Claiborne settlement were probably resting beneath the Chesapeake. Their condition and integrity was undoubtedly another matter. But it was worth a shot. I suggested that before any further investigation be undertaken, a comprehensive research design and an honest budget be developed. Funding and competent, scholarly input would be of paramount importance. And we would have to be prepared to accept failure as well as success, for it was by any measure a remote chance that if the site had eroded, any significant identifiable component of it had survived intact. Locating such remains with the conventional technology would prove difficult if not impossible. Excavation and survey, even with state approval, would constitute a major undertaking even on a very limited basis. And conserving artifact collections could prove as expensive as the rest of the project combined.

Neither Pohuski nor McNamara was deterred from the challenge. Swayed by their ardor—and, I must admit, by the prospect of missing out on a potentially important project—I agreed to join. I suggested that we name the effort the Claiborne Project, in honor of the founder of the Kent settlement in 1631, and that Fred Hopkins be brought in as a fourth coinvestigator. Not only was Fred a professional academician, superb historian, researcher, and long-time colleague, but he had connections that could lead to financial assistance for the project and, through the university, access to the latest computer technology. The suggestions were readily accepted, and the Claiborne Project was off and running.

❏　❏　❏

Thunderhorse approached the spear of Bloody Point Light, barely a nautical mile southwest of Kent Point, less than an hour after departing West River. With one eye on his fathometer and another on the shore, John Kiser managed his boat with economy and grace. He deftly turned the wheel, rounded Kent Point, and brought her onto a due north heading into Eastern Bay. It was a snappy twenty-eight degrees, and the water was tinged with whitecaps. The sky seemed to be darkening by the minute as clouds began scudding in from the north. Below deck, the middies were suiting up in dry suits, while vigorously swapping tales of football, their diving acumen, and the opposite sex. In the galley, Pohuski and McNamara sat hunched over a pile of maps and notes. I stood alone on the bow, unrigging the Zodiacs lashed to the forward deck.

The objective for the day was simple: to conduct a series of visual underwater surveys with divers radiating from set datum points along a several-hundred-yard stretch of beach between two small stream outlets called Hullica Snooze and Scaffold Creek. It was here that we had elected to begin our preliminary field reconnaissance. Our principal goal was to secure hands-on data on the near-shore environment along the south end of the island between the Snooze and Scaffold Creek.

We had many reasons for beginning our investigation here, although the historic record had indicated only two clues to the location of Kent Fort. These two pieces of evidence, however, were of enormous significance. The first seemed almost a dead giveaway. When Leonard Calvert invaded Kent Island in 1639, he reported that he landed "at the southermost end thereof where Capt. Cleybornes howse is seated wthin a small ffort of Pallysadoes fast barred in the inside."[1] The second clue was lodged in Calvert's instructions to his two spies, Mark Pheypo and John Genalles, to

151

sail to Poplar Island (the eroding remains of which lay due south of Kent Point) in such a secret manner as to keep their shallop hidden from view, "discovering forehand if any vessel be riding against the Southern pt of Kent . . . & not to go on shore at Kent point or thereabouts until you had information. . . ."[2] Moreover, the site was clearly visible from Poplar Island, which lay, in 1639, approximately two and a half miles to the south of Kent Point.

Our evaluation of secondary sources from early chroniclers of Maryland history, such as John Leeds Bozman (1837) and George Davis (1855), suggested that Kent Fort was located on the first "navigable" creek northeast of Kent Point or directly on Kent Point, on Eastern Bay. We soon came to view these descriptions with caution as no references had been cited, nor had we been able to find any that directly confirmed the settlement's proximity to a navigable creek.[3]

Fortunately, Pohuski's and Hopkins's research into title and probate records provided additional, albeit fragmentary, data on the subsequent history of the lands upon which Kent Fort had been ensconced. After Claiborne's settlement had been seized by Leonard Calvert and then transferred to the ownership of Giles Brent, the plantation had been passed on to Brent's son, Giles Jr., then to his grandson, Giles Brent III, then to William Brent, and finally to William Brent Jr. In 1737 the lessee of this last Brent, an absentee landlord, successfully ejected Benjamin Tasker, who, for forty years, had maintained posssession of the property, for his predecessors. About 1750 the old house built by Claiborne more than a century earlier was destroyed by fire, and another was built upon its foundations. In time, that structure also disappeared. For years thereafter, the land was owned by the Chew family, until it was divided up, and the vestigial location of the actual site of Kent Fort survived as little more than a dim memory. By 1769, when one William Eddis recorded his own visit to the island, all evidence of the settlement had disappeared. For the next 134 years, the location of Kent Fort was forgotten.[4] In the process, William Claiborne was presented by such Maryland historians as Bozman and Davis as the greatest villain Maryland had encountered (with the possible exception of Richard Ingle) during its early history.

In November 1903 a pair of historians from Johns Hopkins University, DeCourcey N. Thom and Bernard C. Steiner, became the first actually to visit the island to conduct research for a history of early Maryland and to try to identify the specific location of Kent Fort. "From Stephensville, the chief village on the island," Steiner later reported,

> we drove along an excellent country road through level fertile country with interesting old farm houses standing at a distance. These were often built telescope fashion, each successive owner placing a larger and higher section next the older building. At Norman we passed a quaint old shingled house and a small negro settlement. Further along

we reached Mattapex Post Office, whose name recalls the Indian tribe. We learned that we had just passed Indian Spring farm, but that the spring had been filled up. . . . Finally the high road ended, a gate barring our passage, and we turned aside to the house of Mr. J. Frank Legg, to learn that we were in Kent Fort Manor. Mr. Legg went with us to show us the point which tradition marked as the site of the Claiborne settlement. We found it just where Bozman led us to expect it, on a slight elevation back of an old landing on the bank of the first navigable creek on the Eastern Bay side above Kent Point. To the north of the site, now known as Chew's Gardens and cultivated as a field, is a little valley which was probably once an inlet, so that the site was then surrounded on three sides by water. We found a number of fragments of glazed bricks about seventy yards from the shore, which we fancied must have been part of the Brent Manor house. Looking southward across Eastern Bay we saw Popley's (now called Poplar) Island, about two miles away where Claiborne's men had a branch settlement, and thought of the wonderful pertinacity with which he pressed his claims to [the] island, sending his last petition to Charles II forty-five years after he settled the island.[5]

We had read Steiner's delightful description cautiously, but his report of the local tradition regarding the location of the settlement had been encouraging. Though he failed to name the creek he mentioned, his description of the area fit well the description of the north side of Scaffold Creek as it was charted in 1903.[6]

In 1937, Dr. Henry Berkeley produced yet another study and a map placing the location of Kent Fort on a narrow peninsula called Tanners Point, a ten-foot-high strip of land dividing two waterways, Tanners Creek and Cove Creek, before they merge and flow into Eastern Bay at Long Point, approximately two miles northeast of Kent Point. William Claiborne, Berkeley claimed assuredly, had arrived at this very point in 1631 aboard *Africa* and had found the site to his liking. Once past the narrow gut of the entrance to the creek, the wide cove within could protect and "hide two ships or galley Ships of five hundred tuns." Tanners Point was Berkeley's candidate for the location of Kent Fort. To back his hypothesis, he quoted Calvert as saying that Kent Fort was situated on "an Isthmos of low hard ground like a Tongue environed with fresh water," an apt description of Tanners Point. Berkeley attributed his locational data to a document in the Maryland Historical Society's Calvert Papers 880.[7] Hopkins's research, however, had revealed that no such location had ever been mentioned in any of the Calvert Papers. But it sounded great! Unfortunately, Berkeley's flawed account was soon to become the basis for several subsequent hypotheses that also placed the location of Kent Fort on Tanners Point.

Melted Beads

In 1951, Nathan Claiborne Hale wrote what many have considered to be the definitive biography of William Claiborne, entitled *The Virginia Venturer*. Unfortunately, Hale accepted Berkeley's false data entirely, and quoted from it freely. Six years later, Eric Isaacs, an Israeli scholar, published his doctoral dissertation, *The First Century of Settlement on Kent Island*, a geographical, geological, and historical study of the island. Isaacs's work incorporated a detailed summary of the Kent Fort title and probate records, a history of the settlement, and, of course, his own theory as to the location of Kent Fort. Isaacs had also drawn upon Berkeley's phony data but accepted Long Point as a logical solution to the mystery rather than Tanners Point. His reasoning was based upon the discovery that in the mid 1600s, Kent Islanders paid their taxes at a mill located near Kent Fort. One of the taxation days was September 29, Michaelmas. Title and probate records had indicated that a farm once situated on Long Point was known as St. Michael's Farm, and this appellation may have been derived from Michaelmas. Employing this linkage, Isaacs surmised that Kent Fort had been located on Long Point.[8]

The majority of subsequent historical accounts relied upon Bozman, Davis, Steiner, Berkeley, Hale, and Isaacs for their views on the location of Kent Fort.[9] But no one had discovered verifiable, datable evidence of the site. Wisely, Pohuski had decided to cast out all such hypothetical locations and attack the problem using only original documentation, title, and probate records. Hopkins began to sift through the microfilm records of the Colonial Records Project at Colonial Williamsburg to glean the official Virginia side of the story, while Pohuski and I focused on Maryland's title and probate records in the Maryland Hall of Records in Annapolis, transcripts in the manuscript and general collections of the Library of Congress, and the voluminous files of the Maryland Historical Society. A computerized database of all source material, in manuscript form and published, was soon under development for ready information cross-referencing and retrieval.

Systematic evaluation of historic maps was to become an integral component of the group's research effort. We compared all available seventeenth-, eighteenth-, nineteenth-, and twentieth-century maps. The most intriguing comparison was the Augustine Hermann map of Virginia and Maryland, engraved at the behest of Lord Baltimore in 1670 during Claiborne's lifetime, and a map of the same region by Herman Moll, which first appeared in John Oldmixon's *The British Empire in America*, published in 1708. The Hermann engraving, which featured the south end of Kent Island, indicated two plantations, one on Kent Point and a second on Long Point. The Moll map, the first truly popular cartographic effort to represent the Chesapeake region since the Hermann map and which was published thirty-eight years after it, showed only the Long Point plantation (St. Michael's Farm?) as extant.[10] Although Moll may have omitted a few plantations, it was of considerable note that land records of the period indicated the virtual abandonment of the southern end of Kent Island by 1700, although it remained under the ownership of absentee landlords.

A more accurate map of Kent Island was not published until 1844, when the U.S. Coast and Geodetic Survey, founded in 1807, finally produced a chart of the area. We had managed to acquire copies of the 1847 version of the chart, as well as scores of successive maps and hydrographic charts from 1892 to 1986.[11] Several dozen charts were evaluated, then reduced or enlarged to a common scale based upon stable benchmarks. Acetate overlays were then created, allowing a chronological sequence of the probable evolution of the island's coastline from 1847 onward. Simultaneously, through the auspices of the University of Baltimore's Academic Computer Center, Hopkins began an intensive computerized reconstruction of the Kent Fort Manor lands based upon title and probate records. In concert with the geographic analysis, I began to conduct a comprehensive review of the geological evolution of the island. The product of the synthesis of our combined efforts was stunning. For the first time, we could plot the depredations caused by eustatic change, the erosion and accretion process along the entirety of the island's shores. The probability of Pohuski's original hypothesis, that Kent Fort may well lie beneath the sea, was no longer a longshot; it seemed, judging from the enormous loss of land to erosion, a distinct likelihood.

❑　❑　❑

If Captain John Smith, the first European to produce a reasonably accurate map of the Chesapeake Bay, were to visit the region today, he would recognize very little of it. His confusion would not stem from the vast tracts of development that have sprung up along much of its seven thousand miles of coastline so much as from the simple fact that the shoreline he explored and mapped in 1608 is no longer there. Indeed, in many places today, beaches range from two hundred to two thousand feet or more farther landward than their seventeenth century positions.[12]

The 4,316 square miles of the modern Chesapeake is, in fact, a geologically ephemeral component of the Coastal Plain. As a result of fifteen thousand years of global warming following the Wisconsin glaciation, commonly referred to as the last Ice Age, sea level rise has been estimated at between 150 and 300 feet. Between seven thousand and ten thousand years B.P., glacial melt and crustal subsidence—that is, the sinking or settling of sectors of the earth's crust—resulted in the drowning of the ancient trunk of the lower Susquenhanna Valley, creating the Chesapeake Bay in the process. Within the last two thousand to three thousand years, eustatic change brought the Chesapeake to within an average of 10 feet of its present height. A consequence of these dynamics has been the conversion of the Chesapeake into a vast sediment trap that captures eroded materials from the uplands and diminishes its depth by as much as an inch per year in certain areas.[13]

The siltation process, especially since the arrival of European civilization and the systematic stripping of great swaths of land for agriculture, mining, and development, has accelerated well beyond the natural rate. For instance, in 1965 the 110 miles of the Patuxent River, which drains over 9 percent of Maryland's territorial landmass, produced an average of 235 tons of silt per square river mile annually.[14] And the Patuxent is

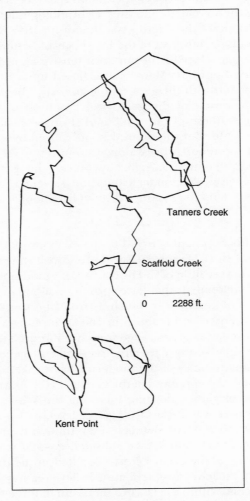

A computer-generated re-creation of Kent Fort Manor in 1802.
Courtesy University of Baltimore

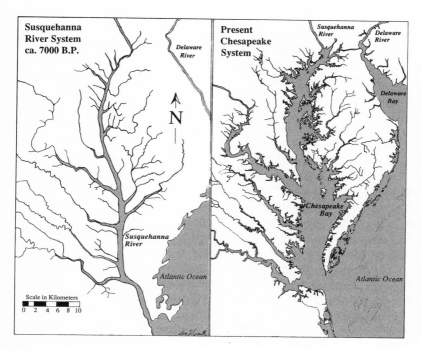

A schematic comparison of the probable Chesapeake and
Delaware Bay regions circa 7000 B.P. with today.

but one of 48 river systems, with 102 branches flowing into the Chesapeake. The impact upon an estuarine system currently averaging only 27.4 feet in depth was, is, and will continue to be significant.

Many islands and archipelagoes have been severely damaged if not altogether lost. Sharps Island, for example, off the mouth of the Choptank, 800 acres or more in extent in the seventeenth century, had been reduced to 438 acres by 1848. By 1910 it was down to 53 acres. A 1915 study by J. F. Hunter predicted its complete demise by 1951. Hunter was off by only three years.[15] In 1965, geologists were estimating that 300 acres of land a year were being lost in the Chesapeake to erosion. The impact upon the low-lying island systems of the Chesapeake, such as Kent, Poplar, Tilghman, and others, and upon the Delmarva Peninsula itself, is predictable.

Given the abundance of documentary and archaeological evidence concerning prehistoric and historic settlement patterns along the waterways of the Tidewater, it was readily discernible to us that marine transgressions on the archaeological resource base, such as we suspected had occurred at Kent Island, have been, and will continue to be, significant. That such transgressions in the Chesapeake are not entirely destructive, however, had already been proven by a number of projects carried out

157

over the previous fifteen years. At the site of colonial London Town (Londontown), Maryland (1683-1776), during the first underwater archaeological survey in Maryland history, I located and surveyed (but not excavated) in the South River trash pits, a possible brick building foundation, and a barrel well which had survived the erosion process to become submerged archaeological sites.[16] Investigations that I had also directed at Point Lookout, Maryland, to locate and evaluate inundated resources related to Camp Hoffman, a massive Civil War prisoner-of-war installation and fortification complex, revealed that even fragile organic architectural components can survive marine and microbiotic assault in high-energy surf zones, given the right circumstances.[17] Even prehistoric sites had survived, as evidenced by archaeological discoveries in the Patuxent River between 1977 and 1980.[18] That such site preservation might exist in the waters surrounding Kent Island was therefore entirely possible, indeed probable.

Kent Island was no different from the rest of the Chesapeake island systems. All had been and would continue to be heavily affected by sea level rise and the resultant erosion processes. But how much had been lost since 1631, and at what rate? Was it indeed possible to accurately reconstruct the early seventeenth century coastline of Kent Island from a synthesis of the geological and historical record? Fortunately, extensive environmental research focusing on the problems of erosion loss had recently been carried out and conveniently dovetailed with our own inquiry. A 1988 Critical Areas study of the fifty-nine miles of Queen Anne's County, Maryland, shoreline, much of which belonged to Kent Island, had documented loss rates precisely. The study had revealed that 57 percent of the shoreline was losing up to two feet a year, 29 percent from two to four feet per year, 7 percent from four to eight feet, and 4 percent more than eight feet. At the same time only 3 percent was adding land through accretion. Along Eastern Bay on the south and Chester River on the north, where the shoreline is protected from prevailing wind-driven wave attack, erosion rates were measurable over the long run but relatively minor over the short run. On the Chesapeake, or western side, of the island, with its dramatic long fetch, erosion was the most severe, especially at the northernmost and southernmost tips of the island.[19]

The historic record indicated that the settlement established in 1631 was substantial, multifaceted, and dynamic. By late 1637, six years after its founding, it boasted a population of 120 men and their families, possibly as many as 300 souls, which was barely a score shy of the number of immigrants who had come over aboard *Ark* and *Dove*. With its defenses, buildings, industry, and agriculture, it had become a major settlement in every sense of the word. Here had been established the first fort, church, plantations, brewery, mills, and industrial production center (for staves) in what would one day be Maryland. Buildings of brick and thatch alike, windmills, fenced fields of tobacco, corn, and cattle, and even a shipyard had been erected long before Lord Baltimore's colony had even been planted. Here was a complex English society replete with the trappings of English law, the Anglican Church, free trade, slavery, indentured servitude, agriculture, and industry. The first white woman to make her appearance on the upper Chesapeake had made her home on Kent Island, as had the first black slaves and white indentured servants. Unquestionably, the archaeological record of Kent Island Hundred and its vital nucleus, the Kent Fort settlement, was once substantial. Its continued existence beneath the waters of the Chesapeake was a definite possibility.

All we had to do was find it.

❏ ❏ ❏

John Kiser brought *Thunderhorse* to a stable anchor 800 yards off the mouth of Scaffold Creek at 10:30 A.M. With a young midshipman to assist me, I immediately set off in a Zodiac to take soundings along the nearshore and determine the best position to establish a datum and transit station on the beach. Mike remained on board to coordinate operations by radio. Unfortunately, the weather refused to cooperate. By noon the surf was kicking up even more than we had anticipated and I was obliged to work 150 yards offshore to prevent being capsized. A freezing saltwater spray, skimmed from the froth of whitecaps, did its best to chill us to the marrow and dilute our enthusiasm. Still, we persisted in assembling as much bottom data as possible before returning to the boat to pick up McNamara, the first group of navy divers, and survey gear for the ferry ride to shore. By now, the sky had darkened into a canopy of thick, gunmetal-gray clouds, and a fine, wind-driven rain had begun to fall.

As the Zodiac circled, awaiting a hole in the breakers to run ashore and offload, my walkie-talkie crackled. It was Pohuski: *Thunderhorse's* anchor was losing its hold in the soft bottom against the wind and waves. But worse, a northeaster was rushing down on us and would be hitting within an hour or two. Storm warnings and small-craft advisories had been issued for the entire upper Bay region. The day's effort would have to be scrubbed. The Claiborne Project was, indeed, off to an awful start.

Pohuski was despondent at the inauspicious beginning. But the storm that lashed the Bay for the next eighteen hours proved a blessing in disguise, for a freak weather condition rare to the Chesapeake had prevailed. Referred to by Bay watermen as a "blowout," the condition was caused by a combination of strong northerly winds and extremely low tides. The consequences of the blowout were to force vast amounts of water southward and out of the Bay and to cause the complete exposure of great tracts of bottomland, normally covered by three to five feet of water, even at low tide. The Chesapeake had, incredibly, rolled back her mantle to reveal the secrets hidden within her bosom.

Melted Beads

Early on the morning of December 3, taking advantage of this unique blessing, Pohuski and McNamara began to walk the exposed shoals off Kent Island. Near the mouth of Hullica Snooze, the two investigators stopped in their muddy tracks. For here, temporarily exposed by the blowout, they encountered what would soon prove to be the first dramatic evidence of William Claiborne's long-lost settlement.

FOURTEEN

Well, Well, Well

Among the many definitions that *Webster's New Collegiate Dictionary* heaps upon the word *well* is that of "a pit or hole sunk into the earth to reach a supply of water."[1] When most of us think of a well, we see a quaint little brick structure, sheltered by a red tiled roof, beside some bucolic country byway, with a fair-haired maiden lowering a bucket into its crystal spring. In many children's stories, it is the hiding place for trolls, treasures, or dashing heroes escaping the king's men. But for Michael Pohuski and Joe McNamara, on that cold December morning in 1989, the remnants of three primitive barrel and box wells they had discovered on the bottom of Eastern Bay, where dry land had once been, now exposed by the blowout, held the potential keys to the successful search for Kent Fort.

There really wasn't much to see, merely the circular outline of two barrel tops and a single square box, reinforced by timber braces, all of them eroded almost level with the Bay floor. Indeed, a casual bather wading these waters under normal circumstances would have had a difficult time even stubbing a toe on one. Yet these finds excited both investigators. Of particular interest was the presence of a fragment of dark green bottle glass common to the seventeenth and early eighteenth centuries, partially buried beside one of the barrels.

Quickly, the two men took out their measuring tapes and compasses to triangulate and record the positions of the three features relative to a datum established at the end of a line of riprap along the shore and to a pair of nearby concrete breakwaters. The thirty-three-inch square box well, designated as Well No. 1, was only twenty-seven feet four inches from the riprap datum. Well No. 2, a thirty-nine-inch diameter barrel well, was fifty-two feet seaward, and Well No. 3, only two feet in diameter, was eighty-seven feet six inches from the datum.[2]

The discovery of the barrel and box wells was a stroke of fortune that would have been overlooked by most laymen. But both investigators were exhilarated at the promise the wells held—both as architectural features and for the diagnostic data they might contain within. They knew that the sites were nothing less than potential calendars of the unwritten past.

Ever since the first well shaft had been dug by prehistoric man in search of fresh water, abandoned wells have also served as receptacles for house-

161

hold refuse. For the archaeologist, as Ivor Noël Hume once wrote, "wells hold all the promise of both privies and rubbish pits; the moisture preserves organic materials and metals, as well as cushioning the fall of large objects and enabling them to be recovered intact."[3]

Why would one want to fill a well with refuse? And why would a well be abandoned in the first place? There are, of course, many answers. Common sense dictated that an unused, open well would become a danger to

The remains of a colonial box well, designated Well No. 1.
Photograph by Michael Pohuski

Well No. 2, a barrel well, may well have been constructed as early as 1631 and remained open as late as 1725. Photograph by Michael Pohuski

Well, Well, Well

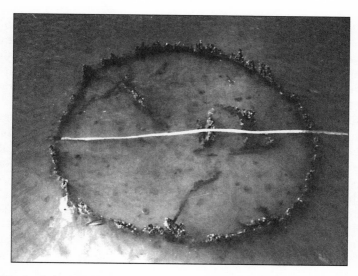

Well No. 3, a barrel well opened about the time of the closure of Well No. 2, near the beginning of the eighteenth century, was undoubtedly a distinct improvement over its predecessor. A primitive filtering system was discovered in its base during archaeological excavation of the site in 1990. Photograph by Michael Pohuski

people and animals alike and had to be filled for the sake of safety. Wells were abandoned for a variety of reasons: contamination of the water supply; the water supply fails and a new shaft must be opened to replace the last; property boundaries change and the site of a well becomes inconvenient; or the area in which a well was erected is abandoned and later reoccupied as a result of natural causes, social unrest, and so forth. But one fact was immutable: wells were frequently abandoned and filled more often than not with the detritus of the society that built it. Throwing rubbish into a well disposed of it for good. But as one archaeologist once aptly noted, one man's trash is another's window to the past.[4]

The method of well construction varied little from the Romans of the first century A.D. to the English settlers in the Tidewater of the seventeenth and eighteenth centuries. Shallow wells such as those dug by William Claiborne's contemporaries at Jamestown and Accomac rarely exceeded fourteen feet in depth and the construction technique employed was simple. First, a hole somewhat bigger than the intended well shaft was excavated, after which a wood, barrel, or brick lining would be built from the bottom. As the structure was completed, the area surrounding the shaft lining would be backfilled in the same manner as a builder's trench surrounding house footings. Frequently, fragments of building materials, trash, and other contemporary components of the period of construction would be deposited in the backfill, providing a *terminus post quiem,* or date of origin. The tradition of the box wells, once favored by the Romans, was frequently used in the Chesapeake region in the seventeenth century.[5] The wooden box well form was built up from frames of mortised timber and laid in the base of a squared pit. As the well was built, the hole around it was backfilled with stones, gravel, and brick rubble, which would serve as a water filter.

Another common well form of the seventeenth century Tidewater frontier was the barrel well. To construct a barrel well, one was merely obliged to knock the ends out of the barrels and stack them one on top of the other. A more refined variation of the stacked barrel well was the sleeved well, which consisted of an inner and outer sleeve of barrels, often with the spacing between them stuffed with crushed chalk to act as a filter. A third variation was the cased barrel well, that is, stacked or sleeved barrels reinforced by a wooden box casing. Box and barrel wells were usually less than thirty feet from the dwellings, as evidenced from at least seven sites excavated between 1934 and 1958 at Jamestown and eight sites excavated in 1987 near the mouth of Nassawadex Creek in Virginia.[6] Significantly, all of the aforementioned wells had been constructed during the seventeenth century (although box wells dating from as late as the mid-nineteenth century had been discovered and archaeologically excavated on the Mississippi, at Lucy, Louisiana).[7]

With the growth of English civilization in the Tidewater and the retreat of the frontier, the more primitive barrel and box wells were replaced by brick or stone wells by the early eighteenth century, possibly because the earlier well types, though easy to construct, frequently proved as unhealthy as they were useful. As early as 1610, Sir Thomas Gates noted that the Jamestown water supply came from a well "fed by the brackish River owzing into it from whence I verily believe, the chiefe causes have proceeded of many diseases and sicknesses which have happened to our people. . . ."[8] Nor was the hazard limited to those who would consume the water, for those who constructed such wells were also in jeopardy. "When you dig for a Well," wrote one Richard Neve in 1703 about the construction of wells in England, "great Care ought to be taken not only in stewing the Sides, to keep the Earth from falling in upon the Workmen; but to take Care that the Effluvia's of the Water (if bad) do not hurt them; for it has been often found, that the Water which is under the Earth, hath many bad Qualities, and emits Vapours, which often stifle those that work in the Well, after it has been dug."[9]

The signs for Michael Pohuski and Joe McNamara, however, were anything but foul. An interview with local property owner Fred Skove, whose house and yard abutted the waters in which the wells had been found, revealed that the site had been known to him for several years, and he had a dried-out, shrunken barrel stave to prove it. Both Skove and his next-door neighbor, Wayne Mason, had bulkheaded their waterfronts only recently (and at great expense) to halt severe erosion of their property. Mason revealed that during the construction of his bulkhead, he had been obliged to backfill a large area on the landward side of the structure, and in so doing had buried beneath ten feet of soil yet another well. He had saved several of the wedged-shaped brickbats, known as compass bricks (suggesting eighteenth century construction), with which it had been originally built .

Invigorated by their discoveries, the two investigators continued their reconnaissance at an accelerated pace. Off the mouth of Hullica Snooze, an unidentifiable wooden structure, barely discernible but of obvious human manufacture as indicated by the presence of wooden treenails, was found embedded in the bottom muds. Was it the fragments of a forgotten shipwreck cast into the shoals, the foundations of an eroded waterfront structure now inundated and buried, or merely floating debris that had finally settled to the bottom? The questions abounded and each question spun off into a dozen avenues of inquiry. Could the site be related to the tales of the origins of the unique name of the creek? Some said that Hullica Snooze was a derivative of Hooligan's Noose, the site where Leonard Calvert, according to folk tales, had executed Claiborne's faithful lieutenants, Tom Smith and Edward Beckler. Or had the executions been carried out on Scaffold Creek, to the north, as others championed? Jackie Ringgold, a veteran waterman living near Chestertown who had worked the shoals off the Snooze for years, had run into the remnants of a worm-eaten structure, possibly a wreck, with his dredge more than once and had recovered wood fragments to prove it. Waterman Steve Ruth had reported finding glass bottles, brick fragments, and other artifacts, including the lead top of an ancient inkwell, from the same area. The area was a potential archaeological hotbed but not nearly as hot as the Kent Point shoals.[10]

Jackie Ringgold had informed the two investigators that approximately twenty years earlier, while clamming off Kent Point immediately southwest of the Snooze sites, in less than five feet of water on a hard clay bottom, he had dredged across a concentration of bricks and pottery, sorted through the spoils, and kept some of the more interesting samples. One of the most prominent finds, recovered three hundred to four hundred feet south of Kent Point, had been a Bellarmine seal sherd featuring the right-side profile of a hook-nosed aristocratic-looking man wearing a crown of laurel and a mustache that flowed back to below the ear. He had given the piece to waterman Steve Ruth as a gift years later. The redware sherd dated from the end of the sixteenth century and was the second-oldest piece of pottery to come from the waters of Kent Island.[11]

Despite the promise offered by such random discoveries, Pohuski and McNamara failed to relocate the concentrations of pottery and brick off the Snooze or Kent Point during the blowout. The bottom, they discov-

Melted Beads

A Bellarmine fragment recovered by a waterman from the waters of Kent Point, only a few hundred feet from shore, dates from the end of the sixteenth century. Photograph by Michael Pohuski

ered, was no longer exposed clay but had been covered by shifting sands that masked features that may once have been exposed.

The two investigators were now nearing the end of their first tantalizing reconnaissance. The watery mantle, which had briefly been removed to expose the seldom-seen bottomlands of the Kent Island nearshore, had returned. The last hours of daylight would thus be devoted to exploring inland anomalies reported in the Maryland Geological Survey's archaeological site files and from data extracted from the archival collections of the late Mildred Schoch, a noted collector of Kent Island lore and history. Of special interest were the ruins of foundations of an unidentified brick structure,[12] known to but a few locals who simply referred to it as "the old trench." [13]

Pohuski and McNamara discovered the site amid a dense copse of trees, strangled and all but invisible beneath thick vines and ground cover. As the two men quickly began to clear away enough underbrush to examine the brick-strewn ruins, they became increasingly excited. The cold December sun was lowering toward the horizon, casting tall shadows in the late afternoon. Finally, amid the bracken and vines, the site was revealed. It was a collapsed burial vault.

❏　❏　❏

On January 27, 1990, we prepared to clear the vault in its entirety, to document its architecture, and to discern everything we could from its remains short of a full-scale excavation of the surrounding features. There had been no mention of such a structure in any of the title or prob records we had surveyed, and its very identity and age were a mystery

The structure once possessed an arched brick roof, which had long since collapsed. A spread of brick, partially buried in the soils to the west of the site, had probably been removed from it, undoubtedly when a wooden roof had been put in. From the rotting timber lying on the floor, with machine-cut wire nails still in place, it was obvious that the roof had been of recent origins, at least after 1850, and most likely during this century. The caps of several shotgun shells and decoy fragments suggested that the vault had probably been recently used for a duck hunter's blind.

The structure was in poor condition, with its southern side and eastern end, through which one entered, in danger of imminent collapse. A four-foot-long and one-foot-wide gray stone, which had once served either as a stepping stone down into the vault or, more likely, as a lintel across the head of the door, all but blocked the entrance. At the southern end, a semicircular section of brickwork opposite the door had obviously been rebuilt using modern Portland cement, most likely during the early twentieth century. The structure measured seven feet two inches long and eight feet eight inches wide at the floor, with the exterior at nine feet two inches wide, twelve feet two inches long, and five feet two inches high at its western and most complete end. Five rose-headed nails were still embedded in the shell-flecked concrete matrix of the door jamb, indicating possible colonial construction. The extant brickwork of the original structure was a three-course common bond, standard during the latter half of the eighteenth and early nineteenth centuries. That the structure

Local legends suggested that the Kent Island Vault Site may have served as a temporary burial for English soldiers who died during the British occupation of the island in the War of 1812. Although the brickwork in the structure was common to the latter half of the eighteenth through the early nineteenth century, the vault's use by the British, who were encamped nearly fifteen miles away at the north end of the island, seems unlikely.

had been intended as a vault was suggested by the presence of a narrow ledge running along both sides of the building, a feature most commonly found in vault design of the eighteenth and early nineteenth centuries. The ledge, as architectural historian Orlando Ridout V later pointed out, was used as a prop for the wood "centering" that supports the masonry vault while it is being laid up. Once the vault was completed and the mortar had set, the centering was knocked out and removed.

It was a unique "rediscovery," for few such structures were known to exist in the Maryland Tidewater. Although the structure had been noted, no one had paid it the least bit of attention or attempted to put it in a historical context. Ironically, one of the most recent vault finds had been in 1987 at the site of Darnall's Chance, near my home in Upper Marlboro, and was being excavated even as we worked on Kent by archaeologist Donald Creveling, of the Maryland National Capital Park and Planning Commission.[14] Of greater interest were the similarities of the two vaults; both featured similar brickwork and design. But when had ours been built?

Ridout noted that the earliest dated examples of three-course bond brickwork in the Tidewater were in a house of the mid-1740s in Cecil County, Maryland. "This is an exceptionally early example, however, and seems more likely that we have a Federal period structure," he wrote after reviewing our findings. "The general character of the bricks reinforces my feeling of dating—they appear Federal in character rather than colonial."[15] It wasn't exactly what we wanted to hear, but it was clear that Kent Island had many secrets yet to yield.

Despite the false start to the project, the discovery of both the wells and the vault had provided us with an impetus to move forward with confidence to implement our project design, beginning with an intensive aerial photographic survey of the south end of the island and adjacent water, followed by site-specific ground truthing of the target area in representative transects. All we needed was the money to do it.

Infrared

The $175 charter flight of the little Piper Cherokee that took off from Bay Bridge Airport on the morning of February 8, 1990, was one of the best birthday presents Michael Pohuski's wife, Barbara, could have given him. His project had so far failed to secure any financial support, and the continuing field recons and archival research were being funded entirely out of the four principal investigators' pockets. All were prepared to accept any aid possible—including the gift of an aerial photographic survey of southern Kent Island.

When the plane swung out over Chesapeake Bay, Pohuski's assistant ignored the scenic view of the Bay Bridge, far below, as he readied several banks of cameras loaded with false-color infrared and Ektachrome film and high-resolution VHS videotape. To aid field investigations as well as the aerial survey, the southern end of the island had been divided into ten discrete survey transects, beginning at Kent Point and running north as far as Chews Creek on the Chesapeake side and across to the headwaters of Tanners Creek on the Eastern Bay side. Target areas would also include potential seventeenth- and eighteenth-century sites outside of the ten transects, on Warehouse Creek, Philpots Island, off Matapeake, and off Chesapeake Estates, as well as sampling units selected from earlier historic map evaluations. Three complete runs were to be made along specified flight lines above each targeted transect or site, at altitudes varying from 250 feet over water to 1,000 feet over land, to produce overlapping individual pictures as well as continuous video. The first pass over each target was to be a video run, the second would be devoted to infrared (IR), and the last to true-color photography. It was imperative that the flight be conducted on a cloudless day, when the tide was lowest and good water visibility prevailed, preferably during the early morning hours with eastern sunlight. Only on three days in February would predicted tide and weather conditions coincide in Michael's favor. February 8 would be the first, and proved, as weather degenerated throughout the month, the only day favorable for the aerial photosurvey.

The aerial remote-sensing survey was primarily intended to assist in detecting hitherto unknown sites, distribution patterns, spatial data, and features over a relatively large area of land and shallow water. The surficial geological framework of the target areas would be detectable through differences in color chroma and tone. These differences are influenced by vegetation and moisture in underlying deposits on land areas. The survey would provide superb delineation of bare-earth areas in which archaeological sites are undetectable up close. Ground-cover types, soils, geological features, and other environmental photointerpretive characteristics could be precisely charted, providing data on contemporary as well as earlier parameters for habitation. In the wide band of shoals surrounding the southern end of the island, the spectral signatures of features such as scars, stream-delta channels, shellfish beds, and even man-made features such as collapsed wharves, ruined jetties, and, we hoped, clues to inundated archaeological sites would be detectable through the use of false-color IR. A great deal of reliance was to be placed on the use of both true-color and IR film transparencies, as opposed to black-and-white negative film, for they provided superior color rendition, definition, and flexibility of use, both interpretively and diagnostically.

The photointerpretation data would later be transferred directly onto the project base maps. The ten transects forming our study area would then be broken down into manageable sampling units for hands-on field investigations and ground truthing, both on land and in the water. These units would be documented and, if conditions were right, evaluated through surface collection and/or test excavation.

As the little Cherokee approached Kent Point, Michael Pohuski strapped on his safety harness and leaned out. The freezing winter wind numbed his face as he picked out the tiny features and well-defined shoreline a thousand feet below, an area that we had begun to scour only two months earlier. He could see the markers he had erected near the three barrel wells, and to the west the copse of trees in which the mysterious burial vault was hidden from all but the most discerning eyes.[1] But of the greatest interest were the strange dark splotches in the water. Then the cameras began to roll.

Within days after the aerial survey was completed, intensive evaluation of the IRs, color transparencies, and videotapes had begun. Working in Pohuski's well-equipped photography studio in downtown Baltimore, Fred Hopkins, Michael, and I pored over hundreds of photo images, transferring data to larger site maps, quadrangles, and the master base map. An amazing array of detail began to dot each transect, on land and in the water. A delightful panoply of features appeared at the edge of the undersea dropoff off the Snooze and in the shoals off Kent Point, near Green Point, below Chews Creek, in Tanners Creek, off Long Point, off Philpots Island, and at a score of other places. A peculiar unidentified feature, estimated to be over 150 feet in length, appeared in the nearshore of Kent Point. And elsewhere along the coast, the shoally bottomland close to shore, festooned with hundreds of small black and gray craters,

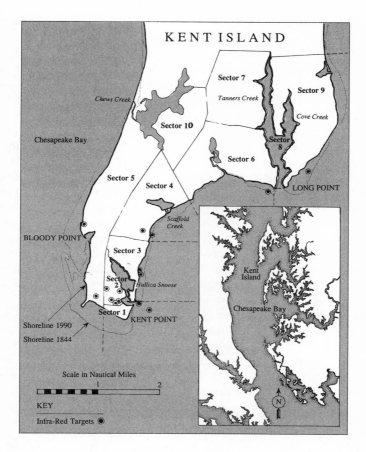

Kent Island survey transects.

appeared as if it had been carpet-bombed. Ashore, scars and depressions and subtle color variations invisible to the naked eye on the ground were clearly revealed in the fields near the tip of the island and near the vault. The ghostly images of paths and walkways long since forgotten were now plainly defined crisscrossing unplowed fields and across the expansive yards of the larger estates. And on the shores, the signs of erosion were everywhere.

The next phase of the project—the systematic comparison of our data with aerial photographs of the same areas produced by the U.S. Department of Agriculture between 1952 and 1964 (the only holistic aerial photo survey of the area available), preliminary ground truthing of targets, and the identification of other features revealed by the aerial survey, on the land and in the water—began almost immediately. On February 18, even before the final transferral of data to the base map was completed, Pohuski and McNamara began field investigations of the targets.

The fieldwork was rewarded almost instantly—and with some surprising finds. Several of the scars and mottled color images led them to concentrations of brick fragments and pipe stems, particularly in the vicinity of the vault ruins. Failed breakwaters, long ago enveloped by the sea, were everywhere, offering sad evidence of the relentless persistence of the Chesapeake. The long, unidentified feature just offshore at Kent Point, adjacent to a private marina cut, was perhaps among the most unusual breakwaters discovered. Approximately 150 feet long and 8 feet wide, it was constructed of hundreds upon hundreds of tombstones. When exposed at low water, these markers of past lives, torn from the resting place of people long forgotten, awash and eroded by the unceasing actions of the sea, posed both a stunning and moving sight. An examination of the names inscribed on the stones indicated that the markers had originally been erected in a graveyard (or graveyards) with a largely Germanic population. The stones, trucked in from somewhere in Baltimore at a cost of fifty dollars a ton, we later discovered, ranged in date from the early nineteenth to mid-twentieth centuries.

The tombstone breakwater was not the only such structure of rather unusual composition to be discovered protecting (or attempting to protect) the shores of Kent Point from erosion. Much of the southernmost tip of the island, east of the failed graveyard breakwater and south of Hullica Snooze, belongs to Jack Willard, an amiable man who, like many Kent Islanders, has fought the good fight against the Chesapeake. Willard's tenuous victory, or more appropriately, holding action, did not

Aerial infrared photograph revealing sand wave action near Long Point.
Photograph by Michael Pohuski

Infrared

A failed breakwater, discovered as a result of the aerial infrared survey of lower Kent Island, proved to be unique, composed entirely of gravestones.

come cheap. An expensive riprap stone bulkhead had to be constructed along the entire eastern frontage of his property. Willard's works are composed of some of the more interesting building materials. The stone, Willard said, had been procured, sight unseen, from a contractor and trucked all the way over from Washington, D.C., after the great race riots of the 1960s. Much consisted of granite blocks, cornices, and circular sandstone pillar sections which, he was informed, had been removed from the rubble of a Washington church damaged during the riots.

Although the tombstone breakwater and the Willard riprap were anything but relevant to the Claiborne settlement, they were certain to momentarily confound the unwitting marine archaeologist of the future who happened upon them. Just how could any rational explanation be made to explain the presence of a German graveyard and a Washington church resting serenely beneath Chesapeake waters?

A hundred yards south of the Snooze, we identified yet another anomaly. This time, it was the remains of a large wooden vessel, broken in half and driven ashore by some past storm. The wreck was identified

Melted Beads

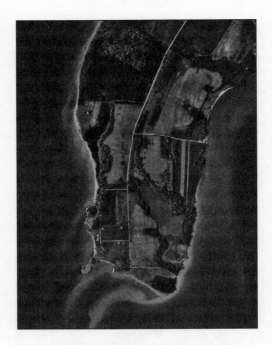

A 1964 aerial photo of Kent Point.
Courtesy National Archives and Record Service

Bloody Point today reveals evidence of repeated attempts to hold back the Bay
and stem the erosion that may have claimed the Claiborne settlement and
other early colonial sites on Kent Island. Photograph by Michael Pohuski

as that of a barge of late-nineteenth- or early-twentieth-century construction. As continual reconnaissance efforts were carried out over the next year to monitor erosion along the shore, the wreck was discovered to be migratory and had left evidence of its visit at several separate locations. Lifted from one spot by occasionally high flood tides, or during a storm, she would float along the Kent coast and eventually be deposited at a new location. How many times, we wondered, had this sad old boat been moved in pursuit of her final resting place?

One of the more relevant targets we visited lay along a stretch of beach to the immediate north and south of Scaffold Creek. Here we discovered the remains of a large shell midden eroding from the shoreline and now bisected by the meandering creek. Pottery sherds and lithics suggested the midden was of the Middle to Late Woodland period (A.D. 200–1600). The midden's discovery brought to mind the comments of one noted Englishman's first encounter with the Native American's favorite seafood. In April 1607, Sir George Percy, one of the founders of Jamestown, encountered a party of natives at Cape Henry: "We came to a place [Cape Henry] where they [the natives] had a great fire and had been roasting oysters. When they perceived our coming, they fled away to the mountains and left many of the oysters in the fire. We ate some of the oysters which were very large and delicate in taste."[2] Was it possible that the natives who had created the piles of shells after innumerable feasts near the creek were the ancestors of those amiable Matapeakes who had greeted Claiborne's settlers in 1631? Had the Kent Islanders themselves contributed their own shell pile to the heap when they had been faced with starvation during the tragic Evelin administration in 1637?

Although the ground truthing of targets revealed by the aerial photographic survey had just begun, apparently more questions were being posed by the findings than were being answered. And the underwater anomalies had yet to be tested.

We soon began to explore and examine hundreds of locales on the southern end of Kent Island, each of which was blessed with its own unique peculiarity. On our first visit to Craney Creek, on a freezing, gray winter morning, ice lay heavy on the little waterway, with a cloud of mist hugging the shoreline and utter stillness prevailing everywhere. It was a scene of incredible visual pleasure, not unlike a seventeenth century Japanese watercolor. We visited historic Romancoke Wharf, where one of the grandest views of Eastern Bay at sunrise is to be savored. We hiked the edges of Tanners Creek, which were still beautifully festooned with wild geese riding at anchor amidst rime ice bordering the shores, and explored to the tip of Tanners Point. Although Berkeley and Hale had placed the settlement here on this eminently defensible peninsula, a survey by archaeologist Kit Wesler in 1983 had failed to discover any evidence of seventeenth-century occupation.[3] It was clear that Wesler had been cor-

Melted Beads

Tanner's Creek, believed by many to have been the site of the William Claiborne settlement. Courtesy National Archives

rect in his assessment of the site: there was a total absence of archaeological evidence supporting the Tanners Point location as the site for the Claiborne settlement. Indeed, as Hopkins pointed out during our investigation, the waterways shouldering the peninsula could hardly have hosted an oceangoing sailing vessel such as *Africa*, owing to the extreme narrowness of the entry passage, the swift downstream currents, and the prevailing northwest winds which would have obliged any vessel to beat hard against the wind to enter.

We visited potential sites on Batts Neck and scoured the shores of Warehouse Creek, Chews Creek, and Bloody Point. We walked and rewalked the beaches around the entire southern end of the island, meeting local residents, evaluating private collections of artifacts, and documenting eroded sites and artifact concentrations as we went. We shovel tested a forty-year-old spoil pile composed of sand and gray clay dredged from the Snooze and intently studied and analyzed its sparse contents of coal, charcoal fragments, and nineteenth-century glass and pottery sherds. We poled and pushed a small johnboat into the Snooze and up the marshy, mucky channels of Scaffold Creek to probe the bottoms for structures and possible wrecks whose locations had been related to us by local inhabitants or revealed by the aerial photography. Our testing of targets seemed endless. One thing, however, was becoming abundantly clear: aside from the prehistoric sites, only sites later than the end of the eighteenth century were in apparent evidence ashore.

Nevertheless, our search was a source of endless personal pleasure, for along the way we met marvelous, straight-talking islanders who took us out with them on their boats and into their shops and homes, fed us pie and coffee, told us tales of their lands and waters and of the way it used to be before the developers came. We attended the meetings of the Kent Island Heritage Society in the modest county library at Stevensville, and we gorged ourselves at the local firehouse bull roast. We besieged watermen with questions. And we listened attentively as the islanders told us of their heritage and spoke of William Claiborne in almost reverential tones.

Few island natives have any dealings with the folks of the western shore or the bureaucrats and "establishment" historians in Annapolis and Baltimore who had ignored or stonewalled Kent Island's claim to hosting the site of the first European settlement in the state. There were vested interests elsewhere supporting Maryland's presently acknowledged founding father, namely Lord Baltimore, they told us, that could not afford to be challenged by an avowed foe, and a hated Virginian at that, namely William Claiborne. Several curmudgeonly "oysterbacks," irate over the state's perennial refusal to put up a historic marker, had even spoken of secession, the islanders said, until a marker had been grudgingly erected on the superhighway leading to the Bay Bridge.

Yet, history was everywhere, seeping from the land and sea, circulating in the veins of the natives, and transfused to the newcomers. Some islanders, such as waterman Billy Baxter, could trace their lineage directly back to the settlers of 1631. Others, later immigrants to the island, such as the famed marine biologist and centenarian Dr. Reginald Truitt, were no less zealous in their spirited support of their adopted heritage.[4]

The legends and myths that had become inextricably blended with island history had served to unite many of the islanders in a common bond alien to the suburban societies of other regions of our state. It was, moreover, a blend decidedly unacceptable to the purportedly biased establishment history of Maryland and to the state-funded institutions that had championed the founding father icons. The absence of material archaeological evidence had served only to reinforce the historic prejudice. After all, if Claiborne's settlement had been so important, why was it that not a single sherd, brick, or bead with verifiable archaeological provenance had ever been found?

For many, there was a willingness to accept *any* potential evidence of linkage to the Claiborne past. Two small "millstones," discovered in 1957 near Craney Creek and ensconced on the estate of former Delaware Governor Elbert N. Carvel at the purported site of Crayford, had been enthusiastically adopted by the islanders as the stones imported by Claiborne for the island's first mills.[5] The authenticity of the stones had even been attested to by Eric Isaacs himself. Unfortunately, a reexamination of the two items by Hopkins and me revealed them to be little more than poured concrete post or stanchion bases of modern manufacture.

Among the most ardent proponents of "the Claiborne thing" (as some islanders called it) were the watermen—clammers, oyster divers, and fishermen—who regularly worked the waters off Kent Island and knew the bottoms like the veins on the sunburnt backs of their own weathered hands. One such man was Fountain John Davidson, a rugged, bearish, furnace-faced, sixty-five-year-old islander and vice president of a Baltimore construction firm, who has carried on a lifelong love affair with the Chesapeake. Davidson managed the Carvel estate in his spare time and had devoted every other moment hunting on or fishing around the island. Once, while escorting us about the Carvel property in his pickup, he regaled us with tales of his many adventures hunting the redoubtable island foxes, geese, and other critters; of the tragedies and amusing anecdotes of island history; and of the terrible invasion of his beloved Kent by western shore yuppies.

Davidson's experiences on the waters off Kent, however, like those of most of the watermen we met, both sportsmen and professionals, were of enormous interest to us. His accounts were typical of the lot. While he was fishing at one favorite spot, approximately five hundred yards off a certain

A Rhenish blue-gray stoneware jug of the early seventeenth century was dredged from the waters off Long Point by a Kent Island waterman. It is typical of materials of the period of the Claiborne settlement which have been found only in the water and not on land. Photograph by Michael Pohuski

point on the west side of the island, his anchor had become wedged in an obstruction in eighteen feet of water. When the anchor was finally retrieved, it had come up with mud and small, smooth, gray stones six to eight inches in diameter lodged around it. The event occurred not once, but on several occasions in the years thereafter at the same location. When he finally brought out an oyster diver to examine the site, the diver discovered a large spread of bricks lying on a sandy bottom and, on another visit to the site (which had been altered somewhat by the currents), had found two corners of a brick foundation, standing a full three feet off the bottom, and the top of a circular brick well.

Typical seventeenth century ceramics recovered in clam dredging operations from the waters surrounding Kent Island. Photograph by Michael Pohuski

Colonial musket flints from inundated sites off Kent Island recovered by clam dredgers. Photograph by Michael Pohuski

Another islander, a waterman-cum-blacksmith named Bobby Aarons, who regularly works the waters with his clam rig, had dredged up pipe stems from the Davidson site, while also encountering a spread of brick, in a north-south alignment and approximately sixty feet long along a strip named Brickhouse Bar. Aarons had also discovered a shipwreck, approximately sixty-five to seventy feet in length and 16 feet abeam, in 1970 off the Queen Anne Marina. By running his clam dredge right up the center of the wreck, he managed to recover four intact earthenware cups and a number of pipe-stem fragments (undoubtedly while inflicting great damage to the wreck itself in the process), but was unable to relocate the site later on.[6]

One of the most magnificent finds recovered by a dredger had been an intact gray Rhenish stoneware jug with cobalt blue floral motif. The piece had been brought up by clammer Reverdy Saddler off Long Point, in the vicinity of one of the untested anomalies revealed by our aerial survey. But it was only one of many elegant artifacts to be recovered from the waters off Kent Island. In my view, however, one of the most beautiful sherds to be found was a Westerwald medallion dredged up by James Coursey, a waterman from Wye Mills, while working his clamming vessel *Vigilante.* This almost-perfect jug fragment, though somewhat discolored by the bottom muds, had been produced in the Westerwald district of the Rhineland and had been incised, stamped, sprigged, and painted with cobalt blue decorations, with the large letters "GR" (George Rex) topped by an unpainted crown. The piece had probably been produced during the reign of the first Hanoverian King of England, George I (1701–27), for export to the American colonies.[7]

One of the most avid relic collectors among the watermen of Kent is Billy Baxter, who claims direct descent from Roger Baxter, who had arrived on Kent Island with William Claiborne. Billy Baxter is a friendly fellow, proud of his heritage and his trade, which rarely takes him more than a few miles from his beloved island. His favorite line is, "I've been on Kent Island for over 350 years, and I have traveled thirteen miles to see the world." Baxter, who says he is fifty-four (but varies his age with a wink, and almost as frequently as the weather changes), had been a professional clam dredger for thirty-two years.[8] We went out with him one cold winter morning to obtain positions of several sites he knew about.

Commercial clamming is a relatively new industry on the Chesapeake and, owing to the declining clam population, is in danger of being one of the shortest-lived. Its focus is the harvesting of soft-shell clams, which are found locally throughout the Chesapeake Bay region. Yet, unlike crabs and oysters, which have traditionally been harvested for local markets, the soft-shell clamming industry in Maryland had been developed in the 1950s to serve New England, when the industry there could no longer meet consumer demand because of overfishing and disease. A typical dredge rig

Infrared

Inundated aboriginal sites are frequently encountered by watermen. This
Woodland Period pot, lithics, and other prehistoric artifacts were recovered
by clam dredgers near Eastern Bay. Photograph by Michael Pohuski

can be lowered to a depth of seventeen, eighteen, and even twenty feet
and dig a trench eighteen to twenty-four inches deep. In the process, not
only clams but inundated archaeological sites of every kind can be
discovered. And destroyed.[10]

Like many of his colleagues, Billy Baxter, in his more than three
decades of dredging the Chesapeake, has found scores of sites. On one
occasion, while working off the Thomas Point Light on a shoal that had
once been the Three Sisters Islands, he dredged up a sizable collection
of human remains, lithics, and pottery, enough to fill two large boxes. The
Smithsonian Institution was informed of his find, which proved to be an
inundated Middle Woodland site. But fear of losing access to this rich
clamming ground prompted Billy to keep the location secret.[11]

History was repeating itself. Baxter, like most of the clammers we met
during the project, was no different from the rugged and wary sponge
divers who had guided the pioneers of underwater archaeology in the
eastern Mediterranean to practically every underwater site of antiquity
found. Without the sponge divers, there would have been nothing, and
if the archaeological finds were to continue, the vested interests of the
divers could not be jeopardized.[12] The clammers of Kent Island were our
sponge divers, and their trust was imperative.

Clamming is the only form of underwater excavation exempt from
antiquities codes in Maryland, and many clammers such as Baxter, who
are antiquarians or relic collectors, wish to keep it that way. Yet most were
eager to share their knowledge and understanding of the history that they
alone for years have realized lay beneath the waters. Baxter, like many
other watermen, readily shared his knowledge, acquired from hard

decades of working the waters, with strangers whose only common link to him was a keen interest in Kent Island and the desire to explore, discover, touch, and document its past.

Billy worked his boat by instinct and experience and never used navigational equipment. He knew precisely where he was at all times by mentally triangulating his position from landmarks and by compensating for running time and data on his bottom sounder. And usually, on a clear day, he could put himself on the same site within fifty feet. Expensive navigation systems, radar, digital sounders, and the like, Billy said, were for the kids in the Department of Natural Resources marine police, and not for a real Bay waterman.[13]

For the Claiborne Project, however, dead reckoning wasn't enough if we hoped to return to any specific site for ground truthing for the archaeological record. A portable, hand-held global satellite positioning system receiver, called a Micrologic Voyager Sport NAV portable Loran C, was borrowed to provide us with accurate position and navigational data. With this thirty-ounce, hand-held unit on board, we could record the locations of any sites Billy Baxter or his colleagues chose to reveal to us. And the rewards were considerable.

On one of several exploratory voyages with Billy in early April, traveling from Matapeake to Bloody Point Light, we documented no fewer than four sites, including one shipwreck, two aboriginal sites, and a possible inundated colonial site. A photographic survey of Billy's artifact collections, which had been dredged up over the years, verified his claims. There were projectile points and axe heads from the Late Archaic to

Waterman Billy Baxter operates his clam dredger in the waters of Eastern Bay. Artifacts recovered by watermen provided important data on potential inundated seventeenth-century settlement sites off Kent Island. Photograph by Michael Pohuski

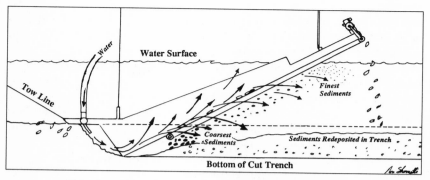

Side view plan of a hydraulic clam dredge in operation.

the Middle Woodland periods, stone pendants, scrapers, handmade bricks from the colonial era, silver spoons, a butt plate from a flintlock, blown-glass bottles, ceramic pitchers, pharmaceutical bottles of the nineteenth century, and potsherds from the seventeenth and eighteenth centuries. Billy's most prized recovery had been an intact colonial serving dish, possibly late seventeenth century, which had been donated to the Smithsonian and exhibited in the National Museum of History.[14] And Billy Baxter was but one of many who had been dredging the waters of Kent for the last thirty years.

❏ ❏ ❏

Ground truthing of underwater targets revealed by the aerial survey and local informants like Baxter was not as easily accomplished as land targets. The bottom of the Chesapeake, with tides, currents, and weather influencing conditions, is ever-changing. Sites exposed one day may be covered by sand and mud the next. Expensive remote-sensing equipment, such as magnetometers, side-scan sonar, and sub-bottom profilers, would likely prove unsuitable or deficient for our purposes owing to the types of buried targets, primarily small and nonferrous, which we were seeking. Although hands-on investigations might provide us with some clues (if bottom conditions permitted and the sites were not sanded over), actual underwater sampling strategies that were discrete and cost-effective, without major underwater excavation, had never been developed.

As we investigated numerous upland sites and examined private collections assembled from both dry land and from under water, it had become clear that seventeenth- and eighteenth-century materials were being recovered *only* from the water and not from the land. Our hypothesis that the major components of the Claiborne settlement were inundated seemed to be growing stronger. But nothing could be proven until controlled ground truthing was conducted underwater. Yet without funding, the best we could hope to accomplish was to identify anomalies that were exposed. At one of our frequent organizational meetings, I had even proposed the controlled use of a clammer's hydraulic dredge working in concert with an underwater observer.

The concept was not implausible, although it had never been done in the United States. There was, indeed, a certain paradox in that there was a substantial potential for site disturbance by advocating such use. However, watermen who were exempt from Maryland antiquities codes had already been doing it for nearly forty years, and with remarkable discoveries that few archaeologists had paid even the slightest attention to.

A dredge boat survey could be conducted, under supervision, like a land-based transect survey. Land-based surveys involved controlled shovel test pitting and trenching during preliminary archaeological reconnaissance or more intensive intervention with the mechanized removal or scraping of overlying soil (overburden). The most important factor, of course, would be the degree of archaeological control. When the survey was run with Loran-C, microwave positioning systems, or even land-based transits, then precision data assemblage and provenance for sites, transects and spatial distribution of artifacts could be assured. But as usual, funding was necessary, and we had as yet been unable to secure a sponsor, and among traditionalists, the suggested methodology was far from orthodox, and definitely controversial.

We had already spent a great deal of time and money preparing presentations and grant applications, but to little avail. On one typical fund-raising effort, Fred Hopkins, who was a member of the Maritime Committee of the Maryland Historical Society, had arranged for us to present a proposal to that organization, requesting fifty-seven hundred dollars. The society had just been the recipient of a three-hundred-thousand-dollar bequest from a noted maritime historian, the late Marion V. Brewington, and Fred thought we had a good shot at a small piece of it. After a well-received formal presentation to the committee in the Radcliffe Maritime Museum, all the signs were positive. One committee member was even heard to comment, "Hell, they will never find the damned site, but all we have done for the last five years is eat crab cakes every three months [at quarterly committee meetings]. Let 'em have the money. Maybe they'll get lucky." But it was not to be. The available money, we were told, was earmarked for bookshelves and a small exhibit in a proposed maritime center in Baltimore Harbor. "I've dug many dry holes in my time," Society Director Charles Lyle informed us, "and that's what you will be doing."[15] We later discovered the real reason for the lack of support. The society had been informed that the Maryland Historical Trust was now considering launching its own survey of the island waters, and the society was not about to spend its money on our modest endeavor when state professionals were about to enter the search.

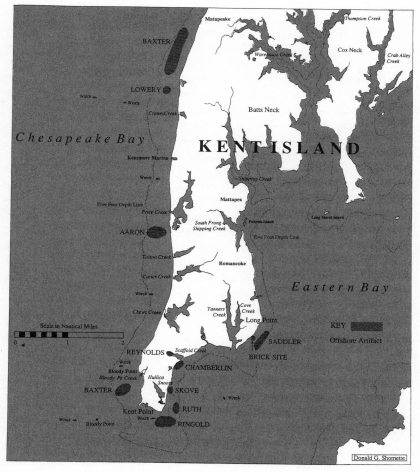

Distributions of offshore artifact concentrations
located by watermen and other collectors.

Later, when we made a similar formal pitch for support to the Kent
Island Heritage Society, our presentation was preceded by a lecture by
Orlando Ridout V, the senior architectural historian for the Trust, who
was there to solicit five thousand dollars in matching funds from the
islanders to permit a graduate student to conduct an archaeological
survey of the island. Despite our cordial relationship with the Heritage
Society and the Trust, it was impossible to compete with a state agency.

In the meantime, we had begun to conduct underwater investigations
of select targets provided by informants and the aerial survey. Targets
revealed a thousand feet off the Snooze by the infrared photos were
investigated by underwater radial surveys by divers but produced only

duck-blind pilings, several large stones, and sunken tree trunks. Several sites revealed to us by Baxter, Davidson, and Ringgold were visited in late April in waters from seven to twelve feet deep off Bloody Point and Kent Point. Again we conducted exhausting radial surveys, frequently against heavy currents and bottom sandstorms, which caused the terrain to alter by the minute. Nothing was found but a few modern derelict boats. The team was growing increasingly discouraged with each failure.

Finally, during an intensive, combined land-and-sea investigation off the Long Point and Tanners Creek transects, we finally struck pay dirt. Assisted by six volunteers and a borrowed twenty-four-foot boat, we had hoped to examine approximately twelve major anomalies in the area. One of the most significant targets had been revealed by a color aerial photograph of the Long Point transect as a dark, mottled area several hundred feet from shore, off a modern bulkheaded housing tract. When Joe and I plunged in from the boat to investigate, we were stunned to discover a large spread of densely compacted brick, mixed with some stone, distributed over a wide area in waist-high water and standing off the bottom a full eight inches. With zero visibility prevalent, we were obliged to investigate by touch and probes—perhaps not scientific, but adequate. We soon determined that we were on the top of a fair-sized site. With the resources at hand, we established a random datum, took shore coordinates and a Loran-C fix on the site, and began a radial surface survey at five-foot increments to determine the pattern of distribution.

The main concentration of brick was seventy-five feet in length and forty feet maximum width, with scatter extending even farther, and oriented roughly from north to south. A second, smaller concentration south-southeast of the main site was almost linear in shape. Unfortunately, no diagnostically useful artifacts were encountered, although we were all well aware that this was near where waterman Reverdy Saddler had dredged up several items, including an intact Rhenish stoneware jug of the seventeenth century. As we had no permit from either the Historical Trust or the Corps of Engineers to excavate or alter the bottom, the site was left as found. Our spirits, however, were renewed a hundredfold.

We resolved to begin the arduous permitting process with the Corps and the Trust to excavate the Skove wells, test the Long Point site, and conduct a dredge test trenching operation off Kent Point. In the meantime, we would continue our search for financial assistance.

In June I traveled to England to conduct further research on William Claiborne and to visit Cleborne Hall in the tiny hamlet of Cliburn, in Northumberland, one of several places purported to be the site of his birth and the ancestral estate of the Claiborne clan.[16] Unable to locate the hamlet on the British Ordnance Survey maps of the area, I resorted to the obvious, the tourist board in the little town of Keswick. "Why would anyone want to visit a wretched place like that?" they asked me. "And who the hell was William Claiborne anyway?"

When I finally located the hamlet, a pristine little working-class agricultural village set astride a scenic brook in the countryside, it was anything but wretched. The town church, surrounded by a weathered stone fence with a wrought-iron gate and a graveyard on one side, could have been drawn from an eighteenth-century engraving. Although I had not seen a soul from the moment of my arrival, I ventured in. The doors were unlocked, although the church was empty. At the entrance, two stones from the second-century Roman garrison station at Kirkby Thore, some two miles distant, and a carved Norman lintel graced the passage. One of the Roman stones had come from a bath, and the second from a pagan altar. I later learned that in 1886–87, the porch itself had been rebuilt from coffin lids and later plastered over, with the stones and lintel placed in for decoration. And I thought the gravestone bulkhead at Kent Point had taken the prize for innovative recycling![17]

Inside I noted the beautiful hand-carved church font, which dated from the twelfth century. I was delighted to discover that the oak font cover had been presented as a gift to the church by Captain C. J. Cleborne, USN, a direct descendant of William Claiborne, in memory of his father, Admiral Christopher James Cleborne, M.D., USN. Nearby, a beautiful cut-glass window in the north chancel wall had been erected by Admiral Cleborne in memory of his cousin, General Patrick Renayne Cleburn, USA, as well as a marble plaque in memory of his own wife, and in return for the hospitality offered him by the rector, the Reverend Clarke Watkins Burton. In 1874, the admiral had also presented the church with an antique Jerusalem Cross, believed to be the Cross of Saint Giovanni di Vallambrossa, and a silver communion service inscribed with the Cleburne coat of arms. The cross had been ensconced for seven hundred years in the Vallambrossa Monastery until the reign of King Victor Emanuel, when it fell into antiquarian hands. Sadly, the service and cross had been purloined during a church benefit in 1987.[18]

Across the road from the church was ancient Cleborne (now Cliburne) Hall, which had for centuries been the property of the Lowther family until 1963 but was now a massive dairy farm under the ownership of one Derrick Bowness. As I walked up to the main house, I encountered Derrick's wife, Dreen, who graciously consented to show me about. The Claiborne family and Lowther estate records that I had come to examine were, she said, no longer in the possession of the estate. Only two or three years earlier, Americans claiming to be descendants of William Claiborne had come to see them, asked if they could make copies in the nearby town of Kendall, took the documents, and never returned. I was ashamed of my countrymen as never before.[19]

Melted Beads

Dreen Bowness, the epitome of British civility, took me on a tour of the estate. There, she told me, pointing out over the stone stables, they were just removing, for the first time in the estate's half-millennium history, the original slate shingles, which were to be replaced by modern tarred shingles. In her beautiful garden stood two large millstones from the nearby Cliburn Mills. The naked stone manse, which had stood for centuries largely unadorned, had only recently been covered with stucco to help fend off the cold winter winds. The only portion of the house surface left as it had been was a large sandstone relief, inset into the wall. It was Claiborne's coat of arms. And it was, I surmised, about as close to the old adventurer as I was likely to get.

Not long after my return from England, Michael Pohuski called to inform me that he had spoken with Paul Hundley of the Maryland Historical Trust. We need not apply for a Corps permit to excavate if we did the work directly through the Trust. Moreover, two thousand dollars had been dangled before him to support a small excavation—not enough for everything, but enough to excavate two of the barrel wells and provide for conservation costs. The choices were clear: either work through the state or wait six months for a Corps permit, raise the money elsewhere, and pray for approval of our program by the Trust. We immediately set to work on a revised project design, to excavate Wells No. 2 and No. 3.

On September 5, 1990, Michael called me from his vacation retreat at Chincoteague, Virginia. Our revised project design and the money had been approved.[20] The excavation was on.

S I X T E E N

Baubles, Barrels, and Beads

The salt marsh mosquitoes of the Eastern Shore, *Aedes sollicitans* and *Aedes taeniorhynchus,* are without question the most bloodthirsty of all of God's creatures residing in the state of Maryland.[1] Early on the morning of September 21, 1990, as Michael Pohuski, Fred Hopkins, John Kiser, and I assembled at the Skove site to begin the excavation of Well No. 2, we were unexpectedly ambushed by swarms of these vampirelike insects and continued to serve as their main course throughout the day. We nevertheless managed to proceed with the construction of a prefabricated, eight-foot-square cofferdam, as well as a platform to station beside it and on which to mount a water pump and sundry excavation gear. These structures were to be hauled out to Well No. 2 and planted over it. With the assistance of a powerful hydrojet and a good sledgehammer or two, the coffer's four corners would be driven five feet into the bottom to anchor it. With a berm built up on the sides, and forty dollars worth of Hefty trashbags filled with beach sand to further seal off seepage, we hoped then to be able to pump out the coffer and excavate the well dry. The three well sites were quickly relocated and their perimeters marked by flags to prevent personnel from tripping over them during the excavation.

Within a short time, the archaeologists from the Maryland Historical Trust began to arrive to monitor our operations. Betty Seifert, level-headed master of perspicuity in matters of archaeological conservation from Jefferson Patterson Archaeological Park, had also arrived to set up shop on the beach. Betty was to handle the cataloging as well as the field and long-term conservation of any artifacts that might be found. But she did much more.

By late afternoon the cofferdam had been firmly planted. Water depth over the site was three feet. As Michael started up the pump to drain the coffer, we all crossed our fingers. Slowly the waters declined, and the dark, circular outline of barrel staves began to take shape. Suddenly, with barely six inches of water to go, the external pressure forced a blowhole under the coffer and the containment instantly refilled. Again the pump was started, and again a blowhole punched through. The observers from the Trust quietly departed. On shore, Betty filled more bags with sand, while the rest of us hauled them through the water to reinforce the coffer—but

189

to no avail. Nothing, it seemed, could prevent the Chesapeake's waters from percolating into the structure.

The following morning was gray and drizzly when I returned to the Skove site accompanied by my brother Dale, who had volunteered to help. I feared the worst, for the weather had been miserable during the night. My anxiety was shared by Michael, who had gone ahead with Joe before sunup to survey the scene. When they arrived, Eastern Bay was frothing with whitecaps and had already ripped the coffer from its foundations. It was clear that we would have to start again from scratch. By noon, the coffer had been replanted and reinforced with eighty sandbags. Again, we attempted to pump it out in a halfhearted hope of success. It was, as before, a vain gesture.

We now determined to excavate the site wet, although it was still surrounded by the coffer to shelter the excavation from wave activity. A sixty-inch cross frame was rigged diagonally across the full thirty-nine-inch diameter of the barrel, leveled two feet above the site, and its elevation shot from the transit station ashore. From the crossbar a plumb bob on a measured line was dropped at regular intervals to determine the depth of penetration as excavation proceeded. Horizon levels were divided into three-inch units, as tighter controls in zero visibility would prove impractical. As soil was carefully removed from the site with trowels, it was transferred into a small container on the bottom.

Fred Hopkins and the author lower a plumb line on one of the barrel wells at the Skove Site while Dale Shomette takes notes. Photograph by Michael Pohuski

Baubles, Barrels, and Beads

When each new container was filled and then carried ashore, Joe and Betty directed several teams of volunteers in the careful sifting of every bucketload of sediment. Sediment samples from each stratum were retained for later flotation and pollen analysis, soil study, and documentation of floral and faunal remains. Any artifacts found were bagged, tagged, and logged in.

A team of divers worked in tandem from opposite sides of the barrel, excavating the site in pitch black water, while a second team manned the bucket brigade to shore and transferred the excavators' drawings and measurements of the site to mylar. As penetration into the barrel slowly progessed, the excavators were obliged to work in a nearly vertical, upside down position. The water within the coffer began to stink as we penetrated the sand to a black, gooey mud, which suggested that we might even be digging into the base of a privy, and I recalled how dismal Sir Thomas Gates's 1610 account of how unhealthy wells could be.

Although gloves were a recommended accoutrement, I preferred to dig barehanded, feeling for both solid and soft features before placing the contents into the bucket. It was important to have some tactile sensation in the darkness, even though encounters with the occasional edge of a razor clam inflicted several evil-looking cuts. Although we were working under barely three feet of water, in the inky blackness it might as well have been a hundred feet. When the first identifiable artifact, a honey-colored slipcoated Staffordshire sherd, was recovered, it was treated as if it were the Crown Jewels.

As each team spelled the next, penetration downward within the big barrel progressed at a snail's pace. By the end of the day, I had spent five hours in absolute darkness, mostly upside down within a barrel, the contents of which no one was yet certain. And I was sick and nauseated from ingesting occasional mouthfuls of its putrid, slimy black contents. Nevertheless, our efforts were magnificently rewarded. The sifting operation on the shore had yielded splended results: a small brass pin, a fragment of a polished kaolin Dutch pipe from Level 6, and three colorful beads plucked from the muck of Levels 6 and 7. By the time I finally waded ashore, the artifacts had already been bagged, tagged, and cataloged. Here, at last, might be the evidence we had sought—retrieved in a controlled excavation, with three archaeologists from the state of Maryland looking on. But were the artifacts datable to the period of 1631–45?

The following day was the fall equinox, and extremely low tides had been forecast. Well No. 2 could be wrapped up if everything fell into place. That evening, however, as the foul waters I had ingested began to take effect and my stomach revolted, I cared little if we ever found evidence of the settlement or, for that matter, whether I lived or died. When I arrived at the site late the next morning, still nauseated from my intestinal ordeal,

Conservator Betty Seifert (right) and a volunteer from the Archaeological Society of Maryland sift through sediments excavated from a barrel well at the Skove Site.

The author measures the barrel staves of Well No. 2 before a collapse of the cofferdam reflooded the site. The well and the artifacts contained therein provided the first archaeological clues to the probable location of the Claiborne settlement, as well as definite data on the oldest European site on the island discovered to date. Photograph by Michael Pohuski

the team was already hard at work. Michael was upside down in the well and, I was told, annoyed at my delayed arrival. And he was justified.

Although the start had been retarded by the need to reexcavate the recent fill, progress was excellent. Just as the three Historical Trust archaeologists arrived, artifacts began to turn up in the sift box: rose-headed nails, a brass tack, small seeds, and stave fragments from the upper well structure which had collapsed into the shaft as it eroded. Finally, the bottom of the well was reached at the same time the lowest tide of the season arrived. The site was now barely covered by a foot of water.

We decided to make one last attempt to pump the coffer and well dry. Within minutes the greasy black waters trapped within the coffer were being drawn out. The well, possibly manufactured by the first pioneer settlers in what would one day become the state of Maryland, was exposed to the light of day for the first time in centuries. Yet there was little time to savor the moment. Fearing that the coffer's collapse might be repeated at any minute, I jumped into the three-foot-deep barrel to take precise measurements of the staves, even as Michael began to take photos of the exposed site.

It was, for all of us, a most rewarding moment, one on which to capitalize. Michael and one of the Trust archaeologists immediately jumped into the coffer and began to excavate a vertical shaft down the exterior of the barrel, to ascertain the positions and types of hoops that might still be affixed to it and to examine and sample the colonial backfill around the barrel for artifacts. The excavation proved only partially successful: three square-edged, tapered wooden hoops, fitted to the staves with iron tacks, were discovered on the exterior of the barrel. The fill, unfortunately, was sterile.

We now had to make a strategic decision. Should we attempt to resurrect the entire barrel, or rebury it and return at a later date for its recovery? The tide was again rising, the coffer had sprung a small leak, and there was precious little money available for conservation of an entire barrel with twenty-one staves. Besides, we still had another well to excavate. The barrel was backfilled with thirty five-gallon cans of sand toted from the beach, and the coffer was dismantled.

❏   ❏   ❏

Excavation of the second barrel well was delayed for nearly two weeks, as we awaited the most promising weather and tidal conditions. On October 4, we learned that adequate sea conditions and an extremely low tide would occur two days later. This time we would attempt to excavate Well No. 3 wet and without benefit of a cofferdam.

Unlike No. 2, Well No. 3 was excavated simultaneously both outside, in the backfill zone, and within the barrel. We almost immediately discovered a fragment of green bottle glass and a whiteware sherd in the

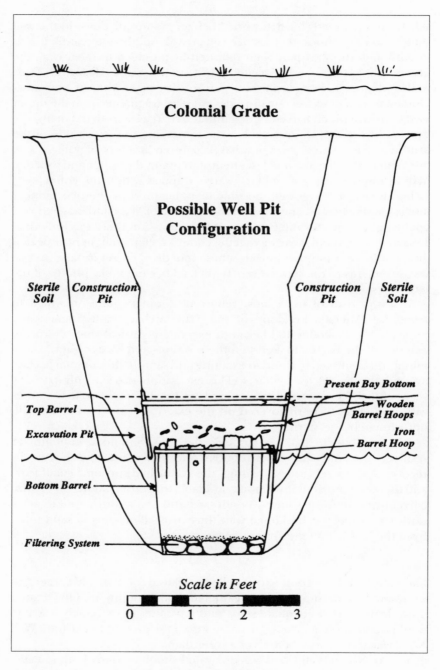

Colonial Grade

Possible Well Pit Configuration

Sterile Soil   *Construction Pit*   *Construction Pit*   *Sterile Soil*

Present Bay Bottom

Top Barrel   *Wooden Barrel Hoops*

Excavation Pit   *Iron Barrel Hoop*

Bottom Barrel

Filtering System

Scale in Feet

0   1   2   3

Plan of Well No. 3.

fill, both of them datable to the first quarter of the eighteenth century. Well No. 3 contained remnants of a second sleeve barrel as well as a wooden bung and portions of disarticulated wooden wicker hoops. The upper sleeve barrel had almost entirely eroded away, leaving only several wooden hoops and the lower seven to fifteen inches of standing staves. One wicker hoop was recovered intact. Unlike the sleeve, the lower barrel was held together with metal hoops. Unfortunately, the interior was devoid of artifacts. However, a filtering system of tightly fitted river cobble overlaid by a layer of sandy white pulverized chalk or limestone was discovered at the base of the well. It was the first time a filtering system had been found *inside* and at the bottom of a Tidewater barrel well.[2]

But what did it all mean, these two ancient wells and their sparse, mundane contents? For starters, Well No. 2 could conceivably have been opened as early as 1631 and remained open until as late as 1725. Well No. 3, with its primitive filtering system and metal hoops, was opened about the time of the closure of No. 2 and was a distinct improvement over its predecessor. No. 1, the box well, which was destined to remain unexcavated, was probably either the first or the last well to be erected, having been deemed inferior early on, or superior after the failure of the first two. That box wells rather than barrel wells continued to be erected

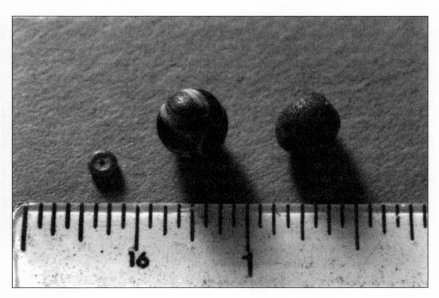

Beads recovered with archaeological provenance from Well No. 2 suggested the structure may have been associated with the oldest Euro-American site in Maryland, possibly even the Claiborne settlement itself. Photograph by Michael Pohuski

during the succeeding two centuries suggests that No. 3 was probably the last to be built.

It was, however, in the contents of the wells that our greatest interest lay. The slipcoated Staffordshire sherd recovered from Well No. 2 and identified by Dr. Henry Miller, the new director of archaeology at St. Mary's City, was identical to samples excavated at the Van Sweringen Site in St. Mary's from a context of 1680–1725.[3] The nails recovered along with it were associated with one of the top-end hoops no longer extant. But we were most interested in the brass straight pin and the beads recovered from the barrel.

The three beads were checked against a sophisticated classification system devised by K. and M. A. Kidd, were compared to bead collections archaeologically excavated throughout the Chesapeake Tidewater and along the lower Susquehanna River drainage, and were evaluated by Karlis Karklins of the Canadian Parks Service, one of the foremost experts on colonial beads in North America.[4]

The most attractive bead recovered was deep blue with pairs of white, striated lines and was promptly classified as Kidd Type IVb33; the second was a plain, light blue color and was identified as Kidd Type IIa40. The third was an unidentifiable white bead, possibly made of bone, which could not be readily classified. Both the IVb33 and IIa40 had been recovered in abundance from numerous sites in the Chesapeake Tidewater. Type IVb33 had been excavated at St. Mary's City in contexts of 1638–60, at Jamestown without context, at a Piscataway Indian ossuary on the Potomac in a context of 1630–50, and in Susquehanna area sites with contexts of 1575–1680. The IIa40 had been excavated at St. Mary's City in various contexts ranging from 1638 to 1720, at a site on the James River in a context of 1680–1710, and at various northern Seneca and Mohawk Indian sites in the north in contexts between 1560 and 1687. Bead expert Karlis Karklins suggested that the beads were probably of Venetian manufacture, although since a smaller, darker version of IIa40 had been excavated at a bead manufacturing site in Amsterdam with a 1600–1680 context, Dutch origins could not be ruled out.[5]

The findings were both exhilarating and frustrating. Hard and circumstantial data had been extracted from the excavation. Well No. 2, with bead types ranging in period from as early as 1560 to as late as 1720, and which had remained open as late as 1725, was possibly the earliest Euro-American site found in Maryland, and definitely the earliest ever documented from archaeological evidence on Kent Island. The evidence provided by two identifiable beads and a pin suggesting that the well may have been opened and used as early as the first Claiborne occupation was slender. But it was the first hard archaeological evidence ever found of early European settlement in the vicinity of Kent Point.

Baubles, Barrels, and Beads

Although the use of beads as a trade commodity with the natives of the Tidewater and the lower Susquehanna is barely attested to in the historic record, their employment is richly confirmed by the archaeological record. Claiborne's possession and use of beads as items of trade from the very founding of the settlement was evidenced by mention of the loss of his first stock during the October 18, 1631, warehouse fire, wherein the company's supply of trade beads was melted into worthless lumps of glass. That new supplies of beads were obtained and had been forwarded to Palmers Island for use by Claiborne's traders is attested to by the inventory of goods taken as booty during Calvert's attack on that place in 1639, booty which included a "parcel of blue beads." The evidence, albeit hinging on only two tiny, fragile pieces of blue glass, seemed more than promising.[6]

❏   ❏   ❏

On January 10, 1991, the principal investigators on the Claiborne Project—Michael Pohuski, Joe McNamara, Fred Hopkins, and I—formally presented our findings to our peers in the American archaeological community at the annual meeting of the Society for Historical Archaeology in Richmond, Virginia. Our symposium was entitled "The Underwater Search for William Claiborne's Seventeenth-Century Settlement in the Upper Chesapeake" and was well attended and received. Our papers would soon be published as the lead articles in the *Underwater Archaeology Proceedings* for 1991.[7] A month after the symposium, we received an invitation from the Maryland Historical Trust to present our findings to the Trust and the Maryland press.

In mid-February Pohuski received an urgent call from one of our Kent Island informants, an amateur archaeologist named John Chamberlin, who had for months been monitoring, in our behalf, the eroding beachfront between Scaffold Creek and Hullica Snooze. After every spate of rough weather and whenever his schedule allowed, Chamberlin walked the beach, collecting artifacts eroding from the shore and plotting their positions on a master chart of the coast. When Michael answered the phone and heard John's voice, he expected to hear that yet another batch of pipe stems or prehistoric lithics had been collected from the eroding shore.

This time, Chamberlin was more than excited. A recent storm, he said, had exposed as many as three great depressions in the bluff immediately north of the Snooze. He believed they might be grave sites. Moreover, he had just collected a large number of dark blue beads south of Scaffold Creek approximately five hundred feet north of the Skove wells, some of which were similar to those recovered from Well No. 2. But his most significant find had been several lumps of melted blue glass, striated with mangled but clearly discernible white lines. Melted beads!

Melted Beads

On February 23, Michael, Joe, Fred, and I joined John Chamberlin in the field to examine his discoveries. It was not the best of times to be on the open beach, as the thermometer was hovering at the ten-degree mark and the windchill factor on the water was minus thirty. But zeal can work wonders. Two of the depressions near the Snooze and only several hundred feet south of the Skove sites were readily judged to be natural concavities caused by recent erosion. The third, however, was something else. A large six-foot-deep crevice had been exposed in the shoreline bluff face, barely five feet from the water's edge at mean low tide. Its interior lines were perfectly static and straight. At the entrance lay a perfect rectangle of organic soil, as if someone had laid a doormat down in front of it. The site presented the appearance of a precise cutaway of a squarely dug grave with perfectly vertical sides, hefted from the clay and then backfilled with black, organic soils, traces of which were still evident. In the immediate shoreline, not six feet away, John Chamberlin pulled a basal fragment of a Rhenish stoneware flagon of the mid-seventeenth century from the surf. As we measured and pondered over the site, we became increasingly convinced that the cavity was indeed the remnant of a grave, its occupant having long since turned to dust and his or her remains carried away by the erosive assault of the sea. Yet, without a systematic excavation of what was left, the validity of our surmise would remain merely problematical. And time was against us. The site would not long endure the onslaught of the winter's wrath. Perhaps a few days, a week, or even a month, and it

Erosion of the shoreline above the now-bulkheaded Skove site revealed a possible colonial burial site, seventeenth-century artifacts, and a handful of melted glass trade beads. Photograph by Michael Pohuski

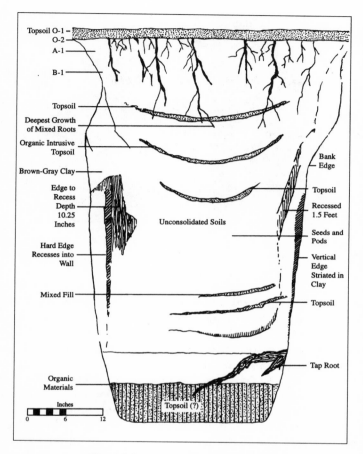

Plan of the Chamberlain grave site.

would be gone. Measurements and photographs were taken. Then, hoping to buy time against the inevitable, at least until a more thorough investigation could be launched, we spent the rest of the day building a pitiful barrier of stone, dirt, and rip-rap around it and then covered the whole with fragments of plastic sheeting that had washed up on the beach. It was a futile gesture at best, but it was all we could do.

On February 25, in a briefing room at 45 Calvert Street in Annapolis, the Claiborne Project investigators again presented the fruits of over two years of research to a specially assembled group from the Maryland Historical Trust. The Trust's Chief of Archaeology Richard Hughes welcomed the guests.

Somehow, it all seemed so surgical now, so clinical and unimportant as we read our tracts and showed our slides and videos to an audience that

199

Melted Beads

Melted and intact trading beads, recovered from the eroding shoreline adjacent to the Skove site by John Chamberlin and dating from as early as 1600–25. Photograph by Michael Pohuski

seemed to be only going through the motions of being attentive. After the presentations, there were no questions. Indeed, there was no reaction at all. Only dumb silence. Had our work been that bad?

Soon after the symposium, we pressed key members of the Trust and other archaeologists present about supporting or conducting further work on the sight. Again, there was little interest. We approached the Trust for even modest aid to continue our research, to complete an excavation of Well No. 1, a survey of the Long Point site, or even to conduct a one-day test trenching experiment to locate one of the myriad offshore sites with a clam dredger. Although the following year a small grant would be awarded to other researchers for further work on Kent Island, for the time being, there was no money available for the salvage excavation or survey. Moreover, the dredging experiment was considered too dangerous to the resource, too revolutionary.

At our request, John Chamberlin had driven from the Eastern Shore to attend the symposium, bringing with him the beads, both melted and whole, which he had recovered from the eroding shoreline below Scaffold Creek. All told, he had assembled a total of twenty identifiable beads and five melted clusters. One of the new beads, unlike any excavated or collected to date, was Kidd Type IVb31, dated in a Susquehanna context only of 1600–25. It was, given the context, the earliest glass bead with local provenance ever found in the state! The probable association with the Kent Island settlement of 1631–45 could not be ignored.[9] But for the present, Maryland was not interested.

After all, William Claiborne *was* a Virginian.

PART THREE

THE GHOST FLEET OF MALLOWS BAY

*The road to victory, the guarantee of victory, the absolute
assurance of victory, has to be found in the word "ships," and a
second word, "ships," and a third word, "ships."*

David Lloyd George

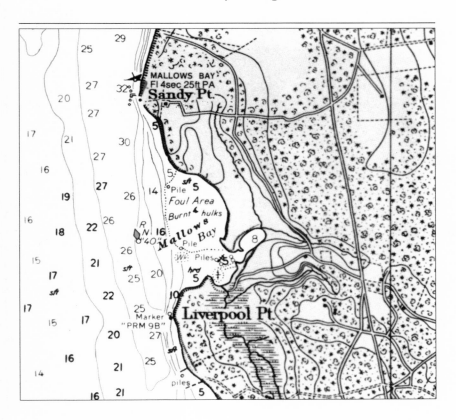

SEVENTEEN

A Forgotten Alcove of Time

It was a frosty, brisk morning when we shoved off into the open Potomac from the dock at General Smallwood State Park on Mattawoman Creek. The candied colors of early autumn were splashed in bright, irregular patterns along the shore, and the October sky was cloudless, marred only by the vapor trail of a jet flying somewhere near the edge of its earthly envelope. For a day so perfect, however, the river appeared devoid of its usual boaters. With the singular exception of a young whitetailed deer swimming across the creek from the appropriately named Deer Point, nothing seemed to stir. It was perhaps fitting that all signs of human activity had seemingly disappeared from the scene, for our objective was a place of a somewhat peculiar, indeed, unique nature. By the map, we were bound for an obscure, marshy indent on the Maryland shore, a forgotten alcove of time inhabited only by creatures of fur, fin, and feather, and the vestigial remnants of a maritime era long dead.

Upon entering the main channel, Pete Petrone of *National Geographic,* my father, Grady Shomette, and I were instantly struck with the wide majesty of this most historic of American rivers. Between our point of embarkation and our ultimate destination, only a few miles along on the watery highway from the nation's capital, many pivotal events of American history had taken place. Here, in 1608, the indomitable Captain John Smith had explored, searched for precious metals, and gauged the measure of the native inhabitants. Here, shiploads of colonists had landed to challenge and then push back the Tidewater frontier, founding hamlets, towns, and cities as they went. Here, Loyalists and Patriots had engaged in bloody riverine warfare during the Revolutionary War, and British invaders, hell-bent on the capture of the city of Alexandria during the War of 1812, had arrived to chastise President "Jemmy" Madison for daring to declare war on the mightiest seapower in the world. And here, between Mattawoman Creek and Liverpool Point, tens of thousands of Union troops had fortified the coastline to counter a feared Confederate invasion of Maryland during the early days of the Civil War; Professor Thaddeus S.C. Lowe had monitored rebel movements from one of the first balloon reconnaissance missions of that terrible conflict; and the U.S. Navy's hard-pressed Potomac Flotilla had kept constant vigil, intercepting contraband, shelling rebel positions at Cockpit, Possum, and Freestone Points, and blockading the lone rebel warship on the river, the CSS *George Page*, ever so tightly in Quantico Creek on the Virginia shore.

As we passed closely along the sandy cliffs of Stump Neck and neared the mouth of Chickamuxen Creek, the rusted bones of a retired and decaying U.S. Navy assault craft, perhaps a veteran of a more recent conflict, lay hard against the shore. Her machine gun turrets were empty and her once-strong back appeared broken, a rusting memento of the more sinister side of civilization. Soon, the shallow cliffs of Moss Point, once known as Budd's Ferry, and the shoally indent of Goose Creek, both sites of Union waterfront batteries and breastworks, were far behind us. Only the giant, modern web of power lines sweeping across the river from the power station above Quantico Creek spoiled the pristine panorama. The visible evidence of the sprawling U.S. Marine Corps Base at Quantico seemed but a defect on the far horizon. A few miles ahead of us was the modest protrusion known as Sandy Point, on the northern perimeter of our area of investigation. Beached on the shores of the point, and all but hidden from view by the forest that was gradually enveloping it, lay a giant, silent guardian, the skeletal remains of a once-great ship.

As we approached the point, the wreck was invisible against the brilliantly colored backdrop of autumnal foliage. Full-sized trees had grown from its heart, and underbrush camouflaged its waist. A sand spit had grown up around its starboard side as vessel and earth had gradually begun to merge into one after decades of unremitting action by wind, waves, and tides. I dubbed the ancient ship "The Sentinel Wreck." Soon, we bumped ashore and began to explore the great old wooden hulk and the thickly covered terrain surrounding her. I was intrigued by the degree of structural integrity remaining despite the ongoing natural integration process even now under way. Iron pins which had once held its planks in place still stood in orderly rows, beneath canopies of pretty pink wildflowers and brush, as if awaiting marching orders. The area was, indeed, lush with life: evidence of myriad insects, birds, fish, and even deer, raccoon, and otter was everywhere. A great blue heron, flushed from his cover by our arrival, lifted majestically off the stern of the wreck, leaving his half eaten meal behind. Nearby, in the thick underbrush, the remains of a large wooden ship's bulkhead lay adjacent to a pile of weathered vine-covered ship timbers. The Sentinel Wreck, it appeared, had been abandoned while in the very process of being broken up. To the immediate south of the hulk, near the ruins of an ancient wharf, lay the bones of yet another victim of time, a massive wooden barge, hauled up for the last time on the debris-strewn beach an eon before us.

Our destination was an obscure mile-long indent in the Charles County, Maryland, shore fed by a pair of even more obscure streams. As we rounded the northern lip of the embayment, the full and stunning scope of its unique contents was suddenly revealed to us. For almost as far as we could see, masked by the green mantle of nature, lay the greatest assemblage of historic shipwrecks in one discrete location in all of America, more than one hundred vessels dating from the period of the American Revolution to the Space Age. Here, in a place that time had forgotten, slept the Ghost Fleet of Mallows Bay.

❏ ❏ ❏

It is a minor geographic feature on the big map of the Potomac River drainage system, this little indent of shoreline known as Mallows Bay. Surrounded by low bluffs of up to fifty feet in elevation that frequently meet the water's edge, it lies more than thirty miles south of Washington, D.C., and sixty-five miles from the Chesapeake. The heavily wooded highlands surrounding its narrow beaches between Sandy Point on the north and Liverpool Point on the south are here and there gouged and sliced by ravines of some depth. Two short, meandering creeks, Liverpool and Marlow's, feed into the river near its southern end and drain substantial and scenic wetlands. It is a shallow embayment, situated directly on the salt water–fresh water interface of the river and as such is a natural spawning ground, nursery, and habitat for anadromous and semi-anadromous fishes. Its bottom consists of soft muds and silts in which myriad forms of microscopic life thrive. And its beaches, shores, and forested bluffs, like much of Charles County, host animals of innumerable varieties, from the majestic American bald eagle, osprey, and egret to the playful river otter, beaver, and painted tortoise. As they say, biodiversity at its finest. It was not always so. And its history? Well, let's just say it is checkered with a different form of diversity.

The first European to explore and document fully the navigable length of the Potomac River, Captain John Smith of Virginia, was also undoubtedly the first white man to lay eyes upon the little geographic feature now known as Mallows Bay. Yet Smith, more occupied with the search for precious metals than with minor geological landmarks, failed to even note the tiny embayment in his *General Historie of Virginia, New-England, and the Summer Isles.* Nor would those who came after him, such as Henry Fleet, Henry Spelman, and Leonard Calvert, bother to comment on the place. Indeed, the little bay was simply too remote and insignificant to bear much attention for more than half a century.

Although the white man's occupation of the river shores in the vicinity of the embayment was certainly under way by the late seventeenth century, as evidenced by indications of two plantations on Augustine Hermann's famed 1670 map *Virginia and Maryland,* [1] by 1708 only one of the two sites was noted by name. This may have been the estate of Zachariah Wade, who lived on a shallow shoreline indention to the south of Mallows Bay as early as 1665 (adjoining waterfront acreage that would eventually be purchased by George Washington).[2] Not until 1735, when Walter Hoxton published his *Mapp of the Chesapeak,* did prominent landmarks about the bay actually begin to appear on published maps and charts of the region. For the first time, the southern lip of the embayment was identified as Liverpool Point.[3] In 1776 its northern lip was named for the first time on Anthony Smith's *A New and Accurate Chart of the Bay of Chesapeake* as Sandy Point.[4] Yet, the area was still isolated and occupied by only a few residents who gained subsistence from agricultural pursuits and possibly from seasonal fishing for shad and herring.

By the onset of the American Revolution, at least one residence stood upon or near the shores of Sandy Point, although the unnamed embayment to the immediate south may well have already begun to serve as a convenient natural refuge and anchorage for shallow draft workboats and other vessels plying the Potomac. Indeed, it offered the first sheltered anchorage on the Maryland shore for in-bound vessels after rounding Maryland Point well to the south, and the last on the same shore for outbound vessels after passing Chickamuxen Creek until they approached Nanjemoy Creek. Yet, for all of its strategic location, the bay itself appears to have remained nameless and unconnected to the rest of the world by either road or trail. Indeed, not until the onset of the American Revolution would it even experience its first significant brush with history.

❑ ❑ ❑

In July 1776 the Potomac River reach between what would one day be called Mallows Bay and the opposite shoreline of the Old Dominion was destined to suffer from stinging depredations by British and Loyalist naval forces under the direction of James Murray, the Earl Lord Dunmore, Virginia's deposed royal governor. Driven from Virginia by patriot forces, but still in command of a great armed flotilla largely manned by Loyalist refugees and freed slaves, and supported by several Royal Navy men-of-war, Dunmore was desperately short of water and provisions. He had first entered the waters of the lower Potomac hoping to find the resources to keep his forces afloat until a reinforcement of British regulars might be sent to help him regain his province. Dunmore first tried his luck at St. George's Island, near the mouth of the river, but was deterred by local militia forces and then by the lack of potable water on the island. He resolved to conduct a watering expedition farther up the river. Leaving the bulk of his flotilla anchored off the island, and assisted by Captain Andrew Snape Hamond, commander of HMS *Roebuck,* 44 guns, he proceeded in his flagship, *Dunmore,* up the river with a force of armed vessels bent on securing the necessary water and "to harass & annoy the Enemy by landing at different places."[5]

A Forgotten Alcove of Time

On the afternoon of July 22, the little squadron dropped anchor a mile west of Sandy Point. The following morning, as the British filled their water casks on the Virginia shore, a body of local militia estimated at three hundred strong assembled at the home of William Brent, three miles south of the Stafford County–Prince William County border. Hamond immediately dispatched a tender and row galley with a force of 108 men belonging to the Royal Marines and the Fourteenth Regiment of Infantry. Their mission was to attack the Brent estate, known as "Richland," and break up the forces assembling there. The affair was concluded after a brief skirmish. Brent's elegant brick manor house and several outbuildings were destroyed. The Virginia militia, many of whom were in no condition to fight after a night of "Drunking Frolick" before the battle, retreated.[6]

Dunmore and Hamond then turned their attentions toward the Maryland shoreline between Mallows Bay and Sandy Point. The engagement that followed involved a small group of men from the Virginia Potomac Flotilla galley *Protector* who had come ashore to join a force of Charles County militiamen commanded by Colonel William Harrison. The Virginians, who had arrived in the bay aboard two boats, included Captain Robert Conway, commander of *Protector,* Second Lieutenant John Thomas, and five recently enlisted seamen. Colonel Harrison's force may have numbered several hundred. Conway's ship, unfortunately, was at that moment at Alexandria awaiting the return of the captain from a recruiting expedition to the lower Potomac.[7]

According to a later report by Thomas, it had become evident on the afternoon of July 23 that Dunmore's forces were preparing to seize the two vessels that *Protector*'s men had arrived in and beached near Sandy Point. Conway and Thomas did the most expedient thing by staving in the bottom of one of the vessels to prevent capture but had counted on the strong Maryland militia force to repel any British attempt to capture their other boat. The stove boat was to be the first of a long line of vessels lost or abandoned in the vicinity of Sandy Point. To the disgust of the Virginians, Harrison's men were quickly intimidated by the approaching enemy row galley, which had been sent out to destroy or capture the craft, and fled with little fight. He later provided a description of the scene, one which was quickly challenged by other eyewitnesses: "When the enemy saw them [from *Roebuck*'s masthead] running off they hollowed at them, and called them sundry names, they made signs for the row galley to pull ashore, which they did, and launched our boat off; they gave them three huzzas, and fired several shots, both small and great, at the house where our baggage had been taken to; then returned to their ships with their booty, without having one gun fired at them."[8]

The statements of Thomas and other members of *Protector*'s crew, which were sworn under oath before John Carlyle in Alexandria, soon appeared in the *Virginia Gazette* and aroused a storm of controversy over the alleged conduct of the Maryland militiamen on the scene. On August 20, *Dunlap's Maryland Gazette* carried a series of charges and counter-charges regarding the incident. Finally, a sworn refutation by John Finley, William Hunter, and James Lawson, in behalf of Harrison and his men, was issued. The statement was sworn before Justice of the Peace William Ramsay at Alexandria on October 4 and published in the *Maryland Gazette* on November 7:

> On Tuesday the 23rd of July last, we, the subscribers, set off from this place with intention to see the enemy's ships, which we were informed were proceeding up Patowmack, and arrived opposite them at Sandy-Point, in Maryland, about half an hour past 6 o'clock in the evening, when we found a body of the militia stationed, who informed us there were more men a little lower down the river; to whom we immediately went, and were by them told that col. Harrison, with a detachment of 25 men, was gone down to prevent the enemy's taking off capt. Conway's boats, by means of a gondola and armed schooner, which had left the ships for that purpose, as we conceived. We saw the Roebuck under way turning down, and firing now and then across the field, between the detachment and main body, and heard some other great guns, which we supposed were from the gondola and armed schooner. We returned to the main body where we immediately heard a brisk firing of small arms and swivels, which was thought to be an engagement betwixt the detachment and the enemy. We think about sixteen cannon were fired in the whole. The men appeared to be all drawn up ready with their arms, and during the firing seemed in good spirits, and we heard several of them ask if they might not go to the assistance of the detachment. We saw, nor discovered, nothing like cowardice; but on the contrary, a willing spirit seemed generally to prevail.[9]

Interestingly enough, the incident drew no mention from Hamond in his famous *Narrative* and was only noted in *Roebuck*'s log thus: "Tuesday 23d . . . at 4 Saw a Number of Arm'd men about a Boat in a Creek Sent the Galley which brot the Boat off."[10]

Two days after the engagement, the British completed their task of taking on fresh water and proceeded down the Potomac unopposed.[11] The Marylanders, whatever the tumult in the press may have been, appeared satisfied with their efforts. Three days after the engagement, Joseph Hawkins wrote from Charles County, Maryland, to Daniel St. Thomas Jennifer: "I have the Satisfaction of informing you that our Militia have prevented the Enemy from Landing or plundering if they intended it and that we have sustained no damage except the Loss of a couple of boats, & the fleet have gone down the River again this day."[12]

A Forgotten Alcove of Time

❑ ❑ ❑

Mallows Bay returned to its rural obscurity following the American Revolution. Not until 1822, probably as a consequence of the infant fisheries industry which was already taking root on the river, would Sandy Point be considered important enough for a road to be constructed linking it to Port Tobacco, the county seat of Charles County. Yet, by 1833, the point had again slipped into such obscurity that the road disappeared from the map.[13] In 1841 contemporary maps indicate that one of two creeks that fed into the embayment had finally taken on a name, that of the Marlow family which dwelled upon its banks. By the onset of the Civil War, the bay itself was being called Marlow's Creek.[14] Yet, settlement upon its shores was sparse and, as elsewhere in southern Maryland, poor. Liverpool Point was under the ownership of Robert A. Clarke and Samuel Barnard, both of whom were so impoverished that they could not make their tax payments. In 1851 the two men were obliged to surrender their property to the state for payment of back taxes.[15]

The documentary record regarding Mallows Bay during this period is limited, but considering the bountiful marine resources of the site, it is quite likely that it was already serving as a major staging area for commercial fishing on the Potomac, probably as early as the 1830s. Indeed, by 1837, Sandy Point was definitely hosting one of thirty known major fisheries on the river. And, judging from the reported take at mid-decade, it was a most productive, if rigorous, enterprise.[16]

Although commercial fishing on the Potomac had begun as early as the 1760s, it was not until the onset of the nineteenth century that the river's vast finned bounty began to be exploited on an industrial scale. In 1835 a Virginia gazetteer stated that 22,500,000 shad (*Alosa aestivalis*) and 750,000 herring (*A. pseudoharengus)* were being caught per year in the river, though only a few fishing methods, such as the use of simple short tongs for harvesting shallow water oysters and small seines, weirs, and primitive fish hooks for bringing in finned fish, were being employed at the beginning of the century.[17] Fishing technology, however, was destined to improve rapidly.

The shores of Marlow's, from Sandy Point to Liverpool Point, would have served admirably for haul seining, which was to become the most efficient manner of commercial fishing prior to the Civil War era. The operation based at Sandy Point would probably have varied little from others on the river. The fishing camp would be established on the beach near the hauling grounds where the seine haulers lived during the fishing season. The crew, usually slaves, varied from five or six men at the beginning of the season to approximately thirty men when fishing was intense. In addition to slaves, one or two men were hired as seine managers, one as a seine mender and another as a clerk for the fishery. From six to eight marker boats were utilized to transport catches from the landing to market in Alexandria, Virginia. The round-trip by sailing or rowing could take more than two days. The run boats returned with salt, fish barrels, and various other items of clothing and equipment used in the fishery.[18]

A typical seine was 350 yards long. Its dimensions, according to the journals and records of one prominent Potomac haul seine fisherman of the early nineteenth century, George Chapman, were "going out wing 130 yards 2½ inch mesh 144 meshes deep, middle 120 yards, small, 2 inch mesh 180 meshes deep, coming in wing 100 yards 2½ inch mesh, 144 to 168 meshes deep." Cork floats were used on the headrope. The footrope was not leaded, but probably hung with a heavy line to keep the net on the bottom. Tar was used as a net preservative.[19]

Some seining operations were enormous in extent. By the late 1830s tremendous seines employed on the Delaware and Susquehanna Rivers had been introduced to the Potomac. "Extending nearly across the river, one thousand to two thousand two hundred fathoms in length [6,000 to 7,000 feet] with an equal length of rope attached to one end," these massive seines were then "dragged up and down the stream with the tide, so as to sweep away anything within its bed." The use of such equipment, of course, had the effect of severely impacting or destroying the spawn and shutting down many of the small fisheries that lined the river.[20]

In 1858, however, another important fishing technology was adopted on the Potomac. This was the utilization of pound nets to block large areas of the river, from shallow to moderately deep waters. Stake gill nets were also being employed on an ever-widening basis. Employment of this fishing method was primarily in the upper Potomac above Mathias Point. Nets were usually put in in early spring, about March, to catch the ascending schools of such anadromous fish as striped bass and shad and were discontinued by the end of April. Stake gill nets were most frequently deployed from Sandy Point to Douglas Point and were usually carried out from the edge of Mallows Bay all the way across the Potomac to the shoals of Widewater. The new fishing methods, of course, rapidly began to deplete the resource base. Indeed, concerns about overharvesting the Potomac were being expressed as early as 1817, but frequent efforts at punitive legislation in both Maryland and Virginia did little to stem the tide that was even then measurably reducing the bounty of the river.[21]

❏ ❏ ❏

By the onset of the Civil War, Marlow's Creek had begun to appear in contemporary maps as Marlow's Bay, on the shores of which a landing known as Main Wood Landing had been established. A quarter mile inland from the headwaters of Marlow's Creek was a settlement referred to as Jacksontown, although neither the "town" nor the landing was connected by any formal road system to other sectors of the county.

Both Liverpool Point and Sandy Point, by this time, had been connected to Port Tobacco and to the road system leading north. In 1862, a contemporary military map of the region notes that a family named Waters occupied the waterfront at Sandy Point, while another named Price occupied Liverpool Point. A ferry landing called Cooke's Ferry had also been erected at Sandy Point, undoubtedly somewhat prior to the war, for it connected with another landing on the Virginia shore at Widewater which was cut off from Union access in the opening days of the conflict.[22]

During the Civil War, southern Maryland, particularly Charles and St. Mary's Counties, was notoriously sympathetic to the Confederate cause. Charles County was immediately occupied and heavily fortified by federal troops under General Joseph Hooker, as much to quell possible insurrection and halt the traffic in contraband goods across the Potomac as to protect against a feared Confederate invasion of southern Maryland. Despite such precautions during this period, information and mail were frequently smuggled across the river to Virginia from the more isolated reaches of the county, such as Marlow's Bay.[23]

Federal control of the Marlow's Bay area was maintained from Camp Wool, only 4.5 miles from Liverpool Point. During the fall of 1861, at the peak of Union fears over a possible Confederate invasion of Maryland from the Virginia shore, Liverpool Point was held by a forward unit of Smith's Fifth Excelsior Brigade, an element of Colonel Charles K. Grahams' Seventy-fourth New York Infantry, attached to Hooker's division. Fortunately, neither Marlow's Bay nor any other sector of southern Maryland would suffer from an outright invasion, emerging from the hostilities unscathed by fire or sword.[24]

During the years immediately following the war, the Marlow's Bay region appears to have resumed its previous state of remoteness, although in late 1871, William L. Chiles and James M. Harvey of Nanjemoy, Maryland, purchased the Liverpool Point tract and erected the first known wharf there to open up the point to steamboat traffic.[25] Then, in 1885, an expatriate Virginian, Captain Morgan L. Monroe, rented a farm on Sandy Point which "proved to be the most lucrative location for fishing on the river, due to the deep channel close to shore." Monroe was born at Chancellorsville, Virginia, on May 2, 1863, in the very midst of the epic Civil War battle being fought there, and had migrated to the hamlet of Riverside, in Charles County, at the age of twenty. From his home at Riverside, he had managed to carry on a successful gill net operation for two years before deciding to move his fishery to Sandy Point.[26]

In 1888, three years after opening his Sandy Point operation, Morgan Monroe erected a sturgeon fishing station and caviar processing plant at Liverpool Point. He did not, however, enter the business of caviar processing unprepared and had first educated himself by hands-on study of caviar plants at Richmond. After fully familiarizing himself with the processing operation, he returned home with a supply of sieves, casks, and salt, ready to go to work.[27]

Monroe purchased at least five Philadelphia sturgeon fishing skiffs and two mules and procured the services of ten men, many of them family members, to carry on the operation. His boats had been shipped by train from Philadelphia to Widewater and were the last so-called "foreign vessels" to gain popularity on the Potomac.

Many local mariners employed in the fisheries industry, following Monroe's lead, soon began to frequent Marlow's Bay, several of whom began to call the place home port. From the late nineteenth century on, such Potomac River steamers as the big 315-ton steamboat *Potomac,* of the Mount Vernon and Marshall Hall Steamboat Company, had begun to stop regularly at the old wharf at Liverpool Point to take on and off-load passengers, produce, livestock, and mail.[29]

One of the vessels that had begun to call Marlow's Bay its haven was the square-sailed bugeye *Lola Taylor,* a vessel owned and operated by Captain Andrew Kendrick and employed, off and on, carrying general cargoes and firewood between Alexandria and Fort Washington. *Lola Taylor* was a typical Potomac workboat, of ten tons burthen, 56 feet in length, 16.2 feet abeam, and 2.3 feet deep in hold. She had been built in Westmoreland County, Virginia, in 1886 and would serve under Kendrick until sold to Captain Randolph Thomas of St. George's Island, Maryland. On September 29, 1939, after fifty-three years of service, and having out-lived her usefulness, *Lola Taylor* was abandoned at Cross Road, Virginia.[30]

Another vessel that would hail Marlow's Bay as home port during this period was *Bessie Lafayette,* which may have served under one of Kendrick's relatives who also plied the Potomac. Unlike *Lola Taylor,* but like many other working craft, *Bessie Lafayette* would end her days in the little embayment, stripped and abandoned. Only her trailboard would survive, saved by Potomac River historian Fred Tilp and displayed at his home in Alexandria until his death.[31]

Despite its now more frequent callers, Marlow's Bay continued to retain its patina of isolation, a remote sector of the Potomac known only to the river's diminishing population of watermen, a handful of rural farmers along its shores, and the steamboat captains who routinely stopped at Sandy Point and Liverpool Point. Yet, with the onset of World War I, its very isolation was destined to play a significant role in the transformation of the embayment from a serene little backwater into the largest and most densely populated ship "graveyard" in America.

A Bridge of Wooden Ships

By April 2, 1917, the day President Woodrow Wilson issued a national call to arms against Imperial Germany, the entire continent of Europe, and much of the rest of the world, had already been immersed in a terrible and costly conflict for nearly three years. The entry of the United States into the Great War, however, came at a most crucial moment. America's allies, in particular Great Britain and France, were already reeling from the devastating onslaught of Germany's new campaign of unrestricted submarine warfare. In February and March 1917, only a few weeks before Wilson's declaration of war, over one million tons of merchant shipping, more than two hundred ships per month, had been destroyed by German submarines and mines, and the rate of destruction during April was destined to be even worse. By the end of the month, one in every four ships leaving England, nearly one hundred vessels a week, would perish. More than five million tons of Allied merchant shipping had been destroyed by the Central Powers since the beginning of World War I in 1914, and there seemed every indication that the new and devastating undersea campaign pursued by German submarine forces would be carried out with increasing vigor during the coming summer months. With barely twenty million tons of merchant shipping still afloat for all of the Allied nations combined, the outlook appeared grim. England's starvation and probable elimination from the war seemed imminent.[1]

It was patently obvious to the Allies that it would be up to America to offset the losses to enemy submarines if the war were to be won. Thus, in April, following Wilson's declaration of war, a general, indeed frenzied, speeding up of merchant ship construction in the United States was initiated. Yet to gauge the enormous logistics necessary to wage war on the other side of the submarine-infested Atlantic, it was necessary only to look at a few comparative—and sobering—statistics. In 1915 the merchant tonnage of the entire world was estimated at 49,262,000 tons, of which 43.5 percent was British, 12 percent American, 10 percent German, and 5 percent French. Between 1899 and 1915 the shipyards of the United States had launched only 540,000 tons of blue water shipping, or 14.6 percent of the world production total of 3,685,000 tons. Hitherto preoccupied with its own westward expansion and domestic struggles, the nation had, in fact, largely forsaken merchant shipbuilding following the Civil War and permitted foreign vessels, primarily British, to transport most of its sea commerce. At the onset of World War I, the United Kingdom launched an incredible 1,683,533 gross tons as compared to only 200,762 by the United States (most of which was, in any event, for foreign owners).[2]

The expectation that the war would continue for several years prompted American shipbuilders to accelerate production; they launched 192 ships totaling 228,016 gross tons during the first half of 1916. By April 1917 the United States had achieved some progress, although a large share of its modest shipbuilding energies had been expended upon foreign rather than domestic accounts.[3]

With growing public concerns over possible entry into the war in Europe, as early as 1914 William G. McAdoo, Wilson's secretary of the treasury, independently conceived of a shipping corporation that the federal government would own. In 1916, after several failures to act, Congress finally enacted a shipping bill. The bill provided for a Shipping Board charged with the promotion and regulation of the United States water transport which could also commandeer private lines if it were determined that they were not serving the public interest.[4]

It is doubtful if Shipping Board officials had expected to establish a shipbuilding program or could have foreseen the then-radical concept of wooden steamship construction as a component of such a program. After all, it was common knowledge that wooden steamships had gone out with the Civil War. Yet, the severe toll being exacted by German submarines upon Allied shipping was soon to emphasize clearly the immediate need for ships of any and all types. In 1917, Germany's institution of unrestricted submarine warfare sparked a review of the Shipping Board's functions. These circumstances led to the creation of the United States Shipping Board Emergency Fleet Corporation in April 1917 under provisions of the Shipping Act of 1916, which empowered the Board to form a stock corporation. The Emergency Fleet Corporation, with a capital stock of $50 million (which eventually grew to $3 billion), could purchase, construct, equip, lease, charter, maintain, and operate merchant vessels in the service of the United States.[5]

In January 1917, William Denman, a California Democratic Party leader and prominent San Francisco attorney with experience in admiralty law, was selected by President Wilson to head the Shipping Board. The choice was not without its critics, some of whom pointed out that the new chairman's largest clients had been the biggest shipbuilding yard on San Francisco Bay and a number of large timber companies. Not long afterwards, in mid-February, F. A. Eustis, a prominent New England blue blood, Harvard graduate, mining engineer, and politically well-connected yachtsman only lightly acquainted with ship design, suggested to Denman the concept of a large shipbuilding project that would focus on the construction of wooden steamships rather than steel-hulled ships. For Denman, who also knew little about shipbuilding, the concept seemed to have great merit, particularly at this important juncture.[6]

Within days of Wilson's declaration of war, Denman unveiled the Shipping Board's primary steel construction program but at the same time introduced an incredibly ambitious corollary plan, based on Eustis's concept, to augment the steel ship fleet by building no fewer than eight hundred to one thousand wooden ships in eighteen months. A rapid overhaul of the six million tons of German shipping in American ports which had been seized by the U.S. government and the probable temporary suspension of work on naval contracts that could be completed within three years was also planned. These efforts were to make available facilities for building at least 500,000 tons of wooden merchant ships in addition to the large volume of business then in hand in the steel shipyards on the coasts and Great Lakes. Much to the Shipping Board's chagrin, the press quickly focused its attentions on the novel concept of the wooden steamship program. Shipping trade publications charged that the program had been made public without investigating how it could be done and before designs had been produced. Denman was incensed that the press, by claiming that he intended to build "a bridge of wooden ships from New York to Liverpool, over which the victorious army of American people and the sutlers' wagons were going over to succor Europe," had ignored all but the wooden ship project.[7]

At first glance, the project appeared to have merits. Fleet corporation planners concluded that the country owned abundant timber reserves and at least a nucleus of wooden shipwrights, although blue water wooden shipbuilding, as an industry, was largely extinct in all but a few areas along the east and west coasts. The U.S. Forest Service estimated the merchantable timber reserves of the nation at a stupendous 2.5 trillion board feet. In 1915 production of the two principal kinds of ship lumber, namely southern yellow pine and Douglas fir, were respectively placed at 17 billion feet of pine and 5.6 billion feet for fir, although by 1916 the fir states had increased production to 7 billion. Moreover, there were 29,941 mills in operation across the land, and it was estimated that if only 10 percent of the annual Pacific Coast cut were made available for ship production, as many as four hundred 3,000-ton ships could be produced a year. Because of the smaller size of pine timber, the same percentage from the pine states could provide enough lumber for 500 to 600 more ships.[8] Program advocates optimistically reasoned that, with such resources at hand, how long could it possibly take to train an army of patriotic shipwrights to build the fleet?

Within short order, forty shipbuilding yards were being brought on-line to build wooden ocean-going vessels of various types. But the plans of the Shipping Board to build an emergency fleet of hundreds of medium-sized wooden ships to aid in carrying foodstuffs, munitions, and men through the war zone to the Allies meant an immediate and unprecedented overnight expansion of an industry that had only months before been little more than a ghost of its former self. Still, the project was enthusiastically endorsed by the president and at his request Major General George W. Goethals, world famous builder of the Panama Canal and a national hero, was placed in charge of the enterprise as general manager of the Emergency Fleet Corporation.[9]

Before entering upon this project, however, the United States Shipping Board conducted a thorough investigation of the lumber interests, the smaller machine and boiler shops, and steel plants throughout the country. The Board optimistically advised the president and the Council of National Defense that it would be possible, without disturbing the steel making or the steel shipbuilding industries, to produce in the neighborhood of 200,000 tons of wooden shipping each month, beginning about seven or eight months after the work was initiated.[10]

Goethals had long been a strong advocate of steel ship construction. Although cajoled by Denman into endorsing the wooden ship concept (albeit in a lukewarm manner), he now berated it and the creators of the concept. Upon launching his own investigation, he had determined that the program would require an army of between one and two thousand practical shipwrights to build the fleet—an insurmountable problem, for there was barely a fraction of that number in the entire country. Although the timber reserves were plentiful, seasoned timber was almost nonexistent. Wooden ships would simply not do. On May 25, 1917, he issued a public declaration of disapproval, declaring, in effect, his own war on the wooden steamship program and its champions, Denman and Eustice.[11]

Denman defended the program vigorously. The president, empowered by the passage of the Urgent Deficiencies Act of June 15, 1917, with broad powers to requisition, construct, and operate merchant ships, supported the corporation's direction, and the wooden ship program moved forward. However, the Denman-Goethals Controversy, as the dispute would later be called, refused to die and markedly retarded the program's forward motion. In July the president asked for and received both Denman's and Goethals's resignations.[12] Edward N. Hurley replaced Denman as Chairman of the Shipping Board, and Rear Admiral Washington Lee Capps, chief constructor for the Navy Department, succeeded Goethals as general manager.[13] The wooden shipbuilding program, still fraught with flaws, pressed forward.

The Emergency Fleet Corporation's initial plans for the wooden steamship program were seemingly comprehensive. They provided for the building of vessels of 3,500 tons deadweight or more carrying capacity and capable of about ten knots sea speed, for which propelling machinery of about 1,500 horsepower would be required for each vessel. Combined with the output of steel merchant ships produced for the same period, production was expected soon to exceed or, at the very least, keep pace with the highest rate of shipping losses caused by enemy submarine action, thus neutralizing the German submarine blockade of Europe.[14] Indeed, it was strenuously argued by some that wooden ships of up to 5,000 deadweight tons, which required more than 1.5 million board feet of lumber per ship for construction, would have a lifting buoyancy or lifting power of 1,335 tons and would thus be nearly unsinkable.[15] Denman once enthusiastically remarked that even if they could be sunk, the United States would soon turn them out faster than the Germans could build torpedoes to sink them![16]

In carrying out this ambitious program, it was optimistically considered unlikely that any difficulty would be found in securing the necessary timber, although the supply of seasoned lumber, which was preferable, was admittedly far from adequate. It was also obvious that the resources of the engine, boiler, and machinery builders, as well as of the labor market of woodworkers, would be severely taxed.[17] Although 80 percent of aspiring wooden shipbuilders were without adequate experience at the outset, as many as five contract applications a day were soon being forwarded to the Shipping Board. Companies that had specialized in such varied but unrelated enterprises as wooden bridge construction and home building were soon contracted to build wooden ships, the likes of which had never been built before. Fleet Corporation estimators initially anticipated the cost for the construction of each wooden hull at $300,000, while they expected machinery installation to approximate $200,000. The actual total expense would eventually exceed $750,000 per vessel.[18]

The leading and most formidable proponent of the wooden ship concept was Theodore E. Ferris, a prominent New York naval architect with an impeccable reputation. Largely because of his extensive experience and grasp of the tenets of wooden ship construction, Ferris had been appointed to the position of official naval architect for the Shipping Board and, acting upon the instructions of Denman, proceeded to produce the first official plans for the standard vessel type of the program. By July 1917, having successfully weathered the vicious infighting that had accompanied the Denman-Goethals Controversy and the reorganizations of the Emergency Fleet Corporation which followed, Ferris had completed plans and specifications for a standard 3,500-ton wooden steamship that was to bear his name and would become synonymous with the program.[19] The Ferris plan called for a standardized vessel 281 feet 6 inches in length, 268 feet over planking between perpendiculars, 46 feet abeam, a molded depth of 26 feet, a load draft from bottom of keel shoe of 23 feet 6 inches,

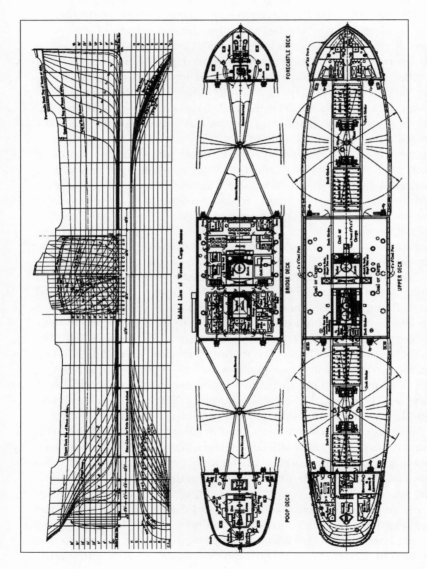

Lines and deck plan of the standard 3,500-deadweight-ton wooden cargo steamship designed by Theodore E. Ferris for the U.S. Shipping Board. Courtesy Steamship Historical Society

a total estimated deadweight of 3,500 long tons, a sea speed, loaded, of 10 knots, and an indicated horsepower of 1,400. The ships were to be built of either yellow pine or Douglas fir.[20]

Although the Ferris type would serve as the primary wooden cargo vessel of the program, other vessel plans would also be designed and adopted to avoid the costly, time-consuming, but necessary alterations to shipyard facilities already in place that would be required to build the Ferris model. These included: Allen, Daugherty, Grays Harbor (or Ward), McClelland, Pacific American, Peninsula, Seattle (or Geary), Supple and Ballin, and Hough. A single wooden steamship would be produced to the design of the Lake, Ocean and Navigating Company for service on the Great Lakes. McClelland and Supple and Ballin represented experimental variations of the basic wooden steamship called a composite. Given dimensions similar to the wooden steamship, the composite consisted of a steel frame with wooden planking intended both to provide added structural strength and to alleviate the problem of obtaining large timbers for the keel and keelsons. These ships proved to be quite expensive and very difficult to synthesize, and only a few were built.[21]

For the most part, however, the wooden steamship types were of similar configuration, although they ranged in size to 5,000 tons. The Hough design, produced by Edward S. Hough of San Francisco, would eventually gain the second widest acceptance of wooden vessels constructed during the Emergency Fleet Corporation program. Unlike the Ferris type, for the greater part of the length of this vessel the sides were flat and the bottom slightly V-shaped, with a deadrise of three feet. With this form of hull, the majority of the frames were straight twelve-inch by twelve-inch timbers—a common stock size of timber, generally known as "mill run" lumber. Most of the planking and ceiling was also straight-line work and could be completed in a minimum of time with a minimum of hand labor.[22] The construction of the Hough design closely resembled that of a barge and required far less shaping and molding than the Ferris model.

Securing building materials for construction of the fleet, it was soon observed (as the realities of the supply situation began to set in), was likely to produce considerable problems for the program. For the necessary timber, the Fleet Corporation selected dense varieties, indigenous yet believed to be plentiful to the region where the ships were built—white pine in the Maine shipyards, longleaf yellow pine in the south, and Douglas fir on the Pacific Coast. The typical Ferris yellow pine ship required approximately 1.5 million board feet and the Douglas fir about 1.7 million.[23]

Not surprisingly, given the few wooden shipbuilders in business in America at the onset of World War I, problems were destined to plague the program from the fall of 1917 until the end of the war and beyond. Although as early as July 1917 massive orders for suitable timber for the construction of keels, frames, and hull planking had been placed with such organizations as the Southern Pine Growers Association, it was not until October that actual orders for the first 433 ships were approved. Another month passed before construction contracts for 310 ships were finally let. Paperwork and bureaucracy proliferated. Critics charged that all that was necessary to secure a government wooden shipbuilding contract was "a piece of land and a keg of nails as a plant." Still, the Fleet Corporation was optimistically predicting that 6 million tons of shipping would be produced by the end of the following year, but now wisely downsized the wooden steamship estimate to 255,000 tons.[24]

By November, organized chaos had befallen the program. Problems included difficulty in obtaining timbers of adequate size, overestimation by lumber dealers of their ability to deliver promptly, a scarcity of railroad cars to transport timber, labor shortages at all levels, the sheer inexperience of many shipbuilders, and the excessive sale by lumber mills to other buyers of choice timbers required by the Fleet Corporation. Pine mills on the Atlantic and Gulf coasts failed to deliver in quantity many of the timbers required by the Ferris model, which called for some as large as 16 feet 24 inches by 40 feet. The years of clear-cutting forests in the south were having a telling effect on the size of timber now available. Pacific Coast lumbermen partially relieved the situation by forwarding thousands of carloads of Douglas fir to Gulf and Atlantic shipyards. Indeed, in a single month, Oregon produced a record 90 million board feet, enough lumber to build 52 ships. Ferris was soon obliged to modify his original design to reduce the need for larger timbers; the lumbermen then complained, however, that, in the process, he added 100,000 board feet to the total amount required per vessel. Great quantities of timber were often side-railed on train cars owing to priority snafus in the shipments of strategic materials, sometimes for months, thereby exposing the lumber to weather, which often warped it entirely, making it useless. That which reached the constructors properly shaped was green, but was employed nevertheless.[25]

The unavoidable use of green timber drew repeated criticism. One captain, facetiously complaining of the materials used in the construction of his ship, later stated: "They sent out oak shoots in spring and provided pine cones for Christmas."[26] Yet, the supply logjam was more than a joking matter. As early as October 1917, the Committee on Public Information at Washington, D.C., had announced that shipyards building wooden ships were desperately in need of white oak construction timbers or logs of good quality. Logs twenty-eight inches in diameter at the smaller end were being valued at from fifty to sixty dollars per thousand board feet, measured in the log. Sticks, hewed or sawed, of this size, at seventy to eighty dollars per thousand board feet, loaded on the cars under two hundred miles from the shipyard, were sought with an almost religious fervor.[27]

Frustrating delays cropped up with regularity. Rear Admiral Francis T. Bowles, chief of the Emergency Fleet Corporation's Construction Division during 1917, reported that, by December, lumber dealers had delivered only one-third of the timbers promised. Although implying that his reasons were more than justifiable, the admiral admitted that he had also contributed to construction delays by directing that his office conform to a request by Lloyd's Register of Shipping to move the engines and boilers more abaft and to increase the depth of the flooring in each vessel.[28]

Many first-time steamship contractors lacked building sites with essential railroad connections and living facilities for employees, while their frequent and often total lack of business experience, coupled with under-capitalization, further added to their burdens. The Fleet Corporation compounded these difficulties by releasing hull designs months before machinery details, neglecting the creation of installation yards to fit out the hulls, and failing to establish a priority system for the delivery of the large timbers critically needed by the Fleet Corporation. By December 1917, the Fleet Corporation was obliged to place an embargo on the sale of timbers with ten-inch widths or larger and lengths of twenty feet or more.[29]

While the Fleet Corporation attempted to manage the national ship-building crisis, the first wooden steamship hull was finally prepared for launching. On December 1, 1917, the first wooden bottom of the program to be launched, *North Bend,* a vessel of 240 feet in length and 4,000

The steamship *North Bend,* launched by Kruse and Banks December 1, 1917, was the first of the wooden steamships of World War I to hit the water. She would also be among those to end her days in Mallows Bay.
Courtesy Steamship Historical Society

221

deadweight tons, slid into the blue waters of the Pacific Coast after a record 120 days of construction, but a full 8 months after America's entry into the war. Not until May 24, 1918, however, would she finally be outfitted, undergo sea trials, be readied for sea duty, and delivered.[30]

On March 18, 1918, an announcement was made that the first wooden Ferris-type ship to be readied on the Atlantic Coast would be launched into the Passaic River at the Kearney plant of the Foundation Company at 3 P.M. the following day. The ship was to be christened by Miss Phyllis Hughes, daughter of the late U.S. Senator William Hughes, who had been selected for the honor by Hurley. The keel of the ship, to be named *Coyote,* had been laid on November 12, 1917. At the appointed hour, the signal for launching was given as the Newark Police Band crashed into a lively patriotic song. The affair was viewed by a crowd of nearly ten thousand invited guests.[31]

Coyote was a single-decked cargo ship rated Class A1 for fifteen years by the American Bureau of Shipping. She was driven by a 1,400-horsepower, triple-expansion engine and was capable of speeds of up to ten knots. She was 281 feet 6 inches in length, 46 feet abeam, and 3,500 deadweight tons. Her construction had required 1,320,000 feet of timber, 715,000 pounds of metal fastenings, 58,000 pounds of steel strapping, 2,800 pounds of oakum, 2,600 pounds of pitch for caulking, 6,000 gallons of paint, and 4,000 pounds of white lead and oil.[32]

The construction contract had been awarded to the Foundation Company during the summer of 1917, but the shipyard itself had to be built from the ground up before the first keel could be laid. Work on ship construction, which was finally started in October 1917, had been retarded because of transportation delays and severe weather. Nevertheless, *Coyote* had been the first hull in the program to hit the water on the eastern seaboard, and though months more work would be required before she could enter service, Admiral Pryor offered his congratulations to H. I. Crosby, superintendent of construction, for getting the hull in the water so soon.[33] By December 7, 1918, the ship had entered the service of the Potter Transportation Co., Inc., of New York. She was soon employed in making voyages, not to Europe as many expected, but to the West Indies and in the coastwise trade.

Coyote had numerous problems which, since she had been one of the first off the mark, were bound to draw more attention than would have otherwise been the case. Her principal problems were the weakness of the wooden rudder stock, troublesome feed pumps, and other auxiliary nuisances. Recaulking had been required throughout the hull soon after her first voyage. The engines and boilers had been satisfactory, but her operators considered her too small and expensive for profitable long-distance service, "but suitable for use in coastwise and West Indian trade if remunerative rates could be maintained." Yet, her construction was totally inadequate for the New England coal trade, for which she had been intended, and her average speed was computed to be slow enough to make her more than an easy target for enemy submarines.[34]

The shipbuilders of the Chesapeake Tidewater were counted among the first in the nation to mobilize for the wooden steamship program. In Maryland, the Henry Smith & Sons Company of Baltimore, the Maryland Shipbuilding Company of Sollers Point, the M.M. Davis Shipyard at Solomons, and others readily secured contracts to build practically every type of wooden steam vessel required by the Shipping Board, from the great 3,500-deadweight-ton Ferris steamships to tough little harbor and military tugs. In Virginia, the Newcomb Lifeboat Company (later to become the Newcomb Shipbuilding and Dry Dock Company) and the firm of Charles H. Tenney & Company, both of Hampton, the York River Shipbuilding Corporation of West Point, and the Potomac Shipbuilding Company of Quantico, had also entered the arena. Some companies were freshly minted for the occasion, while others, such as the Missouri Valley Bridge and Iron Construction Company (which took over the Potomac Shipbuilding Company yard at Quantico), had been specialists in other areas of construction but had never launched a ship before.[35]

Despite constant snafus, the great American can-do philosophy seemed all pervasive. The Newcomb Company, on the banks of Sunset Creek at Hampton, soon had two ships on the way, the 3,500-ton steamers *Luray* and *Kahoka*. The company boasted in its promotional posters that its resources included a work crew of 830 men (with a weekly payroll of $25,000) and 39 buildings. No fewer than 24 Ferris-type steamboats were being planned for construction. Although the shallow creek that was to receive the big ships was far from adequate, the company had soon dredged it to the required 18-foot depth. Unfortunately, the first launch would not come until well into 1919, long after the war was over, but just in time for another crisis in the shipping industry.[36]

The lives of the men who were to build the wooden steamship fleet were often less than ideal. Most of them had never worked in shipbuilding before, much less on wooden vessels. Training programs to instruct the raw manpower needed had to be established, as few of the tens of thousands of men who sought jobs in the industry knew a gudgeon from a keelson. The few older shipwrights who had actual experience in wooden ship construction were often treated as highly treasured commodities. Yet patriotism, good pay, and a sense of inter-industry rivalry helped to facilitate the program and the amazing production records that were set, despite the bureaucracy.

When young Garnett Arnold, of rural St. Mary's County, Maryland, entered the work force of shipbuilders in mid-1917, he was somewhat better equipped for the task than most. Born on September 27, 1894, the son of a Potomac River waterman and grandson of a Potomac River waterman, he had started working the waters at the age of sixteen haul seining for his father. When his father died in 1913, Arnold suddenly found himself the sole support of his mother and sister. With the outbreak of the war, his mother quickly secured a sole support exemption for him. But Arnold needed work, and the labor shortage caused by the war provided it. In late 1917, he traveled to Alexandria and secured a job working on the construction of 110-foot submarine chasers for the princely wage of 29½ cents an hour. In March 1918, when the contract had been completed, he secured work in a local ice plant but kept a keen watch for any defense-related jobs that might come along. When word circulated that a bridge-building company contracted to build wooden steamships was hiring at Quantico, Garnett Arnold was one of the first off the mark. The firm was the Missouri Bridge and Iron Construction Company.[37]

When Arnold traveled to Quantico, having no car, and public transportation to then such an out-of-the-way place nonexistent, he was obliged to do so by the Richmond, Fredericksburg, and Petersburg Railroad, which departed daily from Union Station in Washington. Making the trip with three colleagues, Marion Gibson, Charley Huseman, and Val Clark, with whom he had worked building sub chasers, he first paid a call on the company recruiter, a likable man named Kellum, who hired the four men on the spot. The pay was an incredible sixty cents an hour, more than twice what he had been making at Alexandria. "God, I was tickled to death," recalled Arnold while revealing his reminiscences to me nearly eighty years later.

The shipyard, which had been erected at Quantico in 1916 by the Potomac Shipbuilding Company with the intention of building ocean freighters, tankers, and, later, passenger ships, was located on Shipping Point (on lands eventually occupied by the post hospital). In mid-1916, railroad sidings had been extended to the site, and foundations for three steel-framed buildings had been laid. By 1919 the yard would include no fewer than forty-six buildings and two great marine railways. Despite its size and growth, however, the living facilities were less than spacious. Like all of the seven hundred men employed at the yard, Arnold was housed in a barracks run by a couple named Owens. Many of the men were provided used military clothing, primarily uniforms recycled from the war front in Europe. Although it was free, many shipbuilders refused to wear it. Arnold, like most of his colleagues, thought the uniforms were bad luck; his had bullet holes in the back.

Because of his shipbuilding experience, Arnold was made a supervisor over eight men and would work on one vessel for nearly eighteen months. His team was assigned, among other duties, to riveting the iron strappings in place, placing the bronze gudgeons, and mounting the rudder. The company had been contracted to build two ships. The ship Arnold worked on was initially known as Hull No. 303, later dubbed *Abra*, and then christened *Portland*. The second vessel in the yard, Hull No. 304, was eventually launched as *Bango*. Begun before the war, Hull No. 303 was intended to be only 185 feet in length and a far cry in both size and design from the standardized wooden steamers of the Fleet Corporation. Midway through construction, which had been started by the Potomac Shipbuilding Company at Quantico, the builder's contract was terminated by the Shipping Board with the claim that the company lacked sufficient manpower, was poorly managed, and was falling too far behind to complete the job. On June 28, 1918, the contract was taken over by the Missouri Bridge and Iron Construction Company. On July 17 Missouri Bridge took over the Potomac facilities to complete the two ships. Then, the designs for the two hulls were changed, and the ships were dismantled. Construction was begun anew. This time Hull No. 303 was to be on the Ferris plan, 268 feet in length, outfitted with galvanized fittings and iron or steel strapping. Arnold was proud of his work, and with his assistant, Arnie Carneal, he enjoyed the competitive spirit of construction from the beginning, when their team engaged in contests to finish their appointed tasks first.

There were occasionally exciting incidents to relieve the daily demands of work. One such event was the unannounced and unauthorized arrival of a purported "inspector" whose curiosity, ignorance of shipbuilding, accent, and foreign demeanor incited Arnold to suspect him as a spy. He reported the inspector to his superiors, but by that time the mysterious visitor had departed for Washington. The stranger soon resurfaced at the naval weapons testing center at Indian Head, Maryland, where he was arrested for espionage. It was rumored that he had planned to blow up both the shipyard and the testing facility.

The off-hours for the workers were less than stimulating. The most accessible urban area was the town of Fredericksburg, and Arnold and his friends would occasionally travel there by train to attend dances and other social activities. There were organized sports, of course. And then there were women and alcohol. The first were appreciated only on pay day. But the second was another matter. As early as 1901, the beginnings of statewide prohibition of alcoholic beverages in Virginia had begun with the organization of the Anti-Saloon League. On October 31, 1916, Virginia officially became a "dry" state. In 1920 passage of the Eighteenth Amendment to the Constitution ushered in the era of prohibition. Drinking at the isolated Quantico shipyard was both against the law and, thus, even marginally consumable alcoholic beverages were worth their weight in gold, as Garnett Arnold would soon find out.

Ghost Fleet of Mallows Bay

The Missouri Bridge and Iron Construction Company of Leavenworth, Kansas, was in many ways unique. Its original reason for being was to build bridges, tunnels, dams, and wharves. It owned its own steel plant and enjoyed the favor of Texas Senator Morris Sheppard who, it was said by some, had pressured the Shipping Board into awarding the company contracts to build seven Ferris-type steamships. Its principal owner was a forty-three-year-old English woman named Tellack, a divorcée and one of the hardest bosses Garnett Arnold would ever work for. The company, though under contract to the Shipping Board, was obliged to work in close harmony with the adjacent Quantico Marine Corps base through a liaison officer, one Colonel Blackman, who had a marine's penchant for an occasional sip of strong spirits, which were now illegal in Virginia.

One night, at a dance in Fredericksburg, Arnold became a close friend of Blackman's secretary. Through the secretary, the colonel engaged the young shipwright to procure something better than the awful Virginia moonshine that seemed to be the only available alcohol on base. He even promised to make available a military vehicle for him to bring the booze from Baltimore. The young entrepreneur eagerly sought to appease the officer—and at the same time supplement his own income—by making twice-monthly runs to the city on the Patapsco. Within a short time, Garnett Arnold was making eleven dollars for every dollar spent in running liquor to Quantico. The dealers who distributed it were purported to be making as much as one hundred dollars a quart. When Arnold eventually left the yard for good a year later, he took with him a healthy bank account of seven hundred dollars that would help see him through the lean years to come.

Portland, ex-*Abra,* like her sister *Bango,* would be launched successfully, amid much fanfare, into the Potomac River and towed to Norfolk by a pair of tugs for final fitting out, albeit not delivered for sea duty until July 19, 1919. Sadly, she would serve not as a steamship but, in her final incarnation, as a sailing barge. But Garnett Arnold, whose work had been completed, had already returned to Maryland.

❑ ❑ ❑

As the bloody war in Europe ground on, bureaucratic infighting and yet another complete reorganization of the Shipping Board's top management could do little to stem the growing criticism of the wooden ship program. Repeated charges that the ships, most of which had, of necessity, been built of unseasoned wood and were unseaworthy, drew heated denials from the Shipping Board. The Board vehemently refuted repeated charges that the first hull launched had sunk in ballast and the second had gone down after being outfitted. Scores of rumors abounded that the U.S. Navy refused to take over the operations of all U.S. wooden steamships because they were unseaworthy and little more than floating coffins. Proposals for congressional investigations appeared as early as December 18, 1917, when Representative George W. Edmonds of Pennsylvania threatened a House of Representatives inquiry into the activities of the Shipping Board. New Hampshire Senator Jacob H. Gallinger prophetically declared in February 1918 that ". . . when the war closes, whether it be within one year or five years, we shall have a lot of worthless ships on our hands that will have cost this country an enormous amount of money. . . ."[38]

Such concerns were not without some foundation. On May 1, 1918, the Shipping Board's Planning and Statistics Division released a report expressing serious doubt as to the efficacy of wooden steamships for ocean service. It criticized their limited cargo capacity, uncertain life expectancy, and interference with the more necessary steel ship production. By May 1918, not a single completed wooden cargo vessel had been delivered. The causes were legion. In addition to the aforementioned criticisms, slow arrival of machinery, an unwise policy of paying a disproportionate amount for the laying of keels which caused neglect of advanced stages of construction, and the absence of a procedure for monitoring the state of progress in each shipyard had also retarded production.[39]

Recommended administrative changes soon improved conditions, and production accelerated. By September 1918, although loss of Allied shipping for the previous month totaled an incredible 21,404,913 deadweight tons, an excess of building over losses per month finally appeared in August for the first time since December 1915. In less than eighteen months, by sheer dint of energy, abundance of resources, and the can-do optimism of the American labor force, the United States had taken rank for the first time in history as the world's leading shipbuilder.[40]

Production miracles abounded as many shipyards competed to be the fastest shipbuilders in the nation. One such marvel was the building of the wooden steamship *Aberdeen* by the Grays Harbor Motorship Corporation of Aberdeen, Washington. It was later stated that the company had entered the project "with the view of demonstrating that the Grays Harbor Motorship Corporation had the most efficient shipbuilding organization in the entire world," and after a conference with Fleet Corporation representatives, "decided to enter the game of speed." The company had been given contracts to build four wooden steamships about July 1917 and had been ordered to deliver the first ship on January 15, 1918. Lack of supplies and the growth in federal red tape, however, caused the project to be delayed for more than a year. Yet it was the company's unswerving decision to attempt to break the world shipbuilding record that gave birth to *Aberdeen,* a steamship that, in the very process of its creation, would gain a reputation as having been constructed in quicker time than any vessel of similar tonnage in the world, "thus perpetuating the name of the greatest shipbuilding district on either continent."[41]

227

Aberdeen was adapted from the Ferris plan format and designed by M. R. Ward, general manager and designer for Grays Harbor. It soon became known as the "Ward" type (although it was later referred to as the Grays Harbor type). She was 290 feet overall, 49 feet abeam, and 28.2 molded depth, 4,000-tons-deadweight capacity, and equipped with twin engines of 700 horsepower each.[42]

In building the ship, every historic record in the construction of a ship was smashed. Three shifts, working 7½ hours each, were employed. The following record stood as benchmarks for later constructors: laying of keel, 10 seconds; assembling, building, erecting, and shoring 73 square frames, 29 hours, 26 minutes; ceiling, 151 hours; planking, 228½ hours; from keel laying to launching, with superstructure 96 percent complete and auxiliary engine installation 40 percent complete, 17½ days. Her keel was laid at 8:00 A.M., September 9, 1918, and the launching took place September 28, at 9:00 P.M. Engine installation required six days. On Sunday, October 6, *Aberdeen* set off on her trial trip into the Pacific Ocean, laden with two hundred passengers.[43]

By the fall of 1918, anticipating the war's end, Hurley proclaimed an intended cutback in wooden ship construction. The wooden shipbuilding program was barely off and running when the announcement came.[44] Then, on November 11, 1918, Germany surrendered. Not a single wooden ship built during the wooden shipbuilding program had sailed into a European port.

By the time the Armistice was signed, a total of 189 companies in 26 states had been contracted to build ships, 86 of which were to produce

The hulls of three wooden U.S. Shipping Board steamships
take shape at a Pacific Coast shipyard circa 1917–18.
Courtesy National Archives and Record Service

The U.S. Shipping Board steamer *Utoka*, built at Rockland, Maine,
works up a head of steam. *Utoka* would end her days in Mallows Bay,
ignominiously designated by the Corps of Engineers as "hulk 92."
Courtesy Mariners' Museum

wooden vessels and 5 to produce composites. Yet, contractors had completed and delivered only eighty-seven wooden and nine composite vessels ready for sea. Only fifty-five wooden and seven composite ships had either carried cargoes or sailed in ballast for loading ports. Most were engaged in either Hawaiian or coastwise service and bore light and general cargo. The Fleet Corporation had lost only three wooden ships during 1918—bad weather had wrecked the steamer *Blackford* near Arica, Chile, and the steamer *Coos Bay* off the coast of California. Lightning had struck and burned the steamer *Dumaru* near Guam.[45] Yet, their limitations were legion. "The wooden steamers," recalled Robert Dollar, a noted shipping captain, "were too small for long voyages in normal times. Cost of operating one of these vessels after the war would be more than the cost to operate an up-to-date modern, steel, 10,000-ton foreign steamer." Moreover, he felt, "There was no current solution of what will be done to save the ships from the scrap heap."[46]

Within days of the Armistice, the voices of powerful critics of the Shipping Board and its wooden ship program reached a crescendo. Senators Warren G. Harding of Ohio and William M. Calder of New York called for a senate investigation only ten days after the close of hostilities.

The senate probe was unsettling to many. By the onset of the hearings, of the 731 wooden ships that had been contracted for, 134 had been completed, and another 263 were less than half finished, but only 98 had been delivered. Of these, only 76 had actually carried cargo in trade or sailed for loading ports. The vessels, critics claimed, were of inferior design, weakly constructed, poorly caulked, leaked excessively, and were generally too small and expensive for long-distance cargo hauling—the very mission for which they had been intended. Improperly bolted rudders shifted, and structural defects were universal, owing to the green timber employed. They were, it was charged, unable to withstand even their own engine vibrations. "A wooden freighter steamship," noted A. H. Bull, a well-known shipping operator, "is something that ought never to exist, and when built will not exist long." Senator Calder demanded that Hurley order an immediate cessation of all wooden ship construction. Acting Shipping Board Chairman John A. McDonald vigorously defended the program. He cited reports from wooden steamship operators who had observed that, although the ships revealed minor repairable deficiencies and perhaps possessed insufficient bunkering capacity for sustained long-distance operations, they had performed rather well to date under transoceanic conditions.[47]

There were, in fact, many examples of excellent field performance of the wooden and composite steamships available to counter the program's critics. One such example was the composite ship *Obak,* the fifth of a fleet of six composites of 3,500 deadweight tons, which had been reported completed in early 1919 by the Mobile Shipbuilding Company of Mobile, Alabama, and confirmed by a member of the Fleet Corporation's office in New Orleans. Begun as Hull No. 314 and christened *Obak,* on her March 27 sea trial trip in the Gulf of Mexico, she had averaged 12.01 knots, an excess of 2.01 knots an hour above the contract requirement. From full speed ahead, she was brought to a complete standstill in two minutes, which was one and a half minutes faster than any known on record to that date.[48] Such performances, however, failed to stem the mounting tide of alarmist criticism.

The program simply had to be brought to an end without wasting the valuable maritime resources that had been produced. Several ways, in addition to canceling contracts and selling completed wooden ships to private purchasers, were suggested. These included conversions of completed hulls to barges, employment of wooden steamships in the rivers and inland waters of the United States, transformation of hulls into barkentines and schooners for offshore routes, and the sale of completed hulls to foreign countries.[49]

While suggestions continued to emerge, the shipbuilders finished uncancelled contracts. Despite congressional indignation, ships continued to slide off the ways, although immediately after the armistice, production slackened. Many vessels were soon being integrated in the coastwise trade and in transoceanic commerce. By December 1, 1918, a total of 101 wooden ships had been completed, 94 of which had entered active service. Of 85 of those for which tracking records were available, 305 voyages had been made covering a total of 490,422 statute miles. The record revealed that 194 of these voyages were with cargo representing a freight movement of approximately 485,000 tons and total mileage of 319,092 statute miles. The fleet had been active in the Atlantic and Pacific coastwise trade and had traveled to Hawaii and the Philippines, to South America, and to Africa. The movement of cargo, reported the February 1919 edition of the prestigious trade journal *International Marine Engineering*, had been accomplished with no loss to the shippers.[50]

By mid-1919, 174 ships had been placed into service, even as the government began to consider selling off the fleet piecemeal. In June, the Shipping Board advertised twenty Ferris, Hough, and other type hulls in various stages of completion at Puget Sound shipyards to be disposed of. Yet, more than 462 contracted hulls remained unlaunched, and over 150 more would remain uncompleted. By late 1919, deliveries had finally begun to drop off sharply, falling to one or two a month in early 1920 and ceasing entirely by July of that year.[51]

The return of two million men from Europe, the European relief program, and development of foreign trade routes by the United States reintensified national shipping needs. By early 1919, wooden and composite ships were engaged in European commerce, in the Caribbean, and in South American waters. During the summer and fall of 1919, 167 wooden and composite ships traveled to and from Europe, and 49 carried cargoes along the East Coast. It was, unhappily, little more than a false blush, for the following year, except for a slight rise in Caribbean traffic, shipping to all regions decreased dramatically. Despite criticism about them, wooden and composite steamships continued to conduct more business with European and East Coast ports than all other types combined. Indeed, optimism over the future of the American merchant marine was still sufficient enough to warrant the Shipping Board to designate six wooden steamships to be fitted out as cargo-carrying training cruisers for use in instructing merchant marine crews. By March 1919, three of the vessels, *Utoka*, *Alabat*, and *Brookdale*, had been officially assigned to training stations. *Utoka*, a Ferris-type ship, built by the Gilchrist Yard at Thomaston, Maine, was to be outfitted at Portland with accommodations for three hundred apprentices and then assigned to the Atlantic Training Station at Boston, where *Alabant* was already being fitted. *Brookdale*, a Grays Harbor (or Ward) type, built at Aberdeen, Washington, was assigned to the Seattle Training Station. Unfortunately, optimism—and the training programs—were to be short-lived, for the heyday of the wooden steamship was passing even as the last of the breed was sliding down the ways.[52]

The decline in world commerce and the consequent depression in shipbuilding during the early 1920s soon resulted in a vast withdrawal of both wooden and steel vessels from active service. Technological advances further diminished the utility of the wartime fleet, both wood and steel, as oil burners succeeded coal burners, turbine and turboelectric drives replaced reciprocating engines, and the internal combustion engine supplanted steam almost overnight. Sale prices plummeted: wooden steamships, which had cost between $750,000 and $1,000,000 in 1918 and sold for $650,000 in 1919, brought only $100,000 in 1921.[53]

In 1920, the Emergency Fleet Corporation was obliged simply to tie up many of the steel and most of the wooden ships in the 3,000- to 5,000-deadweight-ton class. The so-called "great 1920 tie-up" had begun. By early 1921 more than 400 steel and 264 wooden steamers were inactive in ports around the country. In 1920–21, Rear Admiral William S. Benson, the new Shipping Board chairman, ordered the majority of these vessels assembled and moored in the James River off Claremont, Virginia, about thirty-five miles northwest of Hampton Roads, in order to curtail maintenance expenses.[54] Other smaller contingents were mothballed at anchor off Staten Island, in the Delaware River, at New London, and off Long Island. It was determined that most of the hulls were unsuitable for conversion to barges, as they were too heavy to tow in foul weather, too deep to enter many coastal harbors, and simply too large for general use. A few on the Pacific Coast were converted to sailing vessels as six-masted schooners and five-masted brigantines, but even their careers were short-lived. In the Chesapeake, the freighters *Dover, Ashland,* and *Fort Scott* were purchased by the Davison Chemical Company of Baltimore and employed as barges to haul pyrite oar from Cuba until 1923, when they were abandoned in Baltimore Harbor. Some, such as *Harish* and *Agria,* were dismantled at Newport News. One vessel, *Mayo,* was employed as a break-water at the Kiptopeke ferry landing. *Caponka* was simply run aground in the Rappahannock River and abandoned. For the vast majority of the shipping, however, there now seemed to be no expedient left but the auction block.[55]

The move to dispose of the U.S. Shipping Board's wooden steamship fleet formally began on April 15, 1920, when a special committee appointed by Admiral Benson and chaired by Eugene Meyer Jr., managing director of the War Finance Corporation, convened to make recommendations as to prices, terms, and conditions for the sale of the ships owned or still being constructed. Then, on December 27, 1920, the Shipping Board moved to dispose of what was now being considered by some as one of the greatest white elephants ever produced by a nation at war—

over 300 leaking wooden ships totaling 994,235 deadweight tons. They were barely being kept afloat, pumped out by two tugs and an army of men at a cost of $50,000 a month. Efforts to sell off the fleet piecemeal came to naught. In 1920, only four vessels were sold to United States and foreign buyers. In 1921, only twenty-two more were sold.[56]

In the fall of 1922, the Emergency Fleet Corporation, stung by repeated congressional criticism, finally offered the fleet for sale as a unit "as is and where is." At the time, 211 wooden steamships were riding at anchor at Claremont, Virginia, 13 were at Orange, Texas, and 2 more were at Beaumont, Texas. Only four bids were submitted, the highest being $12 per deadweight ton. Not surprisingly, the bid was refused. A second call went out for bids. This time the high bid was $430,000 for the entire fleet: Congress protested that this, too, was far too low, and the offer was rejected. Finally, in September 1922, a third bid was solicited and accepted. The greatest portion of the fleet was sold for only $750,000— about the wartime price of a single 3,500-deadweight-ton wooden steamship.[57]

During its life, the Emergency Fleet Corporation had completed 296 wooden and 26 composite steamships through the termination of the building program; 283 of the former and all of the latter actually carried cargoes. Assigned primarily to supplement basic United States sea commerce during the war emergency, they had transported a wide variety of commodities. Coal and lumber headed the list, which included sugar, grain, fruit, hides, and fertilizers. They had hauled suphur from Texas to the great munitions factories on the Delaware, coal and cotton to New England ports, and sugar from the Hawaiian Islands to California. Too late their worth had been proved, but their day had passed. The Emergency Fleet Corporation sold a combined 293 wooden steamships, lost 27, and transferred 2 of them to the Navy Department. Of the 293 ships sold, 16 were to foreign buyers, more than 40 were to various firms and individuals in the United States, and the greatest number of all, well over 200 vessels, were to a pair of California lawyers who immediately transferred ownership of the fleet to what would briefly become the largest wooden shipbreaking firm in the United States, a company that only months before hadn't even existed.[58] The lawyers had paid only $1.14 per deadweight ton, a steal in anybody's book!

And the largest portion of that fleet was destined to eventually come to rest on the muddy floor of the Potomac River.

NINETEEN

Widewater

On September 12, 1922, the bid for 233 mostly wood and composite ships belonging to the United States Shipping Board, totaling 855,931 dead-weight tons (or 614,713 gross tons), 90 percent of which was then anchored in the James River, was formally tendered by a San Francisco attorney named George D. Perry and his then-silent boss, William F. Humphrey. The bid was made with the intention of turning the fleet over to the newly incorporated Western Marine and Salvage Company of Alexandria, Virginia (WM&SC), a firm specifically formed to acquire, dismantle, and scrap the wooden Emergency Fleet for its metal content. As a result of the bid, WM&SC acquired 218 wooden and 9 composite ships, as well as half a dozen other vessels, which had cost the government $300 million to build less than four years earlier, for $750,000. Although the bid had been formally submitted by Perry it was his partner Humphrey who served as the company's president and held the controlling interest in WM&SC with a silent partner named Herbert Fleishhacker, a million-aire San Francisco banker. Once the bid was formally accepted by the Shipping Board, custody of 227 wooden and composite ships was immediately assumed by the purchaser, relieving the federal government of an operational maintenance cost of $50,000.[1]

Prior to the sale, the Shipping Board fleet had been lying at anchor in the James River, under the very lax administrative aegis of the War Department. The loose regulatory conditions did not go unnoticed by Humphrey, who, it was soon deduced by the government, was actually the moving force behind WM&SC in all of its affairs. Even before the purchase had been finalized, the attorney later noted in a telegram to Assistant Secretary of War Ralph V. Sollit, the company had been assured by representatives of the Shipping Board that the various control conditions governing the fleet anchorage on the James would be continued once the fleet became the property of WM&SC. It had been implied by the War Department, with whom the company would be obliged to deal for a temporary anchorage site, that stringent rules and regulations would not be imposed. But Humphrey demanded more than verbal assurance. One Shipping Board representative, Albert Lasker, eager to insure that no obstructions to the sale occurred, quickly "obtained from Secretary [of

War] Weeks a letter consenting to [the] continuance of the James River anchorage without any conditions under which these ships were anchored while owned by [the] Shipping Board."[2]

With one end securely tied down, WM&SC, "with the consent of the War Department," was further assured that a "secondary, temporary anchorage" for dismantling the hulls at Widewater, Virginia, approximately thirty-one miles south of Washington, D.C., on the Potomac River, would be approved once the company assumed ownership of the ships and posted a $7,000 bond for every vessel moved to the new site.[3] The bonds were required to protect the United States against possible loss if the government were obliged to assume the responsibility of disposing of the fleet should WM&SC fail. Approval of the secondary (and soon to be primary) anchorage on the Potomac River was imperative, for the company's main dismantling operation was to be at a shipyard facility in nearby Alexandria. The yard had recently been owned by the Virginia Shipbuilding Corporation and was typical of many that had been quickly erected during the war and then forced into bankruptcy by the post-war depression in the shipbuilding industry. Yet, having gone out of business in the late summer of 1922, the facility was still well-equipped with extensive wharfage, four marine railways, and warehouse space adjacent to a rail line spur. It was eminently suitable for the dismantling operations planned for the Emergency Fleet. Here the hull of every ship could be quickly and efficiently stripped of engines, boilers, and other highly profitable

The steamer *Bedminster,* still bearing her camouflage coat, had already been stripped of her rudder as she awaited the final denouement.
Courtesy Mariners' Museum

and easily removable components and stored until they could be shipped off by rail.[4] The hull itself, however, was an entirely different matter.

The Widewater anchorage area was only a few dozen miles to the south of Alexandria and set against a rural sector of the Virginia shoreline near Brent's Point and southwest of Marlow's Bay. Established well off the main shipping channel, the fleet anchorage, it was felt, would pose only a minimal hazard to navigation. Moreover, its rural location was likely to generate few objections from local residents, as the shoreline was sparsely inhabited. Yet, the anchorage area itself was a location of some historic note and of some commercial consequence to the Potomac fisheries industry, as WM&SC would unhappily soon discover. From well before 1862 to at least the 1880s, Maryland and Virginia had been served by a ferry running from Sandy Point to Widewater, linking the town of Clifton, Virginia, with southern Maryland. The waters off Widewater were considered to be among the most bountiful commercial fishing areas of the entire Potomac and had, for two centuries, yielded herring, shad, rockfish, and sturgeon. By the 1880s, the sturgeon industry was being serviced by a railroad terminal at Widewater, to which point Philadelphia-built fishing vessels were brought in on rail cars and put to work by local watermen, while fish and caviar were transshipped to consumers in such cities as New York and Boston. Sport fishing was also a rewarding pastime for many who took the trouble to travel to Widewater. Among those who did was President Grover Cleveland, who had made it one of his favorite retreats. In 1903 Professor Samuel Pierpont Langley, working under a War Department contract, made history at Widewater when he flew his model of a "heavier-than-air plane" three thousand feet in ninety seconds.[5] Such considerations, however, were of absolutely no interest to the managers of WM&SC.

Once assured of an anchorage at Widewater, the company moved aggressively to assume command of the fleet. The company was initially given wide latitude by the government in developing procedures for the dismantling and disposal of the vessels and "from time to time fully advised the Office of Engineers, U.S. Army." Indeed, if the anchorage at Widewater was to be maintained, a good working relationship with the Office of Engineers was an absolute necessity. At first, company officials were optimistic and noted that "we have every right to anticipate that we would have the cooperation of various departments of the Government in carrying on these operations." That view would soon change radically.[6]

By October 1922, the first vessels destined for dismantling at Alexandria, *Mojave* and *Alanthus,* had arrived at the Virginia Shipbuilding Corporation wharf. The project, however, suffered an almost immediate setback when a fire broke out and engulfed both vessels. Although the conflagration was later termed "one of the most stubborn Alexandria fire fighters have battled," both ships were ultimately saved, then stripped, and towed down the river to Widewater to await final disposal.[7]

The effects of the fire upon the facility were apparently enough to delay work on any more ships for another four months. Finally, on February 19, 1923, the dismantling operations were resumed at an accelerated rate, for by April 17 no fewer than twenty-six ships had been brought up to Alexandria. "Work of scrapping the government's 'wooden navy,'" reported the *Alexandria Gazette*, " is now being pushed at the plant here at the rate of about two ships each week." The hulls were systematically relieved of metal, engines, boilers, and valuable superstructure materials, usable timbers, and other fixtures valued at over $10,000 per ship. With the government netting little more than $3,300 per vessel, the company's potential profits were conservatively estimated at over $1.6 million. The company's problems, however, had only begun, as it chose to focus only on the most profitable aspect of the project—the removal of the large bulks of scrap such as engines and boilers—and to ignore the security of the fleet itself, which was anchored down river almost untended.[8] Further disasters were inevitable.

At 8:00 A.M. on April 18, a report was received by Captain E. G. Huefe, fire marshal at the United States Marine Barracks at Quantico, Virginia, that a number of ships were afire on the river several miles south of the base. Huefe and six marines armed with axes and accompanied by a photographer from the First Aviation Group, also based at Quantico, immediately secured a motorboat and sped to the site of the conflagration. The fire proved to be directly in the midst of the WM&SC anchorage at Widewater. There the marines discovered at least ten ships belonging to the salvage company at anchor, three of which were burning furiously, and a fourth just catching fire.[9]

When Huefe and his men boldly boarded one of the burning ships, they discovered that the entire fleet had been left to the care of a pair of watchmen. The ships had all been bound together in a group by steel cables, and the two watchmen were engaged in a desperate attempt to unlash one of the burning vessels to prevent the fire from spreading to the remainder of the fleet. Their feeble efforts would have been doomed to failure without the timely arrival of the marines.[10]

Quickly Huefe, the coxswain of the motorboat, and another marine, all armed with axes, joined in the attack on the cables bonding the two center vessels together. After an hour's hard work, the cables were finally severed, just as the USS *Owl*, a former minesweeper which had been converted to a tug, arrived on the scene and successfully breasted the burning vessels away from the unburned ships. The tug crew quickly passed firehoses to Huefe's burning ship and then proceeded to pump water into the flames from five of its own hoses. Huefe would later report that the "prime factor in saving any of [the vessels] was the arrival of the Navy tug."[11]

As the grim battle continued, agents of WM&SC from Alexandria, alerted to the conflagration by the military, arrived on the scene by land, escorted by a Major Manney, chief of staff at Quantico, and a Lieutenant Geotage. Geotage and the agents had soon transferred to a small motor launch commanded by a gunnery sergeant named Thruman and bravely sailed in amidst the burning fleet. Four ships were now completely ablaze. Quickly the party joined Huefe in his desperate fight aboard one of the vessels. Then, about noon, the fire tug *Diligent,* hastily chartered by WM&SC at Alexandria, also arrived and began to pump streams of water on the burning ships, albeit with considerable difficulty as several hose lines quickly burst when pressure was applied.[12]

Soon the battle was being observed from above as a U.S. Navy DH-4 seaplane circled to record the disaster on film. By midday, believing the fire to be checked and the situation well in hand, Huefe and his men returned to Quantico, leaving the two tugs to bring the remainder of the conflagration under control. Unfortunately, the conflict was far from over, as the fire suddenly gained renewed fury. Aided by the government tug *Shenandoah,* which arrived on the scene after Huefe's departure, the fight continued well into the night. Indeed, not until 4:00 A.M., April 19, would the blaze finally be completely drowned.[13]

Reports by H. E. Whitaker, general manager for WM&SC at Alexandria, and Major E. W. Fales, the U.S. Army infantry liaison officer at Quantico, had soon reached the district engineer's office in Washington, and they were anything but good. Five of the ten ships at the Widewater anchorage, *Okiya, Catawba, Quidnic, Gray Eagle,* and the historic *Aberdeen,* had been burned to the water's edge and finally come to rest in shallow water partly heeled over on the bottom. The ship *Wasco* was scuttled in place to prevent destruction. Fortunately for WM&SC, although the vessels had gone down well out in the river, they were still a half mile away from the deep water channel.[14]

An investigation by WM&SC soon revealed that the fire had been caused by the explosion of a kerosene cook stove accidentally overturned by one of the watchmen while preparing his breakfast. The chief delay in cutting the burning ships away from the others had been caused by "their being fastened together by steel cables." Whitaker offered the suggestion that the steel cables be replaced by manila cables to allow a quick release in case of a similar occurrence in the future.[15]

Despite it all, Whitaker found the event to be a mixed blessing by noting that five other ships had been "saved by the splendid work of the government boats." But more important, no one had been injured.[16]

Then disaster struck anew.

Sometime before April 28, a heavy gale started one (or possibly several) of the burnt hulks near Brent's Point and set it adrift, causing an immediate hazard to navigation. In a panic, Whitaker reported the problem to District Engineer Major M. C. Tyler by telephone and then set off to obtain a tug to return the hulks to the anchorage area and remoor them all securely. Tyler was angered over the recent events and warned the company "that unless immediate steps are taken to remedy the condition, I will recommend that legal action be taken." Without a War Department permit, WM&SC's right to the anchorage, which had been approved only on a *pro tem* basis, could be removed at any time until the department finally issued a standing permit.[17] The Army's bellicosity, however, was little more than fuss and feathers, for both sides were fully aware that the fleet would have to be anchored somewhere and managed by someone, and it certainly wasn't going to be the federal government!

Despite Tyler's protests, on May 24, 1923, Major General Lansing H. Beach, the chief of engineers, recommended to the secretary of war that WM&SC's application for anchoring about two hundred ships at Widewater be accepted. He suggested, however, that the privilege be supported by stringent regulations to insure that no menace to navigation on the Potomac be produced, and that the United States not be exposed to any expense. He further recommended that the rules and regulations be adopted under certain articles of the Rivers and Harbors Act of March 4, 1915, and submitted a draft of the proposed regulations to the Secretary of War.[18]

The War Department acted promptly. At Tyler's suggestion, rules and regulations "solely applicable to this [Widewater] anchorage" were developed. Principal among these were: (1) all ships being brought into the Potomac were to be anchored together in groups of five; (2) all ships were to be provided with fire protection equipment; (3) a watchman was to be assigned to every unit of five vessels brought into the anchorage; (4) a tugboat was to be permanently assigned by WM&SC to the anchorage at all times; and (5) all expenses incurred in the dismantling of the ships and board and lodging of government inspectors assigned to monitor company activities in the anchorage ground and the Alexandria dismantling operation be paid by the company. The logistical and management concerns were well founded, for by mid-June 1923 it was predicted that a total of 215 vessels would soon be anchored off Widewater, a figure that would eventually be topped off in several months at 218 ships.[19]

WM&SC was, of course, extremely unhappy with the new restrictions. Appeals for more lenient regulations were immediately sought, over the head of the chief of engineers, from the assistant secretary of war and from influential members of Congress, by the well-connected company executives. Wealth and personal connections, the officials of WM&SC

were confident, would win the day on the anchorage issue. On June 13, Herbert Fleishhacker telegraphed Congressman Kahns seeking relief from the regulations. From his plush office in San Francisco, William D. Humphrey telegraphed Assistant Secretary of War Sollit, repeating Fleishhacker's communiqué almost verbatim.[20]

WM&SC's complaints were legion. The cost of tug, security, and fire protection, it was stated, "will involve this company in unnecessary expense which will result in severe loss in its operations," pointing out that no such conditions had been required by the secretary of war for the anchorage of the ships on the James while they had been under the ownership of the U.S. Shipping Board.[21]

Yet, while complaining of the expense, the company officials sought to allay any concerns that WM&SC might be fiscally challenged by the project and assured the government leaders that the "company is financially able to carry out any obligation it undertakes and is willing to obligate itself in a legal agreement to cover this contingency." All they wanted to do was "to be relieved of the above conditions which require such unnecessary expenditures."[22]

Well aware that the last word with the Office of Engineers came from above, Humphrey concluded his direct appeal to Sollit with a personal plea that the assistant secretary himself intervene on behalf of WM&SC. As bait, the company simultaneously moved to offer its own modified—and less expensive—plan for the anchorage of the fleet.[23]

On June 19, WM&SC General Manager H. E. Whitaker proposed placing the ships in single units with a minimum of one hundred feet between each, rather than in multiples of five lashed together, with the bow of each facing upstream "and properly anchored with a single bower anchor" in shallow water. The seacocks on each ship would then be opened to permit just enough water through the hull to sink the vessel and firmly hold it on the bottom to prevent movement by wind and tide. In so doing, he suggested, practically all obstruction to navigation would be removed as the ships would be out of the channel area and close to shore. Should a fire occur onboard any vessel, only that portion above the waterline would be burned and would not materially influence the cost of pumping it out and removing it from the anchorage ground to some predetermined burning park nearby for final disposal. Thus, the requirement for watchmen, fire equipment, and an ever-present tug would be removed. Indeed, the cost of reclaiming a burned hull in this manner "would be very materially less" than that of a ship, "as usually anchored so that the bond called for could be reduced to a small fraction of that required."[24] The company, it seemed, now wanted to sink the whole fleet in shallow water to prevent it from floating off!

The following day, Major F. B. Dowling of the Office of Engineers called upon the assistant secretary of war to respond in person to Humphrey's June 14 communiqué to the secretary. Judging from the presentation Dowling was prepared to make, it would appear that the behind-the-scenes lobbying of company officers in the marble halls of Capitol Hill and the War Department had been unquestionably successful. The major appeared, hat in hand, to try to explain, based upon past experience, the condition of affairs and to defend the manner in which the Office of Engineers had conducted itself with respect to the anchorage issue. He approached the meeting now prepared to agree that if the company submitted a formal request for modification of details regarding their anchorage permit, for sinking the vessels in place, and a reduction of their bond, "the case [would] be considered by the Department on its merits." Secretary Sollit, however, was absent (or, more than likely, unwilling to meet with the major) and would not be available until June 25. The major dutifully left a request that he be contacted and then, lest he be accused of being neglectful of duty, drafted an unaddressed memo documenting his attempt to visit the secretary and explain the willingness of the Office of Engineers to negotiate the situation.[25]

The problem of what to do with the largest assemblage of shipping ever to be convened at one time and place on the Potomac River was soon dropped in the lap of District Engineer J. A. O'Connor, who had suddenly—and mysteriously—replaced Major Tyler on the project. After considerable study and calculations, utilizing the case and condition of the scuttled *Wasco* as a model, he observed that with depths ranging between fifteen and eighteen feet throughout the anchorage area, the vessels *could*, in fact, be sunk from five to eight feet before resting on the bottom. Once sunk, each vessel's buoyancy would be neutralized by the water within its hull, and the weight of the exposed ship would act as an additional anchor. In the event of accidental fire in which the upper works of the vessel were burned, the removal of the hull, after closing off the seacocks and pumping the water out, would, as Whitaker had suggested, actually be "greatly simplified." In O'Connor's view, it would indeed be permissible then to remove all requirements for a tug, fire equipment, and all but two watchmen.[26] Perhaps, the now happy officers of WM&SC must have thought, we have a man we can deal with! But their wish was little more than a chimera.

How the fleet was to be finally disposed of was a matter which, although O'Connor had not been requested to comment on, was of key importance to the company's liability. The engineer now expressed his own opinion rather forcefully, and in a manner not at all to the liking of WM&SC, which had hoped to remove the expensive bonding requirements altogether. Continuing the requirement for bonding was, in the engineer's view, necessary to "safeguard the Federal Government from expense in the event the Western Marine & Salvage Company should fail and leave many vessels for the government to remove." Indeed, many methods for disposal had already been considered, but the most feasible and least expensive of all, said O'Connor, was to fill the ships with sand, tow them to sea, batten down their hatches so that the sand couldn't be dumped, and scuttle them off Cape Charles, Virginia. An informal inquiry at the Navy Department had yielded the advice that if such an effort were to be undertaken, the ships should be hauled at least 75 miles out and sunk with at least 250 feet of water over them to permit the "maneuvering of submarines."[27] Moreover, owing to the initial cost of assembling the necessary wrecking outfit such as pumps, dredges, derricks, tugs, etc., should it ever be necessary to remove the hulls at government expense, a change in the application of surety bonds would be necessary. Since it was now proposed to accept only bonds for units of not less than five vessels, the bond would have to be available for the removal and disposal of any and all vessels in the group. He reasoned that the bonds should specifically name the vessels covered by each bond and that substitutions of new vessels in a bond unit, because of the removal of existing vessels, be authorized by the district engineer's office. Each unit of five vessels should, he suggested, require a bond of $35,000.[28]

On July 26, 1923, General Beach recommended to the secretary of war that the revised WM&SC plan be accepted on the condition that "satisfactory surety bonds" to protect the United States be produced by the company. The general, all too prophetically, pointed out that the "raising of sunken craft may not prove to be costly, but the disposal of the hulls is a problem which offers possibilities of considerable expense."[29]

Beach accompanied his recommendations with descriptions of the set boundaries of the Widewater Anchorage Grounds, as well as the text of the new rules and regulations. On August 2, the assistant secretary of war approved the rules and regulations and advised the general to inform WM&SC of the action and to make the action public. By August 21, O'Connor had formally informed the company of the implementation. The following day WM&SC submitted an application for a permit to anchor the first great batch of sixty vessels of the fleet in the now formal Widewater Anchorage Grounds established on July 26.[30]

As the dismantling process continued unabated at Alexandria, WM&SC began considering a variety of plans for the disposal of the empty hulls, dismissing one after another as either too expensive or impractical. Finally, in early September, it was decided that a test be conducted on one of the five vessels that had been accidentally burned and sunk in April. The ship was to be raised and hauled close to shore, burned once more, stripped of all loose metal (primarily fittings and bracings), then hauled upon the nearby beach and burned yet again. The scheme was submitted to the district engineer for approval, and on September 6 a permit was issued for the experiment to proceed.[31]

To avoid the possibility of objections being raised from local residents along the shore, a witnessed affidavit consenting to the beaching of the hulks was secured from the riparian property owner, one W. B. Lee, before the test could move forward at the planned beaching site. Finally, on September 21, the first disposal test was carried out. The sacrificial vessel, the famed wooden steamer *Aberdeen,* was raised, placed with its bow about one hundred feet from the edge of Brent's Marsh in five to six feet of water, with its stern channelward approximately two hundred feet and in eight feet of water. Once the burning was completed, a floating derrick began removing an estimated two hundred tons of scrap metal consisting of strapping, bolts, and the like. With this weight removed, the vessel was pulled farther up on the beach and again set afire for the last time. "If deemed necessary," the Army engineer who reported on the test later wrote, "the beached hull will be filled with dredge or other material to securely anchor the hull and prevent its getting back into deep water." It was later reported, however, that the second fire had been entirely effective and that the hull had been "completely disposed of."[32] *Aberdeen* was just one week shy of her fourth birthday when they killed her.

The test was deemed a total success, and it had been completed none too soon. By mid-October it was being reported that a total of 218 vessels were already at, or would soon be ready to, anchor at Widewater. On October 3, based upon the successful destruction of *Aberdeen,* a second permit was granted to the company to dispose of an additional ten hulls (which included those burned in the April fire). It was anticipated that the hulls would be placed side by side no more than fifty feet apart, as close to the beach as feasible, then burned, and hauled upon the beach as far ashore as possible.[33]

A week later the second hull, that of *Gray Eagle,* was raised, burned, beached, and burned again. The destruction of the third hull, *Blythedale,* however, proved less than successful. The ship sank while afloat and afire, and the tests were temporarily called off.[34] But now, even more significant problems were threatening.

Although the company had taken precautions to address the possibility of protests by local inhabitants, little note had been made regarding those who relied upon the bounty of the Potomac for their incomes. On October 5, 1923, Secretary of Commerce Herbert Hoover received a letter dated September 29, 1923, from a Fredericksburg lawyer named Alvin T. Embrey. Embrey had been employed by a body of Potomac River watermen to represent them as a group to protest officially the activities of WM&SC. Duplicates of the letter had also been sent to the secretary of the interior and the secretary of the navy. The Virginia commissioner of fisheries was also strongly urged to intervene on behalf of the watermen.

Dear Mr. Secretary:

On behalf of numerous fishermen along the Potomac River; on both the Maryland and Virginia shores—and by fishermen I mean men who make their living by fishing and thus add to the country's food supply—I desire to file a protest against the practice of some salvage company which has purchased a number of wooden hull boats from the Government and make their anchorage in about sixteen feet of water in the Potomac River between Quantico and Arkendale, that is the point opposite the United States Marine Post and the mouth of Aquia Creek.

It seems that this salvage company takes these boats to Alexandria for dismantling the machinery and then returns the hulls to this anchoring ground and then sets them afire. This "flat" on which these boats are anchored is the best fishing ground for gill nets for shad and herring on the Potomac River between its mouth and Washington.

When these boats are burned large portions of the hull, with nails and bolts in them, fall off and as soon as they strike the water the fire is put out and they sink. The hulls burn to the water's edge and sink, and I am informed, their propellers and ribs inside are often on them and these sink. This has a double effect; first the wreckage catches the nets and cause them to be cut to pieces; second—the charred wood, being otherwise clean water on the fishing ground, has a tendency to drive away the fish.

In addition to this, the presence of these hulls on this flat is a menace to navigation endangering the sailing vessels that cross these flats coming from the mouth of Aquia Creek and going up to Stone Landing and Coal Landing. . . .

Yours very truly,[35]
Alvin T. Embrey

Embrey's letter to Hoover, forwarded for comment by the secretary's office through normal channels, did not reach the office of the chief of engineers until October 9. However, a telegram from Virginia Commissioner of Fisheries McDonald Lee from Richmond sent on October 4 arrived only a day after the permit for burning the ten vessels had been granted to WM&SC.

Lee's telegram was far more strident in tone than Embrey's protest and received instant attention by the chief of engineers. "Serious complaint," it read, "that wooden derelicts being burned below Alexandria will for years break up fishing and duck feeding grounds in Aquia Creek and Widewater particularly. Will you not stop this immediately and designate some other burying ground not injurious?"[36]

Lee's complaint was immediately forwarded to the district engineer with instructions that he immediately produce "a full report as to what is being done with the derelicts, and the condition in which they are being left."[37] By October 9, in the absence of the district engineer, Captain W. A. Snow, his assistant, dispatched a complete and succinct report of the key events regarding the fleet to that date and the manner in which the disposal project was being conducted.

The operation of burning the hulls, Snow reported, "is a rather local one," which was carried out mainly in the open river. Each hull took from eighteen to thirty-six hours to burn down. From all indications, it was expected that the entire project would be completed within two years, although an anticipated speeding up of operations planned by WM&SC could materially reduce this time. Indeed, if the present testing continued to produce successful results, Snow proposed that permits be granted to beach all of the hulls "not exceeding 218 in number."[38]

In concluding his report, Snow took issue with Lee's charge that the disposal activity would "for years break up fishing and duck feeding grounds in Aquia Creek and Widewater," and suggested that if details could be furnished to prove the statement, "some consideration may be given to arrangements looking to overcome the objections noted," saying, in essence, put up or shut up.[39]

Snow's report was soon dispatched to the chief of engineers and quickly synthesized into a more diplomatic reply to Lee by Acting Chief of Engineers Brigadier General Harry Taylor on October 16.[40]

On this same date, O'Connor responded to Embrey's protests. The engineer tactfully suggested that the lawyer had been "somewhat misinformed as to what actually takes place at Widewater." He noted that by this time, only three ships had been burned, described the procedures that had been adopted for their disposal, and assured him "that very little, if any, material such as would catch or cut the gill nets drops overboard," and that a government inspector was kept on the job to insure that any materials that were dropped overboard were properly removed. As to the presence of dangerous obstructions such as propellers, shafts, bolts, etc., he pointed out that the salvage company was, in fact, specifically in the business of recovering such scrap metal and would most certainly remove any that was present. With regard to the charge that the charred wood drove away fish, he submitted that "it is a well known fact that charred wood has a sweetening effect, being used as a filtering or purifying agent." He concluded with an offer to meet with any fishermen at Widewater on any mutually agreeable date.[41]

Although the Office of Engineers had responded as promptly as possible to the watermen's protests, their concerns—and political clout— were not taken lightly. Indeed, revisions of the rules and regulations governing the anchorage were soon being drawn up. A halt to burning operations after November 1, 1923, was imposed upon WM&SC. On December 5, 1923, a modification of the rules and regulations was formally submitted, specifically "to better serve the fishing industry." The recommended changes were significant in that they suggested that the anchorage grounds be relocated and that improvements be instituted in the handling and disposal of the dismantled materials.[42] Accordingly, a new anchorage area was defined and laid out and revised rules and regulations drafted. WM&SC might have clout with the War Department, but the local citizenry, it appeared, were not without their own champions.

Unlike the changes in the anchorage area, modifications of the rules and regulations were not as severe and were ostensibly produced not as a reaction to the complaints of the fishermen but merely to provide "a greater flexibility in control so that the results of the experience in handling these vessels can be taken advantage of without requiring further changes."[43] Recalling the events of April 1923, when several vessels drifted away, it was now deemed mandatory that ships that were in no condition to be navigated under their own power were to be placed in the anchorage area in a manner to be approved by the district engineer, specifically to secure them against movement caused by wind, storms, floating ice, current flow, and so forth. Specifications that they be placed bow pointing upstream and anchored by a single 4,000 pound anchor and then sunk in position were dropped. The requirement that they be placed in the anchorage area in an orderly and uniform arrangement, working out to a central point, with open lanes not less than seventy yards maintained around each vessel, was also dropped.[44]

Overall, the east-west boundary had been withdrawn about 400 yards farther from the channel of the river and the anchorage moved 750 yards farther north. The modified anchorage was now approximately 3 miles in length and 1⅓ miles in width. The movement of the anchorage area closer to the Virginia shore now provided a more comfortable width of about 2 miles off the Maryland shore. Moreover, the anchorage no longer obstructed "the best fishing ground" on the river, a fact that tended to smooth the ruffled feathers of the Potomac watermen, if not extinguishing all of their concerns about the hulls themselves.[45]

By the end of 1923, WM&SC's massive scrapping operation, billed as the largest enterprise of its kind in American history, had met with mixed results. Two more vessels would be burned before the spring of 1924, but neither was able to be beached on Brent's Marsh as had been planned. The dismantling process at Alexandria had proceeded in an orderly fashion, almost without incident. Yet the fleet anchorage and disposal program had incurred nothing but problems from the very inception of the project. By December 31, only five ships had been burned in test disposal operations, but only two, *Aberdeen* and *Gray Eagle*, had been beached and effectively disposed of.[46] Although quelled for the moment, continued protests from the Potomac watermen was a factor that was likely to become a recurring headache. Not surprisingly, WM&SC began to consider alternatives and countermeasures to the expanding field of difficulties expected in the days ahead.

TWENTY

A Horde of Squealing Rats

By the spring of 1924, unhappy with the anchorage and disposal problems at the Widewater Anchorage Grounds, and after months of engineering studies and consultation with numerous experts in such matters, WM&SC had decided to seek and secure an even more remote tract of shoreline upon which to beach and burn the fleet. The most adequate and convenient site proved to be the tiny embayment on the Maryland side of the river known as Marlow's Bay.[1] The little bay was close to the main anchorage, sheltered, shallow, and, best of all, the surrounding shore frontage from Sandy Point as far south as the north shore of Marlow's Creek was owned by a farmer named Henry Koester and was for sale. On April 21, 1924, Koester transferred title to the entire tract, totaling 566¼ acres, to WM&SC.[2]

The company planned to maintain the anchorage at Widewater but tow the dismantled shipping to Marlow's Bay, where they would be burned, hauled ashore on a marine railway system specifically constructed for the purpose, and then further reduced. The remains of the hulls could then be permanently beached, burned, and buried beneath spoil dredged from the river. To facilitate the effort, four great marine railways were to be constructed at Sandy Point, less than two miles from the Widewater Anchorage Grounds. The Office of Engineers, which had final approval over any change of methodology, termed the operation "a positive and satisfactory method for disposing of these dismantled hulls." With the official blessing of the office of engineers in hand, the company began construction work at Sandy Point, installing such machinery and equipment as was necessary to the operation."[3]

Yet controversy over the Widewater Anchorage Grounds was far from over. On April 21, the day WM&SC sealed the deal with Koester, the commanding officer of the Tenth Marine Regiment (artillery) at Quantico complained to his superiors of the impossibility of securing a suitable range at the base for 150-mm guns and anti-aircraft artillery without firing over portions of the Potomac south of the base because of the ships in the anchorage grounds. A week later, the commandant booted the complaint up to the major general commandant of Marines. The commandant of Marines formally contacted the U.S. Army chief of engineers regarding the problem and noted that the ships "are in the way of good spotting and in the danger zone," and requested that a decision be made "as to whether or not it would be practicable to move the Anchorage Ground and also provide regulations for control of navigation on the Potomac River for artillery firing from Quantico, Virginia."[4] In the best military tradition, the chief of engineers bumped the question upstairs to the secretary of war. WM&SC was dumbfounded. Did this mean that the anchorage would again have to be moved, this time so that the military could practice with their guns? The secretary of war, after considerable study, replied in the negative.[5]

WM&SC and the Office of Engineers, however, were not out of the woods yet, for the local watermen would continue to play havoc with the company's plans, as accidents on the river continued to crop up. One typical complaint surfaced on May 14, when R. W. Power, of Widewater, grumbled to R. Walton Moore, U.S. representative from the Eighth Congressional District of Virginia, about "the old boats in Potomac River at Widewater." Walton forwarded the complaint to Chief of Engineers Beach on May 21, along with the notation: "Is there not something that can be done to relieve the condition of which he complains?"[6]

Two days later, as was now normal practice, the complaint ended up on the desk of District Engineer O'Connor. By May 26, O'Connor had prepared yet another reply. Mr. Power, he stated, was misinformed as to the operations under way. In previous plans, he reported, a total of five hulls had been burned and beached downstream of Brent's Marsh, two miles below Widewater. Adverse weather conditions (the storm of April 1923?) caused two to sink about seven hundred yards off Brent's Marsh. Of the five vessels accidentally burned in the anchorage area, three still remained where they had sunk. While in the area, five other vessels had been blown away before anchors could be laid for them, although recent inspection had shown that all were now properly anchored. Of the five blown away, three were still aground off Widewater, but the other two (as well as the scores of dismantled hulls) were in the anchorage ground, the upper end of which was three quarters of a mile off Widewater.[7]

O'Connor went on to report WM&SC's plans for the development of the marine railway facilities at Sandy Point to haul the hulls ashore before their final burning. There were even plans now, as soon as a current spate of bad weather had settled, to remove all of the burned vessels more than three hundred feet offshore (including the burned hulls at Widewater). Steps were also under way to remove, over the next few months, all debris from the areas where ships had been burned in the river. The report was concluded with a promise to get in touch personally with Power and other interested parties to fully explain the project.[8]

By June, although O'Connor had apparently not yet met with Power, General Beach was able to report to Congressman Moore: "The hulls are now hauled out on skidways at Sandy Point, Md., and burned on the beach in five to eight feet of water." A log boom had been erected around the burning area in Marlow's Bay to prevent any wreckage from floating away. But an even more comprehensive approach was being matured as a full-scale marine railway complex was soon to be built (presumably at Sandy Point) to haul the hulls out on dry land before burning.[9]

Not until early August was O'Connor able to meet with Power and other complainants from Widewater.[10] Four hulls *(Okiya, Catawba, Quidnic,* and *Blythedale)*, O'Connor was informed, were lying 1,500 feet off the Widewater shore and had completely spoiled the ducking grounds and "were an eyesore and nuisance to the waterfront." One complainant reported that wreckage lay about in the river, and, in an allusion to malfeasance by WM&SC, charged that some of the ships had anchor chains overboard without anchors attached. Although he wouldn't agree to put his charges in writing, he was more than willing to "supply information in the field." O'Connor dutifully promised to take up the issue of the removal of the four hulls and the presence of loose debris in the area with WM&SC and then to take whatever necessary steps were required to correct the situation. "No further action," he reported to his superior, "is necessary."[11]

As the end of the third year of work approached, and the Office of Engineers continued to contend with the staccato of complaints, WM&SC had finally begun to move forward with construction of its facilities at Sandy Point. The work was now doubly important, for by March 1925 the dismantling operations at Alexandria would be concluded. The most profitable stage of the project was almost over, but the most expensive problems lay ahead. Although construction work on the four marine railways had been initiated early in the year, due to "inequalities of the bottom on which the skidways were placed and the inability to secure an even pull from the four pulling units," the arrangement proved to be an awful failure. The railways were next to useless. Indeed, by late April 1925, the company had managed to pull out and burn only five hulls.[12]

Protests from watermen were now extended to include the burning grounds at Marlow's Bay. One typical complaint was issued on April 27, 1925, when one Walter F. Schwab of La Plata, Maryland, took objection to the company's "placing old wooden ships in Marlowe's cr. with the object of burning them." Claiming that "this is the only harbor for river boats betw. Nanjemoi and Chicamuxin Crks [sic]," he demanded that immediate consideration of the matter be given to "prevent the loss of a harbor that means so much to all who have traffic on the Potomac."[13]

Facility construction problems also abounded. The company sought permits to build two wharves at Sandy Point to promulgate the handling of salvaged materials, but construction was soon stymied. Finally, in April, one wharf built "supposedly under permit" was completed but failed to meet the approval of the Office of Engineers which considered it "an illegal structure," as it was not to specifications. Fortunately for the company, since the wharf had not been built to full length according to plan, it could not be considered a hazard to navigation and was allowed to stand. It would continue to stand for the next half century.[14]

On March 25 a permit had also been requested by the company to burn and beach five dismantled hulls in Marlow's Bay or haul them out at Sandy Point on the railways "as an experiment of the feasibility of such a method of disposal." The hulls were to be burned, five vessels at a time, encompassed by log booms draped with approved netting to snag submerged drift. The burning area was in $7\frac{1}{2}$ to 13 feet of water and approximately 1,400 feet from the north-central shoreline of Marlow's Bay. Refined conditions of the plan stated that once the burning had been completed, the five charred hulls were then to be drawn up in a line against the central shoreline of the bay. By early May, work on the test operation, with a foreman and six men, under the watchful eye of an inspector appointed by the district engineer, had commenced. At Sandy Point, a "Mother Ship," *Obak,* later to be joined by *Botsford,* was permanently anchored to serve as a dormitory for company workers.[15]

O'Connor was cautious in his assessment of the newest scheme for the reduction of the hulls. Indeed, he was becoming more critical of the company's efforts with every passing day. "There have," he wrote, "been four different regimes of control in the lower Potomac to secure results but none have solved the problem. While considerable money has been spent at Sandy Point on the marine railway scheme it was poorly managed and financed. In my opinion the disposal operations have been hampered and retarded by inadequate expenditures and a false economy where positive results are necessary."[16] His views of the company's financial maneuvers were equally negative. They were only reinforced in late April when WM&SC President William F. Humphrey and Executive Officer Ray Baker sought a meeting with Major General Taylor, the chief of engineers. On April 24, the company executives and the engineers convened to discuss WM&SC's desire to substitute bonds with personal sureties for certain bonds on file in the district engineer's office covering the dismantled hulls in the Widewater Anchorage Ground. General Taylor requested that the reasons for the request be set down in writing, which was done and communicated to his office the following day.

"Our dismantling operations at Alexandria have been completed," Humphrey wrote.

> We are now concentrating our operations at Sandy Point, Maryland, with a view to the prompt and expeditious destruction of the dismantled hulls. The operations at Sandy Point have already entailed a large expenditure of money, and the future operations for the destruction

of the hulls will probably be conducted at an expenditure greater than can be recovered through the disposition of the salvage material to be obtained in such operations. It is therefore important to us to curtail expenditures at every point where we can legitimately do so. The furnishing of bonds with corporate surety subjects us to an annual premium charge, based on the number of hulls now in the anchorage, or nearly $15,000. It would be greatly to our advantage, and we believe it would be to the advantage of the Government from the standpoint of having the destruction of the hulls expedited, if this amount could be transferred for expenditure in the active prosecution of the work.[17]

An investigation of WM&SC and the financial status of it two principals, Herbert Fleishhacker and William F. Humphrey, who were to offer sureties (and who had immediately resigned from their positions as officers in order that they could serve as bondsmen for the company they still controlled), was quietly carried out by the District Office. A credit check provided by the Bradstreet Commercial Rating Agency indicated "that they enjoy a good personal and professional standing with responsibility for any reasonable credit." Indeed, both men were quite wealthy! Fleishhacker's net worth was estimated at between $5 million and $25 million, and Humphrey's at between $200,000 and $600,000.[18]

While the Office of Engineers continued to consider a verdict on the bond issue, the company pressed on with the project, albeit with less than aggressive speed. On July 3, 1925, the ships *Colona, Saris,* and *Wonatabe* were released, meaning that they had been burned down. Then, on July 24, after more than a year's delay, the company was finally granted a permit by the War Department "to ground, burn and beach in Mallow's Bay, Potomac River, about two hundred hulls." A new methodology had been specified to protect the river from the recurrent problems of hulls periodically floating away and creating navigational hazards. Noted in paragraph 18 of the permit, it was stated: "When all hulls which it is intended to permanently ground in Mallows Bay have been placed in the grounding area [in the bay], the hulls on the riverside shall be filled with dredge material and a bank of dredged material thrown up against their riverward sides and in the gaps between the hulls."[19] The permit, which was to expire on December 31, 1928, was equally significant in that it was the first time that the name Mallows, instead of Marlow's, was employed to define the geographic area of the bay.[20] It was a name that would be retained forever after.

WM&SC had little choice but to attempt to move forward while the War Department continued to wrangle over whether it was legal or not to accept personal sureties. In the fall of 1925, the company busily prepared for the largest mass reduction of hulls to date. On November 7 a total of thirty-one ships, nearly 110,000 deadweight tons, which had cost the nation well over $31 million, were bound together by a great steel cable, covered by a wire net shroud, and prepared for the monumental conflagration, the greatest of its kind in U.S. history. Oil soaked waste was spread around the decks of the ships to insure that the fire would take hold. At 5 A.M., just before sunup, with federal representatives, inspectors, salvors, and the press hovering about in a squadron of tugs, motorboats, and a lone plane circling overhead, the *coup de grace* was administered. On a given signal, ten men raced about the flotilla touching lit torches to the oil soaked materials. "As the torch was applied," noted one observer from the *Washington Post,* "a horde of squealing rats plunged into the water." From upriver at the Quantico Marine Barracks, which had not been forewarned of the event, the flames appeared "like the red ball of the sun rising in the East, silhouetted against the thick forests which abound on the Maryland side of the river." Again, the U.S. Marines, believing a disaster was under way down river, turned out to battle the flames, only to be turned back after discovering the actual nature of the conflagration. For hours, the glow of the fire could be seen ten miles away.[21]

For WM&SC the successful controlled burning was a significant demonstration of the company's willingness to press on, but, more important, it was strategically timed to facilitate government approval for the work

Thirty-one wooden U.S. Shipping Board steamers go up in smoke on November 7, 1925, the greatest destruction of shipping at one time in the history of the Potomac River. Courtesy National Archives and Record Service

ahead. The three-year period for anchorage was about to expire on August 21, 1926, and there were still many scores of ships moored off Widewater or awaiting disposal in Mallows Bay. On May 12, 1926, the company applied to the district engineer for another three-year permit. More than a month later, after obvious procrastination, O'Connor finally approved. WM&SC was granted another three years, but only to anchor the sixty vessels now remaining there.[22]

The utilization of Mallows Bay as anchorage and burning ground was not without its own apparent impact upon the local fishing industry. Some correlation between the demise of the Monroe sturgeon fishing operations and caviar processing plant at Liverpool Point in 1926, the final beaching of the remaining vessels of the Monroe sturgeon fishing fleet, *Black Bottom, W.S. Child,* and *Edythe,* and the sudden occupation of the entire reach of Mallows Bay by the wooden Emergency Fleet hulls was probable.[23]

The wealthy corporate executives of WM&SC had little concern for a small, family-operated fishery. Despite the enormous success of the November conflagration, however, progress was slow. The millions of melted and contorted iron fittings and strapping released by the fire had to be plucked from each hull by clam bucket and by hand, transferred to a barge (if on the outer perimeter), landed at Sandy Point, hauled up the steep slopes of the shoreline to a road (if within the perimeter), and carted away.

By July 13, 1926, only four more vessels had been released. On August 6, three more followed. Indeed, progress at reducing the hull population appeared to have been so slow that it would not be until the summer of 1927 that bonds for replacements were warranted. Company efforts accelerated in 1928. On March 17, nine ships were released. On June 15 fifteen more vessels followed, including the venerable *North Bend,* the first wooden steamship built during the war. On October 12, twenty-six vessels were released. Four days before Christmas, on December 21, an additional eleven ships followed suit. On April 27, 1927, another seventeen vessels would be released after being burned and their charred hulls hauled into Mallows Bay, like all those that had gone before.[24] Slowly, but perceptibly, the once pristine little embayment was becoming clouded and cluttered with the burnt out skeletons of a once great fleet.

As the shipwreck density of the bay increased, the government became increasingly concerned with its management. To assess more effectively the status and disposition of the fleet, the Army Office of Engineers was soon conducting its own comprehensive survey and mapping of the Mallows Bay anchorage, from Sandy Point to Liverpool Point. The project, completed on August 11, 1929, identified 152 Emergency Fleet vessels by name and a corresponding number, noted their positions, dates of release, landmark features, property boundaries, netting lines, grounding areas, the U.S.C. & G. Monument Site, light and range stations, geological features, soundings, and even the positions of two nonrelated schooner wreck sites.[25] But vessel releases now came even more slowly than before.

Another permit was granted to WM&SC by the War Department on January 3, 1931, wherein it was recited that application had been made "for authority to extend the area in Mallow's Bay, Potomac River, now used for grounding, burning and beaching wooden hulls, two hundred (200) feet channelward." The bay was simply becoming too densely packed with ships to admit any more. Yet, company operations, now seriously hindered by the decline in the market price of scrap metal and the general economic malaise triggered by the onset of the Great Depression, were already winding down. The days of the big money scrap salvage had passed, and all that now remained for the company was the increasingly expensive obligatory work of burning and disposal. In March 1931, WM&SC finally "abandoned the project," taking care only to leave a watchman in charge of the personal property at Sandy Point Farm and to guard the company equipment left on the beach.[26]

WM&SC's operations, said company executives, had been completed. A total of 169 ships had been brought into Mallows Bay to end their days, and the company declared its mission at an end, although in reality, the job was far from finished. Declaring the project completed, however, and receiving a clean bill of approval from the Office of Engineers were two different things. The district engineer did not agree with WM&SC's declaration that they had met all of the criteria necessary for the release of all bonds and steadfastly refused to relinquish them until all the work was completed.[27]

As in the past, the company appealed to higher authority. Although he was no longer officially an officer of WM&SC, Humphrey attempted to use his connections at the highest levels of the U.S. Army in behalf of the company. On June 17, 1931, he met in Washington with Major General Douglas MacArthur, commander of the United States Army, and informed him that "the District Engineer refuses to recommend the release of the bonds filed by the company" until WM&SC raised and moved the four sunken hulls accidentally lost in April 1923, and built a levee "around the hulls grounded in the area set apart for that purpose [in Mallows Bay]." The company stockholders, he said, requested relief since hundreds of thousands of dollars had been tied up in the bonds, but conveniently failed to mention that the stockholders primarily consisted of Fleishhacker and himself. After briefly sketching the story of WM&SC's salvage operations on the wooden fleet, and the difficult position the district engineer's demands had put the company in, he departed for Chicago with a promise to brief the general more thoroughly by letter.[28]

The following day, from the fashionable Blackstone Hotel on South Michigan Avenue and East Seventh Street in Chicago, Humphrey drafted a long letter to MacArthur, filling in the blanks left open during his brief conversation the day before. Writing "from memory, chiefly," he provided a long synopsis of the events since September 1922, when George D. Perry purchased the wooden ship fleet from the U.S. Shipping Board, to the recent demands of the district engineer.

"We disclaim any desire or intention," he diplomatically stated,

> to criticize Major Arthur Jr. [the then-current district engineer] who has always been most courteous and accommodating, however, the plans and specifications prepared by his office at our suggestion would require the expenditure of approximately $50,000 and in the judgment of engineers who surveyed the situation, the hulls without any further safeguard do not menace navigation.
>
> Ordinarily, abandoned wrecks are removed by and at the expense of the Government and it is an added burden to impose this obligation on the Company even if under the permit it is technically obligated to do so. The wrecks have remained in their present location without light or other warning signal for more than eight years without in any way menacing navigation.
>
> The Western Marine and Salvage Company has lost on its operations to date over $255,000.00 as is shown by Haskins and Sells's audits which are available if desired. Of course, this may not be a reason for excusing the performance of an obligation; but this fact, joined with advantage accruing to the Government by the removal of this fleet and the good faith shown throughout the years of onerous work, merits some leniency. The company desires to safeguard navigation but believes it is now fully safeguarded and if not, the necessary additional protection may be obtained without the excessive cost of building a levee.
>
> While we hope that the Company may be relieved of the obligation of raising the wrecks and building the levee, in any event we will always be deeply obligated to you.[29]

MacArthur, of course, circulated the letter to the Office of the Chief of Engineers, Major General Lytle Brown. A special field investigation of Mallows Bay and the Widewater Anchorage Grounds was then undertaken by the Office of Engineers, which reconfirmed the district engineer's view that the four vessels sunk at Widewater constituted "a dangerous hazard to navigation, the continuance of which cannot be permitted."[30]

Brown was adamant and unforgiving regarding the company's obligations. Pointing to Humphrey's assurances to the assistant secretary of war made on June 13, 1923, in which it was stated that WM&SC was financially able to carry out any obligation it undertook and was willing to obligate itself to a legal agreement to guarantee that the dismantled vessels in the area would be removed whenever they were deemed a hazard to navigation, the general dismissed the attorney's excuse that the costs for meeting its obligations were now too high. As for the issue of the levee, the general was willing to bend, or at least relinquish judgment to a higher authority. "While the vessels grounded in Mallows Bay constitute a decidedly objectionable local condition, it may be questionable that the interests of local navigation make it essential that these wrecks be enclosed within a levee, and I suggest that you make formal application to the Secretary of War for relief from the requirement of this condition of your permit."[31]On July 23 Humphrey appealed to Brown for relief in the Widewater issue, again requesting that the government, not WM&SC, remove the four sunken hulls. He claimed that the hulls had been accidentally set afire and had sunk before the bonds were extracted from the company. Therefore, he reasoned, the War Department would be justified in removing the hulls as abandoned wrecks without cost to the company. Yet, if full relief was not possible, the attorney suggested, would the War Department remove the hulls at its own expense, if the company contributed up to $10,000 toward overall cost? As for the hulls in Mallows Bay, the company soon made formal application to the Secretary of War for relief from the proviso that they be enclosed by a levee.[32]

Citing the record of bonds, Brown responded on July 31 to the attorney's letter of July 23 and effectively scuttled any argument WM&SC had that the four vessels sunk at Widewater had been lost prior to their being bonded. The four hulls, *Okiya, Catawba, Quidnic,* and *Blythedale,* had, indeed, been covered by a bond dated August 9, 1929. Therefore, the expense of removing the hulls could not be borne by the government. The company would be required to meet its obligation.[33]

The following day, in response to Humphrey's formal application for relief on the Mallows Bay levee requirement, General Brown fired off a note informing the attorney that he would meet with him on the issue "if . . . it is found that a personal conference with you is advisable."[34]

At Mallows Bay the company had entirely ceased all work by June, although the permit would not expire until December. Yet, in the vacuum created by WM&SC's cessation of activity, the wrecks quickly became the target for scores of local scavengers, mostly unemployed men, many of whom had once worked for WM&SC, who began to pick over the beached hulks for whatever scrap metal they could remove and sell. Their endeavors were soon being conducted on a remarkably large scale. A "scrap rush" was soon on. In July, when a party of Sea Scouts on a cruise of the Potomac entered the bay, the scout leader, Fred Tilp, recorded in his journal: "About 20 boats here are loading scrap iron being removed from the burned wooden ships ashore. Thousands of snowy white egrets nest in these old hulks. In a small bight on the south shore we find a bugeye being painted for use as a scrap-metal carrier to Washington."[35] Still, the negotiations between the Office of Engineers and WM&SC continued without letup—or apparent forward motion—even as the secretary of war considered the levee issue. By December 31, 1931, when the permit for work in the bay expired, it was not renewed. Indeed, the company had failed even to begin construction of the levee. Although the company continued to maintain a watchman at Sandy Point Farm to monitor company property until the summer of 1932, it repeatedly insisted that its work was done. In the meantime, the company's request for relief from the levee construction requirement was finally presented to and reviewed by the secretary of war. In this matter, the lobbying effort by Humphrey and his associates had apparently been intense, off the record, and remarkably successful. On January 2, 1932, WM&SC was officially notified "that this part of the stipulated work [the levee construction] was not considered necessary for the protection of navigation and they were relieved of the requirements. . . ." Moreover, the issue of the company's responsibility for the removal of the four ships sunk at Widewater was now, for the first time, conveniently overlooked. On January 20, 1932, the Office of Engineers, U.S. Army, filed its final report, stating that "all work required under the permit as granted and modified" had been completed.[36] The company was finally and irrevocably off the hook. The government's decision, as later events would unfortunately demonstrate, would return to haunt it for the next half century.

On November 20, 1932, WM&SC conveyed the Sandy Point Farm tract by deed of sale to the Potomac Realty Company, Limited, a San Francisco–based corporation, without including any mention of the burned and sunken hulls in the riparian property areas covered by the deed. It is probable that the government was entirely unaware of the change of ownership or that it was but a clever, albeit transparent, legal maneuver by WM&SC officials who also controlled all interests in Potomac Realty. Indeed, it would appear from subsequent events that the transfer was undertaken in a deliberate effort to remove any possible recurrent legal responsibility that could arise from the Mallows Bay hulks or those at Widewater which might eventually become hazards to navigation. Not surprisingly, WM&SC left it to its successor, Potomac Realty, to remove the machinery and equipment left behind at Sandy Point Farm.[37]

Then, in December 1932, to destroy all possible legal entanglements, WM&SC was dissolved as a corporate entity. The official reason was eventually stated in a formal letter drafted on December 22, 1934, from the Potomac Realty Company (whose executives and personnel were the same as WM&SC) to E. Cortlandt Parker, a Washington attorney who had represented the interests of WM&SC. The official cause given for the company's demise was: ". . . due to the heavy overhead for maintaining the office and a large force of men, it was deemed too expensive to continue salvage operations, and for the further reason that the stockholders of said salvage company at that time desired its dissolution in

The detritus resulting from the destruction of nearly eight score wooden
steamships in Mallows Bay, more reminiscent of a bomb blast than an
industrial salvage operation, would prove to be a magnet for scrap salvors
for decades. Courtesy National Archives and Record Service

order that they might ascertain what loss had actually been sustained by
them as stockholders . . . if conditions again warranted any further
salvaging they could do so in the nature of a joint venture without the
formality of a corporate existence.[38]

WM&SC had indeed orchestrated a masterful legal sleight-of-hand
maneuver. And the once placid waters of Mallows Bay, cluttered with the
detritus of the greatest wooden shipbreaking operation in American
history, looked for all the world like a bombed-out version of hell.

TWENTY-ONE

Fastened His Eyes on These Hulls

Almost as soon as WM&SC ceased operations at Mallows Bay, "the public and the residents in the neighborhood began the removal of metal from the burned and sunken hulls without interference [even] while the watchman was there." Indeed, it was then, "when, to all appearances, the wrecking business of the Western [Marine and Salvage] Company was at an end, that the people living in the neighborhood took this view they there saw and began to gather the junk remaining in the burned, submerged hulks, and sold it to junk dealers in and around Washington."[1]

Some would later claim that when WM&SC abandoned operations, "they told the residents that any material left on these abandoned hulks could be salvaged if they so desired." Soon, between fifty and seventy-five residents of Charles County could be found on any given day actively engaged in picking over the hulls for marketable scrap metal. Local salvors, such as Preston Dent, who owned a barge, began to work the wrecks even though the price of scrap was now so low that "it was barely worth getting." For Dent, who made regular forays to Washington with barge loads of seventy to eight-five tons of scrap each trip, which he sold for six dollars a ton, the profit was marginal, considering the labor involved. But for many others, unemployed and penniless as a result of the Great Depression, the scrap provided at least a subsistence income.[2]

Within a short time an unorganized but relatively efficient ad hoc system evolved at Mallows Bay involving labor, middlemen, haulers, and sellers. Lorenzo D. Crouse was one typical entrepreneur. By September 1932 Crouse, who had worked for WM&SC the previous year, began his own salvage operation removing lead, brass, copper, and iron scrap. Like most, he recovered and sold small lots of scrap, usually marketing the material to a middleman named Sinclair, in parcels of thirty tons each. Sinclair, who bought scrap from scores of salvors like Crouse, in turn sold the combined lots to one Harry Steinbraker.[3] A few dealers from Piscataway bartered for the scrap directly with the independent salvors using bootleg whiskey as the medium, then hauling the material to Washington where they sold it for a considerable profit.[4]

In mid-1934, increased Japanese interest in American scrap metal began to drive prices up again. One of the first to observe the possibilities for increased profit from the burned, gutted, and submerged hulls was Steinbraker. Yet, he was not alone in his assessments. In early July 1934, one Irwin Bowie, a resident of the nearby town of Ironsides, in Charles County, sought the assistance of a La Plata attorney named J. Read Bailey to determine whether the wrecks "at Sandy Point, in the Western Section of this County, are still the property of the Navy or War department." Bowie reported that some parties unknown had acquired the property adjacent to the abandoned hulks and had refused to give permission for anyone to board them. Undoubtedly being one of the many small salvors who had been working the wrecks, Bowie was determined to find out if the hulls still belonged to the government or some private individual or concern. Bailey, in turn, queried Congressman Stephen W. Gambrill, who turned the query over to the Office of Engineers.[5]

On July 16, 1934, Brigadier General G. B. Pillsbury, acting chief of engineers, replied to Gambrill's inquiry with a brief review based upon the War Department's files. "Completion of the work under the permit, was reported on May 23, 1932. The War Department has no interest in the boats in question and their present ownership is not known to this office." The attention that the general gave to the query was, perhaps, indicative of his interest in providing an answer. If the former owner had relinquished rights to the property, Pillsbury suggested, Bowie should contact the attorney general of Virginia "regarding the ownership of such abandoned property under the laws of that state." That the hulls lay in the Potomac River, within yards of the Maryland shoreline, and were clearly in Maryland waters, seems to have passed right over his head.[6]

Maneuvering for control over the wrecks, however, intensified. As the price of scrap continued to climb, Steinbraker was the first actually to attempt to corner the market on Mallows Bay metal. Tracing the current owners of Sandy Point Farm, probably through land transfer records in La Plata Court House, he "called the Potomac Realty Company on the West Coast on the telephone" to secure salvage rights to the wrecks. The call resulted in the "stockholders" of WM&SC, that is Humphrey, Fleishhacker, and Perry, by agreement dated December 1, 1934, assigning, releasing, and quitclaiming unto the Potomac Realty Company, Limited (mainly themselves) all the "right, title or interest which they or any of them may have in and to all lead, copper, brass and/or other metals of whatsoever kind and nature located in or around each of the 169 vessels or hulls . . . situated in Mallow's Bay, near Sandy Point, Maryland." By agreement made on December 3, 1934, nearly two years after the transfer of the Sandy Point tract to the Potomac Realty Company, Limited, the land was again transferred by deed of assignment, this time to Steinbraker, and recorded in Charles County, "all the right, title, and interest of the said the Potomac Realty Company, Ltd., in and to all lead, copper, brass and other metal of whatever nature owned by it, or to which it has title in and around the hundred and sixty-nine (169) vessels, which said vessels were formerly owned by the Western Marine & Salvage Company, the said vessels being located in Mallow's Bay, near Sandy Point, in Charles County."[7] The same metals were assigned "as is, where is, if is, without any warranty of title whatsoever or otherwise." The price to be paid was two dollars per ton f.o.b. railroad cars, with a deposit of five hundred dollars to be applied on the last payments due the purchaser. A bond of ten thousand dollars was guaranteed noninterference with navigation.[8]

Steinbraker moved forcefully to secure his holdings, and soon "a large number of workers" were in his employ "steadily engaged" in removing metals from the hulls. To recover large quantities of metal from this remote setting required a considerable manpower base, which was to be readily had in the terribly depressed economy of southern Maryland. It was also necessary to provide adequate support and living space for the workers. In June 1934 a derelict four-masted merchant schooner, *Ida S. Dow*, was permanently moored on the southwest edge of the basin to serve as a dormitory for workers and "for officials of the salvage firm," presumably those employed by Steinbraker.[9]

Ida S. Dow had once been a graceful, indeed beautiful, ship and must have appeared wholly out of character with the war zone ambiance of the embayment. Built in 1918 at Thomaston, Maine, by the Atlantic Coast Company, the 1,411-ton, 225-foot merchant schooner was one of the last of the classic four-masters to be constructed. Although she had managed

The elegant schooner *Ida S. Dow,* built at Thomaston, Maine, one of the last of the four masters, is pictured here during her halcyon days as a freight hauler. She would end her days as a dormitory for wreckers at Mallows Bay. Courtesy Mariners' Museum

to survive the war and the "great 1920 tie-up," misfortune finally overtook her on November 30, 1931, when she was severely damaged in a collision with the German steamship *Hermen Frasch*. Ignominiously towed stern first into Hampton Roads, Virginia, she was soon thereafter abandoned at Newport News and drawn up to await the wreckers. In the spring of 1934, however, she was granted a new, albeit brief, lease on life, when she was acquired by salvors who towed her up the Chesapeake and dropped anchor in the Mallows Bay graveyard.[10]

Steinbraker's legal efforts notwithstanding, the Mallows Bay hulks continued to be the subject of salvage by numerous county residents acting in their own behalf, all of whom conducted their work openly and without permission from him. Steinbraker angrily moved to halt the salvage of what he now construed to be his property. On December 22, 1934, hoping to set an example, he filed a bill of complaint against one of the salvors, Lorenzo D. Crouse, in the Circuit Court of Charles County, Maryland, charging that Crouse, "his agents, servants and employees, disregarding the interests of 'the plaintiff' in and to the lead, copper, brass and other materials contained in said vessels . . . have entered upon and seized said vessels and are at present engaged in shipping and selling such metals to parties unknown" to the plaintiff. As a result of "such depredations" the "value and interest" of Steinbraker's "holding in said vessels and metal is being permanently injured." The bill prayed for an injunction and an order was passed to that effect. Then the case was appealed and again heard in court.[11]

Crouse answered the charges against him by denying that "Steinbraker ever acquired any right, title or interest in and to the lead, copper, brass, and other materials" mentioned in the bill of complaint. The defendant freely admitted that "he, his agents, servants and employees, have heretofore entered upon the sunken hulls of certain vessels mentioned in the bill and engaged in the removal, shipment and sale of certain materials salvaged therefrom, but deny that in so doing they committed trespass, or disregarded any right, title or interest of the plaintiff for the reason that the materials taken by them were a part of the abandoned wreckage of certain ships that had therefore been dismantled, sunk and abandoned by the Western Marine and Salvage Company."[12] This time the court was quick to observe that although Crouse was the only person actually named as a defendant, "this suit is really directed against numerous residents of Charles County, variously estimated by witnesses at from fifty to seventy-five, who had been engaged in the same business, on the same wreckage, as the defendant."[13]

Testimony was heard relating to the history of the Mallows Bay wrecks from the date Perry had acquired the ships (reported in testimony at 232 vessels) to the sale of salvage rights to Steinbraker by the Potomac Realty

Company, Limited. Testimony was also presented by many of the independent salvors on their own behalf.[14]

One of those so employed had been J. W. Cox, who lived in the neighborhood and testified that he "was engaged in this work on his own initiative and was not employed by any one to do it. He considered this was abandoned property because it had been lying in the water, some of it, for four or five years." Cox further stated that although he was no lawyer, "he had always heard that when a ship or anything of that kind was down and the tide rising and falling over it for a number of years it was abandoned property." There had not been a watchman at the site since 1932, and no one had attempted to interfere with his work, although there had been seventy-five people working the sites.[15]

Another witness was James L. David, who had, on his own, visited the War Department to inquire whether anyone had a permit to remove the metal from the vessels. "I went to several different members, but they told me there didn't anybody want the thing. . . . Then I went back and went to work" removing and selling scrap from the sunken hulls. David, like millions of Americans, was unemployed and "had nothing to do at the time and realized wages from his operation." He noted that there were at least fifty men working the sites at any given time. He stated that his reason for going there "was because he understood it did not belong to anybody; everybody all over the community, from Washington and other places were going there and helping themselves and they explained that it did not belong to anybody and that it was free for anybody to partake of."[16]

Preston Dent testified that he had visited Mallows Bay in June 1932, worked a short time, and came back again in August 1934 to resume salvage work "without any authority from any one, just because he heard that it was open and nobody had anything to do with it. He had seen Mr. Steinbraker down there . . . but had no dealings with him." At the time, he observed that "most of the wreckage is beneath the water but some parts are sticking above the surface. The wreckage is surrounded by water."[17]

Lorenzo Crouse, the defendant, had once worked for WM&SC as a crane operator. When the company operations ceased, his fellow workmen informed him "that they were quitting." In September 1932, following the departure of the watchman, he began his own salvage work and continued in that employ for the next two years, selling the recovered metals to either Sinclair or Steinbraker, until the latter "undertook to buy the submerged hulls and enjoined him" to cease work on the sites.[18]

Throughout the proceedings, the court was repeatedly provided with evidence from which it was finally concluded: "that for over two years the wreckage had been abandoned so far as the community affected did or could know, and with this impression, under very great difficulties, anywhere from fifty to seventy-five persons had removed hundreds of tons of metal from these hulls, and their principal customer was either Sinclair or Steinbraker; or both, and all without interruption or interference from Western Marine and Salvage Company or any one interested in it."[19]

That was until Steinbraker, whose own interest in the sites was further spurred by the rise in scrap metal prices, contacted Potomac Realty Company, Limited.[20] "The rule of law," the court observed, in forming its opinion, "with respect to abandoned property is very simple. Property is abandoned when the owner walks off and leaves it with no intention to claim it again or exercise rights of ownership over it. When this was done, it belonged to anyone who took possession of it. With respect to real estate, it was not quite so simple, as the one entering was obliged to serve his time of prescription and possession before he can acquire a legal title. In the case of the abandonment of an easement, which was the most frequent occurrence, abandonment means revision of the then owner of the fee." The court then cited a precedent wherein it was stated that "he who takes possession by the owner, immediately becomes the proprietor of it by occupancy."[21] The court further stated, with respect to the abandonment of an easement, that the rule in Maryland was the same principle as that just stated concerning personal property. Indeed, it was stated in Charles County Circuit Court in an opinion by one Judge Avery:

> It is now very well settled, by authorities of the highest character; that a party entitled to a right of way or other mere easement in the land of another may abandon and extinguish such right by acts *in pais*, and without deed or other writing. The act or acts relied on, however, to effect such result, must be of a decisive character; and while a mere declaration of an intent to abandon will not alone be sufficient, the question, whether the act of the party entitled to the easement amounts to an abandonment or not, depends upon the intention with which it was done, and that is a subject for the consideration of the jury. A cesser of the use, coupled with any act clearly indicative of an attention to abandon the right, would have the same effect as an express release of the easement, without any reference whatever to time.[22]

The record had clearly shown that WM&SC was a "temporary corporation" formed specifically for the purpose of wrecking and salvaging all that it regarded as valuable, marketable, and profitable of 232 vessels [sic] purchased from and discarded by the U.S. government. The court further observed that the wrecked hulls were not located on the property of the Western Marine and Salvage Company, but were in navigable waters, occupied by permission of the War Department, which expressly stated that the permit was subject to any other rights of the state or its citizens, public or personal. The vessels were located on land belonging to the state, to which the federal government disclaimed any intention of asserting title. The interest of the government extended only to control of the water over the land, not to the soil.[23]

So long as it was engaged in the wrecking and junk business, WM&SC had secured permits from the government to employ the waters. When the company was through with its work, however, and was dissolved in December 1932 after conveying its lands to Potomac Realty Company, Limited, the court stated, "the Western [Marine and Salvage] Company was out of business so far as the salvage of these vessels was concerned. It was then, when, to all appearances, the wrecking business of the Western [Marine and Salvage] Company was at an end, that the people living in the neighborhood took this view of what they saw and began to gather the junk remaining in the burned, submerged hulks, and sold it to junk dealers in and around Washington."[24] Citing the testimony of the many witnesses who had worked on the sites, their unhindered activities, and the various proceedings regarding the delayed transfer of rights to the scrap aboard the ships, the court noted:

Inherent to possession is the right to exclusion; and, if through a duration of many years no act or attempted act of exclusion is exercised by a presumed possessor; and through all that time the thing . . . is openly, freely, and continuously depleted, taken, and carried away in vast quantities, without compensation or permission asked, the intention, if it ever existed, to exclude others, has disappeared; and, when there never was, before and after these open appropriations, assertion of title or acts of dominion exercised, the conclusion is inevitable that the legal possession has been relinquished and the thing abandoned.[25]

In summing up its opinion, the court ruled:

It requires no stretch of the imagination to believe from the evidence in this record that, if the plaintiff had not fastened his eyes on these hulls, the so-called 'depredations' of the defendant and others in the vicinity of Mallow's Bay would have continued uninterruptedly to this day. The sequence of events from the time the stockholders of the Western Marine and Salvage Company conveyed the land from themselves to themselves under the name of the Potomac Realty Company, Limited, the sale of the equipment to outsiders, the invasion for over two years of the wrecked and sunken vessels, and the continuous, uninterrupted, and open carrying away of the scrap therein, without compensation or permission asked, show clearly in our opinion, an intention to abandon and an actual abandonment, not to be recalled by the subsequent negotiations and agreement between the former owners and the plaintiff and the decree of the chancellor should be affirmed.[26]

Ghost Fleet of Mallows Bay

Ida S. Dow in her last days at Mallows Bay. Courtesy
Mariners' Museum, Newport News, Virginia

On January 15, 1936, the decree of the court was affirmed with costs. Steinbraker had lost. The Mallows Bay wrecks were open to salvage by anyone and everyone.[27]

Not long after the court's ruling, title to the Sandy Point Farm tract was conveyed by the Potomac Realty Company, Limited, to the Anglo-California National Bank of San Francisco. But the local salvage operations on the hulls in Mallows Bay continued unabated, as ever larger numbers of workers descended upon the embayment to tear out a living from the boneyard. Living facilities were spartan. By September 1, 1936, the leaky *Ida S. Dow* had apparently become unsuitable for service as a barracks ship (or perhaps was being denied to the scores of independent salvors by Steinbraker), and was now incapable of even being towed away. She was thus hauled to the southern line of the hull containment area, filled with mud, sunk in place and abandoned. According to Frederick Tilp, the legion of wreckers, who were now working on the hulks or beach combing the shoreline for scrap, began taking up residence in five "Potomac Arks," inexpensive houseboats, easily constructed, and occasionally mounted on pilings, which provided convenient and cheap lodging.[28]

Salvors who were fortunate enough to own vessels worked upon the more easily accessible hulks, principally those located along the outer line of wrecks nearest the edge of the Potomac channel. Frequently, dynamite was employed to break up ships and to loosen banding straps, drift pins, and bolts. The work on the outer line was carried out primarily because of easy access, as most of the wrecks were so tightly clustered together in very shallow water that they defied direct approach by watercraft. Concentration on the removal of metal from these wrecks soon began to produce a most unexpected by-product. As the metal was removed, the ships became lighter, more buoyant, and inclined to float. Yet, as late as October 4, 1935, when the Army Office of Engineers conducted one of its periodic inspections, all had appeared in order in Mallows Bay. On the Virginia shore it was another matter.[29]

On several occasions, the hulls beached at Brent's Marsh (which had also been subjected to their share of local salvagers) had been reported to be moving. "Two or three times," reported Major W. D. Luplow, the district engineer, "they have been found to have drifted various distances up to several miles out into the ship channel." But the moves were usually addressed right away. On February 8, 1937, one hull drifted from Brent's Marsh and was found fifteen miles downstream in the channel. It was recovered before causing any damage to navigation and returned to its former resting place. Then, on April 26, during an abnormally high tide, two vessels moved out of Mallows Bay. One of the ships was quickly relocated by the district engineer down river near Maryland Point. The other had been blown ashore upriver, in the mouth of Chopawamsic Creek. The vessel in the channel near Maryland Point was dragged to shoal water on the Virginia shore near Chatterton's Landing and temporarily secured. The hull at Chopawamsic, however, had grounded itself so firmly that it could not be moved with ordinary methods."[30]

For the army engineers, it was now clear that the provision in WM&SC's permit requiring that a levee be constructed over the riverward hulls in Mallows Bay and that the hulls at Widewater be removed had been more than justified. Yet, with WM&SC's demise, bemoaned District Engineer Luplow, "there is now no one this office can hold responsible for remedying the situation at the grounding area." And, it was too dangerous to permit the condition to exist "with the possibility of some vessel slipping out into the channel and causing a serious accident to navigation."[31]

In an effort to rectify the situation, Major Luplow submitted to the chief of engineers, on May 8, 1937, a request for funds and authority to dredge at Mallows Bay and to use the spoil to erect a dike such as called for in the permit issued to WM&SC in 1925. Seven isolated hulls along the Virginia shoreline should, he recommended, also be filled with dredge material in order to prevent further movement. He estimated that to return the hulls at Chopawamsic and Chatterton's Landing to their former positions in Mallows Bay and to construct levees by depositing dredge spoil over the wrecks would cost $9,500. "It is considered, in view of the work," he wrote, "that this can be done most expeditiously and economically with Government plant and hired labor." He recommended that the hydraulic dredge boats *Talcott* or *Dalecarla* and the clam shell dredge boat *Atlas* be employed for the project.[32]

Another inspection was called for. On May 19 Inspector G. D. Ritten-house personally investigated the condition of the hulls beached in Mallows Bay, at Brent's Marsh, and off the Quantico Flying School in Chopawamsic Creek. He observed that all of the hulls on the outside line at Mallows Bay had been "fairly well cleaned of scrap iron and are much lighter than at the inspection of October 4, 1935." Two of the hulls had moved from the area and several others had shifted their positions in the bay.[33]

One of the hulls mentioned above, No. 153 (which had apparently been brought into Mallows soon after the August 11, 1929, survey of wrecks in the bay, as only 152 numbered hulls are listed at that time), had been found in the main shipping channel of the Potomac by a Captain Read. Read had towed the vessel to the Virginia shore and left it about 2,000 feet off the home and property of W. B. Lee, in 8 feet of water and approximately 500 feet downstream of the hulls at Brent's Marsh.[34]

The other hull, unnumbered, had drifted ashore at the Quantico flying field. Rittenhouse discovered that hull lay about 600 feet upstream from a newly cut channel in Chopawamsic Creek, bow in and about 100 feet from a riprap wall. The bow sat in 2 feet of water. The hull had been secured by a cable and anchored to the shore.

As for Mallows Bay itself, the situation was serious. The ship *Yakima* (Hull No. 117) had moved about thirty feet channelward. An unnum-bered hull lying between the hulls of the *Casmalia* (Hull No. 34) and Hull No. 157 (another post–August 11, 1929, addition) had moved out of position and was discovered lying on a north-south axis, but had been made fast to another unidentified hull upstream of No. 157 by a cable. Yet salvage by the locals was continuing on many of the hulls despite the hazards. Indeed, during his visit the inspector had observed from fifteen to thirty men gathering iron which, for the most part, was being sold to one A. M. Scott, a buyer for a dealer named Jake Levin of Washington, D.C. Part of it, however, was being bought directly by one G. H. Morgan, a local resident of Mallows Bay.[35]

During his inspection, Rittenhouse noted that the salvors were using dynamite vigorously and that several charges had been set off on the hull of *Congaree* (Hull No. 125), which lay in the second line of ships in the bay. Observing the lightened condition of the outer line, the inspector had asked Scott "to keep the men from salvaging from the outside line of hulls" and "intimated that if this was not done all salvaging in the area would be discontinued by this office."

"The conditions at Mallows Bay," the inspector wrote in his final report,

are considered dangerous and a distinct menace to navigation on the Potomac River. The main ship channel at this point is approximately 1,000 feet from the hulls and in the event of high water and high tides, such as experienced the latter part of April, very little time would be consumed by a hull floating out of the Bay into the channel. Recent observation proves that the hulls now have the necessary buoyancy to break loose on high water and it is possible that this contingency should be remedied as soon as possible. I believe the most permanent and least costly method of securing the hulls is to put several hundred yards of mud in each of the outside hulls, about 35 in number. This would cover the remaining scrap iron and effectively stop salvage in these hulls.[37]

From the Rittenhouse study, it was reported that Hull No. 153, ashore at W. B. Lee's, was in an open area traversed by small pleasure craft and by fishermen conducting drift net operations and was, without question, an obstruction to navigation. The hull lying immediately upstream of the new channel in the Chopawamsic was deemed a menace to small pleasure and fishing craft as well as to the crash boats attached to the flying field units at Quantico.[37]

Even as the engineers mulled over the serious threat posed by the wrecks, on May 26, 1937, three more hulls floated out of the grounding area, one seriously obstructing navigation, the other two menacing the shipping lanes. Fortunately, an Army Office of Engineers "plant" was scheduled in the area for a week. The local engineer, one Bullock, quickly recommended the hulls be returned to Mallows Bay and that the dike, mentioned so many times in the past, be built. It was now simply the most direct and economical procedure possible.[38]

After reviews by superiors and revisions of recommendations had been made, $4,600 was officially requested for placing the errant hulls (and presumably those noted by Rittenhouse) back in Mallows Bay and for the building of the dike. The only alternative solution seemed to be to maintain an inspector or observer on site at Mallows Bay at all times. But that would require a long-term commitment and an expenditure that was out of the question.[39]

"Without an inspector actively employed on the job," complained the District Engineer,

this office would be unable to learn properly when any hull floats out of the grounding area, as the only way in which advice of this condition would be received would be from local parties sufficiently interested or from navigation interests encountering or observing the drifting wrecks. Even so, some time for preparation and transportation would be involved before wrecking activities could begin at the site after authority therefore had been requested and secured. The employment of some local resident is considered unsatisfactory. The only way in which prompt and reliable information could be furnished this office would be through the full-time services of an inspector on 24 hours per day observation at cost of above $500 per month. In view of the fact that it has been "customary" to safeguard navigation from possible danger by removal or otherwise mitigating conditions that result from wrecks or abandoned equipment classed as menaces to navigation, it would seem that funds can be properly devoted to the elimination of this menace to navigation by filling in the outer ring of abandoned hulks.[40]

There should be no legal objections to such an event, noted the engineer, since the Charles County Circuit Court had already ruled that the wrecks were abandoned property. Thus, the district engineer recommended that the proposed allotment be approved to remove the main hazard to navigation by "construction of a dike over and between the outer row of these hulks and that this office be authorized to perform the work with Government plant and hired labor."[41]

On June 6, 1937, the allotment was made. The work, however, would not be the last attentions heaped upon Mallows Bay by the Office of Engineers, soon to be known as the U.S. Army Corps of Engineers. Yet, the project proved to be but a temporary expedient for, although sand and gravel were piled upon the ships (and presumably between them), many were soon washed clean by the Potomac waters and Tidewater weather (so much for engineering solutions). In the meantime, on February 26, 1941, the Anglo-California Bank of San Francisco sold a non-waterfront section of the Sandy Point Farm to Hugh and Grace Murdock. On March 6 the remainder of the tract, that which embraced the waterfront of Mallows Bay, was sold to Walter R. and Blanche Wilson.[42]

Despite the Office of Engineers' dire predictions for the hulks of Mallows Bay, the last of the disasters appeared to have come to an end and the wrecks could once more be forgotten. But not for long.

TWENTY-TWO

These Strange Islands

On September 1, 1939, Germany invaded Poland, and the United States began its inevitable drift toward the next great war. The price of scrap metal skyrocketed. Not surprisingly, the Mallows Bay hulks once again became of considerable importance when, on June 28, 1940, the Metals Reserve Company (MRC) was established by the federal government to organize and manage the stockpiling of strategic metals. Then, on December 7, 1941, Japan attacked the United States Pacific Fleet at Pearl Harbor, Hawaii, guaranteeing America's participation in World War II.

Within months of America's entry into the conflict, the War Production Board (WPB), which had been formed to coordinate national production for the war effort, began to orchestrate a monumental nationwide salvage effort to recover scrap metal. On July 16, 1942, the WPB Salvage Program Office forwarded to the MRC a special project directive regarding the recovery of strategic metals from the Mallows Bay fleet. By October 10, 1942, Mallows Bay had been designated a special project of consideration by the Salvage Section of the MRC. The many hulls still in the embayment, it was then estimated, were capable of yielding as much as 20,000 tons or more of scrap for the war effort.[1]

Within two weeks, a U.S. government–sponsored project was launched to recover the scrap fittings in the burned hulls of more than one hundred ships still lying in Mallows Bay. On October 19, 1942, the WPB instructed the MRC to initiate the project. Anticipating the WPB directive, the MRC had apparently already begun negotiations with the Bethlehem Steel Company, "with reference to the recovery of the said metals." The negotiations resulted in a contract providing that the MRC take steps "as it may deem necessary to acquire title and that Bethlehem will do all things that are necessary to recover the maximum amount of metals from the vessels in the water and also in the vicinity thereof." Upon allocation by the WPB, Bethlehem was to transport the metal to its sprawling plant at Sparrows Point, Maryland. The MPC would then sell the recovered metals to Bethlehem Steel at Office of Price Administration (OPA) prices. In turn, the MPC would reimburse Bethlehem for the price of the work. Settlement would be effected upon completion of the work with the provision that "if the amount of the metal recovered is in excess of the cost of the

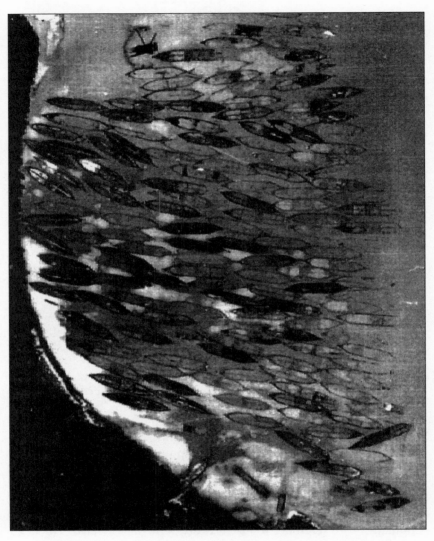

A 3,000 percent computer-enhanced enlargement of a 1942 aerial photo
showing the disposition of the fleet in Mallows Bay.

work, Bethlehem will remit such excess to the Metals Reserve. While, on the other hand, if the cost of the work is in excess of the price of the metal recovered, Metals Reserve will reimburse Bethlehem for such amount."[2] It seemed to company executives like a no-lose opportunity.

Although no accurate estimate of the cost or the precise amount of metal to be recovered had been made, the MRC judged, from the "best appraisal available," that it was unlikely that the cost of the work would be very much in excess of the price of the metals recovered, "provided unforeseen circumstances do not intervene."[3] On October 21, only two days after the WPB authorized the project, G. W. Nichols, Vice President of the MRC, recommended acceptance of the proposed contract.

As a windfall, the MRC was also hopeful that "an estimated 5,000 tons of steel believed to have fallen in the water in the graveyard of the ghost ships," comprised a reported 150 anchors and parts of chains which had been removed when the fleet was moved from the Virginia shore to Mallows Bay. It was even reported that the Salvage Section was canvassing the nation for a floating electromagnet unit capable of raising this lost resource, as well as odd scrap from the bottom of the river.[4]

Bethlehem moved quickly. A portion of the property surrounding Mallows Bay which had belonged to the Wilson family had been sold on December 31, 1942, to Frank O. and Mildred Morgan, and the steel company's first action, presumably, would have been to lease the waterfront areas from both the Wilsons and Morgans.[5] Then the company's efforts focused upon the excavation of a great earthen basin and the construction of a pair of cofferdams and gates, at the outlet of Marlow's Creek and on the seaward end of the basin. The initial basin design (which may have later been expanded) called for the excavation of a facility 900 feet in length by 250 feet in width and capable of dry-docking 15 bottoms at a time. Cuts running from the main river channel and from the heart of the anchorage area in the bay to the basin also had to be excavated wide and deep enough to allow passage of the hulls and barges necessary to haul out their remains. Two earthen berm walls were constructed, one at the outlet of Marlow's Creek, and a second several hundred yards upstream. The outer dam was to be reinforced with concrete and sheets of corrugated steel and could be closed off by great floating iron or wooden gates. The inner coffer wall was to be bulkheaded with timber. On the outer gate berm a small pump house was to be erected, and surrounding the facility, several small houses, storage sheds, and the like were also to be built.[6]

The methodology of the salvage work is only presumptive, based upon scattered newspaper references, the surviving remnants of the facility and the vessel remains themselves, and the testimony of local residents. It appears, however, that the *modus operandi* was to float several of the hulls into the newly created basin, close the gate, pump the basin dry, or nearly so, burn the hulls down in a controlled, dry environment, remove the metals, reflood the basin, and open the gates to begin the cycle anew.

As with the WM&SC efforts, the Bethlehem project appears to have met with difficulties early in the game. Dredging of the channel into the burning basin was stymied owing to the soft silts, which slumped back into the dredged line as soon as the spoil was removed. The first group of eleven hulks moved into the burning area became hopelessly mired in the bottom when the water was removed, and the fire which was intended to reduce them was literally smothered by mud oozing back over them.[7] Sometime during the first half of May 1943, a devastating and costly breakthrough of one of the dams occurred. Engineers from the MRC felt that a portion of the mishap was due to "the lack of attention by Bethlehem in supervising the engineering details of the construction."[8] A flurry of telegrams was dispatched by C. W. Nichols of the MRC to the company regarding who was to cover the expenses incurred. Haggling over the subject would continue into the next year. By December 31, 1943, Bethlehem's agreement "to do all things necessary to recover the maximum amount of metal from certain vessels requisitioned at the request of the War Production Board" had cost the company $360,000 but had yielded "a very small recovery of metal." Within two months company expenditures on the project had become substantial enough for Bethlehem to request that it be reimbursed in the amount of $200,000 as partial payment.[9]

Despite the difficulties, Bethlehem persisted in its operations. In May 1944 the MRC requested that the company salvage the hulk of the SS *Bodkin*, ex-USS *Nokomis*. The company was instructed to move the ship to Mallows Bay and to remove only that metal that could be remelted.[10]

Bodkin had been built by Pusey and Jones, of Wilmington, Delaware, and launched in May 1914 as the yacht *Nokomis II*. She had been purchased by the U.S. Shipping Board from Horace E. Dodge, of Detroit, Michigan, on June 1, 1917, and renamed *Burke*. Taken into service by the U.S. Navy soon afterwards, she was again renamed *Nokomis* on November 19, 1917, and commissioned at Philadelphia on December 3, 1917, as a submarine chaser (SP-609). *Nokomis*, after being fitted out at Philadelphia, was a sleek, fast, and powerful vessel. She had a displacement of 1,265 tons and was 243 feet in length, 31 feet 10 inches abeam, and 12 feet 10 inches draft. Originally built as a composite steamer of steel construction but with wood planking, she boasted two decks and traverse framing. Armed with four 3-inch guns and manned by 191 officers and crew, she was a formidable naval asset.[11]

Nokomis had sailed to Bermuda, with a French submarine chaser in tow, and from there departed on her first mission for Brest, France, on January 8, 1918, stopping only twice en route, at the Azores and Lexicoes, Portugal. Operating with the U.S. Patrol Squadron for the remainder of World

War I, *Nokomis* helped protect American troop transports approaching the coast of France. Terminating this duty in 1919, she had returned to the United States in August. Reclassified PY-6 in 1920, she was decommissioned at New York on February 25, 1921. Soon afterward, in July of the same year, she was outfitted as a tender for the Naval Governor of Santo Domingo but did not assume this duty, conducting instead surveys in Mexican and Caribbean waters under direction of the U.S. Hydrographic Office. Returning to Norfolk on September 24, 1934, *Nokomis* was again decommissioned on February 15, 1938, and struck from the Navy Register on May 25, 1938. Yet, like many mothballed ships, she was destined to be recalled for duty in World War II. Renamed *Bodkin* on June 1, 1943, she was loaned by the Navy to the Coast Guard (then operating under the direction of the Navy Department), but her condition had by that time deteriorated from five years of inactivity. Nevertheless, she was soon undergoing conversion work at the Coast Guard Yard at Curtis Creek, Maryland, for service as a submarine chaser assigned to EASTSEAFRON and stationed at New York, New York. However, after more than $150,000 in conversion costs, work was soon suspended due to the decline in German submarine activity on the East Coast. *Bodkin* would never see service again. She was to have the dubious distinction of being the last vessel Bethlehem Steel would scrap at Mallows Bay, for on June 22, 1944, the company agreed to carry out the final shipbreaking operation on the bay.[12]

By the fall of 1944 the market for scrap metal had slowed measurably, and the government no longer saw the necessity of subsidizing the movement of iron and steel scrap. Thus, on September 22, 1944, the government recommended that all work under the contract between the MRC and Bethlehem Steel Company, except the work on the hull of *Bodkin*, be halted. The recommendation was approved and on the following day Bethlehem was instructed to cease all operations on Mallows Bay except on *Bodkin*. By mid-January 1945, the book on Bethlehem Steel's Mallows Bay Project was finally closed.[13]

After more than twenty-two years of efforts, the salvage work on the U.S. Shipping Board's once-heralded wooden steamship fleet, the largest concerted shipbreaking operation of its kind to that time in American history, had finally come to an end, with scores of partially burned ship hulls still lying scattered about the bay in great and sad profusion. The once beautiful bay itself, hitherto filled with nature's bounty, was now a vast wasteland, hopelessly cluttered with the ruins and detritus of one of the greatest maritime industrial experiments in national history. The fallibility of the can-do-at-any-cost attitude had asserted its terrible price at last. The refuge of the snowy white egret was now a giant junkyard. The sturgeon, bass, herring, and menhaden were gone, destroyed by the construction, fires, and dynamiting that had ripped asunder the ingenious, albeit flawed, maritime artifacts of Yankee ingenuity and commerce. And as the bickering and blame-casting gradually subsided, a terrible silence descended on Mallows Bay. Finally freed from the machinations of man, nature set about to make things right.

The Mallows Bay wrecks, the Widewater hulks, and the sundry vessels that had floated free from both sites were rapidly forgotten by the public and the government which had spawned them as they settled more firmly than ever into the Potomac muds. Their remains, now incorrectly reported by some to be those of great troop ships from the War to End All Wars, aroused interest only from the weekend excursionists aboard the Potomac Line steamers that passed by. In February 1948, during a particularly nasty freeze, Gus Chinn, a photographer for the *Washington Star* newspaper, while on a flight down the Potomac to take pictures of ice breakers opening the frozen river to bring in fuel for Washington, noticed the Mallows Bay graveyard and snapped a photograph. At least one hundred of the World War I steamship hulks and several derelict wooden barges, left behind by the various salvage efforts, were recorded, but no one seemed to know anything about them. The newspaper inquired at the U.S. Maritime Commission but "failed to elicit any information about these old hulls." Indeed, no one seemed to know a thing about them. They were noted by the papers only "as an infrequently seen reminder of the waste of war."[14]

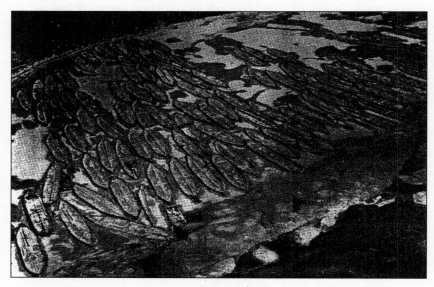

The Ghost Fleet of Mallows Bay, frozen in place by river ice, as it appeared to photographer Gus Chinn of the *Washington Star* in February 1948.
Courtesy Library of Congress

The years rolled by and the battlefield contours of Mallows Bay softened, as wind-borne seeds took root in the rich, soil-filled holds of burnt-out ships, as creatures large and small began to return, as the green chain of life was slowly reforged.

On August 20, 1954, the Sandy Point Farm tract fronting Mallows Bay was again sold, this time to a development company called Sandy Point Estates. It was ostensibly the company's aim to develop the waterfront tract for recreational housing, but the move failed to materialize.[15] And the shipwrecks of Mallows Bay slipped ever deeper into their beds.

In June 1958, a young construction contractor and his two children set out on a weekend camping and boating trip on the Potomac, bound for Mallows Bay. The father knew little about the recent history of the embayment or its occupants, only that it was a place of some interest. The trio traveled downriver from Mattawoman Creek in a creaky old second-hand johnboat powered by an engine that coughed for its life each time the propeller turned. Their destination, the father promised his two boys, would be a place unlike any they had ever visited in their lives. He had often seen it himself as a child, but only from the distant vantage point of a passenger on weekend steamboat excursions with his parents and siblings. He told the children of the great fleet that lay in the river, said by most to be troop transports from World War I, and added the delicious prospect that they were probably haunted. By the time they arrived at Sandy Point, darkness was setting in and they camped on the rickety remains of an ancient wharf and told ghost stories until the evening mists obscured all but the faint red glimmer of a nearby navigation light.

The older boy, though fourteen years of age, didn't sleep much that night, half filled with the residual terrors of the storytelling, and half with the expectations of what lay ahead. He was not disappointed, for the following day, in the early morning fog, they entered into a place that time had seemingly forgot. It was, for the two children, as if they had trespassed into a lost city in the heart of some remote jungle at the far ends of the earth, a place enshrouded in mystery and enchantment and populated only by the great and hoary relics of ages past. It was a hidden world that filled two young boys with the excitement of discovery that most children only dream about. A grizzled old watermen, working his pound nets nearby, had called the great old hulks the "ghost fleet," which only added to their allure. Though the boys infrequently returned after that, their first visit to the graveyard of ships was laminated forever in the elder son's memory, for it had been one of the greatest gifts his father ever gave him. It was, indeed, one of the most memorable events in my life.

❏ ❏ ❏

Not until the 1960s would the Mallows Bay hulks again catch the public's attention, this time spurred by a group of Charles County residents who began to lobby actively for their removal. The group's contention was not new. The wrecks, they said, were hazards to navigation. In 1962 the group, possibly backed by another development company, declared that it was "interested in improving the appearance and enhancing the property values of the vicinity."[16]

The urgings of the Charles County citizens group were not without results. The Army Corps of Engineers ordered that yet another study of the Mallows Bay hulls be undertaken. In 1963 the investigation was carried out by the Baltimore District's senior civilian employee, John L. Reynolds, chief of the operations branch. Reynolds did his homework well. "He determined," it was later reported, "that the hulks, lying in shallow water close to shore, were not a menace to navigation." They were, however, still capable of becoming such if any should float out into the channel, as some had during storms in the past. He recommended that thirty of the hulks around the perimeter of the bay be filled with stone (as the sand had presumably been washed away), to form a bulkhead to prevent the escape of the others, and estimated the cost of the project at $50,000.[17]

In the meantime, the great tract of land surrounding the bay was again changing hands, this time to a firm with far more aggressive intentions than the former landlords. On the surface, their objective was to improve the property for real estate development. But, as is often the case, all was not as it seemed. On October 31,1963, Sandy Point Farm was conveyed to a Maryland corporation called Idamont, Inc. The firm's officers were reported to be the partners of the La Plata law firm of "Mud & Mud [sic], their wives, and a secretary in the office."[18] Idamont, it seemed, wanted the wrecks entirely removed, not stabilized—and quickly.

On July 17, 1964, the Corps of Engineers director of civil works formally withheld approval of Reynolds's recommendations regarding the stabilization of the Mallows Bay hulks on the grounds that the Charles County group's interest in having them removed was "primarily because of their effect on the property values and for aesthetic reasons." He advised the Baltimore district engineer to resubmit the Reynolds proposal only when and if he could furnish evidence of concurrence by "state and local interests and property owners."[19]

Acting on the advice of the director of civil works to seek concurrence of the property owners, Reynolds visited La Plata on July 29 and explained to Idamont President J. Maurice Flinn his plan to fill thirty hulks with stone. The following day, Flinn's senior law partner, F. DeSales Mudd, wrote Reynolds that "access to, and use of the waterfront on the bay as well as the river, is the essence of the value of this property." He stated that Idamont needed more detailed information about the proposed work before being asked to consent and requested a copy of the plans and specifications. The Corps promptly sent him a drawing of the general plan, not yet having advanced the project to the stage of making up definite strategy and specifications.[20]

On November 4, 1964, apparently having been fully apprised of the July 17 comments of the director of civil works, Mudd wrote to the Corps' Baltimore office as follows: "I regret to advise that Idamont, Inc., owner of the Sandy Point property, cannot agree to positioning the hulks around the perimeter of the area and filling them with stone, to form a barrier against the escape of the other hulks from the Mallows Bay area. Such a barrier may prevent the hulks from becoming a future hazard to navigation on the Potomac River; but the proposal could place serious limitations on the development of the Sandy Point property."[21]

As a result of Idamont's rebuttal, the Corps began the development of an alternative plan—one with an all-too-familiar concept. This scheme called for the mud to be cleaned out of the hulks, which could then be pulled ashore and burned. The cost was now placed at $350,000.[22]

Support for the removal of the hulks by some Maryland politicians was strong. In 1962 Samuel C. Linton Jr., a member of the Maryland House of Delegates and a resident of Charles County, became interested in the wrecks after a man drowned because of them. Linton, possibly at Idamont's urging, soon began investigating the old hulks and discovered that many residents were bothered by them. "Big fragments drift up on the shore," he later reported, "and sometimes they weigh from 10 to 15 tons. Then the people have to call the Corps of Engineers to come down and remove them. These hulks are a real navigational hazard, as well as an eyesore."[23]

In 1964, as Idamont continued to press the Corps of Engineers for the removal of the hulls, Linton backed the company's efforts in the Maryland State Legislature by introducing a joint resolution to the General Assembly. The resolution called for that body to recommend to the president of the United States, Lyndon Baines Johnson, that federal action be taken to remove the ships. Copies of the resolution were sent to every Maryland congressional representative. One congressman, Carlton Sickles, became deeply interested in the problem and traveled to Mallows Bay to investigate the situation first-hand. Support for the removal project accelerated when another Maryland congressman, Hervey Machen, joined the movement to clean out Mallows Bay. Ultimately, both Sickles and Machen would introduce bills calling for the total destruction of the hulks.[24] Few now paid any heed to the travails of those, including a giant of American industry, who had tried and failed to do just that.

Though initially unsuccessful in his quest, Machen aggressively pursued the issue. In 1966 he again introduced a bill for the removal of the hulks, but the effort died when the secretary of the army recommended that no action be taken pending the release of a major study on the

Potomac Basin then under way by the Department of the Interior. President Johnson, it seemed, was now intent on making the Potomac America's model river and nothing was going to stand in the way.[25]

Again, in January 1967, Machen introduced legislation for the removal and destruction of the hulks. By February it had progressed to the House Public Works Committee, and the congressman was hopeful that forward motion would continue. "We're hoping," he told reporters, "it will receive favorable attention this time and that hearings will be held so that this problem will finally be settled."[26]

Despite Machen's optimism, it was readily apparent that forward motion would be held back until the Department of the Interior study on the Potomac, which was far behind schedule, was completed. By mid-February, however, Kenneth Holum, assistant secretary of the interior for water and power, could only state, "We're still getting all the reports together. This was a bigger job than we anticipated." When queried whether the study would address the issue of the abandoned ships, Holum commented, "At this point, we just can't say what the study will include."[27]

In 1968 Machen introduced yet another bill, this time to the Eighty-ninth Congress, requiring the Corps of Engineers to remove or destroy the Mallows Bay hulks. The timing seemed appropriate. The Department of the Interior report had finally been completed, and Congress was then considering the new River and Harbor Act of 1968 which would soon become law. Again the bill was held up, this time by a critical Corps of Engineers report that the project would result in the expenditure of public funds for the benefit of private landowners.[28] Machen, and presumably Idamont, fumed over the seemingly unending bureaucracy.

The effort to secure federal support in removing the hulks, however, was resumed in 1969 in the Ninetieth Congress. This time Machen's bill was approved and became section 116 of the 1968 River and Harbor Act (Pub. L. 90-483, 82 Stat. 737) with the amendment, suggested by the Corps, requiring "local interests" to match the federal expenditure. The law applied to all hulks that were in, or had drifted from, Mallows Bay and Widewater. The appropriation authorization, $175,000, was based on half the 1964 estimated cost of beaching and burning the hulks.[29]

On paper, the project seemed feasible. Again, however, disposal of the hulks by burning encountered serious objections. Now it was the environmentalists! Due to increased national concerns over water and air pollution, and the resultant political pressures, the Corps of Engineers was obliged to abandon the plans to eliminate the hulls by fire, and by the end of the following year was "not sure now what method to use to remove and destroy" them.[30] For the Army Corps of Engineers the shipwrecks of Mallows Bay had simply become a nightmare that wouldn't go away.

In the meantime, another unexpected interested party, which had been working quietly behind the scenes during the early 1960s, and which

280

would benefit enormously from the removal of the hulks, at last surfaced. On April 30, 1970, the Potomac Electric Power Company (Pepco), a publicly owned utility which provided power for the Washington metropolitan area, applied to the Public Service Commission of Maryland for a certificate of public convenience and necessity to construct a giant generating station at Sandy Point. The utility stated in the application that it had been the owner of Sandy Point Farm since 1963.[31] The controversy that this statement precipitated, which the company undoubtedly hoped to avoid, was stunning.

Pepco's secret was out: it wasn't a small real estate development company that owned the land, but a giant power company. The removal of the wrecks was necessary for the company to permit the free access for coal barges to its proposed facility, not to remove a purported eyesore that might hinder real estate development or recreational uses. Congressional hearings on the subject followed almost immediately. On July 21, in hearings before the U.S. House of Representatives Conservation and Natural Resources Subcommittee of the Committee on Government Operations, Dorsey F. Hughes, senior vice president of Pepco, produced revealing testimony that would ultimately determine the future of the shipwrecks of Mallows Bay. In attempting to mask the company's long-term objectives and behind-the-scenes methods it had used to achieve them, Hughes stated, "We played no part in the introduction or enactment of section 116 of the River and Harbor Act of 1968, directing the Corps of Engineers to remove or destroy the hulks." He further noted, "We operate in a crystal-clear fish bowl with every step we propose to take being subject to rigorous examination by competent and dedicated experts in various federal and state agencies."[32]

Questioning by the committee, however, revealed that exactly the opposite of Hughes's statement was true. Under congressional interrogation, the Pepco executive revealed that Idamont, Inc., had been a straw company created to enable Pepco "to hold title to the Sandy Point property without public disclosure." F. DeSales Mudd was Pepco's local attorney in Charles County and had no personal interest in the property as the company had stated. In fact, Mudd had been acting in behalf of Pepco and no one else. The power company had for a considerable time been able to disguise its ownership of the Sandy Point property by not revealing the holding in its annual report to the Federal Power Commission and by intentionally failing to list Idamont as a controlled corporation. The company, it seemed, had lied to both the government and its own shareholders.[33]

Asked when they first became aware of Pepco's plans for a power station at Sandy Point, all of the government's witnesses, including federal officials, stated that it was only after Pepco's April 30 filing with the Public Service Commission. John L. Reynolds, the Corps' senior civilian engineer, whose plans for the stabilization of the hulks had been deemed unacceptable, reaffirmed that it was solely Mudd's refusal on behalf of the landowner to accept the plan which led the Corps of Engineers to abandon the scheme in favor of a more expensive one of removal and destruction.[34]

Mudd, it was then learned, was definitely not acting alone. On August 18, 1964, after receiving the plan showing the work proposal for stabilizing the hulks, the lawyer wrote to the Corps the following: "Please be advised that we have referred this plat to our engineer, and apparently it will be necessary that we inspect the property to determine the probable consequence of what is proposed by the U.S. Army Engineers."[35]

The House committee readily deduced that since Idamont, Inc., was a hollow shell, the Idamont "engineer could hardly have been any one but a Pepco engineer." On November 4, 1964, in the letter where Mudd finally refused consent to the stabilization plan, he had written that "the property owner has now had an opportunity to fully consider the matter."

Hughes, Pepco's vice president, explained the actions: "When we bought this property we bought it for a future generating site, but we weren't sure about whether we would develop it as one, and we have played no part in the resolution about moving the ships. The only thing we did was to say we didn't want them to apparently anchor them there permanently."[36] However, Machen, testifying before the House Public Works Committee on June 26, 1968, in favor of the bill which later became section 116 of that year's River and Harbor Act, stated: "The report from the Secretary of the Army of February 9, 1968, on my bill recommends that section 2 authorizing him to receive a contribution from the State be deleted and add the phrase 'Provided, That local interests shall contribute one half of the cost of such work.' I would interpret this to indicate participation by the State of Maryland. I have talked with the owner of the adjacent property of Mallow's Bay and he is agreeable to this recommendation by amendment. Therefore, I support it."[37]

Machen went on to quote from a letter from then Governor of Maryland Spiro T. Agnew, endorsing his proposal and stating: "I would look with favor upon . . . some degree of cost sharing by Maryland."[38]

But, had Idamont, Inc. (Pepco), deliberately sought to mislead both Congressman Machen and Governor Agnew through misrepresentation? According to correspondence in the files of the Maryland Department of Natural Resources, copies of which were made available to the House Committee, Governor Agnew, before taking any position, had carefully referred the proposal for investigation to State Adjutant General George D. Gelston. General Gelston had then visited both Mallows Bay and Mr. Mudd. In a letter dated April 20, 1967, he reported to the governor as follows: "I understand the adjacent land is owned by Idamont, Inc., a corporation of which a Mr. DeSales Mudd, of La Plata, is president. I discussed the matter with him and he states that the hulls preclude use of Mallow's Bay for fishing and other recreational uses, and are also a serious navigational hazard; the hazard being not so much where they are located but that they are breaking up and large pieces are drifting into other navigable areas. Mr. Mudd further stated that long-range planning for the area, an economically depressed one, is for use as park land."[39]

The House Committee was now entirely unwilling to accept either Mudd's or Hughes's stories. Hughes's statement that Pepco "played no part in the introduction or enactment of section 116 of the River and Harbor Act of 1968" appeared entirely inconsistent with the fact that Pepco's agent, F. DeSales Mudd, was clearly one of the strongest moving forces behind adoption of the legislation which contemplated enhancing the value of Pepco's Sandy Point property at federal and state expense— not to mention the intentional avoidance of full disclosure in its actions to both stockholders and the government.[40]

The effects of the findings were dramatic. Once the disclosure of the fact that Pepco would be the only landowner benefiting from the removal of the hulls from Mallows Bay—and the deceptive manner in which it had acquired the land—was made, the state of Maryland quickly reversed its earlier position supporting the proposed removal. On July 2, 1970, the secretary of the Maryland Department of Natural Resources wrote to the House Committee on Government Operations that the removal of the hulls would serve no public interest and that the state of Maryland had no plans to contribute the "local interest" matching funds required by section 116 of the 1968 River and Harbor Act.[41]

The committee's investigation, however, was not yet completed. Now, for the first time, the issue of the ecological status of Mallows Bay was brought to center stage. The little embayment had been changing, almost imperceptibly, as Mother Nature quietly worked to reclaim her lost ground. The official committee report, published in 1970, painted a vivid picture of the bay at that time.

The hulks have been filled with gravel and pilings have been driven around the periphery of Mallows Bay to keep them from floating out into the navigation channel. Nevertheless, from time to time in heavy storms several of them have floated loose. Others seem to have sunk without trace. The Corps of Engineers has identified 99 hulks as still being aground in Mallows Bay, one near Sandy Point, 9 across the river at Wide Water, which is south of Quantico, Virginia, and one on the Virginia shore opposite Maryland Point. Many of the old hulks are now overgrown with bushes. Seen from the air some of the hulks look like huge flower pots. Only the outlines are visible. Over the years, trees have taken root in the earth inside the hulls, and these strange islands are not at all unattractive. Herons and egrets make their homes there.

The American bald eagle nests in the area. The adjacent part of the estuary is spawning ground for striped bass. Until recently Mallows Bay was a great place for fishing, and will be again if the sewage pollution originating at Washington and its suburbs is ever cleaned up.[42]

Testimony in support of the uniqueness of the Mallows Bay ecosystem and the effect the removal of the hulks might have upon it were to have a significant effect in the committee's decisions. Mrs. Hal Margargle, Environmental Chairman of the League of Women Voters of Charles County and Chairman of the Conservation Committee of the Audubon Naturalist Society of the Central Atlantic States, testified before the committee: "The burned-out remains of the World War I troop ships now in the bay have been there for so long—nearly half a century—that it is inconceivable that they are not an integral part of the ecosystem."[43]

Dr. Eugene L. Cronin, director of the Chesapeake Biological Laboratory, endorsing Margargle's assessment, noted that Mallows Bay included the interface between salt and fresh water on the river where salinity varies between zero and five thousands parts of salt dissolved in a million parts of water. The location of the interface varies with the season and from year to year, depending on the fresh water inflow from the estuary. As for the removal of the hulks, he stated: "Shipwrecks, which have existed in Mallows Bay for many years, have no doubt established a special ecosystem. It has functioned to some extent as an artificial reef and attracted some species of fish. . . . The removal of the wrecks would restore the bay to its natural ecological balance, and will during the process cause some temporary readjustment on the part of the existing fauna and flora. We can see no harm to the environment. Since this is a critical spawning and nursery zone for striped bass, it would be wise not to perform the removal during the spring season."[44]

Although Cronin was not against removal of the hulks from an environmental standpoint, the big guns of the Department of the Interior were. In regards to the fisheries, Assistant Secretary of the Interior Leslie L. Glasgow stated: "Fishery use at the present time is largely governed by the polluted condition of the river. If the river were cleaned up, there would be much higher fishery use there." To remove the hulks, however, had ramifications which had not even been addressed by Dr. Cronin. "That is," stated Dr. Glasgow, "the fact that if, in removing these hulks, you disturb the bottom sediment a great deal, and if it is polluted with DDT and other chemicals, you would then by stirring it up repollute the area."[45]

The committee's ongoing investigation soon "clearly established" that the removal of the hulks from Mallows Bay would now cause great ecological damage. Moreover, it would benefit a private landowner (Pepco) at public expense and cost seven times as much as stabilizing the hulks in place. The committee's opinion was clear: the removal of the hulks "is unnecessary, since the good it can do—preventing some of the hulks from drifting out into the navigation channel—can be done as effectively by stabilization."[46]

Still, the U.S. Congress, by section 116 of the River and Harbor Act of 1968, had instructed that the hulks should be removed. But there was, as in most laws, a loophole. The committee's final recommendation was that the hulks "should not be removed from Mallows Bay," an objective that could be achieved simply by the continual refusal of the state of Maryland and other "local interests" to contribute half of the cost. Since federal expenditures on such a project could not legally exceed $175,000, and the cost of such removal operations was certain to rise, it was probable that necessary state and "local interest" funding would not be forthcoming.[47]

Congressional action to remove the Emergency Fleet wrecks from Mallows Bay was thus concluded. The issue of drifting hulks becoming hazards to navigation, however, would continue to resurface from time to time. In 1980 yet another query on the issue was addressed to the Corps of Engineers, this time from the U.S. Coast Guard, apparently as a result of the movements of the more recent derelicts which had been abandoned in the area. Couldn't the hulks be removed from Mallows Bay? On November 26, the Corps informed the Coast Guard it would once again study the situation. By June 1981 a full reassessment of the measures necessary to promulgate such an action was completed.

The fact sheet accompanying the Corps report was succinct:

Removal of the hulks has been authorized under section 116 of the River and Harbor Act of 1968. However; Federal costs cannot exceed $175,000 and local interests must contribute 50 percent of the cost of removal. An estimate of removal of the hulks has been developed by the Estimating Section and Navigation Branch. Removal would involve dredging eleven channels (122,000 cubic yards) into the holding area to provide channel access for the removal equipment which would consist of a crane on a barge, a compressor for cutting equipment and debris barges. The hulks would be cut and loaded onto the barges, towed to a shore station, placed on trucks with a second crane and taken to a landfill. The dredging would be accomplished by bucket and scow and disposal would be upland which would require double handling.[48]

The total cost of dredging and removing the hulks was estimated at $4,830,000 and would take 20 months to complete. An alternative to removal was suggested. This plan called for the reestablishment of the pilings placed around the bay, many of which had long since fallen, to keep the hulks in place. Based on placing 270 thirty-foot pilings (15 feet on center), the total cost was estimated to be $157,000 and performance time would be only 90 days.[49]

On June 24, 1981, Colonel James W. Peck, commander and district engineer of the Baltimore District, Corps of Engineers, informed Rear Admiral John D. Costello, commander of the Fifth Coast Guard District, of the estimate. The removal cost far exceeded the amount authorized by the 1968 River and Harbor Act. Section 116 was the only one specifically addressing Mallows Bay, and as a consequence additional authorization by Congress to produce the funding would be required before any action could be taken, including restoration of the piling system around the bay. In the Corps' view, as the hulks, in situ, were no longer a hazard to navigation, the Corps was powerless to act.[50]

The shipwrecks of Mallows Bay, and the ecosystem that had reclaimed them, would remain.

The metamorphosis of a shipwreck in Mallows Bay into a "strange island."

TWENTY-THREE

Telltale Signs

As our boat pressed into the heart of Mallows Bay on that sunny October day, Pete Petrone, my father, and I spoke almost in hushed tones, as if we had entered some hallowed sanctorum. From the main river channel, the graveyard of ships was barely decipherable, for the bones of many of these long-forgotten hulks, several disguised by a necklace of vegetation and a crown of trees, barely pierced the surface of the still waters within, and were visible in outline form only. Most were indistinguishable from the backdrop of forest that crowded the elevated shoreline. The wrecks at the northern end of the embayment over time had filled with collapsed wooden hull siding, sediments, fire charred timbers, rotting vegetation, and more than half a century's worth of Potomac River flotsam and jetsam, creating incredibly rich soils. In the process, they had evolved into islands, some with mini-forests up to twenty-five feet or more in height growing from their hearts, and so tightly crammed with foliage that boarding was all but impossible. A few had floated ashore or had been pulled up, bow first, hard against the beach, while the noses of others, with rusted steel cables dipping off at odd angles into the water, actually abutted the sides of steep bluffs. And everywhere, there was life, radiant, and in utter profusion.

The waters within the bay were now clotted with thick mats of hydrilla, a Eurasian plant that had been introduced to the Potomac in the mid-1980s to help clean up pollution. It fouled our prop, obscured from view the thousands of obstructions lying just below the surface, and forced us to conduct our explorations under oars alone. White feathered sentinels watched our every motion with spectral eyes from their perch on a line of three score of pilings, marking the southern perimeter of the bay. All about us, untold numbers of ships lay in varying states of decomposition. Many were festooned with the leafy burnished colors of autumn, while others revealed only the wicked crossed teeth of iron strapping that once reinforced wooden hulls long since burned or rotted away. As we passed beyond the piling line, more hulks lay just beneath the waters, adjacent to a giant steel-hulled ship. The great vessel, which appeared to be a relatively recent arrival, apparently had been abandoned while in the very

287

process of being dismantled and pinned to the bay floor by immense piles of cement blocks dumped on her stern.

We circled around the ship and then into the old burning basin, passing smaller wrecks on either side. Several wooden barges, undoubtedly employed at one time or another in the wrecking operations, projected out from the shoreline, half buried by a peninsula of earth. At the corrugated iron and concrete entrance to the basin, a wooden hulk lay off to our left, and the ruins of what appeared to be a dilapidated house on stilts, erected above the water, stood precariously on our right. An old, bedraggled cinder block building stood astride the southern lip of the entrance. At the far end of the basin lay a small, somewhat run-down private marina, with derelict vessels, many of a more recent vintage than those in the bay. Close inspection of a small ship-shaped island on one side of the basin—which appeared to be suspiciously similar to the wrecks in the bay—offered no evidence of any man-made structural features, although parts of wooden ship remains found everywhere else in the area hinted at its possible identity. The hulk of a World War II–vintage dredge and other fragments of salvage and industrial equipment lay partially submerged in the muck or half pulled up on the beach all along the shore.

As we continued to explore the intriguing nooks and crannies of this lost corner of history, I thought back to my first visit to the embayment thirty years before, and then to my last, in 1963, as an art student in college. I was by then too old for ghosts, and there were more practical things to occupy a young man's interests. I had come to shoot footage for

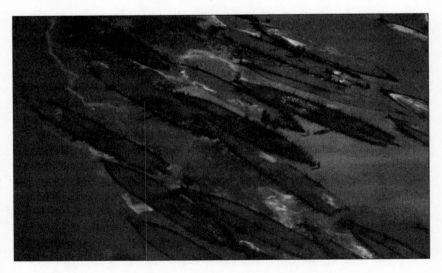

A cluster of steamship hulks surrounded by patches of river ice in February 1992. Courtesy St. Clement's Island–Potomac River Museum

The northernmost clusters of steamship hulks in Mallows Bay, locked in river ice, February 1992. Note the hulks close to shore are the most densely covered by vegetation. Courtesy St. Clement's Island–Potomac River Museum

a short clip for my film production class at Pratt Institute, in Brooklyn, New York, on a subject I was certain would not be duplicated by my fellow students—the Ghost Fleet of Mallows Bay. But in the process, I began to realize, even then, that the bay was changing dramatically. The ship remains were slowly, but perceptibly, being altered as plant and tree roots gouged ever more deeply into the matrix of their old hulls. The still waters of the bay were, in those days, covered by the telltale signs of a river struggling to stay alive. A foul-smelling soup of pea green algae, perhaps a half inch thick, swirled slowly about the surface. The bloated odoriferous bodies of dead fish clustered in every hollow of the bay, lapped by thick, dirty waters of almost molasses-like consistency. The newspapers, during those early years of environmental consciousness, had been filled with accounts of the dramatic increase in river pollution and the life forms that were disappearing because of it.

Yet nature was fighting back. Here and there, as if to punctuate the fact, a great blue heron would rise up, incensed at our intrusion, and escape to a more remote sector of the basin. The wrecks themselves, some even then brimming with growth, seemed to be coming to life despite the poisonous waters of the Potomac. The abandoned hulks were being changed by a strange and wondrous metamorphosis which saw the discarded, wasted products of an industrial society slowly transform into many thriving micro-environments.

The mystery of Mallows Bay was still there, albeit more mired in the black, muddy bottom with every passing year. Just who had built these great ships and why? Why were they here, in this forsaken, albeit beautiful, setting so close to, but isolated from, the civilized world? My father, for me the fount of all wisdom, had no answers. I vowed that day that I would find out.

Now, nearly three decades later, I resolved to act. I would find out all there was to know about the Ghost Fleet of Mallows Bay, whatever it took.

❑ ❑ ❑

As I set out on September 8, 1992, to the wonderful little St. Clement's Island–Potomac River Museum at Colton Point, Maryland, I contemplated the results of my preliminary research on the shipwrecks of Mallows Bay. I was scheduled to meet with Mike Humphries, an ex-Marine, schoolteacher, archaeologist, and, since 1975, director of the museum. Mike was well known in southern Maryland, particularly in St. Mary's County, for getting Herculean cultural projects done, usually against all odds, on time, and within budget. He had navigated his own institution through the treacherous waters of state and national museum politics and had recently secured for it national accreditation by the prestigious American Association of Museums. His museum was one of only two so accredited in all of southern Maryland. I was descending upon him with a proposal seeking his museum's support to conduct a historical and archaeological survey of the Ghost Fleet of Mallows Bay, probably the greatest shipwreck fleet in North America, and possibly the world.

My presentation, replete with slides, photos, and charts, was well received. But, as personable as he is, Mike Humphries is not averse to cutting to the chase. How much will it cost? What will we learn from it? What is in it for the museum and its constituency? How long will it take? What kind of problems are we likely to encounter? I must have said the right things, for his decision was straightforward and positive. He thought it would be a marvelous project, although he needed approval from his board of directors. Then he asked: "Why do you want to do it?" To which I could only reply: "Because I have always wanted to." "Well then," he said with a laugh, "let's get on with it!"

After nearly thirty years, I was at last focusing on a childhood dream— and I was delighted. We wasted little time in frivolities. Our objective focused on conducting a comprehensive inventory and an entirely non-intrusive archaeological reconnaissance of the historic resources of Mallows Bay, centering on the evaluation of the principal wooden steamship vessels built under the auspices of the Emergency Fleet program. But it was also apparent, from my recent reconnaissance, that there were many vessel remains from earlier and later times as well, each contributing to the greater tale of Mallows Bay. We were equally aware that the presence of so many wrecks in such a small place had, perhaps, created a unique combination of historical and ecological micro-environments that could be instructive in any long-term efforts to gauge the effects of the wrecks on the embayment and vice versa.

A first step would be to conduct an aerial reconnaissance of the entire bay, from Sandy Point to Liverpool Point, using infrared, true color, and black-and-white still photography, as well as videotape. A second step would be devoted to conducting a hands-on inventory of the resources, ship by ship, followed by a survey of discrete targets representing the major vessel types. At the same time, an archival survey would be initiated to evaluate the published and manuscript resources pertaining to the wrecks, as well as the wrecking process that had brought them to their present state. This information would permit the construction of the most complete history and site map ever assembled of Mallows Bay and the shipwrecks therein (including those produced by the Army Corps of Engineers). An inventory of flora and fauna found within the perimeters of selected test sites would be undertaken to develop a database suitable for long-term ecological monitoring. Efforts would be made to videotape the sites for later public display and educational purposes and to produce a published history of the ships and the evolving environment of the bay, as well as an exhibition on the Ghost Fleet itself, that could travel around the state to government buildings, schools, libraries, and other places for the benefit and education of the citizens of Maryland.[1]

Although I would serve as principal investigator, I quickly proposed that Dr. Fred Hopkins be recruited to serve as my second and as principal historian. The services of a number of colleagues representing many valuable disciplines would also be solicited, as would volunteers from the museum's Friends organization and from public sector groups such as the Maritime Archaeological and Historical Society (MAHS).

By virtue of state antiquities laws, as the vessel remains fell within the direct administrative jurisdiction of the Maryland Historical Trust, and a permit was, of course, necessary to promulgate our work, it would be obligatory to prepare a presentation to the state to seek not only permission but support as well. It would first, however, be essential to feel out those in authority as to whether or not there was even any interest at the state level for such an investigation. The less-than-systematic reconnaissance which Pete, my father, and I had conducted had produced a considerable photographic reference source and a rough database on just what we might expect, but we needed a project design, a goal, and the semblance of a team to achieve it. But nothing was going be accomplished before we had at least a nodding approval from the Trust.

On Monday, December 14, as Mike and I were scheduled to attend a meeting at the Trust on another matter, we decided it would thus be a most opportune time also to query J. Rodney Little, Director of the Trust, on potential approval and support for the proposed Mallows Bay Project.

Ghost Fleet of Mallows Bay

Selling the Mallows Bay Project, I soon learned, was like selling hotdogs at the ballpark—it virtually sold itself. Without wasting words, Little indicated he was extremely interested in the project and would be willing to permit the Trust to fund it—if we could do it for less than $10,000 and could get a letter of intent and project design to him by December 31. But first, he wanted to sound out the governor.

That afternoon, Mike Humphries and I proceeded to draw up a preliminary twenty-page outline for the survey of the Ghost Fleet of Mallows Bay. On December 29, the polished proposal, letters of recommendation, resumes, project design, budget, time line, and all necessary legal instruments were formally submitted. The project would take a total of 22 days of fieldwork and cost $16,862, of which $8,730 would be provided by the museum in in-kind support and some cash, and the remainder (we hoped) by the Trust. I was well aware that it was likely to take far more than a month to assess the fleet, but recalling the official lack of enthusiasm for the Claiborne Project, I wasn't about to provide our possible benefactors with any excuse to shy away. Yet, we soon had every reason to believe the project would be well supported at the state level, for on December 22, even before our final submission was made, I was notified by a member of the Maryland Advisory Committee on Archaeology that Governor William Donald Schafer was extremely enthusiastic about the project. And well he should have been. The archaeological survey of an entire fleet of as many as one hundred ships, the largest concentration of historic shipwrecks in the nation, at approximately eighty-seven dollars a ship, was a buy in anybody's book![2]

❏ ❏ ❏

With the Trust's assurances that there would be little difficulty in securing the grant, we held the first of several planning sessions on January 5, 1992, attended by a cadre of eager volunteers. Fred Hopkins and I launched into the archival research, mining fields of incredibly rich data hitherto untouched since they had been filed away half a century or more earlier. I would receive in the mail hastily scrawled notes of Fred's finds, discovered in such repositories as the National Archives, the Corps of Engineers Fifth District Headquarters, and the Steamship Historical Society—a steady flow of copies of documents, publications, letters, lists, photos, ship plans, and maps, the likes of which would have impressed Diderot himself.[3]

Although the first organized field work—pending approval of the grant—was scheduled to begin in May, I decided that an intensive pre-survey reconnaissance might prove beneficial. Accordingly, Fred, my brother Dale, I, and several others descended upon the bay at the first sign of reasonably good weather. Our first stop was the Sentinel Wreck, at Sandy Point, where we took some preliminary measurements and photographs, made drawings, videotaped the wreck, and produced a very preliminary site plan. The investigation proved more than instructive.

Fred's remarkable discovery of the 1929 Army Office of Engineers map showing the disposition and indentity of 152 of the 169 hulls in the bay had told us that two vessels, *Obak* and *Botsford,* both of which were McClelland-type composites built of iron and wood, had been anchored on the point. Upon close examination of the Sentinel Wreck, it was readily apparent that the ship was probably neither of the two, as the hull and framing were entirely of wood construction, albeit, like most of the Emergency Fleet, braced with the ubiquitous iron strapping. Examining the Sentinel Wreck was accomplished with some difficulty, since her starboard side was almost entirely buried beneath the shoreline and great portions of her port side were covered by heavy logs and river debris that had become trapped by her strapping during some past flood. The lower aft port area was extremely well preserved, replete with pulleys, compartments, and bulkheading foundations. Her ceiling (floor) and futtocks were constructed of pine, at least to the turn of the bilge, and when deeply scratched with a knife still betrayed the sweet scent of the wood, even after seven decades. Her main keelson and the packing timbers for her engine foundation were thickly festooned with iron bolts and pins which had probably been driven in by pneumatic hammers (one of the technological innovations in wooden shipbuilding in 1917). The well-preserved forefoot was composed of a natural knee and angle blocks but was fitted with both iron and wooden trunnels. Evidence of caulking, and even hexagonal white ceramic tiles from the galley or shower facilities, were noted in profusion. The nearly flat bottomed wreck measured 264 feet 6 inches in length and 44 feet abeam, and had carried a single engine and rudder.[4]

Given her overall base dimensions, and comparison with plans of the major wooden steamer designs, it seemed probable that the Sentinel Wreck had been a Ferris-type ship. Having been built of pine, she was likely to have been constructed on the East Coast or Gulf Coast. She had given us a good idea of what survey work on the other sites might entail. Yet, a visit to a second site was going to prove even more instructive, but in another way.

Under the northern lip of Mallows Bay, several hundred yards south of Sandy Point, lay the most concentrated assemblage of shipwrecks in the area. Here, the scores of vessels are so tightly packed that entry into the embayment by boat is extremely difficult except at high tide. Three free-standing wooden steamboat wrecks and the skeletons of several barges guard the approach to the northern edge of the outer line of ships. Immediately to the east of these, a single shipwreck, designated site No. 1, juts from the shoreline. Masked by a mini-forest of trees, it is connected to the shore and partially buried by a narrow neck of land that has been built up over it in recent years. At least eight ships and two barges lay scattered in disarray near or directly against the beach. All have become virtual islands, crowded with dense vegetation and capped by trees. To the south of the entrance, nearly thirty ships formed an outer barrier line in a more-or-less orderly formation, effectively locking in behind them perhaps several dozen more vessels. At the southern terminus of the bay, beyond a perimeter of pilings, a great steel ship, shouldered by a wooden steamer hulk, marks the lower border of the main wreck containment area.

Passing over the shoals formed by the stern of No. 1, we attempted to board the first entirely dry vessel we met, a heavily forested ship with at least three feet of hull still standing above the waterline. Her bow was close to the shore, but her stern lay clear, and as we approached, we could see two great concrete projections, sheltered by cedar trees, sticking perhaps six feet above her exposed shaft tunnel. I was immediately puzzled since there was no mention in any building specifications regarding the use of concrete in the wooden ship construction program. The hulk was immediately dubbed the "Concrete Wreck." Owing to the density of vegetation all about her, it was necessary to hack a boarding path. As we clambered over her port midship with machetes in hand, like pirates boarding a prize, a pair of beavers, startled by our arrival, splashed into the water from the starboard side. We had, it seemed, come aboard precisely at the site where they had been constructing a lodge!

The Concrete Wreck was nothing less than a natural arboretum. Eastern red cedar, green ash, and other trees grew in profusion, a few as high as thirty feet. Woody shrubs, herbaceous perennials and annuals, and vines had taken root in copious density. As I stood in the middle of the ship, it was virtually impossible to see the water only a few feet away. Signs of birds and animals, their nests, eggs, droppings, and even bones were everywhere. Chewed tree stumps indicated the industry of the beaver, while depressed and matted clumps of weeds and grasses suggested the bedding of larger creatures such as deer.

It was a unique wetland environment and I resolved that the site might well serve as a natural laboratory. Its contents could be systematically inventoried and monitored, conceivably over a long period of time, to gauge the growth and evolution, health and diversity of the ship's bountiful mini-ecology. It might even tell us something about the effects of the wrecking process and the natural collapse that follows.

Moving southward, within the bay itself, we discovered that the farther we proceeded, the less defined the wrecks became by vegetation alone. Many sites were evidenced only by a few timbers or pieces of iron projecting above the surface, while others bore skimpy laurels of false indigo and arrowweed that clung to barely exposed sections. The presence of a few shipwrecks was indicated only by the curious actions of the water as wavelets passed across them. All but a single vessel in the outer line were positioned with their bows pointing eastward, toward the shore. Interestingly, upon close inspection, we now observed that many of the exposed hulks had concrete stanchions positioned along the sides of their shaft tunnels, and occasionally in their bows as well. One wreck appeared to have had her entire lower forepeak filled with many tons of concrete, which now survived in a massive, albeit crumbling, V-shaped block projecting nearly six feet above the water and the rest of the wreck.

As we dodged in and about, seeking out passages between the myriad hulls, it was obvious that a systematic, ship-by-ship inventory would be necessary to gauge the true extent of the fleet and its condition, for in many places it was impossible to determine where one wreck ended and another began. The visible, above-water structural state of preservation of the fleet ranged from poor to excellent. On several wrecks, the stern and rudder posts, replete with gudgeons, still stood a proud ten feet or more above the surface, and hulls, bulkheads, coal bunkers, shaft tunnels, engine mounts, and other features within the ship possessed considerable integrity, even though evidence of burning and wrecking were apparent on most sites. Several vessels, close to or hauled up on the beach, their bows still firmly attached by cables running into the water or onto the shore, were in excellent shape. The beach itself was littered with the washed-up detritus of wrecks. In one spot, a great mound of disarticulated bulkheads, frames, sections of a keel, and rudder fragments, covering an area of approximately twenty-five hundred square feet, jutted up from the bottom to form a hazardous cluster near the southern shore. Had this been a pile of material ripped from many hulls, heaped in a pile in shoal water, and destined for reduction by a fire that was never lit? All we could do, at this point, was speculate.

Our next stop was the great steel ship lodged at the southern edge of the wreck anchorage. The vessel had obviously been subjected to the not-so-tender mercies of scrappers. Her superstructure had been cut away, and her stern, facing the Virginia shore, had all but disappeared, and its original position was indicated only by a great rudder post projecting from the water surrounded by large concrete blocks that pinned the ship in place. The aft end, which had been cut off by scrap salvors, was open to the sea and awash. We boarded, with some difficulty, through a hole in the starboard side and were delighted to discover that here, too, life had sprung up amidst the bones of destruction. Small trees and plants, their seeds having been deposited in bird droppings or by the breeze, gained purchase on sediments that had also been deposited by the winds. Red cedar saplings, swamp roses, sedges and thistles, creepers, and many others were slowly gaining ground. In the still intact but cool, exposed, water-filled hold, floating aquatic and subaquatic vegetation was thriving.

Ghost Fleet of Mallows Bay

I immediately decided to make this ship our second biotic testing and monitoring area. Now we had an all-wooden hulled ship and an all-steel hulled ship.

Making our way up a dangerously decrepit iron stairway to the main deck, we viewed, for the first time from a superior elevation, the breathtaking panoramic spread of Mallows Bay. On the bow, flared sides gave the ship bulky and certainly less than graceful lines. This, together with a pair of great winches and locking assemblages still mounted on the sides, suggested that the vessel may have last served as a car ferry. Here and there hatchways, stitched with spider webs, permitted a view into the very heart of the ship. Corroded iron ladders descending into watery darkness dared us to test them. We did, and in the Cimmerian hold we began to take note of those few features that still stood above the water. Asbestos covered pipes and fittings crisscrossed the area, but even in the hold there were everywhere signs of the wrecker's hand, which had stripped fixtures and fittings from every place imaginable.

What ship was she? That she was the only complete steel ship in Mallows Bay, and a big one at that, was evident. That she had been altered to her present form from a much sharper original design was also probable. She had also arrived sometime after the 1940s as records failed to mention any such vessel prior to that time. She was, indeed, just one more question mark in the book of mysteries that was Mallows Bay.

As I gazed over the vast array of shipwrecks, more tonnage in one place than had been built by the United States in the fifteen years preceding World War I, I experienced the distinct feeling that I had bitten off far more than I could reasonably hope to consume in a dozen lifetimes.

296

TWENTY-FOUR

Buried Boats

To facilitate the archaeological inventory of Mallows Bay, the region between Sandy Point and Liverpool Point Wharf was divided into four transects. The entire area to be surveyed covered as many as one hundred shipwrecks or more, including freighters, fishing vessels and workboats, a sailing ship, a warship, a ferryboat, and recreational craft, dating from the period of the American Revolution onward, as well as land and sea sites pertaining to the Potomac River fishing industry and the great shipbreaking efforts of WM&SC, the independent Charles County salvors, and Bethlehem Steel.

Fortunately, Fred Hopkins's research was continuing to turn up important data, not the least of which was a series of high-level aerial photographs of Mallows Bay, taken from the 1940s to the 1990s, the most recent of which was shot in 1992. I had been able to locate several more, one of which was a high-altitude infrared photo of the region taken during the mid-1980s for the Maryland Department of Agriculture, specifically to determine the impact of gypsy moth infestation. It had also proved to be a valuable interpretive photo showing not only the current distribution of the known wrecks, but also indications of possible shallow underwater sites, abandoned and overgrown roadways, activity areas, and other features. Humphries had been able to secure even more low-altitude photos taken in 1992 by a curious navy test pilot stationed at the Patuxent Naval Air Test Center. The sequence of aerial photographs, together with numerous maps produced by or for the Corps of Engineers from 1929 to 1944, made it possible not only to assess the visible and partially inundated wreck sites, but also to chart their movements as they were shifted about the embayment by salvors and the whims of nature. Thanks to the 1929 map identifying 152 ships, the actual names of many of the hulls still in the bay could be determined. From the aerial photos and maps, it was possible to chart the migration of some vessels as they were moved about the bay by salvors or by nature. It was also possible to determine from which areas the Bethlehem salvage operations had drawn, and where vessels may have simply sunk even before being salvaged. Moreover, from the most recent aerials, it was possible to prepare a preliminary map that would be of key importance to assist in the actual field inventory program.

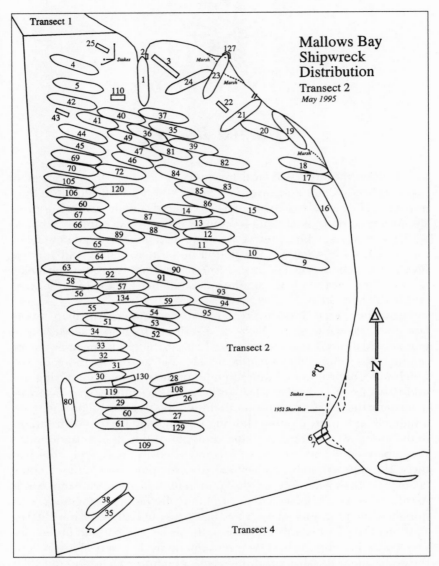

Plan of the disposition of the Ghost Fleet of Mallows Bay, 1995. All numbers are survey site numbers. Rectangular figures are barges.

It was fortunate that we were able to acquire so many valuable resources so early on in the project, for, despite repeated assurances that the grant had been processed, approval of our funding was not forthcoming. On August 25, 1993, Mike received a letter from Governor Schafer, dated the previous day, congratulating him upon the award of the grant, but it would not be until February 24, 1994, exactly six months later and nearly thirteen months after submission of our proposal, that I would be informed that the project had been officially approved. It was thus apparent, early on, that if money was to be spent for the expensive aerial survey, it would have to come from the St. Mary's County government, which wasn't about to assume such an expenditure without an already valid and signed grant. The aerial survey was indefinitely postponed.

It was obvious that we would simply have to do the best we could with the resources in hand. We began to beg and borrow equipment and supplies wherever and whenever possible. Several institutions, such as the National Geographic Society, would eventually provide superb technological support, while volunteer personnel from others, such as the museum's Friends association, and the Maryland National Capital Park and Planning Commission, on their own time and personal expense, were soon lending expertise in many important areas. The project lurched forward.

To avoid the necessity of making a sixteen-mile round-trip voyage each day from Mattawoman Creek (the closest public marine access in Maryland) to Mallows Bay, it was a logistical imperative that we secure direct shorefront access from some convenient private landing directly on or near the bay. Joe Densford, the county attorney for St. Mary's County, member of the museum's Friends association, and an avid sport diver who had generously donated his services and body pro bono to archaeology, immediately set about to contact in writing all of the property owners along the survey transects. He then paid a personal visit to the little Mallows Bay Boat Club Marina located in the burning basin, introduced himself to the gregarious manager of the facility, a much traveled man named Reed Scott, and readily secured permission to traverse club property as needed.

On May 8, 1993, with a working site map already in the hopper, a legion of highly skilled volunteers and divers at the ready, and a handful of borrowed, beat-up old canoes and johnboats to maneuver about the embayment, the Mallows Bay Project formally commenced.

The road to Mallows Bay, once one pushes beyond the chaotic shadow of the Washington metropolitan area, passes through some of the most scenic countryside in all of southern Maryland. The names on the Charles County map are almost as bucolic as the settings themselves: Chicamuxen, Pisgah, McConchie, Nanjemoy, Welcome, Poseys Wharf, and so on. We sped along the single-lane road, beneath green canopies of tall forests, and passed picturesque farmlands, historic homes, churches, country stores, and Civil War encampment sites.

Our volunteer survey team (there were no paid professionals), which normally varied between six and eight persons, was to be divided into two groups. One unit would begin the nonintrusive survey and mapping of exposed sites in the Sandy Point transect, focusing on the Sentinel Wreck, while the other, using the base map produced from the 1992 aerial infrared photo, would tag an assigned site number on the bow of every visible shipwreck in the Mallows Bay transect, after which each site would be photographed. The two teams were kept in contact by walkie-talkie.

The day was bright and warm, and the waters placid. I had hoped the tagging effort, which was to be managed by Fred Hopkins and Larry Pugh, a marine biologist with NOAA, could be concluded in a few days. From the findings of our initial and all-too-brief reconnaissance, it seemed unlikely that fewer than three or four discrete sites of any kind would be encountered at Sandy Point. But, as WM&SC, Harry Steinbraker, Bethlehem Steel, and the Army Corps of Engineers might well have attested, nothing goes as planned in Mallows Bay. Permanently attaching anything to many of the crumbling, almost organic shipwrecks was next to impossible, and ultimately a total of ten days would be necessary to visit all the wreck sites and photograph them. Another ten days would be required to visit and take measurements of basic hull dimensions on a large sampling of nearly forty vessels. Moreover, the Sandy Point transect would prove to be a treasure trove of unexpected sites and archeaological resources that would be examined, off and on, for more than a year.

From the aerial photos, the voluminous manuscript records regarding the Army Office of Engineers ongoing management problems with WM&SC, and the 1929 engineering plan of Mallows Bay, we had learned much about the probable sites to be encountered in the Sandy Point transect. We had ascertained that the company had constructed a short wharf (the very structure I had camped on in 1958), four marine railways, and at least three buildings at the point. The ships *Obak* and *Botsford* had served for some time as a barracks for workers there. And as many as five vessels were said to have been drawn up on the railways and reduced, and presumably buried according to plan, before the operation at the point was terminated as impractical.

Our work here seemed pretty cut-and-dried. All that was required was to survey the Sentinel Wreck, locate at least one of the five buried hulls to confirm the shadowy record on this point, and find four marine railways and related structures without digging a hole. Nothing to it!

The upper end of the Sandy Point transect, immediately north of the Sentinel Wreck, faces a steep bluff and (at low tide only) a narrow strip of sand and pebble beach. Nearly a hundred feet to the east of the wreck, a deep ravine slices the bluff in half, from the southern shoulder of which the vestige of a road descends to the shore from the farmlands above. From this point, the bluff turns gently south-southeastward, and a flat, sandy terrace, only several hundred yards at its widest, extends from its base toward the river.

The survey of the Sentinel Wreck was carried out with little difficulty, although it was impossible to conduct standard mapping owing to a blanket of literally tons of logs, earth, and debris covering major components of the wreck. A datum was erected near the stern, however, and after a path had been laboriously hacked out through the vegetation along the keelson, a baseline was established. Elevations were taken and length and beam measurements were made along the keelson, the latter at ten foot intervals, while drawings of the exposed bow, stern shaft tunnel, aft port bilge ceiling, limberstrakes, lockstrakes, and framing were produced. The wreck had been held in place by steel cables running from the hull to trees at the base of the bluff, a distance of a little over a hundred feet, secured decades ago. Over time, as the trees grew, their bark gradually enveloped the cables, securing the ship more tightly than ever. Slowly, the shallow beach between the ship and the tree line filled with sand, forming new earth, and covering the cable lines to the trees. The venerable old trees still stand, their gnarled trunk bark revealing only here and there the rusted remains of steel cables held fast. From the historic aerial photos which Fred had assembled, it was apparent that the wreck had been deposited at the point some time after 1947, well after the close of the Bethlehem operations. It was thus concluded that the ship had been one of the "floaters" which had drifted from the main wreck disposal area and was later retrieved and towed to the Maryland shore and secured to nearby trees to insure that it wouldn't float again.

Less than two hundred feet to the south of the wreck, concealed in the brush near the beach, a sixty-eight-foot-long, nine-foot-tall section of a great wooden bulkhead, replete with the top half of a doorway still intact, was discovered. Could it have belonged to the Sentinel Wreck? It was, from the evidence in hand, impossible to tell until other wreck sites had been investigated.

Farther along the beach, iron straps, large concrete fragments, and the top of an eight-foot-long iron cylinder, possibly a small smokestack, and other debris could be seen in the surf zone near the wreck of a sixty-foot-long wooden barge. The barge had been drawn up on the beach one hundred yards south of the Sentinel Wreck and lay only twenty-five feet away from the remains of the WM&SC wharf. After being surveyed by Densford and Humphries, it was determined that the wharf, for which only piling stubs remained, was a modest affair. Had it, in fact, been the failed wharf constructed by WM&SC? Or was it all that remained of the Civil War-era Cooke's Ferry wharf, or of a later steamboat wharf?

Below the wharf, the decaying, somewhat fragmented remains of a great wooden ship's rudder, over twenty-four feet in length, was discovered and meticulously measured, drawn, and recorded by Fred Hopkins and Ken Hollingshead, who had volunteered for the project and was destined to provide hundreds of hours of service. The rudder pintals, usually four in number, which permitted the rudder to be hung from the rudder post, were generally bronze castings. As such, they had been highly prized by the scrap salvors, and had long since been removed from the assemblage. The pintals, had they been present, would have fit into bronze sockets, or gudgeons, bolted to a rudder post which was also no longer in evidence. Interestingly, a number of hulks in Mallows Bay bearing intact rudder posts, we later discovered, still mounted gudgeons, but of iron, not bronze. Most of the posts had been trimmed or beveled to permit the rudder to turn at the requisite angle. The trimming, known as bearding, was usually sufficient to allow the rudder to turn about 45 degrees each way. Not for another three months, however, would we actually discover a mounted rudder *in situ* on a steamship wreck.

An accumulation of evidence began to suggest that the low terrace south of the Sentinel Wreck actually covered a substantial debris field of wreckage. Here and there pieces of iron, ship timbers, steel cable, and suspiciously shaped depressions in the earth implied the presence of buried wreckage or structures. In one location, a large iron cylinder, nearly six feet in width, was found poking up from the sand. Excavation within the site to a depth of four feet and probing with steel rods another five feet down failed to locate the other end of the feature. Modest grass-covered mounds abounded everywhere, many with fragments of metal or wood exposed only by wind erosion. At the edge of an idyllic little pond, shaded by trees and occupied by turtles, frogs, and lily pads, several disarticulated ship timbers jutted from a muddy bank, exposed in the root system of a fallen tree. It seemed more than probable that the terrace had served as a platform for wrecking operations. Perhaps, we reasoned, it might also cover the skeleton of a burned-out ship or two!

Early in the investigation of Sandy Point, evidence of the site's usage for something other than shipbreaking had been discovered. Not far to the east of the Sentinel Wreck, and hard against the bluff wall, the remains of an ascetic fisherman's shanty was found. A few feet to the south, the foundations of a second wooden building were found amid the under-brush, as well as a cistern and a shallow, dry trough in the earth running from the well to the beach. Debris of relatively contemporary origin lay scattered about. Were these two of the three buildings indicated on the 1929 map, perhaps reused until finally abandoned in more recent times? Midway between the shanties, three piles of pound net stakes, several hundred in number, forty-five feet in length, and sharpened at one end, lay decomposing in the weeds. To keep them off the ground to prevent rot, the stakes had been laid across several ship timbers from one of the wrecks. Since the stakes had been placed across timbers which had themselves been removed earlier during a shipbreaking operation, they had undoubtedly been cut and readied for use after the abandonment of the point by the shipbreakers. As the Potomac fisheries were, by the mid-1930s, in serious decline owing to pollution and overfishing, they had never been used. Yet, the pound net stakes, abandoned at the site probably many years after the wreckers had departed, testified to the long history of Sandy Point as a fisheries station, from the 1830s probably through the 1960s or later.

By overlaying a contemporary topographical map of the survey area with the early Army Office of Engineers maps and the enhanced enlargements of the historic aerial photos, it was readily apparent that the shoreline of Sandy Point had evolved somewhat since 1929, but more dramatically after 1947, as a result of the shoaling caused by the Sentinel Wreck. But where were the four marine railways? And what of the five ships that were supposed to have been destroyed there? Had they, in fact, been buried ashore beneath spoil, possibly in the area currently formed by the open terrace, as the historic record suggested?

Enlargements of the historic aerial photos of Sandy Point offered some tantalizing clues. Although no photo predating 1943 had been located, it was apparent that the point had become heavily overgrown by that time. However, between 1947 and 1952, trees and underbrush had been removed, exposing the scars of old roadbeds and much more. Using computer enhancement to boost extremely subtle differences in the gray scale of the photos, which had been enlarged 2,200 percent, four long scars situated side by side, ranging in length between 250 and 325 feet, and each approximately 30 feet wide, were discovered. We located the sites of the marine railways without getting scratched by a single briar!

As readily detectable surficial evidence suggesting at least small fragments of a wreck or wrecks had been discovered beneath the soil, I decided to try using ground penetrating radar to see if there had, in fact, been significant buried features or alterations in the subsoil in the areas in which I had calculated the WM&SC facilities to have been. A simple systematic metal detector investigation of the same area would hopefully allow us to plot the distribution of buried iron features.

Ground penetrating radar (GPR), also called subsurface radar, has been employed for many years by archæologists to detect and graphically display variations in the subsoil of land sites and to locate structures, objects, or features beneath the earth, often at great depths. Indeed, GPR had been used successfully by archaeologists to locate everything from lead coffins, burial chambers, and tombs to building foundations, fortifications, and filled-in trenches. Unlike GPR, the simple hand-held metal detector, often used by weekend treasure hunters and relic collectors to search for everything from bullets and accoutrements on Civil War battlefields to coins, rings, and watches lost on public beaches, could also be systematically employed in archaeological survey, such as on the Custer Battlefield in Montana. Like the more sophisticated GPR, it could be a formidable asset if utilized systematically.

As I had often done in years past, through the good offices of my long-time friend and colleague Pete Petrone, head of the Photographic

Special Projects Office at National Geographic, I pitched upon the Society for a one-day loan of its GPR equipment. With Pete's help I secured the loan not only of the equipment, but of the best technician the Geographic had to manage it—Pete himself.

The unit loaned to the project was called a Subsurface Interface Radar System (SIR) and was produced by a New Hampshire outfit called Geophysical Survey Systems, Inc. It consisted of a control unit, graphic recorder, remote control unit, calibrator, and transducer. Power was provided by a twelve-volt battery. The workings of the system are relatively simple. The control unit transmits power to the electronics and a synchronizing signal to the pulse generator in the transducer. Whenever the transducer detects a reflected radar pulse, traveling at near the speed of light, a signal is transmitted to the receiver. The receiver converts this electromagnetic signal, only a few nanoseconds in duration, to an analog signal, tens of milliseconds in duration, and transmits this signal to the control units. The signal is then electronically processed and sent to the graphic line recorder, which accepts the signal from the receiver to produce a permanent chart display on electro-sensitive paper. By recording a vertical intensity modulated scan for every few inches of transducer travel, a continuous profile can be developed showing reflections from subsurface strata and any anomalies therein.

All that was necessary to conduct a systematic GPR survey of a select area was to establish a grid of survey lanes and then slowly haul the transducer along each. Not only would it be possible to locate subsoil features; a profile of the geological strata of the sector might also be produced for analysis. Once discrete targets were discovered, they could then be surveyed, mapped, and either excavated or tested in some other fashion. Since the investigation was to be nonintrusive, however, and excavation had been ruled out, I decided that the only testing possible would be through probing and a follow-up survey using a metal detector. To assist us with the metal detecting, I had secured the services of John Mitchell, an ex-relic hunter turned amateur archaeologist, who was both extremely knowledgeable about the Potomac shores of Charles County and an expert in the use of metal detectors in archaeological survey.

The site I had selected to be investigated was a tract of relatively open ground to the east of the wharf ruins. It was an unseasonably hot Monday in May, with temperatures soaring to the mid-90s, when we arrived by boat and began to unload the boxes of equipment on the beach. Owing to surf conditions, however, we had been obliged to land in the small sheltered lee of the stern of the Sentinel Wreck and manually haul our heavy gear and equipment several hundred yards down the beach, swatting off black flies and mosquitoes all the way. Yet, aside from a few small saplings and a hunter's rusting, derelict trailer that had somehow come to rest in the

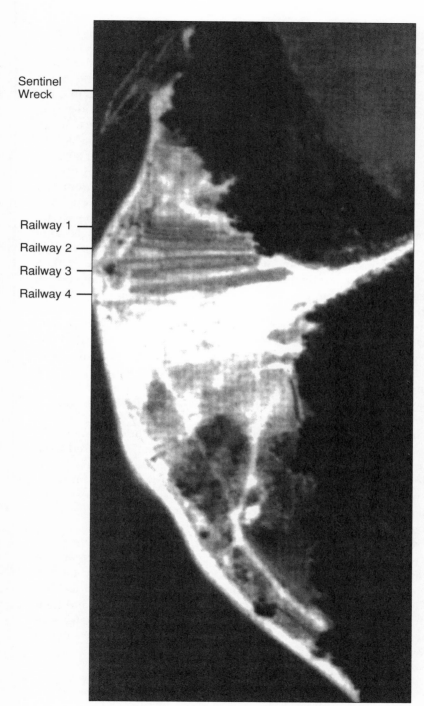

Sentinel
Wreck

Railway 1
Railway 2
Railway 3
Railway 4

A computer-enhanced 1952 aerial photo of Sandy Point showing the position of the Sentinel Wreck and scars of the four marine railways installed by Western Marine and Salvage.

305

area near a copse of trees and the edge of the bluff, there was little to obstruct our investigation.

To assist us in establishing our grid, I had secured the services of a professional surveyor named Rick Moreland, who worked for the Maryland National Capital Park and Planning Commission and who is unquestionably one of the best in the business. By early afternoon, the grid having been established over 32,100 square feet of ground, we were able to begin the survey. Pete wisely selected a shady tree from beneath which to monitor his recorder, while John and I took turns physically dragging the heavy transducer box up and down the survey lanes, and following up with the metal detector. From the GPR signature record it was apparent that the soils in the area had been churned, moved, dug, and distorted in a thousand ways. There were innumerable small magnetic targets mixed in, the probable detritus of the wreckers. But, aside from a single large concrete sleeve inserted into the earth not far from the ruins of the old wharf, there was no indication of any large structures, backfilled earthen troughs, holes, enclosed chambers, or the like to be found. Disappointed, we began to pick up our gear. The survey of the Sandy Point transect had finally been completed.

While Pete and John packed, I conducted one final patrol of the area. Spotting a trio of white tail deer in a small glade of tall grass near the edge of the bluff and perhaps 150 yards from the beach, I called John over to have a look for himself and then returned alone to help Pete. A few minutes later John returned to get his metal detector. "I have a hunch," he said as he bounded back to the glade. Minutes later, he returned again, a Cheshire cat grin cutting across his face.

"Come here. I've found something that you might be interested in."

Pushing back a patch of knee deep grass in the glade, he pointed down to a row, nay, several rows, of iron pins, with helmet-like heads barely visible above the soil. I fell to my knees and began probing with my knife. The pins were lodged in wood, a timber at least several feet wide. Excitedly, I instructed John to trace the lines of iron pins with his metal detector and Pete to follow behind with a tape measure. The mostly buried line ran unbroken for nearly 260 feet. Exploration with the metal detector on either side of the line produced additional targets buried beneath the scenic grass-covered terrace. This was not merely another fragment of a wreck. Indeed, it appeared that John Mitchell had accidentally discovered with his simple metal detector, on the last day and hour of our survey of the transect, what we had spent all day looking for with the most sophisticated, expensive detection equipment available—one of the five buried shipwrecks of Sandy Point.

TWENTY-FIVE

This Is One Evil Place

From high altitude, the shipwrecks of Mallows Bay look, for all the world, like a vast fleet of warships lying at anchor in a snug harbor awaiting orders to sail. Yet, as we were soon to discover, the Mallows Bay transect and all of the ships and features within it were, in reality, an enormous jigsaw puzzle that at times appeared to us so intricate that it might never be reassembled. A single change of tide, which could cover a third of the fleet from view in an hour, made navigation amidst the labyrinthine lanes between hulks, which was never easy, frequently impossible. From late June through early October, hydrilla strangled the bay and everything in it. The still waters of Mallows Bay were now often so densely choked that even a canoe passed only with difficulty, and diving operations were carried out at some hazard. Nevertheless the inventory work proceeded as planned, albeit far more slowly than anticipated.

As Fred and I perused the historic data before launching into the field program for the transect, the immensity and significance of the task before us seemed even more daunting than before. Eight of the ten wooden and composite steamship types built during the war were represented in the steamship population identified by name on the 1929 Army Office of Engineers site map of the bay. Of the total 322 wooden and composite vessels constructed during the war, 218 (67.7 percent) had been brought into the Potomac for breaking up, and at least 169 (52.5 percent), more than half of the ships of the wooden steamship program, had ended up in Mallows Bay. Of those brought into the bay, including the barracks ships *Obak* and *Botsford*, 154 (47.8 percent of total built) were identified in the historic record by name and totaled approximately 554,000 deadweight tons of shipping—more tonnage than had been built by the United States of America in the sixteen years between 1899 and 1915. By far, the greatest number of vessel types represented in the bay were Ferris (117), followed by Hough (12), McClelland (8), Supple-Ballin, Pacific American, and Peninsula (4 each), Grays Harbor (3), Daugherty (1), and one unknown. Only the Allen, and the Lake & Ocean Navigation Company type, of which only one of each had been produced prior to August 1, 1920, were not present. The vessels in the bay included not only the first ship to have been built in the program, *North Bend*, but the last, *Boynton, Munra, Wonahbe,* and *Owatam.* The longest was *Grayling,* which measured 295.9 feet in length, and the shortest *Amoron,* at 258.4 feet. The identified shipping represented the products of at least 58 of the Atlantic, Gulf, and Pacific Coast wooden and composite shipbuilders engaged by the U.S. Shipping Board during the program, including the Maryland Shipbuilding Company of Sollers Point, Maryland, which had built *Arundel* and *Guilford.* In short, the wrecks in the Mallows Bay transect represented the largest archaeological concentration of American ship-building traditions of a given period extant in one place or deposited at one time in the nation.[1]

Enlargements of the infrared and other recent aerial photos indicated that at least eighty-one vessels were still ensconced within the transect, and at least three or four possible wreck sites lay submerged. Over the next two years, *ten* submerged shipwrecks would be found by dragging and systematic underwater survey, bringing the total number of wrecks in the transect up to ninety-two. The transect also contained, besides eighty wooden steamships left after the wreckers had departed, nine wooden barges, one steel-hulled ship, one four-masted schooner, one great debris pile filled with whole sections of ships, at least two primitive marine slips or skidways, a number of unidentified vessels, and hundreds of thousands of vessel fragments. The sites ashore, though less dramatic, were entirely unexpected and of significant importance as well.[2]

In July of 1993 we began in-depth examinations of the shipwrecks, taking basic measurements, photographs, and videotape, and attempting to identify each by type of vessel. Teams of two to four persons, usually working from two canoes in tandem, were required to inventory a site effectively. Often, access was a definite problem and it was necessary literally to walk or swim across several water-filled hulks to get to ones that were entirely closed off from boats. It was, however, often possible to board many of the steamer hulls at low water, or at least to bring our canoes through openings in their sides at high water and paddle around therein, to take measurements of interior features. The interior architecture of a few ships located on the outer line, near the southern edge of the transect, was soon discovered to be in an excellent state of preservation. Normally, between six and nine feet of the steamer hulls lay below the waterline ensconced in the muck, frequently in such good condition that they appeared as if they had just been launched.

As our database expanded, many of the wooden steamers were readily identified by builders class based upon dimensional characteristics, architectural features, and so forth, although usually less than twenty percent of the hull of any given vessel had survived. Others were tougher nuts to crack. Several, initially identified from the aerial photos as smaller ship hulls, proved to be very large wooden barges; and at least one barge, identified as such from the photos, turned out to be a steamer hull with its stern torn away, probably by dynamite.

Exploration and surveying onboard a wooden steamship hull, filled with waist-deep water and frequently populated by snapping turtles, water snakes, and fish and covered by slimy hydrilla which often obscured all surface visibility of the bottom, was something less than an adventure. Even the tiny minnows, ever eager to feed on a bit of peeling sunburned skin, were a nuisance. Adding to these minor difficulties were the distinct hazards caused by thousands of iron pins, fittings, and sharp, broken timbers sticking up from the decks, each of which was capable of tearing a hole through one's foot, wet suit boot and all—and frequently did! Onboard the dry hulks covered by almost impenetrable vegetation, snakes were regularly encountered but proved far less of a vexation than the black flies, mosquitoes, spiders, ticks, and the thousand-and-one other insects that can make life miserable in a jungle-like environment on a 95-degree summer day in the open sun. Of course, attempting to survey hulks in freezing water along the unprotected outer line, directly exposed to the waves and currents of the Potomac on a cold, windy day in March, while struggling to keep from being washed out to sea, was no picnic either. At such moments, knowing that our grant had yet to be formally approved, it was often tempting to chuck the whole thing. But then some

The remains of *North Bend* more resembled a "giant flowerpot" than a ship when first identified in Mallows Bay.

The engine deck of Site 33. Note the shaft casing mounts, still in place, along the centerline, and compartment foundations on either side.

new discovery would make it all worthwhile—until the next unforeseen difficulty. Not everyone was entirely tolerant of nature's diversity or challenges. When a watersnake slid within a few feet of his toes, startling the bejezzus out of him and eliciting a round of serious mockery from us all, Mike Humphries just shook his head and muttered loudly: "This is one evil place."

Underwater work proved far more pleasant. On the Potomac side of the outer line, turbidity usually allowed less than six inches of visibility. But inside, in the hydrilla-choked bay on a warm mid-summer's day, the waters seemed clean and clear. On the Potomac side, living creatures were rarely encountered, yet in the embayment, only a few hundred feet away, fish, reptiles, and amphibians were seen, often in great abundance. Indeed, on one bright afternoon while taking the measurements of a wreck, I looked all the way to the bottom, as if I were peering through a fishbowl, and watched perhaps a dozen giant bass lounging in the ship's cool shadow.

In mid-July a concerted effort was launched on the northern edge of the outer line to explore the area for sunken hulls that had thus far escaped discovery. The survey, however, was carried out with some difficulty. The field log for July 17 reported site conditions thus:

Midday temperatures again reached low 90s. Hydrilla growth has expanded so dramatically that the surface of the entire basin of Mallows

Bay is completely covered by the plant. As a consequence, there is absolutely no surface water activity beyond a few feet of the edge of the growth area because the densely populated area completely absorbs all surface agitation. Waves of six inches are totally absorbed within a few feet of meeting the growth edge. Owing to the lack of agitation, the surface water quickly becomes heated by the sun and is actually hot, and certainly near body temperature. Without clothing to protect the skin, our divers are extremely uncomfortable. The hydrilla itself poses an extremely difficult obstruction to walking, and swimming is nearly impossible. . . . Insect infestation is enormous.[3]

The preliminary investigation, carried out by my brother Dale and me in only ten to fifteen feet of water resulted in the documentation of the better parts of ten known steamer hulls and the discovery of two hitherto unknown and totally submerged barge wrecks. As we proceeded, there were at first few surprises since most of this cluster of vessels had hardly any standing architectural details or artifacts in evidence. One ship featured a loose spread of brick on the deck, and in another hexagonal tiles, similar but larger than those encountered on the Sentinel Wreck. Like all of the steamer hulls encountered thus far, nine of the sites investigated had been stripped of their rudders. Yet on one, site No. 45, the lowest 7½-foot section of a once-massive wooden rudder swung loosely in the current, hanging precariously by a single pintal from the gudgeon in its post. The top, which projected perhaps eighteen inches above the water at low tide, had been sheered off its outer edge, where a protective band of metal once was, had apparently been removed. It was the first rudder found still actually mounted in place, but not the last. Indeed, as we examined the interior features of another hull, site No. 71, only three vessels away, another rudder, the best preserved specimen to be found in the whole fleet, and nearly intact, was discovered on the deck in only three feet of water. How it got there was anybody's guess, for it weighed hundreds of pounds and had probably not moved since it had come to rest perhaps seventy years ago.[4]

It had not been our intention, nor were we able, to conduct a comprehensive archaeological survey of every wreck in Mallows Bay. We did, however, seek to survey a few representative samples. One of those selected for a more intensive analysis had been site No. 37, located in the third line of hulls at the northern end of the bay. The exposed seven-foot-tall remains of the hull were lodged deeply in the mud, in only five feet of water. Her rudder post, separated from the ship by a distance of four feet, was tilted northward at a wild angle and threatened to collapse at the slightest touch. Yet underwater examination of the hull revealed that structural integrity was superb. On her bow stem, a half-inch-thick iron footplate was still firmly attached. Upon taking her measurements, we discovered the ship to be 264 feet 7.5 inches between perpendiculars, 40 feet 2 inches abeam at her midships between uprights, and 44 feet 2 inches planked beam. A pair of 9-inch girder keelsons extended down the hull on either side of the main keelson. Four I-shaped, 6-foot-long wooden platforms for the shaft casings and the elevated engine and boiler bedding timbers were found still in place. The bottom of the propeller shaft boxing beneath the remains of the afterpeak, void of the ubiquitous concrete frames that had been noted on many, if not most, of the hulks, was still largely intact. Two bulkhead foundations were located at 60 feet and 105 feet from the stern. In size and deck layout, the wreck was, in fact, more suggestive of a Ferris type. By comparing the 1929 map data with our developing site plan, it was conjectured that our vessel had been *Bayou Teche*, a Ferris-type steamer built in 1918 at Madisonville, Louisiana, by the Jahncke Shipbuilding Corporation and home ported at New Orleans. The vessel had been ordered scrapped in 1925 and was reduced prior to October 12, 1928, when she was released from bond.[5]

Although not as densely populated by shipwrecks as in the north, the southern end of the Mallows Bay transect was nonetheless mined with intriguing questions. Concrete frames, of varying sizes and shapes, were discovered shouldering the shaft tunnels on many hulls, while the bows of others had bulkheading or forepeaks filled or reinforced with the same materials. The matrix of concrete often varied from vessel to vessel, with some having been produced from sand and small pebbles, while large gravels had been used in others. Naval architect J. Carey Filling, one of the project volunteers, suggested that the concrete had been employed by contractors to provide trim and would thus have varied from vessel to vessel. Yet, these appeared to be architectural components, similar in design and location, but of variable sizes, that had been adopted in the construction of scores of ships in the Emergency Fleet, but had gone unrecorded in the archival record.

Leading experts in historic ship design and construction were questioned about the use of concrete in the Shipping Board fleet and its use in frames, projections, and stiffeners. The noted naval architect Thomas Gillmer was, like everyone queried, somewhat mystified. "It is not uncommon," he wrote, "to pour concrete in the bilges and between the floors (lower frame sections across the keel). This is for several purposes—to prevent bilge water from lying about in these recesses and to make a smooth limber track for bilge water to drain to a sump pump. I personally recommend the use of pitch for this purpose instead of concrete. But this does not explain projections." It may be "for some sort of support . . . for tanks, etc. It may have been an economy in construction to use instead of wood or steel supports. As a substitute for salting the hull—that is pretty far fetched."[6] The best hypothesis that we could come up with was that

The discovery of the poured concete bow section of one ship was typical of the features on the Mallows Bay wrecks not documented in construction plans of the U.S. Shipping Board fleet.

the concrete had served as stiffeners or reinforcements for the fore and aft gun platforms. But it was only a guess.

For several months the wreck of the once-beautiful, four-masted schooner *Ida S. Dow* had taken a backseat to other survey priorities in the transect. Her remains, we knew, were entirely submerged somewhere along the extreme southern border of the wreck impoundment area. And there were ample clues as to her location—such as an Army Office of

Engineers map produced circa 1936–37 showing her permanent anchorage site and then the position of her final resting place. A cryptic notation beside the plan read: "*Ida S. Dow* (abandoned) Pulled to new position & filled with mud Sept. 1936." The plat had indicated that her remains had come to rest alongside the hull of the steamship *Kasota*. [7] Moreover, while conducting an extensive search at the Mariners' Museum in Newport News, Virginia, and at the Calvert Marine Museum, at Solomons, Maryland, for pictures of ships belonging to the Mallows Bay fleet, I had located a number of photos of the schooner, including two showing her at anchor in Mallows Bay, alongside a barge filled with either sand or mud. Her bow was pointed east, toward the shore, and she had been completely stripped of sails, rigging, lifeboat, and other features. I had discovered perhaps the last portrait made of the sad old schooner afloat.

As Ken Hollingshead and I began to drag for her hull, the search for *Ida S. Dow* was rewarded almost as soon as it began. Indeed, we found that the ship's sides projected five feet off the bottom to within inches of the water's surface. Later, underwater investigation of the site revealed that her hull was largely intact for 215.5 feet of its overall length. But a sizable corner of the forward port and starboard hull had virtually disappeared, almost as if it had been bitten off by some giant sea monster—more than likely one that looked like a salvor's clam bucket!

The largest vessel of all in the bay, the big steel ship lying approximately one hundred yards southwest of the *Dow*, and designated site No. 35, was another matter. A number of claims by several authorities had been made about her origins and identity. Indeed, almost as soon as our initial pre-survey reconnaissance had been completed, and before any archival research had started, I began to query a number of experts on the subject and to receive the names of a variety of candidates for the ship. The late steamboat historian Harry Jones said that the ship was *Accomac*, built in 1928 at Quincy, Massachusetts, for the Virginia Ferry Company, a subsidiary of the Pennsylvania Railroad, as the steam screw *Virginia Lee*, and intended for service between Cape Charles and Norfolk. During World War II she had been requisitioned by the U.S. government and loaned to the British Ministry of Transport for convoy duty between Halifax, Nova Scotia, and Great Britain. Owing to frozen pipes and mechanical difficulties, however, she had been returned to New York and promptly outfitted for service to haul rubber, then a strategic war material, from the Brazilian Amazon. After the war, the ship had passed through several owners, until her career was finally terminated by a tragic fire. About 1973, her burnt-out hulk was finally towed to Mallows Bay.[8] It was a splendid tale but, unfortunately, before Harry could provide me with promised documentation, he suffered a fatal heart attack. His loss was deeply felt. As for No. 35, we would have to start from scratch.

This Is One Evil Place

Examining the collections of the Steamship Historical Society in Baltimore, Fred Hopkins was soon able to find that the ship had been converted to diesel power a few years after the war and reregistered under the name *Holiday* for service as a ferry running between Boston, Plymouth, and Provincetown, Massachusetts. In the winter of 1950, while en route for a new operation at Houston, Texas, *Holiday* had been severely battered by a storm off Cape Hatteras, and the following spring she was sold to the Wilson Line and rebuilt for service with the Virginia Ferry Corporation.[9] The ship underwent a major structural overhaul. To permit her to accommodate head-on loading, she was given a new "spoon" bow and was soon capable of hauling 70 cars and 1,200 passengers a trip. Renamed *Accomac*, she would henceforth be assigned to run from Kiptopeke to Little Creek, Virginia. Sadly, as Harry had claimed all along, on May 28, 1964, *Accomac* was permanently put out of commission by a fire. The following year her owner was listed as being the U.S. secretary of commerce. By 1971 she was officially registered as being "out of documentation."[10] But there was nothing, unfortunately, in the literature to confirm the big wreck in Mallows Bay was actually *Accomac*.

Fred began to dig even deeper. An examination of the aerial photographs was undertaken to determine just when the ship may have been brought in. The hull, it was soon discerned, was clearly not in evidence during the 1940s or early 1950s, as one U.S. Department of Agriculture aerial black-and-white photo, taken on June 19, 1952, indicated the site at which the steel wreck now lay was absent of any hulk. Indeed, there were no wrecks of her distinctive deck shape anywhere in the embayment. In late January 1993, Fred began sifting through the voluminous files of the Baltimore District Corps of Engineers in hopes of encountering a reference. There was none. Since the hulk was not in the main channel it was of no concern to the Corps. Yet, as he continued to pour over the documents, he discovered an account dated August 13, 1979, reporting that during a hurricane, a wooden ship hulk or barge had broken loose from the main enclosure in Mallows Bay and was drifting away. Fortunately, the hulk had been secured by the Coast Guard, which towed it up next to the big steel wreck, to which it was then tied.[11] Here was the first archival record of the presence of the steel hulk in Mallows Bay. The time for the abandonment of the ship had been narrowed to the twenty-seven-year period between 1952 and 1979. But was she *Accomac?*

As we continued to probe through the archives and shipping records, several alternative candidates appeared, including a U.S. Shipping Board steel-hulled ship also named *Accomac*, which had been built in 1918 in California by the San Pedro Shipbuilding and Dry Dock Company. This vessel, however, was soon dismissed, for, although she was reported as abandoned, the date was given as 1931. Her length, at 410 feet, was far too long for our vessel, which I had estimated, based on aerials taken in the 1980s, at close to 300 feet.[12]

At the U.S. Merchant Marine Academy at Kings Point, New York, Fred discovered another possible contender, a World War I–era "Hog Islander" called *Commack*. He learned from the librarian at the Academy, Frank Braynard, that the history of the ship had only recently been published in a book called *The Hog Islanders*, by one Mark H. Goldberg. Although Goldberg had reported that *Commack* was demolished in 1938, upon contacting him, Fred was informed that it was, in fact, possible that she was one and the same as our mystery ship.[13] Unfortunately, after locating her specifications, we determined that like the San Pedro *Accomac*, *Commack*, at 390 feet in length, was also simply too long to be No. 35.

Not until the spring of 1995 would the mystery be cleared up. During a small archaeological field session I was conducting with the support of the Maritime Archaeological and Historical Society, I paid a visit to No. 35 with Dr. Ted Suman, an entomologist with Anne Arundel Community College. Our objective was to begin preparations for a comprehensive analysis of the wreck and to search for a potential sampling area deep in her hold for Ted to start collection of data on the insect population of the site. Ted had considerable experience in developing procedures for the analysis of insects in forensic work, and more recently in such major archaeological evaluations as Project Lead Coffin at St. Mary's City, and in the ongoing study of life forms which had inhabited the hull of HMS *De Braak*, a British sloop of war sunk off Cape Henlopen, Delaware, in 1798 and recovered in 1986.

As we approached beneath the starboard prow of No. 35, I was suddenly struck with the prominence of the chief architectural feature of the ship—her "spoon" bow. As I examined the steel deck, I could see that the weld marks clearly indicated that the spoon had not been built into the

The spoon-shaped bow of the ferryboat *Accomac*, initially believed to be the World War I Hog Islander *Commack*, is crowned by an osprey nest.

ship, but added on to the main hull. In addition, as all of the plating and interior metalwork had been welded rather than riveted, the vessel was definitely not of World War I vintage. Then, we began to take her measurements and to photograph many of her prominent features—including her spoon bow. From the measurements taken of the exposed foredeck, utilizing them in concert with the aerial photos to estimate her overall length, I concluded that the wreck was between 290 and 295 feet in length and 50 feet abeam. *Accomac* was 291 feet in length and 50 feet abeam. A few days later, as I perused the recent shots of No. 35 taken from beneath the spoon of the starboard bow, and comparing them with photos of the newly refitted *Accomac*, taken from almost the same exact angle in 1952, there was no doubt in my mind. The late Harry Jones had been right all along.

❏ ❏ ❏

On November 17, 1993, a most unique, albeit accidental, discovery was made while conducting an on-site briefing in the Mallows Bay transect for some of the underwater archaeological staff of the Maryland Historical Trust. The waters of the bay were extraordinarily low as Bruce Thompson, of the Trust, and I proceeded north in my canoe, hugging the shoreline, bound for a cluster of steamship wrecks that had been drawn up on the beach nearly seven decades earlier. At least two of the sites, Nos. 16 and 17, had cables running from them into the water and a wonderful mixture of still-intact architectural features and vegetation upon them that could not help but impress my guest. Yet, as we pulled into the little sheltered box-like cove formed by the juncture of the two wrecks and the beach, my attention was immediately drawn not to the ships, but to what was clearly discernible in the shoal water and extended from the shore: several arrangements of logs, projected perpendicular to the shoreline, positioned in such a way as to suggest boat slips or an elementary marine skidway. We soon discovered that No. 17 appeared to have actually been hauled up between one of the log "slips." Closer scrutiny of the shore revealed that between two such clusters, a deep, V-shaped indenture in the beach was still evident. It appeared that here, overlooked during earlier visits to the area, was some form of marine facility hitherto unknown in the bay. But why had it been built? Not until the spring of 1994 would we find the time to return to evaluate the site and produce a hypothesis.

When I returned to document the "slip" facility (designated site No. 101), I was accompanied by Rick Moreland, Ken Hollingshead, and my wife Carol. The plan was that while Rick and I surveyed and recorded the features in the water, Carol and Ken would take basic measurements on the adjacent shipwrecks and then conduct a walkover of the adjacent littoral. Upon arrival on site, Rick immediately began to hack out a clearing for a station on a slight elevation just above the marsh line, while I probed for and marked the logs and other features in the water at the slip with stakes, about 120 feet away. Each feature was then measured, numbered, and surveyed in, as were the two adjacent shipwrecks.

The logs had all been stripped of bark but were otherwise unformed, bore no tool marks, nails, or other signs of having been worked. The terminus points of each log were physically located and measured by hand in the water and by probing with a steel rod into the marshy shoreline from which they projected. As we gradually pieced together a preliminary site plan, it became evident that the logs had been laid more or less in order to form a rather primitive but usable facility, possibly for the reception of small watercraft. It seemed obvious that they were not railways capable of handling near football-field-length ships such as Nos. 16 and 17. Yet, No. 17 appeared to have been drawn up into one of the slips, and possibly moored there by a steel cable that still extended from the bow into the water. The longest logs were over sixty feet in length and extended seaward for a distance of just over thirty feet, while an equal length was anchored beneath a shoreline of marsh and earth. Smaller reinforcing and shaping logs gave each of the two slips their contours. Still their purpose seemed unclear. Ken and Carol's explorations ashore, however, soon helped to produce a reasonable hypothesis.

Site No. 17 faced directly up the throat of a ravine. The ravine was covered for nearly fifty feet by dense, briary, almost impenetrable vegetation. Beyond the briars, however, the ravine ground cover was light, as a mature forest enshrouded the ground in an eternal shadow. Nearly 120 feet up the ravine from the bow of No. 17, shipwreck fragments were discovered adjacent to a pair of massive steel shackles attached to lines of 1.5-inch-thick woven steel cables which disappeared a short distance later into the earth. Fifty feet farther up the ravine, and almost in its direct center, a V-shaped elevation of earth, surrounded on two sides by a three-foot depression, was found. Findings farther on, however, suggested the earthen feature was not natural, but probably man-made. At an elevation of approximately sixty feet, at the head of the ravine, the vestige of a road, which had been discerned on the infrared aerial photo of the bay area, was clearly definable by the absence of old-growth forest—and by extensive concentrations of steel cables, iron bars, wire rope, and large shackles that littered its path. Of even greater interest was the discovery of cables tied around at least three great trees. As at the site of the Sentinel Wreck, the growth of bark had all but covered the cables. The most extreme cable wrap in one tree was discovered to be thirty feet high. What was the relationship between the situation of site No. 17, the ravine, the earthen feature, the cables and shackles, the tree cable wraps, the road, and the great debris field more than one hundred yards from the wreck?

This Is One Evil Place

Again, John Mitchell and his trusty metal detector were called in to locate and, with Rick and Ken, systematically plot the distribution of metallic features lying above and beneath the soils in the ravine. They not only accomplished their mission with speed and éclat, they discovered similar features, including cabling and shackles in a ravine to the immediate south of site 101! Two days later, Ken, Ralph Eshelman, long-time colleague Nick Freda, and I began surveying site No. 23, another steamship wreck whose bow had been drawn onto the beach near the head of the bay. Although no log slipways were encountered, the bow of the vessel was lodged in a V-shaped elevation of earth at the base of another ravine. A spread of concrete rubble lay in the water to the starboard side of the bow. Large broken concrete forms, similar to those noted on the shoulders of the shaft tunnels of some wrecks, were found farther up the slope, as were sections of ¾-inch steel cable, and the possible vestige of yet a second V-shaped earthen mound. At the top of the ravine, cable fragments were again encountered, albeit in very small concentrations.

Without question, there was a pattern. A thorough reexamination of the aerials was in order. It was immediately discovered that Nos. 16 and 17 had not been moored in the slip areas until after 1952, but had been situated more than 150 feet from the shoreline. No. 23, however, had been in the same position since 1943 and probably earlier. Yet, several hypotheses presented themselves as the pattern became clearer. The slips were probably never intended to serve as railways, or even as permanent reception areas for the shipping. They had, in fact, been constructed from materials at hand to serve as temporary landings for smaller craft, perhaps to facilitate the post-WM&SC scrappers who were stripping the wrecks with only the luxury of small craft to aid them. The road, running along the crest of the bluff at the head of the ravines, provided egress for the removal of salvaged materials, some of which had been accidentally dropped or abandoned alongside its course. But what of the great shackles, the cables anchored in the trees, and the earthen mounds? As it turned out, I would find the answer, not at Mallows Bay, but while visiting the small logging and mining town of Campbell River, on Vancouver Island, over 3,500 miles from the Potomac.

I had traveled to Vancouver in May 1994 to present a paper on the progress of the Mallows Bay Project at the annual conference of the North American Society for Oceanic History and had decided to spend several weeks afterward exploring Vancouver Island. While at Campbell River, which overlooks the scenic, history-steeped waters of Queen Charlotte Sound, I had paid a visit to the new Campbell River Museum. In the yard behind the museum I discovered a grand old steam donkey engine, fully restored, which had been employed in the Pacific Coast logging industry at the beginning of the century. I learned that such engines had frequently been employed to haul logs up steep slopes and even mountainsides. Mounted on log runners set in earthen platforms often cut into the sides of sheer cliffs, the engines were firmly anchored in place by steel cables run to nearby trees. Moreover, utilizing a complex steel cabling system that was also anchored in trees or poles located at higher elevations and funneled through the engines' geared pulling system, logs of great weight and often a hundred feet or more in length could be hoisted up mountainsides with ease. The system, which was called "yarding," had been widely adopted by the logging industry of the Pacific Coast in both Canada and the United States at the turn of the century and had been heavily employed during World War I to move freshly cut Douglas firs from inaccessible areas for transshipment to mills.

Here, at last, seemed a reasonable solution to our mysterious features in the ravines at sites Nos. 16 and 23 and elsewhere. Tons of scrap could be readily offloaded from workboats temporarily moored in primitive slips. The scrap was then hauled from the slips by a moving steel cable system powered by and focused through a donkey engine mounted on an earthen platform midway up the slope. The engine and/or the cable-hauling complex had been anchored in the tree line above. When the scrap had reached the road at the top of the ravine, it was carried away in wagons or trucks. Instead of employing yarding technology to move timber, the salvors had adapted it to move tons of scrap iron.

❏ ❏ ❏

As one of the principal objectives of our research on the shipwrecks of Mallows Bay was to gauge the extent and influence of the environment upon the vessel remains and, conversely, of the wrecks upon the environment, I had selected two sites, No. 24 and No. 35 (*Accomac*), to serve as test laboratories, one of wood and one of steel. The onboard terrain of the two sites offered enclosed aqueous systems, wooded swamp and wetland environments, dry littorals, and, in the case of *Accomac*, a windswept plain (the upper deck). And in each case life had taken root—and control.

Many important studies of the ecology of the Potomac have been carried out. Our investigation was not intended to be comprehensive, since we were neither financially nor scientifically competent to undertake anything more than a limited survey. From a review of previous, more thorough evaluations of the river by such institutions as the famous Chesapeake Biological Laboratory, the Johns Hopkins University, and others, one thing was abundantly clear: from contributed wastes, treated and untreated sewage, exotic chemicals, wasted heat from power plants, silt, and occasional dredging, the Potomac River had been severely impacted, if not irreparably damaged. Shellfish beds in the lower river and fish spawning and nursery areas in the upper river had been threatened or ruined, and spawning grounds were being harmed by urban development. Chemical waste and heat were directly challenging the ability of the ecosystem to survive. Above Mallows Bay the discharges from nine sewage treatment plants poured literally hundreds of millions of gallons of treated and untreated matter into the river daily. Municipal discharge and agricultural, forest, and urban runoff daily delivered many more thousands of pounds of phosphates and organic and inorganic nitrogen into the river, which raised the nutrient load to dangerous levels for aquatic life. Although serious efforts at improving the situation had been under way for years, it was still obvious that the Potomac River was in terrible shape.[14]

The geological status of the Potomac at Mallows was not unlike that of other areas of the river. The average river depth is fifteen feet, and its maximum depth is forty feet, while that of the embayment itself averages approximately five feet. The Potomac estuary itself is gouged out from the sediments of the Coastal Plain. These sediments are, for the most part, blankets of clays, silts, sands, diatomaceous earth, and gravels, in alternating, unconsolidated deposits, overlying hard metamorphic and igneous rock. Some of these layers, formed over innumerable epochs, have been brought down from the slopes of the Piedmont Plateau in the west, while others are of marine origins. The more recent, surficial sediments have been brought in and deposited in the river from upstream and from local tributaries. Not surprisingly, the major surface sediments of Mallows Bay are composed of soft muds, which generally increase with depth. A projection extending from Liverpool Point northward for approximately one-half mile, however, consists of firm muds and clays of moderate to high compaction, locally mixed with sand and other deposits.[15] In many places along the shoreline, sheer, eroding bluffs are exposed to the unprotected assaults of wind and wave, and the annual rate of loss to erosion is estimated at forty-three tons per square mile.[16]

Mallows Bay sits in a unique position on the Potomac. In the months of April and May, during an average year, its waters are tidal fresh. In June its water salinity increases to between .05 and .10 part per thousand. Its average water temperature ranges from a minimum of 1.5° to 2.3° centigrade in January to a maximum of 26.7° to 27.7° centigrade in August.[17] Its northern and southern perimeters are generally considered as estuarine river marshes, normally characterized by such marsh plants as river bulrush, marsh (or rose) mallow, arrowweed, arrow arum, pickerelweed, yellow waterlilly, phragmites, and even wild rice. Yet, rooted aquatic plants, such as sago pondweed, southern naiad, and wild celery, important food sources to both aquatic animals and waterfowl and once considered common to the area, were, by 1970, limited almost entirely to a few narrow strips of the region.[18] Microscopic one-celled phytoplankton, such as

321

algae, whose distribution and density are governed by the complex interaction of such factors as light, temperature, nutrients, and the abundance of zooplanktonic invertebrates that thrive on them, have, in recent years, been prolific in the Mallows Bay region owing to the extraordinarily high levels of nutrients in the water. Sea nettles and winter jellyfish, though infrequently encountered, are not strangers to the area, although the waters are too fresh to support oysters and clams and support only a minimal population of blue crab.

Finfish, both anadromous and semi-anadromous, near the top of the Potomac estuary food chain, were historically among the most significant living features of the bay region. Once upon a time, depending upon the season of the year, freshwater, estuarine, and marine fishes of a wide and wonderful variety could be found here. Indeed, the list seemed endless: sturgeon, white, yellow and silver perch, silver minnow, spottail shiner, golden and satinfin shiner, brown and yellow bullhead, white and channel catfish, bluegill, pumpkinseed, threadfin shad, goldfish, longnose gar, mosquitofish, tessellated darter, black crappie, largemouth bass, quillback, redfin pickerel, Eastern mudminnow, bay anchovy, hogchoker, Atlantic menhadden, bluefish, red drum, black drum, spot, Atlantic croaker, summer flounder, aleback and blueback herring, striped bass, gizzard shad, American eel, Atlantic silverside, and moe.[19]

Birds and mammals had historically been present in great profusion. In 1775 a British traveler named Nicholas Cresswell, while passing through the region, observed that ducks and geese, of "incredible numbers," were so thick that sixty could be killed with a single shot. Cresswell, however, had preferred to dine on other local fare, roast swan. Pheasants, hawks, partridges, and eagles flourished. An eagle kept in the garden at a nearby manor was said to be as big, if not bigger, than a man and would kill any dog that attacked it. Father Joseph Mosley described plentiful supplies of wild turkeys, raccoons, deer, squirrels, and possums, "the fastest animal in winter on the face of the earth, and at that time fine eating." Diving ducks, such as canvasbacks and scaup, and dabbling ducks, such as mallards, black ducks, and wood ducks, could be found in the creeks and marshes around the bay, along with the Canada goose and that greatest of American birds of prey, the bald eagle. Wading birds, such as the great blue heron, egrets, and bitterns, walked about on stalky legs searching for prey in the shoals. Big and small game mammals such as whitetailed deer and rabbit, fur bearers such as gray and red fox, raccoon and mink, rodents such as mice, rats, voles, and lemmings, and aquatic furbearers such as muskrat, as well as snakes, turtles, frogs, snails, insects, and many other creatures great and small had once populated the shores and waters of Mallows Bay and the surrounding countryside.[20]

What were we to find aboard two relatively small, isolated platforms, after more than seven decades of man's misuse of the environment, in a once rich little basin that had been converted into a virtual dumping ground, overflowing with detritus of every sort, then burned, blown up, filled in, polluted, mangled, and finally—perhaps mercifully—forgotten.

Our method of finding out was simple: put a pair of qualified volunteers onboard to collect and inventory every species of plant they could reach, and leave them until they cried for mercy. The two volunteers, Dave Van Horn and my wife Carol, both with the Maryland National Capital Park and Planning Commission, were plopped aboard the wrecks and retrieved at quitting time. Their observations, other than the demeaning innuendoes aimed at the helpless insect population, were invaluable.

On No. 24, the wooden vessel, no fewer than five species of trees were flourishing aboard: sweet gum, red swamp maple, persimmon, green ash, and the most prolific of all, eastern red cedar. Density had been stringently controlled by the space available, and, more significantly, by a family of beavers that had built their lodge amidships. No tree, it was concluded after viewing their handiwork, was allowed to exceed twenty-five to thirty feet in height before it was cut down.

At least seven woody shrubs, twenty-two species of herbaceous perennials and annuals, and nine species of vines were documented. False indigo and groundsel bush were among the most dense populations aboard and were, in fact, the hardiest and most aggressive in colonizing even the smallest platforms offered by the sunken vessels of the bay. It was beginning to appear that the probable frequency of periodic (partial or total) inundation of the site's interior and the equally frequent periods of long-term exposure to dry or drought conditions had little impact upon the survivability of the many species that had colonized the wreck, or upon the hulk itself. Nor had the militant root growth seriously jeopardized the structural integrity of the hull, as had been observed on other ships. Perhaps, we reasoned, the constant competition for the limited space, aided by the untender attentions of such critters as our friends the beavers, which tended to moderate the growth of the deep-root trees and plants, was actually slowing the natural destruction of the ship.

On the other hand, the clean, steel hull of *Accomac*, a more recent arrival in the bay, hardly had time to get comfortable on the bottom before nature had tried to reclaim her surface. Yet, lacking the rich soils of No. 24 and obliged to rely upon aeolian and waterborne sediments, her hostile skin yielded to nature's colonizing efforts far more reluctantly. But yield she would. Red cedar had taken root, yet, not surprisingly, seemed to progress past the seedling stage only with difficulty. Woody scrubs fared better, but not nearly so well as eight species of perennials and annuals, which required less soil. Virginia creeper was the only vine noted. Protected by the hull from the seemingly omnipresent and dominant hydrilla which surrounded the ship, floating and subaquatic vegetation was more plentiful than anywhere else in the embayment. Indeed the duckweed,

Eurasian water milfoil, wild celery, and common waterweed, which had been choked out by the new arrival in the bay, seemed to have maintained control over the deepest recesses of *Accomac*.

Birds and mammals, too, some of which had never been here before, had asserted their presence in the bay. Five bald eagles, only recently an endangered species, were observed near Liverpool Point. Nutria, which had never been observed farther upriver than Port Tobacco Creek, were spotted cavorting in a hull opening on site No. 16. The lodges of beaver, built of bark, twigs, leaves, and limbs of trees, were strong evidence of the resurgence of this once nearly extinct creature. River otter, which had begun to emigrate to the rim of Mallows Bay from the lower river by the late 1960s, had by 1993 settled quite comfortably in among the shipwrecks and in the burning basin. Their presence was attested by frequent sightings and evidence of their diet of fish, turtles, frogs, and even ducks and small mammals, left in tidy piles in closed corners of various wrecks. And then there were the ever-present muskrats which built their homes of plant stems and marsh vegetation and dug their burrows into creek and stream beds, and into the muck-filled bottoms of wrecks.

Were the shipwrecks of Mallows Bay affecting the environment as much as the environment was seizing, recolonizing, and affecting the wrecks? It was, perhaps, still too soon to tell, yet it was most assuredly safe to say that nature, given her freedom, would in time reclaim her due.

TWENTY-SIX

Blowout Redux

The narrow channel leading from the Potomac into the burning basin is well marked by navigational aids erected by the Mallows Bay Boat Club, and in the summer by a distinctive borderline of hydrilla formed along its edges. The passage traverses a shoally flat which, we would soon discern, was filled with the bones of small craft that, having outlived their usefulness, were brought here to die. Access to the burning basin, a roughly rectangular area cut from the mouth of Marlow's Creek, still bears the visible evidence of the great World War II wrecking enterprise of Bethlehem Steel. The seaward entrance to the basin is protected by a concrete and corrigated steel wall which runs directly into an earthen berm, the whole of which is approximately 300 feet in length. The entrance is reinforced by concrete piers upon which the gates that could entirely close off the basin were once mounted. A pump house, which was necessary to drain water from the basin to permit the burning operations within, had been erected on the north entrance berm during the Bethlehem regime, yet a short survey of the now vine-covered area produced no visible evidence of the remaining structure. At the Marlow's Creek outlet, approximately 600 feet to the northeast of the river gate, the vestige of a second wall, 350 feet in length, from 3 to 10 feet in width, and composed of earth reinforced by wooden pilings and timber planking, separates the basin from the wetlands of the creek. The south shore of the basin is a narrow strip of land cleared to the water's edge and fronted with the rusted, decaying relics of World War II, a derelict barge, dredge, wharf, and miscellaneous debris. The opposite shore is covered by dense vegetation. And in the still waters of the basin itself can be found terrapin, river otter, and fish in great abundance—and more wrecks.

In the northeast corner of the basin lies the Mallows Bay Boat Club, a modest affair, with fewer than a dozen vessels tied up at a small wharf, most of which are of a rather "antique" vintage. The club is managed by a colorful, loquacious, feisty, utterly likeable chap, Captain Reed Scott, whose vita, I gleaned after many conversations and not a few friendly beers, reads as if it were honed from an adventure novel. He has a fondness for big cigars which are accentuated by an on-again-off-again stubble of white beard and mustache. At one time or another, he was a colonel in the paratroopers, was imprisoned by Castro in Cuba (where he met Che Guevere), visited the Belgian Congo, fought in Indochina, worked as a naval architect and engineer in Alaska, wrote a book on financial investment, captained a boat on the Pacific Coast, was befriended by Hollywood stars, married, divorced, waged ongoing wars with his neighbors, and now, had retired to the recesses of Mallows Bay to run the boat club. Truth or fiction I could never discern, but it didn't matter. He was our access to the bay and, more important, he was eager to share his wide personal knowledge about the environment which he loved.

There were a number of shipwrecks in the burning basin transect, almost all of which were of a more recent vintage, and most of which Reed was quite helpful in identifying. At the northern perimeter of the basin, a long wooden derelict lay heeled over on her starboard side, her guts gradually spilling out into the shoals. She was said by some to have been a PT boat converted to civilian usage, and by others to have been a search and rescue craft. Reed said that the vessel had come in, damaged and seeking shelter, during a storm in the early 1980s and had been abandoned there. The wreck of another, far smaller vessel, only 23 feet 10 inches in length, lay near the corrugated steel berm at the southern edge of the basin. In a muddy, reed-covered flat nearby, however, the disarticulated remains of a diminutive plank-on-frame vessel lay spread about beneath a great skim of black, nearly organic ooze. While attempting to traverse the purtid smelling mud to investigate the site, I sank to my waste and was retrieved by my colleagues with no small difficulty. The site still awaits investigation—and probably will for some time to come.

One of the more unique sites, located on the northwestern side of the basin, appeared to be little more than a long boat-shaped island. Its outline was suspicious and we immediately assumed that it might have been a hull so completely covered by vegetation and earth that it was no longer identifiable. Examination of its perimeter by boat and by walking upon its surface failed to yield the slightest hint that it was of human design. Probing with iron rods failed to confirm or deny anything. Donning my dive gear and entirely circumventing the feature underwater only added to the mystery. Near its northern extremity, I discovered a steel cable, like those encountered on the steamship wrecks, projecting from the sloping soils of its side. Was the island a vessel in the last stages of total decomposition? Or was there some other explanation?

Within a few feet of the northern end of the "island," I found more underwater wreckage. This time it was, without question, a ten-foot section of the bow of a wooden steamer. Nearby, possibly from the same vessel, another eight-foot section of a wreck, which appeared to be deck planking with both of its ends jagged and torn, sloped gently out into the basin. Here was the first actual evidence of the product of the Bethlehem shipbreaking operations in the burning area. With at least eleven hulks known to have been brought in for reduction, all of which had become lodged in the bottom when the water was pumped out, it was quite possible that whole hulls still lay deeply covered by the muds in the bottom of the little enclosure. Indeed, Reed had informed me that deep obstructions abounded, albeit none of which were impediments to navigation.

Again, the aerial photographs came to the rescue. Enlargements and computerized enhancements produced a dramatic portrait of the basin on June 3, 1943, during the early heyday of the Bethlehem regime, and nearly two years later on April 8, 1945, after its closure of operation. The 1943 photo clearly showed five large ships in the basin itself, which was still under construction, a pair of long barges immediately outside the entrance, and the structure of a large earthen berm running along the northeast and northwest edges of the basin. Marlow's Creek did not spill directly into the basin itself, as we first supposed, but circumvented the northwest berm and drained into the river. The so-called ship "island," was not a remnant of a ship, but the vestigial remnants of the berm. The northeast entrance gate to the basin was not a gate at all, but a break in the wall. The finding was exciting, especially since five ships were shown in the basin awaiting destruction. But where were they now?

In July 1995, I decided to find out by conducting a limited but systematic diver survey of the southwest side of the basin with the assistance of the Maritime Archaeological and Historical Society. Within hours of the start of the investigation, ship fragments were discovered near the extreme western corner of the basin by divers swimming in near-zero visibility along preestablished lanes, probing the bottom as they proceeded. Less than half an hour before the end of the day, two more wrecks were discovered: a small boat lying upside down and nearly covered by sediments and the deeply buried bow of a large ship. It was time to move on.

❑ ❑ ❑

Upon exiting the burning basin, and entering the Liverpool Point Transect, one is immediately faced with a marvelous panorama of the Potomac. The most dominant feature one first observes, however, is not the dramatic silhouette of *Accomac*, approximately six hundred yards seaward, but a small, collapsing structure that looks for all the world like a houseboat. Closer examination, however, revealed that the "boat" is actually a building mounted on pilings. The structure is situated less than twenty feet from shore. Reed had said that it last belonged to a local yacht club for use as a hunting and fishing cabin. The late Fred Tilp, with whom I had been visiting at his home in Alexandria on the sad day of his demise, had told me that the structure was actually a Potomac River "ark." Tilp, who had visited the bay many times during the 1930s while leading a unit of Sea Scouts, claimed that five arks had been maintained as local barracks by sturgeon fishermen until the 1920s. Yet, owing to increasing pollution and the commensurate decline in commercial fishing, most arks, which were purportedly common on the Potomac, were sold off to gamblers, bootleggers, and prostitutes.[1] Those in Mallows had been occupied by salvors.

The alleged Mallows Bay ark was a modest structure, standing in only several feet of water, and still bearing the remains of white paint on its sides, with blue trim and facings. A slatted skirt once surrounded its lower side, concealing the pilings beneath. Underneath the structure, mounds of clam and oyster shells could be seen in the soally waters. The building was but a single story tall, with doorways and louvered windows on all sides. The interior, divided into seven small rooms, revealed it had been used for many purposes. A living room, replete with a now collapsing brick fireplace and extensive shelving, was cluttered with debris dating from the 1950s to the present, as well as several 48-inch home-made iron-fluked anchors. There was a bedroom with a small wooden bed built into the wall, and another room filled with eel traps in their last stages of collapse. There was a bathroom, with shower stall and sink, and a miniscule kitchen. A walkway once surrounded the entire structure at deck level, and on the seaward side, the remnants of a porch could be seen, replete with the vestige of five mattress spring sets hanging from it into the water. And scattered about were enough snake skins and bird feathers that one might readily assume that the site had long since been relinquished to the animal world. Moreover, it was in such a wretched state of rot that it threatened to crash into the river with the next big storm.

Had it been one of the alleged Potomac arks as Tilp had claimed? Or were its origins less dramatic? That the site had been there from at least the late 1950s, as attested to by numerous artifacts, seemed likely however. That it had been used for domestic purposes was obvious. That it had served as a storage area for watermen was also obvious. Had it been employed as a brothel? Probably not. Yet, I had to chuckle to myself as I counted the five bedsprings hanging over the side, and then spotted nearby an empty collection of thin, matchbook-sized cardboard containers yellowing in the sun. They were old condom packages.

❏ ❏ ❏

Approximately 400 yards to the west, between the outlet of the burning basin and the tiny cove at the opening of Liverpool Creek, the shallows were lined with small craft wrecks, or parts of wrecks. The Army Engineers map of 1929 had indicated a schooner lying on the south shore beach of the cove, and a second, noted only as an "old wrecked schooner," submerged in 4½ feet of water approximately eight hundred feet to the north, and in the main approach to the burning basin. A 1944 Corps of Engineers map of the area indicated the presence of three additional wrecks, one of which was over two hundred feet in length, on the opposite shoreline of the cove. In addition, the map showed the locations of fishing

Blowout Redux

shacks, sheds, an "office" (presumably employed by the management of the Bethlehem operations), wharves, soundings, and recently created channels leading from the Potomac and the anchorage area into the burning basin. Many other significant features were also indicated, including an island built across the mouth of Liverpool Cove from spoil produced by the channel dredging operations. A second islet had formed along the north shore approach to the burning basin, covering several derelict barges in the process. The notion that the islands had been created from dredge spoil was at first little more than hypothesis, since one of them no longer exists and the other, which now only partially enshrouds a pair of barge wrecks, has been linked to the mainland by accretion. However, the testimony of an elderly local resident named Rudy Datcher, whose father had worked as a wrecker on the bay and who, as a young boy, had personally witnessed the channel dredging work and the building of the burning basin, confirmed the fact. The cove, he told me, had served as the main deposit areas for spoil from the dredging, and everything in it had been covered by several feet of mud.

The exploration of the little cove was initiated with as much excitement as that of the survey of the main fleet sites. There were at least five wrecks documented, two of which were schooners that predated 1929, and three more vessels (one of which was of substantial size) that had apparently been deposited between 1929 and 1944. There were the facilities ashore. And there was the possibility that beneath the spoils deposited in the cove, even more wreck sites from earlier times might still exist.

Our first limited foray into the Liverpool Creek Cove area was on July 10, 1993. By midday, the thermometer had topped 100 degrees. Surface water temperature was approaching 80 degrees. The hydrilla, which presented the appearance of a solid mat across Mallows Bay, was king. Our canoe could barely cut a path through it.

Yet, setting out from the burning basin at mean low water, we were instantly treated to our first find of the day, not fifty feet from the ark. Two small wrecks, both of them wooden boats, were encountered in close proximity. One lay dangerously close to the channel, with jagged metal fittings projecting just above the surface of the water. The second, which appeared to be only the remains of a deck, on which was bolted a remarkably well-preserved windlass for hauling fishing nets, lay partially on top of and adjacent to a large spread of cobblestones. The 1944 Army Engineers map indicated a wharf in this immediate area. Had the structure been a cob-style wharf, that is, one that is enclosed and filled with stone and soil? Such a structure would have required pilings and timber work, none of which were readily visible. And why was the wreck, probably of early-twentieth-century construction, sitting on top of it? After recording the positions and layouts of the sites, we moved on into Liverpool Cove.

329

Ghost Fleet of Mallows Bay

Minutes later, as we rounded a slight elbow of the shore, we found our first big target, the two-hundred-plus-foot vessel noted on the 1944 map. The ship, hauled up on the shore and reduced to but a few feet of hull, was of composite construction, the only one of its kind encountered in the bay. Her hull was planked with wood, but her traverse frames were of steel. As she had appeared only on the 1944 map, my first notion was that the wreck was that of *Nokomis*. Reduction was begun on the old subchaser by Bethlehem Steel in the summer of 1944 and was still under way by September when company wrecking operations were terminated on all but her hull. The map had been the product of an army engineers' survey of the cove area and approaches to the burning basin completed near the end of October. The prospect of having found our first and only warship in the bay was too delicious to contemplate.

Our next objective was to locate a schooner wreck noted on the 1929 map as on the beach on the south shore of the cove. The search was completed in minutes, for remnants of the vessel, covered by hydrilla but projecting from a soup of porous sediment within a few feet of the shore, were instantly discovered. Leaping into the muck to inspect, we discovered that the wreck was that of a five- or seven-log centerboard canoe.

Only three logs, two frames, and the centerboard well survived, and another log fragment lay a few feet shoreward of the wreck, yet the find was significant as a unit. Although Tilp had reported that schooner-rigged

Site 107, originally thought to be the remains of the USS *Nokomis*, proved to be the only composite U.S. Shipping Board merchantman discovered in Mallows Bay.

log canoes could still be seen as late as 1978 at the Headley Boatyard on Coan River, and at Deagle's Boatyard at Piney Point on the lower Potomac, the Liverpool Cove boat was the only log canoe remains, to my knowledge, that had been located on the upper river. Yet, the vessel type was one of the most common workboats employed in the tidewater from the seventeenth through the very early twentieth century. Its ancestry could be traced to the primitive single-log dugout canoe of prehistoric times, and its adoption from the Indians by the white man was wholeheartedly begun soon after the arrival of the first colonists. Sails were added and architectural modifications to convert the craft for hauling freight, such as tobacco, on the rivers and bay soon made the craft a staple of transportation and commerce. By 1686, colonial settlers had begun to abandon the single-log canoe for the two-log catamaran. The three-log canoe, squared off, joined by mortis and tenon fittings along a centerline, and hollowed out as a single unit by chopping with an adze, soon followed. By the mid-nineteenth century, extra carrying capacity, stability, and sailing capabilities were provided by the addition of wing logs and centerboards. Five- and seven-log canoes, sloop and schooner rigged, were soon commonly found plying the waters of the Tidewater, with a few survivors reportedly working the waters until the onset of World War II. The Chesapeake log canoe was a form of shell first construction, wherein frames were added only after the hull of the boat had been formed and fitted together with mortis and tenon joinery and, after the Civil War era, iron pins. Often the joinery of earlier canoes was reinforced by wooden butterfly fitting.

Within a hundred feet of the canoe, several futtocks of a larger frame-on-plank vessel, with a beam estimate of at least 20 feet, were discovered projecting from the muds. On the south shore outlet of the creek itself, the naked keelson of yet another vessel, over 100 feet in length, was discovered peeking out from beneath a sand bar. And lodged up in a marshy area nearby, the remnants of a vine-covered single log of a log canoe (possibly a component of our first log canoe find) was discovered. Then, as we prepared to depart, the centerboard of yet another wreck, designated site No. 114, was exposed immediately off the northshore outlet of the creek.

It was now certain that the shallow waters of the Liverpool Cove area, with at least five, and possibly six, wreck sites in evidence, was a mini-graveyard of vessels probably predating or at least with the great ships of the Mallows Bay transect. With the exception of the big composite hull believed to be *Nokomis*, the wrecks appeared to be relatively small craft, probably workboats that had outlived their usefulness, and had been brought in to end their days in the shade of the obscure little cove. Here was obviously an important and exciting component of the Mallows Bay story which was hardly anticipated. Had we encountered *Bessie Lafayette*, or perhaps one of old Monroe's sturgeon boats, abandoned here in 1926? Clearly, the sites demanded more attention than our "windshield" survey could provide. Yet, not until May of 1994 would we return to the sector to conduct an intensive mapping of the exposed wrecks and search for other possible sites. The work in Liverpool Cove would, in fact, continue in fits and starts for the next year.

❑ ❑ ❑

The 1994 field activities in the Liverpool Cove sector had been scheduled for May, to take advantage of the best possible weather window before the annual onset of the horrendous hydrilla. I had scheduled volunteers who were willing to brave the snakes, snappers, and slimy mud in return for the opportunity of trading their skills and expertise for free—and to document a piece of history that might otherwise go by the boards.

The cove survey began on May 11. It was, unlike the previous spring, chilly and wet. By early afternoon, a stiff, cold wind had begun to blow out of the north, inducing a state of constant shivers among all of the volunteer survey team. Nevertheless, we proceeded to erect a base station and datum point on the shoreline of the cove and then construct a formal grid over the site of the five-log canoe, designated site No. 96. The grid was manufactured of ½-inch PVC pipes and twine, attached to poles driven into the bottom around the site. Chuck Fithian, the state archaeologist for the Delaware State Museum, who had volunteered a few days of his time, and I began the survey of No. 96, square foot by square foot. The vessel was fifty-six feet in length, iron fitted, with the centerboard box snuggled directly through one of the logs. Although three small frames had been added, no evidence was discovered suggesting additional frames had been incorporated in the craft's architecture. Nor was there evidence of any mast steps, limberboards, or other such features encountered. Much of the surface area of all three logs had been worn down to the very heart of the wood by water erosion. Had it not been for the centerboard construction, the wreck might easily have gone undiscovered.

The sucking muds in which the site was interred obliged us to move about at a snail's pace, waist deep in the slop. Fithian, who had worn hip waders in lieu of a wet suit, was soon carrying around as much glop inside his accoutrements as outside—to equalize the pressure, he said with a laugh. But the temperatures continued to descend and the wind to blow. By sunset, their missions for the day accomplished, all of the volunteers except Chuck had departed—most with comments that there were likely to be more important things for them to do at home if the weather didn't improve. I had visions of working alone in the cove for the rest of the survey, and I was not far off the mark.

That night the wind, blowing from the north-northwest, increased to nearly gale force, and although slowing the next morning, would continue throughout the day. The effect, combined with an extremely low tide, was a blowout—a wonderful blowout, more revealing than had been experienced even at Kent Island. As I had expected, only one volunteer, the ever-reliable Ken Hollingshead, showed up. As we paddled from the burning basin, it was evident that the water was now nearly three feet lower than we had ever seen it in the river, and still going out!

With great anticipation we entered the cove. The composite wreck, site No. 107, was entirely high and dry. I had intended on completing the grid survey of No. 96 before turning our attentions elsewhere, but as we made directly for her, I couldn't help be both excited by what was being revealed and upset that there were not enough hands to address this rare opportunity. Not surprisingly, the log canoe was now entirely exposed above the water, with the grid still in position over her remains. But now, for the first time, the full extent of the second centerboard vessel, No. 114, could be seen in its entirety as well, her hull planking and frames covered only by a skim of mud along its centerline. Immediately off the stern of the vessel, the remains of a centerboard well from yet another wreck lay stuck in the mire. Behind that, a slight sandy extension of the northern lip of the creek was also bared, with a small rudder assemblage lying pancaked into it. And the waters continued to recede.

We went to work immediately and by noon had completed recording the log canoe. We then set about to document the second centerboard vessel, No. 114, a doubled-ended craft, 47 feet in length, at least 14 feet abeam, and with a flat-bottomed sharpie configuration. Two mast steps were discovered, set 2 feet and 34 feet aft the bow. The centerboard well, 12 feet 8 inches in length, was also intact, with the centerboard still present. The sharpie, a distinctive form of watercraft built during the last quarter of the nineteenth century, with lengths usually between 20 and 35 feet, but occasionally reaching 65 feet or more, was usually of a two-masted rig. Its

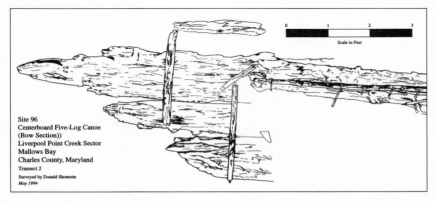

Partial plan of the bow of the Liverpool Cove five-log centerboard canoe.

rise in popularity, mostly among oyster tongers of Long Island Sound, began in the fisheries at New Haven, Connecticut, in the 1870s.[2]

The classic New Haven sharpie may have been introduced to Maryland waters in the early 1870s and was undoubtedly modified to fit Tidewater needs and tastes. Rigged with two leg-of-mutton sails, using sprits instead of booms, mounting a short bowsprit, and an outboard rudder on a skeg, the Potomac sharpie ranged in length from 18 to 28 feet (used mainly for oyster and crab scraping), with a few reaching 38 feet. Although the type never grew to enjoy the popularity of such prominent Tidewater vessels as the pungy, bugeye, or Chesapeake schooner, the larger vessels were occasionally employed in terrapin hunting and were referred to as terrapin smacks. All were shallow-draft vessels which, because of their flat-bottomed construction, were unable to withstand rough weather.[3] Our find was the first to actually document their presence on the Potomac and was perhaps one of the largest sharpies on record in the Chesapeake. But it wasn't to be the last discovery in the cove.

By late afternoon, the waters of Mallows Bay had dropped another foot, revealing sections of beach that were normally immersed. Within minutes, Ken had discovered yet another small wreck, this one totally buried in the

The Sharpie Wreck (site No. 114) in Liverpool Cove, exposed during the May 1994 blowout. Note the fragment of a centerboard well lying in the foreground from yet another wreck.

sand. Within a few minutes more, a second wreck, also buried beneath the beach, was discovered but a few feet away. The first vessel, designated site No. 113, appeared to be a small plank-on-frame boat, 25 feet 2 inches in length, 7 feet abeam, fitted with wood and brass fittings. Her painter peeked from the sand, but her starboard side was entirely buried beneath the shore. The second wreck, a centerboard vessel designated site No. 112, was 75 feet in length, with a 25-foot-long centerboard box squarely in her middle. From the maximum width of her frames, her beam was computed to be least 17 feet.

Both vessels were partially or entirely extant beneath the sands, but as we had no permit to excavate, and as the two wrecks were certainly not going anywhere, we contented ourselves with rushing through a quick gridded survey of the exposed surficial outlines of the remains. But as I hurriedly photographed the site while Ken took measurements, many things raced through my head. Could No. 113 perhaps be Captain Robert Conway's longboat, belonging to the Virginia galley *Protector*, which had been stove in during the fracas in July 1776? Why had the newly discovered vessels escaped inclusion on any of the army engineers' maps? Had they been lost so long that they were only now, by a freak of nature, exposed for the first time? Or were we just lucky? Indeed, how many more vessels lay beneath the sediments of the cove and in the bay that we didn't know about? As the afternoon sun lowered and we sat on a log wolfing down a much belated lunch, Ken answered the last question with another question. "What's that out in the middle of the cove?" he said with a mouthful of peanut-butter-and-jelly sandwich.

All I could see was a long black shape being lapped by waves, emerging ever so slowly as the waters continued to recede. Looking through my binoculars, I replied in exasperation. "Oh no, not another wreck!"

This time, it was an 89-foot 5-inch centerboard frame-on-plank vessel. It was, perhaps mercifully, to be the last wreck located in Liverpool Cove. But not the last to be surveyed.

❏ ❏ ❏

In the days and weeks to come we would make many more discoveries. In the summer of 1995, with the help of the Maritime Archaeological and Historical Society, the wreck of the giant composite hull in Liverpool Cove, once believed to have been the remains of USS *Nokomis*, would be surveyed and mapped. The ship would prove not to be the warship, as I had hoped, but a composite, flat-bottomed steel and wood steamship of World War I vintage of the McClelland type. A total of eight of the twenty-six McClelland composites were known to have been brought into Mallows Bay prior to October 1929, six of which were destined for final reduction. These vessels included: *Balino, Battonville, Borad, Botsford, Dalgada, Obak, Quemakoning,* and *Tuwetanka. Battonville* and *Borad* were re-

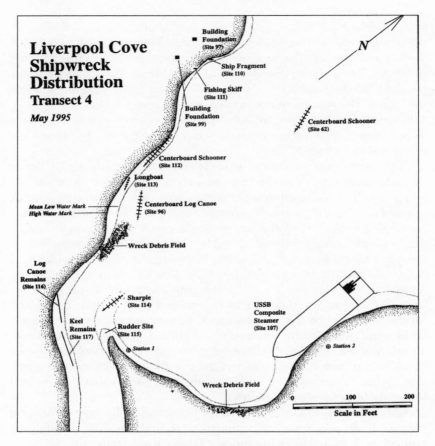

Shipwreck distribution map of Liverpool Cove.

portedly removed to Philadelphia. *Botford* and *Obak* were employed as barracks ships at Sandy Point, and their fortunes are unknown. *Dalgada* and *Tuwetanka* were reduced prior to April 27, 1929. *Quemakoning* was reduced in 1930, and *Balino*'s fate is unknown. Was the vessel either *Balino*, *Botsford*, or *Obak*, one of the three whose dispositions are undocumented? Or had one of the other hulks, perhaps partially reduced, been towed in and further assailed after 1929 and before 1944, as indicated by army engineers' maps? Whatever the answer might be, one thing was certain: the wreck was the only composite ship remains located in Mallows Bay— and possibly the last remnant of the more than two dozen experimental steamships built during the U.S. Shipping Board program.

The south shorelines of Liverpool Cove continued to yield new finds, indeed, almost everytime we went ashore. A large section of steamship hull here, a small rowboat there. The foundations of two wooden build-

Blowout Redux

Volunteers from the Maritime Archaeological and Historical Society erect a survey grid over the box of Site 107 in Liverpool Cove.

ings, one with a standing brick fireplace and chimney, were found where two fishing shacks had been indicated on the army engineers' map of 1944. Evidence of tarring operations, possibly for nets or small workboats, were found between the two buildings, as were artifacts from the 1930s through the modern day.

Yet, it was our last survey target that was to be the most visually dramatic—an intact shipwreck that lay at the southern terminus of the transect. Immediately below the piling stubs of the old Liverpool Point steamboat wharf, drawn up with her bow ashore and her stern in eight feet of water, lies the sad ruins of the North Carolina Atlantic menhaden fishing boat *Mermentau.*

Mementau presents the classic picture of a fatally stranded ship, with her distinctive, graceful hull tilted to one side on the beach and her white pilot house torn askew. On her rounded stern, the shadowy outline of her name can be traced in the darks and lights of the wood. Although her single mast still stands and her aft cabins are intact, she is a sad sight. Built in 1949 at Beaufort, North Carolina, for the Gulf Menhaden Company, she was 199 tons gross, 153 tons net, 121.7 feet in length, 20.6 feet abeam, and 9.8 feet deep in hold. She was an oil screw ship, with engines capable of producing 400 horsepower. Thanks to Fred Hopkins's research, we discovered that she had last been owned in 1981 by the New Smith Meal Company of Maine and was home ported at New York City. Local informants told us that about that time she had been anchored in or near the burning basin but had been removed to the wharf at Liverpool Point by a man who wanted to refit her and live aboard. A tropical storm which struck the area put an end to such notions. Now, she was occupied by beavers and river otters who had taken up residence in her hold, and by a family of osprey living in her crow's nest.

Upon boarding the ship and looking northward toward Mallows Bay, Sandy Point, and beyond, I was struck with all we have seen and discovered

The wreck of the North Carolina menhaden boat *Mermentau,*
ashore at Liverpool Point, before her removal by the Maryland
Derelict Removal Program in 1995.

within the space of less than a few miles and a few months. Here, in the wrecks and ruins of a century, perhaps two, lay an enormous concentration of the physical remains of a pivotal, defining moment in American history, a vast repository of American maritime design and technology sleeping serenely in the environment for which it was intended. We had explored, mapped, and studied the remains of probably the largest shipwreck assemblage in the nation, and possibly the world. We had seen and documented the physical evidence of mankind's genius, stupidity, intellect, avarice, drive, ignorance, and waste. We had plumbed the depths of a fourteen-year-old's fantasy, and we had barely scratched the surface. But the odyssey had just begun.

On February 24, 1996, the Fifth Annual Workshop in Archaeology, sponsored by the Maryland Historical Trust and the Archaeological Society of Maryland, convened at Crownsville, Maryland. In his welcoming remarks to the conferees, J. Rodney Little, director of the Trust, announced for the first time the state's intention to designate the Ghost Fleet of Mallows Bay a Maryland State Historic Shipwreck Preserve.

Appendix:

Disposition of U.S. Shipping Board Emergency Fleet Wooden Steamships Documented in the Potomac River, at Mallows Bay, Maryland, and Widewater, Virginia

The following list has been assembled from the Records of the Chief of Engineers, Record Group 77, 1923–42, Potomac River, housed in the National Archives Annex at Suitland, Maryland, and from the August 11, 1929, Army Engineers Survey Map of the Grounding Area at Mallows Bay, Maryland, housed at Headquarters, U.S. Army Corps of Engineers, Fifth District, Baltimore, Maryland. Of the 218 vessels intended by the Western Marine and Salvage Company for reduction in the Potomac, 152 have been documented as present in Mallows Bay as of August 11, 1929. Another 16 vessels have been documented as having been released from bond after being reduced by fire, but their final dispositions are unknown. Seven known vessels were sunk, burned, or otherwise reduced at Widewater, although army engineers' reports indicate that as many as 10 vessels remained there. Thus, a documented total of 174 vessels can be accounted for. Ships presented herein are first indicated by name, then army engineers' assigned number, then date of release from bond, and finally by vessel type. Variations of official spelling of names are also given.

VESSELS PRESENT IN MALLOWS BAY, AUGUST 11, 1929

Abbeville [15] 12/2/28 (Ferris)
Acrema [122]—(Ferris)
Aculdo (*Aculeo*) [39] 10/12/28 (Ferris)
Adway [36] 10/12/28 (Ferris)
Afalkey [91]—(Ferris)
Afrania [58] 7/13/26 (Ferris)
Ahala [3] 3/17/28 (Ferris)
Aiken [22] 7/28/28 (Ferris)
Alabat [73] 10/12/28 (Ferris)
Alanthus [63]—(Ferris)
Alapaha [114]—(Ferris)
Alcis [88] 4/27/29 (Ferris)
Alector [108]—(Ferris)

Allison [120]—(Ferris)
Alpaco [43] 10/12/28 (Ferris)
Alta [103]—(Ferris)
Amoron [128]—(Ferris)
Anoka [147]—(Peninsula)
Andra [78] 4/27/29 (Ferris)
Angelina [27] 3/17/28 (Ferris)
Anthera [131]—(Ferris)
Aowa [149]—(Ferris)
Arado [26] 3/17/28 (Ferris)
Ardenia (*Ardena*) [71] 12/21/28 (Ferris)
Arundel [86] 4/27/29 (Ferris)
Aspenhill [65] 10/12/28 (Ferris)

339

Appendix

Astoria [72] 12/21/28 (Hough)
Baladan [17] 4127129 (Hough)
Balino [129]—(McClelland)
Bancroft [70] 10/12/28 (Ferris)
Banica (Banicaa) [89] 4/27/29
 (Ferris)
Barabos [132]—(Ferris)
Barrington [97] 12/21/28 (Ferris)
Battahatchee [84] 4/27/29 (Ferris)
Battonville [124] To Philadelphia
 (McClelland)
Baxley [144]—(Ferris)
Bayou Teche [40] 10/12/28 (Ferris)
Bedminster [112]—(Ferris)
Belgrade [148]—(Ferris)
Bell Brook [45] 7/28/28 (Peninsula)
Benzonia [146]—(Ferris)
Berea [127]—(Ferris)
Blandon [145]—(Hough)
Blue Eagle [35] 10/12/28 (Ferris)
Bobring [29] 7/28/28 (Pacific Ameri-
 can Fisheries)
Bockonoff [76] 4/27/29 (Pacific
 American Fisheries)
Boilston [57] 7/28/28 (Hough)
Bologan [37] 10/12/28 (Ferris)
Bon Secour [7] 8/6/27 (Pacific Ameri-
 can Fisheries)
Bonifay [23] 10/12/28 (Ferris)
Boone [16] 12/21/28 (Ferris)
Borad [106] To Philadelphia
 (McClelland)
Botsford [not numbered]
 (McClelland)
Bottineau [116]—(Ferris)
Boxley [62] 12/21/28 (Ferris)
Boykin [118]—(Ferris)
Boynton [95]—(Ferris)
Buhisan [104]—(Ferris)
Bushong [54] 7/13/26 (Ballin)
Braeburn [48] 7/28/28 (Peninsula)
Brentwood [140]—(Peninsula)
Bromela [30] 7/28/28 (Grays
 Harbor)
Brompton [8] 3/17/28 (Grays
 Harbor)
Buckhorn [98]—(Ferris)
Bulana [136]—(Ferris)

Bushrod [56] 7/13/26 (Ballin)
Cabeza (Cabega) [113]—(Ferris)
Cabura [10] 8/6/27 (Ferris)
Calala [32]—(Ballin)
Capines [83] 12/21/28 (Ferris)
Canbou [152]—(Ferris)
Casmalia [34]—(Ferris)
Cheron [46] 7/28/28 (Ferris)
Clodia [11] 10/12/28 (Pacific Ameri-
 can Fisheries)
Coconino [21] 7/28/28 (Hough)
Coloma [20] 7/3/25 (Ferris)
Conewago [52] 10/12/28 (Ferris)
Congaree [125]—(Ferris)
Coulter [85] 10/12/28 (Ferris)
Cumberland [42] 10/12/28 (Ferris)
Dalgada [107] 4/27/29 (McClel-
 land)
Dancey [134]—(Ferris)
Darrah [9] 4/27/29 (Ferris)
Datis [44] 10/12/28 (Ferris)
Dertona [55] 7/13/26 (Ballin)
Dungeness [47] 10/28/28 (Ferris)
Esopus [141]—(Ferris)
Eyota [77] 4/27/29 (Ferris)
Falmouth [130]—(Ferris)
Fassett [121]—(Ferris)
Fernandina [94] 12/21/28 (Ferris)
Flavel [24] 7/28/28 (Hough)
Folsom [111]—(Ferris)
Forster [60] 3/17/28 (Ferris)
Fort Riley [69] 10/12/28 (Ferris)
Fort Sill [5] 3/17/28 (Ferris)
Fort Stevens [67] 10/12/28 (Ferris)
Grayling [1] 7/28/28 (Grays Harbor)
Guilford [137]—(Ferris)
Hokah [142]—(Ferris)
Hoosac [87] 4/27/29 (Ferris)
Horado [6] 8/6/27 (Daugherty)
Itanca [2] 7/28/28 (Ferris)
Kanakee [18] 10/12/28 (Ferris)
Kangi [115]—(Ferns)
Kasota [150]—(Hough)
Katonah [82] 10/12/28 (Ferris)
Keota [110]—(Ferris)
Kickapoo [13] 4/27/29 (Hough)
Kimta [79] 10/12/28 (Ferris)
Kokomo [4] 3/17/28 (Ferris)

Appendix

Laforge [51] 7/28/28 (Ferris)
Latoka [49] 3/17/28 (Ferris)
Lewiston [109]—(Ferris)
Lonoke [101]—(Ferris)
Mahnet [14] 12/21/28 (Ferris)
Marshfield [12] 4127129 (Hough)
Medford [93]—(Ferris)
Mono [99]—(Hough)
Moosabee [53] 3/17/28 (Unknown Type)
Moraine [38] 10/12/28 (Ferris)
Munra [80] 10/12/28 (Ferris)
Musketo [28] 7/28/28 (Hough)
Namecki [126]—(Ferris)
Neeolah [25] 7/28/28 (Ferris)
Nemassa [139]—(Ferris)
North Bend [50] 7/28/28 (Hough)
Nupolela [151]—(Ferris)
Obak [not numbered] (McClelland)
Oraton [135]—(Ferris)
Owatama [31] 12/21/28 (Ferris)
Panga [41] 10/12/28 (Ferris)
Pascagoula [133]—(Ferris)
Quapaw [61] 10/12/28 (Ferris)

Quemakoning [123]—(McClelland)
Quinault [81] 10/12/28 (Ferris)
Saris [19] 7/3/25 (Ferns)
Sewickley (*Swickly*) [102]—(Ferris)
Swampscott [100]—(Ferris)
Tanka [119]—(Ferris)
Toka [96] 12/21/28 (Ferris)
Tuwetanka [105] 4/27/29 (McClelland)
Umatilla [138]—(Ferris)
Utoka [92]—(Ferris)
Wakan (*Wakanna*) [75] 4/27/29 (Ferris)
Wayhut [68] 4/27/129 (Ferris)
Wayuoan (*Wayuean*) [64] 10/12/28 (Ferris)
Wenakee [74] 10/12/28 (Ferris)
Wihaha [66] 4/27/29 (Ferris)
Wonahbe (*Wontatabe*) [59] 7/3/25 (Ferris)
Woyaca [90] 4/27/29 (Ferris)
Yakima [117]—(Ferris)
Yawah [33]—(Ferris)

VESSELS PRESENT AND/OR DESTROYED ON POTOMAC RIVER AT OR NEAR MALLOWS BAY

Chibiabos
Cresap
Dera
Fonduco

Mahaska
Makanda
Nashotah
Waneyanda

VESSELS PRESENT AND/OR DESTROYED AT WIDEWATER, VIRGINIA

Aberdeen (Grays Harbor)
Blythedale
Catawba
Gray Eagle

Okiya
Quidnic
Wasco

Notes

The following is a list of short titles and abbreviations for the notes presented hereafter.

Admiralty	*Admiralty Records*, Public Record Office, London, England
Archives	Archives of Maryland
CMM	Calvert Marine Museum, Solomons, Maryland
C.O.	Colonial Office, Public Record Office, London, England
DGSC	Donald G. Shomette Collection, Dunkirk, Maryland
H.C.A.	High Court of the Admiralty, Public Record Office, London, England
LC	Library of Congress, Washington, D.C.
MGS	Maryland Geological Survey, Baltimore, Maryland
MHM	*Maryland Historical Magazine*
MHS	Maryland Historical Society, Baltimore, Maryland
MVUS	*Merchant Vessels of the United States*
NARS	National Archives and Record Service, Washington, D.C.
NDAR	*Naval Documents of the American Revolution*
PRO	Public Record Office, London, England

Chapter 1: As Her Service May Require

1. Stephen D. Lee, *The First Step in the War*, vol. 1 of *From Sumter to Shiloh: Battles and Leaders of the Civil War* (reprint, South Brunswick, New York, London: Thomas Yoseloff, 1956), 76.
2. Naval History Division, Navy Department, comp., *Civil War Naval Chronology 1861–1865* (Washington: Government Printing Office, 1971), part 1: 7–10.
3. Mary Alice Wills, *The Confederate Blockade of Washington, D.C., 1861–1862* (Parsons, W.Va.: privately printed, 1975), 10–11.
4. Ibid., 11; *War of the Rebellion: Official Records of the Union and Confederate Armies* (Washington, D.C.: Government Printing Office), series 1, vol. 2: 592–93; Richard Walsh and William Lloyd Fox, *Maryland: A History 1632–1974* (Baltimore: Maryland Historical Society, 1974), 351.
5. See George William Brown, *Baltimore and the 19th of April 1861: A Study of the War* (Baltimore: Johns Hopkins Press, 1887) for a complete account of the Baltimore riots.
6. Frank Moore, ed., *The Rebellion Record: A Diary of American Events* (New York: G. P. Putnam, 1861), 1: 33–34, 37, 42, 46, 48, 49; Ralph D. Gray, *The National Waterway: A History of the Chesapeake and Delaware Canal, 1769–1965* (Chicago: University of Illinois Press, 1967), 137–42.

Notes

7. Testimony of Captain Philip Reybold before the Agnus Commission, Senate Document No. 215, 59th Cong., 2nd sess.: *Report of the Commissioners Appointed by the President to Examine and Report upon a Route for the Construction of a Free and Open Waterway to Connect the Waters of the Chesapeake and Delaware Bays* (Washington, D.C.: Government Printing Office, 1907), 44–45.

8. Edward J. Ludwig III, *The Chesapeake and Delaware Canal: Gateway to Paradise* (Elkton, Md.: Cecil County Bicentennial Committee, 1979), 7, 9; Wills, 13.

9. Gray, 143–44.

10. *Civil War Naval Chronology 1861–1865,* part 1: 9, 11; Ludwig, 9.

11. Between 1862 and 1865 annual traffic on the C&D Canal would average 790,000 tons, and in 1864–65, income for canal owners would reach an all-time peak of $424,313, not surprising figures with so many vessels in federal service. By April 1865, a total of 144 propeller-driven steamboats, 89 steam tugs, and 842 freight barges had been seized or "chartered" by federal authorities for military use on the canals, rivers, and Atlantic coastal bays of the Union and in the war zone itself (Gray, 144–46).

12. Richard F. Veit, *The Old Canals of New Jersey: A Historical Geography* (Little Falls, N.J.: New Jersey Geographical Press, 1963), 19–23, 61–65.

13. Ibid., 70, 71; Crawford Clark Madeira, Jr., *The Delaware and Raritan Canal: A History* (East Orange, N.J.: Eastwood Press, 1941), 61.

14. *New Jersey,* Temporary Registration, Baltimore, 23 December 1862, NARS; Steamship *New Jersey,* Master Carpenter's Certification, 23 December 1862, Official Number 18336, Baltimore Customs House Records, RG 41, NARS. In January 1865, *New Jersey*'s dimensions were reported as 166 53/100 feet in length, 22 58/100 feet abeam, and 9 3/100 feet deep in hold (Admeasurement, no. 1321, Port of Baltimore, 6 January 1865, Baltimore Customs House Records, RG 41, NARS).

15. Robert Kipping, *Rudimentary Treatise on Masting, Mast Making, and Rigging of Ships* (London: Lockwood & Co., 1873), 105–6.

16. Ibid.

17. Ibid., 106–7; "Practical Results of the Screw as a Propeller," *U.S. Nautical Magazine and Naval Journal* (New York: Griffith, Bates & Co., May 1856), 4, no. 2: 141–42; Thomas D. Stetson, "On Elevator Screw Propellers," *Monthly Nautical Magazine and Quarterly Review* (New York: Griffith and Bates, April to September 1855), 2: 141–46; W. M. Walker, *Notes on Screw Propulsion: Its Rise and Progress* (New York and London: Van Nostrand Trubners & Co., 1861).

18. [*New Jersey*] No. 1321 Temporary [Registration], NARS; Record of Vessel [*New Jersey*] Official Number 18336, NARS.

19. Proof of ownership of a ship or vessel to be enrolled, No. 1051, NARS.

20. Charter Party of the Steamer *New Jersey,* December 20, 1863, NARS.

21. Ibid.

22. Captain A. D. Collins to Secretary of War Edwin M. Stanton, 16 May 1864, in *War of the Rebellion: Official Records of the Union and Confederate Armies* (Washington, D.C.: Government Printing Office), series 1, vol. 36, part 2: 830.

23. Edwin W. Beitzell, *Point Lookout Prison Camp for Confederates* (Abell, Md.: privately printed, 1972), 41, 58.

24. Commander Renshaw of the USS *Massasoit,* while patrolling off the Chesapeake in search of the CSS *Chickamauga* and *Olustee,* reported on 6 November that he "spoke [to] the U.S. transport steamer *New Jersey,* from New

York, bound to Hampton Roads" (Report of Commander Richard T. Renshaw, *Official Records of the Union and Confederate Navies in the War of the Rebellion* [Washington, D.C.: Government Printing Office, 1894–1922], series 1, vol. 3: 332–33).

25. The troops, belonging to the First Division, 25th Army Corps, were transferred to the steamer *Admiral Dupont* at Hampton Roads. Their horses were transferred to the steamer *Salvor* because *Dupont* had no accommodations for the animals. Off Beaufort, North Carolina, a violent storm forced the soldiers to jettison all their shot. The gale then caused a collision between *Admiral Dupont* and a brig, forcing the former to return to Norfolk for repairs. The unit's mission was to have been participation in an attack against Fort Fisher, North Carolina, but the effort had been delayed by weather (Lt. Colonel Clark E. Royce to Captain S. A. Carter, 1 January 1865, *War of the Rebellion: Official Records of the Union and Confederate Armies,* series 1, vol. 43, part 1: 987–88).

26. Charter Party of the steamer *New Jersey,* 10 June 1865, NARS.

Chapter 2: Burned to the Water's Edge

1. Alexander Crosby Brown, *Steam Packets on the Chesapeake: A History of the Old Bay Line Since 1840* (Cambridge, Md.: Cornell Maritime Press, 1961), 161.
2. Ibid., 71.
3. Ibid.
4. The *Sun,* 28 February 1870; *American & Commercial Daily Advertiser,* 28 February 1870. *New Jersey* is noted as having cleared on 26 February, 7 and 10 April 1869 under the command of Captain Eddens, and on 18 September and 12 October 1869 under the command of Captain Kirwan, with a cargo consigned to R. L. Poor of Norfolk. Her departures were noted in the *American & Commercial Daily Advertiser* a day or two after each clearance from Baltimore.
5. Robert H. Burgess and H. Graham Wood, *Steamboats Out of Baltimore* (Cambridge, Md.: Tidewater Publishers, 1968), 4, 47, 144, 194; Brown, 70; The *Sun,* 28 February 1870.
6. The *Sun,* 28 February 1870; *American & Commercial Daily Advertiser,* 28 February 1870.
7. Alexander Crosby Brown, 41, 58.
8. Edward M. Blunt, *The American Coast Pilot* (New York: Edward and George W. Blunt, June 1863), 252, 803.
9. Ibid., 350–51.
10. *American & Commercial Daily Advertiser,* 28 February 1870.
11. Ibid.
12. Ibid.; The *Sun,* 28 February 1870.
13. The *Sun,* 28 February 1870.
14. *American & Commercial Daily Advertiser,* 28 February 1870; The *Sun,* 28 February 1870.
15. *American & Commercial Daily Advertiser,* 28 February 1870.
16. See *Proceedings of the Nineteenth Annual Meeting of the Board of Supervising Inspectors of Steam Vessels Held at Washington, D.C., January 1871* (Washington, D.C.: Government Printing Office, 1871) for specific operations of the office of the Third District steamboat inspector.
17. Ibid., 46–47.
18. Alexander Crosby Brown, 74.

Notes

Chapter 3: Captain Henry's Mystery Wreck

1. Robert H. Burgess, *This Was Chesapeake Bay* (Cambridge, Md.: Cornell Maritime Press, 1963), 200; Larry G. Ward, Peter S. Rosen, William J. Neal, Orrin H. Pilkey, Jr., Orrin H. Pilkey, Sr., Gary Anderson, and Stephen J. Howie, *Living with the Chesapeake Bay and Virginia's Ocean Shores* (Durham, N.C.: Duke University Press, 1989), 1. By the middle of the nineteenth century Sharps Island contained 458 acres, upon which several prosperous farms and the remnants of a forest were situated. Although erosion of the island was ongoing, a resort hotel was later erected, and its patrons were brought in by steamboat from Baltimore. Water was supplied by an artesian well. By 1910 barely 53 acres of the island remained, and the resort was abandoned. In 1944 the U.S. government took over all that was left, approximately 6 acres of mostly marshland, for use as a rifle range. Within a few decades all visible traces of the island's presence had disappeared. On several occasions, while diving in the area, the author has encountered the remains of farm equipment lying on the bottom of Sharps Island Flats, barely several hundred yards south of the lighthouse.
2. The first Sharps Island Lighthouse was built in 1838 when the island was over 700 acres in extent. In 1881 the structure was torn from its moorings by ice. The following year it was replaced by the brick structure that currently stands on the site. For an excellent mini-treatise on the lighthouse, see Robert DeGast, *The Lighthouses of the Chesapeake* (Baltimore: Johns Hopkins University Press, 1973).
3. *MVUS* (1965), 96, 840, 1264; ibid. (1968), 1164; Bill Miller, "Wrecks of the Chesapeake," *Bay Country Living*, August 1976, 14.
4. *MVUS* (1941), 512, reports that *Bright* was built in 1918 and was lost by stranding. Adrian L. Lonsdale and H. R. Kaplan, *A Guide to Sunken Ships in American Waters* (Arlington, Va.: Compass Publications, 1964), 44, state that there was fifty feet over the wreck.
5. *MVUS* (1928), 406–7; ibid. (1929), 912.
6. Ibid. (1952), 213, 884; ibid. (1953–54), 748.
7. Ibid. (1916), 55; ibid. (1918), 437; Henry G. Granofsky Customs Collection, MS 2231, Box 6, Wreck Report Log, 142, MHS; Miller, 46.
8. Donald G. Shomette, *Shipwrecks on the Chesapeake: Maritime Disasters on Chesapeake Bay and Its Tributaries, 1608–1978* (Centreville, Md.: Tidewater Publishers, 1982), 184.
9. For a review of steam engine development for steamboats, see David C. Holly, *Steamboat on the Chesapeake: Emma Giles and the Tolchester Line* (Centreville, Md.: Tidewater Publishers, 1987), 218–242.
10. On October 7, 1975, Dr. Paul Gardner, without viewing the dated Hobbs sample, stated that the three whiteware samples provided for examination were all simple molasses pitchers manufactured between 1858 and 1890, possibly by the J. F. McKee Glass Works of Birmingham and Pittsburgh, Pennsylvania. (The factory was also referred to as the Jeannette Glass Works of Birmingham after having moved from Jeannette, Pennsylvania. The firm held the patent on pewter lids.) Ceramics and glass expert Orva Heissenbuttle of the Wheeling, West Virginia, Historical Society (where the records of the Hobbs Company are housed) later determined in December 1975 that the

glass was actually a cheap milk glass product commonly sent to Baltimore for marketing throughout the Chesapeake. Paul Gardner, personal communication; Orva Heissenbuttle, personal communication; Charles J. Milton, comp., *A Short History of Early Wheeling Glass* (Oglebay Park, Wheeling, W.Va.: Wheeling Glass Mansion Museum).

11. Field Notes, 26 October 1976, DGSC.
12. Ibid., 4, 13, 26 October 1975.
13. Ibid., 26 October 1975.

Chapter 4: A Cargo of Pottery Vessels

1. Jerome E. Petsche, *The Steamboat* Bertrand: *History, Excavation and Architecture* (Washington, D.C.: National Park Service, Department of the Interior, 1974), 1–11.
2. Ibid., 3.
3. Automated Wreck and Obstruction System File Data, Site 02778 (photocopy), DGSC.
4. Ibid.
5. The site appears as a wreck on NOAA charts 12263, 12266, and 12267.
6. Tyler Bastian to Donald Shomette, 12 January 1983, DGSC.
7. *The Survey. The Newsletter of the Underwater Archaeological Society of Maryland* 1, no. 1 (April 1984): 1.
8. Joseph McNamara, personal communication.
9. Although the possibility of relic hunters salvaging the ship's propeller, a major underwater effort by any measure, may seem farfetched, the capabilities of determined amateur salvagers cannot be disregarded. The giant propeller of the tanker *Marine Electric* was illegally removed by one well-known Maryland relic hunter within days of its sinking in February 1983. See the *Washington Post*, 13, 14, 15, 17, 18, 19, 21, 23, 24, 25 February; 8, 13, 15, 27 March; 18 and 19 May; and 31 July 1983 for a running account of loss of the ship and the alleged piracy perpetrated over her remains.
10. Minutes of Proceedings, Advisory Committee on Archaeology, Maryland Geological Survey, 22 August 1985, MGS.
11. *The Survey. The Newsletter of the Underwater Archaeological Society of Maryland* 1, no. 5 (October 1985): 4–5. Bastian personally invited, by letter, a number of divers known to be visiting the site. He made it clear that "the vessel is considered to be historically significant" yet noted that the state's concern was not with the relics' being recovered but with their not being properly treated afterward. He expressed a strong concern that dredging would result in destructive teredo damage to the site once fragile components were exposed. "It is not our intention to close *New Jersey* to sport divers, but we feel it is in the best interest of the vessel and the diving public that such activities do not diminish the vessel as a cultural resource" (Tyler Bastian to Professor Ed. Hoffman, 13 August 1985, MGS).
12. *The Survey. The Newsletter of the Underwater Archaeological Society of Maryland* 1, no. 5 (October 1985): 4–5.
13. Ibid.
14. When it was learned that damage to *New Jersey* was still being inflicted, Bastian requested the state's Department of Natural Resources Police to patrol the

site to observe for illicit dredging and other violations of the Water Resources Act (Tyler Bastian to Major Harvey C. Cook, 4 October 1985, MGS).

15. *The Survey. The Newsletter of the Underwater Archaeological Society of Maryland* 1, no. 5 (October 1985): 4–5.

16. Donald G. Shomette to Richard Hughes, 7 October 1985, DGSC; "The *New Jersey* Project: Proposed Scope of Operations," November 1985 (Draft), DGSC.

17. Richard Hughes to Donald G. Shomette, 6 November 1985, DGSC.

Chapter 5: The Glass Pit

1. *Herbert D. Maxwell* was 772 tons gross, 640 tons net, and 185.9 feet in length. Two lives were lost when she sank after a collision with a steamboat. The date of her loss has been incorrectly given in the official record as 1910 rather than 1911 (*MVUS* [1915], 35; ibid. [1916], 418).

2. Edward R. Miller to Donald G. Shomette, 2 October 1985, DGSC.

3. Donald G. Shomette, "The Shipwreck *New Jersey* : A Summary of the History, Archaeology, and Destabilization of an Underwater Archaeological Resource in Chesapeake Bay, Maryland," report prepared for the Maryland Geological Survey, 1986, 40.

4. Ocean Survey Vessel *Peter W. Anderson,* Fact Sheet (Washington, D.C.: U.S. Environmental Protection Agency), 1. The *Anderson* was under the command of Captain D. E. Paine during the survey (U.S. Environmental Protection Agency Vessel [OSV] *Peter W. Anderson* Shipboard Guide).

5. Shomette, "The Shipwreck *New Jersey,*" 43–44.

6. Ibid.

7. Ibid., 45–53.

8. Ibid.

9. Ibid.

10. Donald G. Shomette, Memorandum to Participants in the *New Jersey* Shipwreck Survey Regarding Scheduling, 11 November 1985, DGSC; Shomette, "The Shipwreck *New Jersey,*" 53.

11. The Shipwreck *New Jersey,* 54–55.

12. Ibid., 55.

13. Ibid., 55–56.

14. Ibid., 56.

15. Ibid., 58.

16. Ibid.

17. Ibid., 58–59.

18. Ibid., 59.

19. Ibid.

20. Ibid., 59–60.

21. Ibid., 60.

Chapter 6: Flying Eyeballs

1. Estimate for Reburial of *New Jersey* [Project], "Save the Whales," 12 May 1986, DGSC.

2. See Daniel J. Lenihan, Toni Carrell, Thomas Holden, C. Patrick Labadie, Larry Murphy, Ken Vrana, and Jerry Livingston, *Submerged Cultural Resources Survey Study, Isle Royale National Park,* Southwest Cultural Resources Center

Professional Papers no. 8 (Santa Fe, N.Mex.: National Park Service, 1989) for a comprehensive history and archaeological analysis of the Isle Royale shipwreck population.

3. N. King Hubner, *The Geological Story of the Isle Royale National Park,* Geological Survey Bulletin 1309 (Washington, D.C.: Government Printing Office, 1975).
4. Lenihan et al., 187.
5. Ibid., 187–89.
6. Ibid., 191–98, 206–7.
7. Donald G. Shomette, Journal of the Isle Royale Expedition, 28 August–12 September 1986, DGSC.
8. R/V *Discovery* operated by the Maryland Department of Natural Resources, Maryland Geological Survey, fact sheet.
9. Cruise Plan NOS R/V *Laidly,* U.S. Department of Commerce, National Oceanic and Atmospheric Administration, 23 January 1987 (photocopy), DGSC; NOAA Circular 85–52 (Washington, D.C.: National Oceanic and Atmospheric Administration, Department of Commerce, 30 November 1983).
10. Martin H. Wilcox, "The Sonic High-Accuracy Ranging and Positioning System (SHARPS) Net for Underwater Archaeological Survey in Chesapeake Bay" (Paper presented at the Eighth Naval History Symposium, Annapolis, Maryland, October 1987), 1.
11. Ibid.
12. Ibid., 1–2.
13. Ibid., 2.
14. Ibid., 3–4.
15. Ibid., 4–5.

Chapter 7: A Hurricane on the Bottom

1. The project was originally scheduled to begin 9 February but, owing to logistical considerations, was moved forward by one day. The events for this chapter are largely drawn from the daily operations log of the *New Jersey* Project, 8–26 February 1987, and the *New Jersey* Project dive team operations, both of which were maintained by the author and are in DGSC. See also Cruise Plan NOS R/V *Laidly,* 23 January 1987, DGSC; and Larry Murphy, Memo to Associate Regional Director, PCR, SWR from Larry Murphy (subject: trip report on operations in Chesapeake Bay), National Park Services, Department of the Interior H24 PSWR-PCS (photocopy), DGSC. The R/V *Laidly* was 55 feet in length, 14 feet abeam, and 4.5 feet in depth and had a cruising range of 375 miles at 16 knots. She displaced 25 tons and was powered by twin Detroit diesel 8V71-N engines. Among her equipage was a 1,500-pound pull hydrographic winch, a hydrographic crane with a 1,500-pound capacity over-the-stern reach, programmable Loran C, radar, and 12-kilowatt service generator (NOAA R/V *Laidly* 1264 [specification folder]).
2. Michael Pohuski, diary kept during the *New Jersey* Project (photocopy), 8 February 1987, DGSC.
3. Ibid.
4. Peter Carl Fabergé (1846–1920) was the goldsmith and jeweler to the Imperial Court of Russia. His exquisite gold and jeweled eggs, designed and produced for the last czars, are considered to be among the greatest art treasures of Western civilization. For a review of his life and works see Henry Charles

Bainbridge, *Peter Carl Fabergé, Goldsmith and Jeweller to the Imperial Court* (London: Spring Books, 1966).

5. Department of Natural Resources, Maryland Geological Survey, Advisory Committee on Archaeology, Report of the Thirty-fourth Meeting, 22 August 1985, 2.

6. In 1987 Stone chaired the Legislative Affairs Committee of the Society for Historical Archaeology; the committee members were J. Barto Arnold III, of the Texas Antiquities Committee; Marley R. Brown III, of the Virginia Landmarks Commission; Pamela Cressey, of Alexandria Archaeology; Helen Hooper, the SHA's Washington coordinator; and the author (Garry Stone, Memorandum to Members, Legislative Affairs Committee [Society for Historical Archaeology] [Subject: Tasks for 1987]),4 March 1987.

7. Four samples of wood were recovered from the wreck for speciation analysis. On 5 May 1987 the samples were sent to the USDA Center for Wood Analysis, Forest Products Laboratory, in Madison, Wisconsin. On 20 May the USDA reported that all four samples were oak (*Quercus*) of the white oak group (Tyler Bastian to USDA Center for Wood Anatomy Research, 5 May 1987 [photocopy], DGSC).

Chapter 8: Fabergé Eggs

1. Operations log of the *New Jersey* Project, 27 February 1987, DGSC.

2. J. Rodney Little, personal communication; Richard Hughes, personal communication.

3. Richard Hughes to Donald G. Shomette, 9 March 1987, DGSC.

4. In early February 1988 a bill seeking to transfer the operations and jurisdictional authority of the Division of Archaeology of the Maryland Geological Survey to the Maryland Historical Trust, sponsored by Delegate Athey of the Housing and Community Development Committee, was read in the Maryland House of Delegates. The bill was assigned to the Ways and Means Committee and was soon after passed by the House and Senate and signed by Governor Schaefer with minor revision (Maryland Legislature, House of Delegates, *A Bill Entitled an Act Concerning Maryland Historical Trust—Archaeological Property, 8 February 1988,* No. 1304).

5. J. Rodney Little, memorandum to Governor Schaefer through Mark Wasserman, 3 March 1987 (photocopy), DGSC.

6. J. Rodney Little, memorandum to Governor Schaefer through Mark Wasserman and Paul Schurick, 17 March 1987 (photocopy), DGSC.

7. "Underwater Archaeological Resources in Maryland," summary information packet prepared by the Maryland Historical Trust, 1987 (photocopy), DGSC.

8. Governor William Donald Schaefer to Donald G. Shomette, 29 April 1987 (photocopy), DGSC.

9. J. Rodney Little, memorandum to Governor Schaefer through Mark Wasserman, 5 March 1987 (photocopy), DGSC; J. Rodney Little and Richard Hughes, memorandum to members of the Governor's Advisory Committee on Maritime Archaeology, 24 June 1987, DGSC.

10. Bruce F. Thompson, "Maryland's Maritime Archaeology Program: The Formative Years," *INA Quarterly* 19, no. 1 (Spring 1992): 4–9.

11. Garry Wheeler Stone to the Honorable Bill Bradley, 24 February 1987 (photocopy), DGSC.

Notes

12. *Society for Historical Archaeology Newsletter* 21, no. 2 (June 1988): 1–2.

Chapter 9: A Commission to Goe

1. *Bathymetric Map, Chesapeake Bay, Annapolis, Plate 4* (Miami: U.S. Department of Commerce, Environmental Science Services Administration, 1970).
2. Nathaniel C. Hale, *The Virginia Venturer: A Historical Biography of William Claiborne, 1600–1677* (Richmond, Va.: Dietz Press, 1953), 1–7.
3. Edward D. Neill, *The Founders of Maryland as Portrayed in Manuscripts, Provincial Records and Early Documents* (Albany, N.Y.: J. Munsell, 1876), 38; John and J. A. Venn, comps., *Alumni Cantabrigienses,* part 1, vol. 1 (Cambridge: The University Press, 1922), 350.
4. John Herbert Claiborne, *William Claiborne of Virginia: With Some Account of His Pedigree* (New York and London: G. P. Putnam's Sons, Knickerbocker Press, 1917), 4.
5. Hale credits the influence of Claiborne's persuasive mother for securing his position as surveyor (Hale, 26, 55–56). See Neill, *Founders of Maryland,* and Claiborne for comparison.
6. Susan Myra Kingsbury, ed., *The Records of the Virginia Company of London,* 4 vols. (Washington, D.C.: Government Printing Office, 1,906–33), 1: 494; ibid., 3: 477, 486.
7. Ibid., 3:477; Captain John Smith incorrectly notes that "Master Cloyburne" sailed with Wyatt as "the Surgian" (John Smith, *The Generall Historie of Virginia, New England, and the Summer Isles* [London: Printed by I. D. and I. H. for Michael Sparkes, 1624], 140).
8. Kingsbury, 1: 455; ibid., 3: 465, 466, 467; Hale, 57–58.
9. Hale, 68–69, 74–76. See Ivor Noël Hume, *Martin's Hundred* (New York: Alfred A. Knopf, 1982), for the history and archaeology of the 1622 massacre.
10. Hale, 85–86.
11. Henry R. McIlwaine, ed., *Minutes of the Council and General Court of Colonial Virginia 1622–1632, 1670–1676, With Notes and Excerpts from the Original and General Court Records, Ante 1683, Now Lost* (Richmond, Va.: 1924), 3 April 1627, 147.
12. Hale, 85–86, 87, 89; Virginia Land Patent Book 1, part 1: 17, reprinted in Marion Nugent Nell, *Cavaliers and Pioneers, Abstracts of Virginia Land Patents 1623–1800* (Richmond, Va.: Press of the Dietz Printing Company, 1934), 17. The three servants were William Harris, transported in *George,* and William Morris and John Phipps, transported in *Tyger* (ibid., 41).
13. Thomas J. Wertenbaker, *Virginia under the Stuarts 1607–1688* (New York: Russell & Russell, 1959), 61–62.
14. Wertenbaker notes that it was the desire of King Charles I to gain the planters' acceptance through their representatives by an offer to buy all of their tobacco and thus instructed the officials in Virginia to hold elections for Burgesses, surveyor, and a general assembly (Wertenbaker, 63).
15. Kingsbury, 4: 501.
16. For verification of Claiborne's serious attention to his state duties, see McIlwaine, 26, 27, 28, 79, 103.
17. W. Noel Sainsbury, ed., *Calendar of State Papers, Colonial Series, America and West Indies, 1574–1660,* 4 vols. (London: 1889–91), 1: 77.
18. Ibid.

Notes

19. *Archives* 5: 158.
20. McIlwaine (3 April 1627), 147.
21. *Archives* 5: 158–59; C.O. 1/39, f.113, PRO. The permit was granted on 27 April 1627, specifically to discover the "Bottome of the Bay of Chiesepeick" and to conduct trade with the natives.
22. McIlwaine (4 April 1627), 148.
23. Clayton C. Hall, ed., *Narratives of Early Maryland, 1633–1634* (New York: Barnes & Noble, 1910), 88–90. See Emily Roe Denny, "Indians of Kent Island," in *The Isle of Kent: The 350th Anniversary. A Commemorative History* (1981), 10–18, for an account of the history and overthrow of the natives of Kent Island.
24. Hale, 118.
25. On 22 July 1629, Claiborne was appointed by Governor Potts as "Commander" of all forces in Virginia to destroy and pursue the Indians and was awarded the power to govern, punish, and correct all offending persons (C.O. 1/39, f.115, PRO). See also *Archives* 5: 159–60.
26. *Archives* 5: 158.
27. C.O. 1/39, f.114, PRO. See also *Archives* 5: 159–60.
28. Hale, 125–26. Edward Palmer was a graduate of Magdalen College, Oxford, and was described by acquaintances as a "curious and diligent antiquary" deeply interested in education. As a member of the Virginia Company he had received a grant of land at the head of the Chesapeake which included the tiny strategic island at the mouth of the Susquehanna. In his will, Palmer, a man of "plenteous estate," expressed that if his male issue and that of his brother's only son failed, all of this land should "remain for the Founding and maintenance of a universitie." His plans for establishing a college in America were promulgated "at many thousand pounds expense." Although his scheme never materialized, Palmer may justifiably be honored as the first true patron of higher education in America (Raphael Semmes, *Captains and Mariners of Early Maryland* [Baltimore: Johns Hopkins Press, 1937], 310).
29. Smith, 24.

Chapter 10: Unplanted by Any Man

1. See William Hand Browne, *George Calvert and Ceceilius Calvert* (New York: Dodd, Mead, and Company, 1890); Gillian T. Cell, *English Enterprise in Newfoundland, 1577–1660* (Toronto: University of Toronto Press, 1969); and William T. Russell, *Maryland, the Land of Sanctuary* (Baltimore: J. H. Furst Company, 1907), for comments on the Avalon colonization effort.
2. *Archives* 3: 16–17; Russell R. Menard, "Economy and Society in Early Maryland" (Ph.D. dissertation, University of Iowa, 1975), 63.
3. W. Noel Sainsbury, ed., *Calendar of State Papers, Colonial Series, America and West Indies, 1574–1660,* 4 vols. (London: 1889–91), 1: 104; Nathaniel C. Hale, *The Virginia Venturer: A Historical Biography of William Claiborne, 1600–1677* (Richmond, Va.: Dietz Press, 1953), 133–34.
4. Hale, 136.
5. Ibid., 139.
6. *MHM* 71, no. 4 (Winter 1976): 554, 559; *Virginia Magazine of History and Biography* 27, no. 2: 100.
7. Colonial Office Documents, Maryland and Virginia, Transcripts, bundle 98, no. 278, f. 2–3, LC.

Notes

8. Colonial Office Documents, Maryland and Virginia, Transcripts, bundle 98, no. 278, f. 4–6, LC.
9. The surgeon who set Pickne's leg was paid 4.3.0 pounds sterling or 250 pounds of tobacco on 20 November 1631. Bernard C. Steiner, in *Beginnings of Maryland 1631–1639* (Baltimore: Johns Hopkins Press, August-September-October 1903), 45, reports that the surgeon's fee was "doubtless the first medical charge in Maryland."
10. *Massachusetts Historical Society Collections* (Boston: Massachusetts Historical Society, 1886), 5th series, vol. 8: 31.
11. Hale, 144.
12. *Archives* 5: 161–62.
13. C.O. 1/39. ff. 116, PRO; *MHM* 28, no. 1: 30. See also *MHM*, vols. 26, 27, and 28 for H.C.A. Libels, Miscellaneous Books, and Examinations regarding the logistics of founding the Kent Island settlement, its manpower, hardships, and financial cost.
14. *MHM* 28, no. 1: 32; *Archives* 5: 162, 197.
15. Beverly Fleet, comp., *Virginia Colonial Abstracts* (Richmond, Va.: 1937), 18: 35 (mimeographed).
16. *MHM* 28, no. 1: 34; Steiner, *Beginnings of Maryland,* 46.
17. Steiner, *Beginnings of Maryland,* 46; *Archives* 5: 204–5.
18. *MHM* 28, no. 1: 34; Hale, 153.
19. Hale, 155–56.
20. Steiner, *Beginnings of Maryland,* 47.
21. *Archives* 5: 199.
22. Hale, 154.
23. Ibid., 134.
24. William Waller Hening, ed., *The Statutes-at-Large, Being a Collection of All the Laws of Virginia,* 13 vols. (Richmond, Va.: 1819–23), 1: 153.
25. Ibid., 168.
26. *Archives* 5: 163, 198; C.O. 1/39, ff. 118, PRO; Hale, 163. The Reverend James was to receive an annual salary of sixty pounds sterling. Since Claiborne's own salary was one hundred pounds per annum, the Commander of Kent was a very generous patron indeed (Lawrence C. Wroth, "The First Sixty Years of the Church of England in Maryland, 1632–1692," *MHM* 11, no. 1 [March 1916]: 4). Ethan Allen, historiographer for the Bishop of Baltimore ca. 1861, in his history of Christ Church Parish, reports that before Claiborne had become his patron, Jones had served as librarian to the famed English antiquarian Sir Robert Cotton, "and either before or after that, he had been minister on Avalon, Lord Baltimore's Colony in New Foundland, before his Lordship avowed himself a Romanist" *(Christ Church Parish on Kent Island, Queen Anne's County, Maryland,* undated typewritten transcription of *History of Christ Church Parish on Kent Island,* Gertrude Truitt Guthrie Collection, Queen Anne's County, Maryland, 9).
27. Hale, 163.
28. Raphael Semmes, *Captains and Mariners of Early Maryland* (Baltimore: Johns Hopkins Press, 1937), 138.
29. *Archives* 5: 194.
30. Semmes, 138.
31. Ibid., 193, 199, 206, 223; Hale, 164–65.
32. Hale, 165–66.

Notes

33. Ibid., 166.
34. *Mayflower* of London was owned by Samuel Vassall, merchant of London. Along with Vassal's pinnace *George*, *Mayflower* had originally been charged to carry a party of colonists led by Edward Kingswell to America to erect a plantation in "Florida," on the banks of the "River of St Hellena" on the "Coast of Carolana," (St. Helena Sound, South Carolina). The voyage proved difficult, and many passengers died. Mutiny was threatened by John Ripley but was fortunately put down before it erupted. Despite the problems, *Mayflower* reached Virginia safely. With his wife pregnant, Kingswell resolved to winter in that colony and await the spring to press on with the colonizing plan. The delay proved fatal to the effort: Kingswell's resolve softened and then disappeared. In the spring of 1634 he returned to England and a spate of lawsuits by the sponsor of the colonizing effort, Samuel Vassal (Colonial Office Documents, Maryland and Virginia, Transcripts, bundle 92, no. 34, ff.1–12, LC).
35. Hale, 166.
36. Fausz notes that Claiborne's personal servant was a black slave who mastered the Iroquois dialect and frequently visited among the natives (J. Frederick Fausz, "Merging and Emerging Worlds: Anglo-Indian Interest Groups and the Development of the Seventeenth-Century Chesapeake," in *Colonial Chesapeake Society*, ed. Lois Green Carr, Philip D. Morgan, and Jean B. Russo [Chapel Hill: University of North Carolina Press, 1988], 63).
37. For discussions on the role and impact of women on the colonization of Maryland, see Gloria L. Main, *Tobacco Colony: Life in Early Maryland, 1650–1720* (Princeton, N.J.: Princeton University Press, 1982).
38. Hale, 167.
39. In the Chesapeake of the seventeenth and early eighteenth centuries, and-irons were considered not only an important utilitarian household implement, but also a luxury usually owned by middling to upper-level members of plantation society. See Main, 176, 220, 222, 234, 237, for discussion and context of household items in the colonial class structure of the Chesapeake Tidewater.

Chapter 11: The Kent Island War

1. Regina Combs Hammett, *History of St. Mary's County, Maryland* (Ridge, Md.: privately printed, 1977), 3.
2. Raphael Semmes, *Captains and Mariners of Early Maryland* (Baltimore: Johns Hopkins Press, 1937), xi.
3. Clayton C. Hall, ed., *Narratives of Early Maryland, 1633–1634* (New York: Barnes & Noble, 1910), 67–68. The Maryland Charter was closely modeled after that of Baltimore's Avalon. For the full text of the charter, see Hall, 101–12.
4. Ibid., 102.
5. Ibid., 102–3.
6. Ibid.
7. *Archives* 3: 24–25.
8. Ibid., 22.
9. Nathaniel C. Hale, *The Virginia Venturer: A Historical Biography of William Claiborne, 1600–1677* (Richmond, Va: Dietz Press, 1953), 171–72.
10. Hall, 18–20.
11. See Hall, 29–45, for Father Andrew White's description of the voyage.
12. Ibid., 19, 39, 165.

Notes

13. Ibid., 19.
14. Ibid., 20.
15. Hale, 176–77.
16. Hall, 101.
17. *Archives* 5: 164.
18. Present at the pivotal council meeting were Sir John Harvey, William Claiborne, John West, Samuel Mathews, William Farrar, John Utie, Thomas Purfry, Hugh Bullock, and William Perry (ibid.).
19. Hale, 177.
20. *Archives* 5: 165.
21. See J. Frederick Fausz, "Merging and Emerging Worlds: Anglo-Indian Interest Groups and the Development of the Seventeenth-Century Chesapeake," in *Colonial Chesapeake Society,* ed. Lois Green Carr, Philip D. Morgan, and Jean B. Russo (Chapel Hill: University of North Carolina Press, 1988), 67–68, for a synthesis of events leading to the Patuxent crisis.
22. Hall, 55–56.
23. A formal request for action was apparently issued by Calvert directly to Harvey, or so it was reported secondhand by Thomas Yong (who heard it from Thomas Cornwaleys) to Sir Toby Matthew: "That Heerupon the Governour of Maryland complayned thereof to Sr John Harvie, the Governr of Virginia, who forthwth tooke the matter into consideration" (ibid., 56).
24. Claiborne was taken into custody by his friends and fellow councilmen, Samuel Mathews and John Utie (ibid.).
25. Ibid., 56–57. The joint commission was made up of Samuel Mathews, John Utie, William Pierce, and Thomas Hinton, of Virginia, and George Calvert and Frederick Winter, of Maryland, although Thomas Cornwaleys and Jerome Hawley had been selected to officially represent Baltimore. Cornwaleys later informed Thomas Yong that the investigation was to have been conducted at St. Mary's but the Virginians had "inveigled into their company two very young gentlemen [Calvert and Winter]" to represent Maryland and persuaded them to accompany the party to the Indian village of Patuxent. Utilizing his own interpreter, Claiborne and his fellow Virginians promulgated their own very favorable and one-sided investigation and then documented the proceedings in writing for the benefit of the governors of Maryland and Virginia and the authorities in England.
26. Ibid., 57; *Archives* 5: 164–67.
27. Bernard C. Steiner, in *Beginnings of Maryland 1631–1639* (Baltimore: Johns Hopkins Press, August-September-October 1903), 401.
28. This early contention for Palmers Island was not surprising given its strategic position. One of the earliest descriptions of the place (1648) speaks of an island "containing three hundred acres, half meade, halfe wood. On it is a rock forty foot high, like a Tower, fit to be built on for a trading house for all the Indians of the Chisapeack Gulf. The island lieth a mile from each shore in the Susquehannock's river mouth, and there four Sakers [cannon] will command that river. . . . " (Beauchamp Plantagenet, *A Description of the Province of New Albion, 1648,* reprinted in Semmes, 311).
29. Claiborne's shortage of truck for trade, as well as supplies and gunpowder for the Kent Island settlers, is repeatedly cited in *Archives* 5: 189–229.

30. See Semmes, 73–74, for discussion on the construction and fielding of *Long Tayle*. See *MHM* 28 (1933): 26–43, 172–95, for accounting of supplies and artificers employed in shipbuilding.
31. Hall, 88–89, reports three persons were killed.
32. Hale, 189.
33. See *MHM* 28 (1933): 26–43, 172–95, for data on shipment of pelts.
34. *Archives* 5: 235.
35. Steiner, *Beginnings of Maryland*, 402, reports that *James* brought thirty men and a cargo valued at 1,138 pounds sterling, and *Revenge* brought seven men and a cargo valued at 311 pounds. He notes, however, that Claiborne claimed that only twenty-two men arrived. Steiner apparently fails to account for the death of ten men at sea or three who died after arriving. Claiborne, whose bookkeeping has often been questioned, compiled his records after the fact and undoubtedly lumped those who died after arrival with those who were lost in transit, which still leaves a disparity of two men.
36. Hale, 187.
37. *Archives* 3: 29.
38. C.O. 1/8, f. 94 PRO.
39. *Archives* 3: 28–34.
40. Hale, 192–93.
41. Hall, 154.
42. Maryland Historical Society, *The Calvert Papers, Number One*, Fund-Publication no. 28 (Baltimore: Maryland Historical Society, 1889), 141.
43. Ibid., 141–49.
44. Hale, 200.
45. *Archives* 4: 22, 23; ibid. 5: 169–70; Hall, 148–49; Claiborne, 139–41; Hale, 201. According to Mary Foorde, in one contemporary version of the engagement, Cornwaleys was the aggressor. The Kent Islanders were "standing upon their Guards" when Cornwaleys "from his owne lipps commanded the men in his owne boate to shoote at them" and as a result "slew one honest Gentleman, one Mr. Warren, and hurt others" (*Archives* 3: 169). Governor Harvey thought that Claiborne's men "had sought out the Maryland boats, which were trading among the Indians and twice assaulted them, and that there were some hurt and slayne on both sides" (ibid. 39).
46. *Archives* 4: 22, 23; ibid. 5: 169–70; ibid. 3: 32.
47. Ibid. 3: 34, 37; Steiner, *Beginnings of Maryland*, 59.
48. See J. Mills Thornton III, "The Thrusting Out of Governor Harvey: A Seventeenth-Century Rebellion," *Virginia Magazine of History and Biography* 86 (1968): 11–26, for a comprehensive overview of the expulsion and return of Governor Harvey.
49. C.O. 1/8, ff. 166–169, PRO; Mills, passim; Steiner, *Beginnings of Maryland*, 59–60.
50. *Archives* 4: 22, 23; Semmes, 145; Hale, 204.
51. Hale, 204.
52. Steiner, *Beginnings of Maryland*, 62–63; Hale, 203; C.O. 1/8, ff. 174, 175, PRO.
53. The Virginians chose Captain John West as their new governor. Believing that it had been Harvey's encouragement that had prompted Calvert's vigorous and hostile actions, they dispatched Captains Utie and Pierce to Maryland with letters requesting that the Marylanders desist from all violent proceedings. In return, they promised "all fair correspondency on behalf of the

inhabitants of the isle of Kent, until we understood his Majesty's further pleasure" (*Archives* 3: 31–37).

Chapter 12: We Clearly Claime Right

1. Colonial Office Documents, Maryland and Virginia, Transcripts, bundle 98, no. 278, item 16, LC.
2. Nathaniel C. Hale, *The Virginia Venturer: A Historical Biography of William Claiborne, 1600–1677* (Richmond, Va.: Dietz Press, 1953), 166–67.
3. Colonial Office Documents, Maryland and Virginia, Transcripts, bundle 98, no. 278, item 17, LC.
4. *Archives* 5: 181–82, 215.
5. Ibid., 215, 230.
6. Hale, 214.
7. Ibid., 213–14.
8. *Archives* 5: 231.
9. *Archives* 5: 172–73, 231–32, 234; Hale, 215.
10. *Archives* 5: 182, 201.
11. For a comprehensive overview of the betrayal by Evelin, see Sebastian F. Streeter, *The First Commander of Kent Island,* Maryland Historical Society Fund-Publication no. 2 (Baltimore: Maryland Historical Society, September 1868).
12. *Archives* 5: 182–83, 188, 190–91, 195–96, 202–3, 208–9, 212, 215–19, 230–31.
13. Maryland Historical Society, *The Calvert Papers, Number One,* Fund-Publication no. 28 (Baltimore: Maryland Historical Society, 1889), 182–83.
14. *Archives* 5: 185, 190, 203, 208, 217–18; ibid. 4: 2, 3, 13, 29; Clayton C. Hall, ed., *Narratives of Early Maryland, 1633–1634* (New York: Barnes & Noble, 1910), 150.
15. *The Calvert Papers,* 183; Hall, 150–51.
16. Hall, 150–51.
17. *The Calvert Papers,* 184; Hall, 151–52.
18. *The Calvert Papers,* 184–85; Hall, 152–53.
19. *The Calvert Papers,* 185–86; *Archives* 5: 170–72; Hale, 223–26.
20. *Archives* 5: 172; C.O. 1/39, ff. 126, 127; Hale, 227; Hall, 151–56.
21. In 1638 a Swedish settlement was established on the site of modern Wilmington, Delaware. A fort was erected and named in honor of Queen Christina. The settlement was reduced in 1655 by the Dutch. See C. A. Weslager and A. R. Dunlap, *Dutch Explorers, Traders, and Settlers in the Delaware Valley, 1609–1664* (Philadelphia: University of Pennsylvania Press, 1961), chapter 6, for a history of the settlement.
22. *The Calvert Papers,* 186–87.
23. Hale, 225.
24. *Archives* 3: 76; ibid. 5: 72.
25. Ibid. 3: 63–68.
26. Ibid., 32, 71–73, 158; ibid. 5: 178–80.
27. Hale, 231. See H.C.A. 13/113, ff. 124–125, PRO, for Claiborne's response to Lord Baltimore's charges.
28. Bernard C. Steiner, in *Beginnings of Maryland 1631–1639* (Baltimore: Johns Hopkins Press, August-September-October 1903), 90; *Archives* 3: 79, 80, 92–93.
29. Steiner, *Beginnings of Maryland,* 90; *Archives* 3: 79, 80, 92, 93.

Notes

30. See *Maryland Historical Magazine*, vols. 27 and 28, for the Claiborne-Cloberry lawsuits, which are in part transcribed from H.C.A. 13/114; H.C.A. 13/55, f. 288, 289, 527–29, 529, 569–70, PRO.

31. Ibid.

32. *Archives* 3: 92, 93.

33. Edward D. Neill, *Virginia Carolorum* (Albany, N.Y.: J. Munsell's Sons, 1886), 91.

34. J. Frederick Fausz, "Merging and Emerging Worlds: Anglo-Indian Interest Groups and the Development of the Seventeenth-Century Chesapeake," in *Colonial Chesapeake Society*, ed. Lois Green Carr, Philip D. Morgan, and Jean B. Russo (Chapel Hill: University of North Carolina Press, 1988), 75–78. See Raphael Semmes, *Captains and Mariners of Early Maryland* (Baltimore: Johns Hopkins Press, 1937), for a thorough account of the Indian wars of the 1640s.

35. Claiborne's commission was issued by the king from his headquarters at York: "Rex, sexto die Aprilis, concedit Willielmo Claiborne Armigero, Officium Thesaurarii Regis infra Dominium de Virginia durante vita" (Ebenezer Hazard, *Historical Collections*, 2 vols. [Philadelphia: T. Dobson, 1792–94], 1: 493).

36. Fausz, 78.

37. Hale, 246–52.

38. Ibid., 255–56.

39. John H. Latané, "Early Relations Between Maryland and Virginia," in *Johns Hopkins University Studies in Historical and Political Science* (Baltimore: Johns Hopkins Press, 1895), 13: 30.

40. Ibid. On 4 September 1634 Lord Baltimore instructed Leonard Calvert to imprison Claiborne and take possession of his plantation on the Isle of Kent if Claiborne continued his "unlawful" behavior and did not submit himself to Baltimore's patent (C.O. 1/39, f. 123, PRO).

41. *Archives* 3: 161.

42. *MHM* 5 (1910): 373. Braithwaithe had been appointed on 22 April 1638 after Evelin was no longer of viable use (Streeter, 93).

43. *Archives* 3: 161.

44. See Edward Ingle, *Captain Richard Ingle, The Maryland "Pirate and Rebel," 1642–1653*, Maryland Historical Society Fund-Publication no. 19 (Baltimore: J. Mapler & Co., 1884), and Donald G. Shomette, *Pirates on the Chesapeake* (Centreville, Md.: Tidewater Publishers, 1985), 20–34, for complete accounts of Richard Ingle.

45. *Archives* 3: 165; ibid. 4: 281, 435, 458, 459; J. G. Morris, *The Lords Baltimore*, Maryland Fund-Publication no. 8 (Baltimore: Maryland Historical Society, 1874), 38–41; Shomette, *Pirates on the Chesapeake*, 28–34.

46. *Archives* 4: 281, 435, 458, 459; Morris, 38–41.

47. Hale, 264.

48. *Archives* 4: 458, 459; Hale, 265; Semmes, 165.

49. John Leeds Bozman, *The History of Maryland: Its First Settlement in 1633 to the Restoration in 1660* (Baltimore: James Lucas and E. K. Deaver, 1837), 1: 114.

50. Ibid., vol. 2: 246; Frederic Emory, *Queen Anne's County, Maryland: Its Early History and Development* (Queenstown, Md.: published for the Queen Anne's County Historical Society by Queen Anne Press, 1981), 100–1.

51. *Archives* 5: 180.

52. Hale, 268, 273.

53. *Archives* 3: 265, 271–72; Russell R. Menard, "Economy and Society in Early Maryland" (Ph.D. dissertation: University of Iowa, 1975), 235; J. Esteen Cooke, Clayborne the Rebel, *Magazine of American History* 10 (July-December 1883): 97.
54. Report of the Commissioners, *Virginia Magazine of History and Biography* 11: 34; Hale, 279–82.
55. John Herbert Claiborne suggests that William Claiborne's loss of his island dominions was not forgotten by Virginia. "From time to time," he points out, "Claiborne was compensated for his loss in the matter of Kent and Palmer's islands, by grants from the Virginia government aggregating something more than twenty thousand acres" (John Herbert Claiborne, *William Claiborne of Virginia: With Some Account of His Pedigree* [New York and London: G. P. Putnam's Sons, Knickerbocker Press, 1917], 126).
56. Virginia Land Patent Book 3: 34, reprinted in Marion Nugent Nell, *Cavaliers and Pioneers, Abstracts of Virginia Land Patents 1623–1800* (Richmond, Va.: Press of the Dietz Printing Company, 1934); Cooke, 89.
57. *Archives* 5: 158.

Chapter 13: Blowout

1. Clayton C. Hall, ed., *Narratives of Early Maryland, 1633–1634* (New York: Barnes & Noble, 1910), 151.
2. *Archives* 3: 161.
3. John Leeds Bozman, *The History of Maryland: Its First Settlement in 1633 to the Restoration in 1660* (Baltimore: James Lucas and E. K. Deaver, 1837), 2: 166; George Lynn-Laculan Davis, *The Day-Star of American Freedom* (New York: Charles Scribner's Sons, 1855), 45.
4. William Eddis, *Letters from America,* ed. Aubrey C. Land (Cambridge: Belknap Press and Harvard University Press, 1967), 23.
5. Bernard C. Steiner, "Traces of Claiborne's Settlement, Kent Island," *Johns Hopkins University Circulars* (Baltimore: Johns Hopkins Press, 1903), 23: 41–43.
6. Ibid.
7. Henry J. Berkley, "Reconstruction of the Isle of Kent after the Calvert Paper 880" (1937), map and paper in Enoch Pratt Library, Baltimore, Maryland.
8. Eric Isaac, "The First Century of the Settlement of Kent Island," (Ph.D. dissertation, Johns Hopkins University, Baltimore, 1957), 153.
9. See Bernard C. Steiner, "Kent Fort Manor," *MHM* 6, no. 3 (September 1911): 254–55, for hypothesis on the location of the Kent Fort Manor house.
10. Edward C. Papenfuse and Joseph M. Coale III, *The Hammond-Harwood House Atlas of Historical Maps of Maryland, 1608–1908* (Baltimore and London: Johns Hopkins University Press, 1982), 11, 12, 19, 22.
11. The most complete collection of geographic and hydrographic map data for Maryland, from 1670 to the present, is housed in the vaults of the Geography and Map Division of the Library of Congress. Additional data were provided by the U.S. Army Corps of Engineers, 5th District Office, Baltimore, Maryland.
12. Larry G. Ward, Peter S. Rosen, William J. Neal, Orrin H. Pilkey, Jr., Orrin H. Pilkey, Sr., Gary Anderson, and Stephen J. Howie, *Living with the Chesapeake Bay and Virginia's Ocean Shores* (Durham, N.C.: Duke University Press, 1989), 1.

Notes

13. D. F. Belknap and J. C. Kraft, "Holocene Sea Level Changes and Coastal Stratigraphic Units of the Northwest Flank of the Baltimore Canyon Trough Geosyncline," *Journal of Sedimentary Petrology* 47 (1953): 610–29; J. D. Ryan, *The Sediments of Chesapeake Bay,* Bulletin no. 12 (Baltimore: Maryland Department of Geology, Mines and Water Resources, 1953), 4; S. R. Holdahl and N. M. Morrison, "Regional Investigation of Vertical Crustal Movements in the U.S., Using Precise Relevelings and Mareograph Data," *Tectonphysics* 23 (1974): 373–90.

14. The Johns Hopkins University Water Management Seminar; N. L. Fromer, "Sea Level Changes in the Chesapeake Bay during Historic Time," *Marine Geology* 36 (1980): 289–305; Turbit Slaughter, *Historic Shorelines and Erosion Rates,* 4 vols. (Baltimore: Maryland Department of Natural Resources, Maryland Geological Survey, 1975).

15. J. F. Hunter, "Erosion and Sedimentation in the Chesapeake Bay around the Mouth of the Choptank River," *Shorter Contributions to General Geology,* U.S. Geological Survey Professional Paper no. 90 (1915): 7–15.

16. Donald G. Shomette, "Londontown: The Reconnaissance of a 17th–18th Century Tidewater Riverport Complex," in *Beneath the Waters of Time: The Proceedings of the Ninth Conference on Underwater Archaeology,* Texas Antiquities Publication no. 6, ed. J. Barto Arnold (1978), 167–74; Donald G. Shomette, "A Submerged Cultural Resources Survey at Londontown, Maryland," report prepared for the Londontown Publik House Commission (Londontown, Md., 1976). The barrel well discovered at Londontown is not noted in the preceding publications, having been uncovered during a "blowout" in 1979. It was photographed by the author before it was reburied by a second storm.

17. Donald G. Shomette, "The Point Lookout Survey: The Examination of Marine Transgressions against an Historic Civil War Prison Complex," in *In Search of Our Maritime Past: Proceedings of the Fifteenth Conference on Underwater Archaeology, Williamsburg, Virginia, January 5–8, 1984,* ed. Jonathan W. Bream, Rita Folse-Elliott, Claude V. Jackson III, and Gordon P. Watts, Jr. (Greenville, N.C.: East Carolina University, Program in Maritime History and Underwater Research, 1985), 129–39; Donald G. Shomette, "Underwater Archaeological Reconnaissance and Resource Assessment of the Public Beach Nearshore at Point Lookout State Park, Point Lookout, Maryland," report prepared for the Maryland Forest and Park Service, Department of Natural Resources (Annapolis, Md., 1983); Field Notes, Point Lookout Survey, August 1984, DGSC; *Current Maryland Archaeology,* no. 22 (October 1984), 2–3.

18. Donald G. Shomette, and Ralph E. Eshelman, *The Patuxent River Submerged Cultural Resources Survey.* 2 vols. The Maryland Historical Trust Manuscript Series no. 13. Annapolis, Md.: Maryland Historical Trust, 1981, 2:270–73.

19. Chesapeake Bay Critical Area Commission, *Chesapeake Bay Critical Area Program, Queen Anne's County, Maryland* (1988).

Chapter 14: Well, Well, Well

1. *Webster's New Collegiate Dictionary* (Springfield, Mass.: G. & C. Merriam Co., 1959), 971.
2. The nearness of the wells to each other and the historic archaeological precedents established at Jamestown and elsewhere suggesting that most early seventeenth-century barrel well sites were erected close to domestic dwellings

359

Notes

(usually less than 30 feet away) indicated that a habitation once lay close to the wells. This factor was not overlooked by Pohuski and McNamara but was unappreciated by the archaeological community to which the findings were presented. See John L. Cotter, *Archaeological Excavation at Jamestown Colonial National Historical Park and Jamestown Historic Site, Virginia. Archaeological Research Series Number Four* (Washington, D.C.: National Park Service, Department of the Interior, 1958), 152–53, and Nicholas M. Luccketti and Beverly A. Straub, "Excavation of the Church Neck Wells Site, Northampton County, Virginia," report prepared for the James River Institute for Archaeology (Jamestown, Va.: 1987), for findings similar to the Scove Site components.

3. Ivor Noël Hume, *Historical Archaeology* (New York: Alfred A. Knopf, 1974), 146.
4. Ibid., 144–45.
5. Samples of excavated first-century A.D. Roman box wells and hollowed-out tree trunks that served the same purpose were noted by the author during a research visit to the Colchester Castle Museum in England in June 1990.
6. Cotter, 152–53; Luccketti and Straub. Cotter, 152–53, reported that no fewer than twenty-four barrel wells had been excavated at Jamestown, all of early seventeenth-century construction.
7. Ervan G. Garrison, comp., *A Final Report on Archaeological Test Excavation of Two Nineteenth Century Well Sites at Lucy Revetment, Louisiana* (College Station, Tex.: prepared for Department of the Army, U.S. Army Corps of Engineers, by Cultural Resources Laboratory, Texas A&M University, June 1981).
8. Ivor Noël Hume, *The Wells of Williamsburg: Colonial Time Capsules* (Williamsburg, Va.: Colonial Williamsburg, 1969), 12–13.
9. Ibid., 13.
10. Jackie Ringgold to Michael Pohuski, personal communication, notes transcribed in the Claiborne Project File, DGSC; Steve Ruth to Michael Pohuski, personal communication, notes transcribed in the Claiborne Project File, DGSC.
11. Steve Ruth to Michael Pohuski, personal communication, notes transcribed in the Claiborne Project File, DGSC.
12. 18QU201, Archaeological Site Survey of Maryland, Maryland Geological Survey, Johns Hopkins University, Baltimore.
13. Jack Willard to Michael Pohuski, personal communication, notes transcribed in the Claiborne Project File, DGSC; Jackie Ringgold to Michael Pohuski. The vault is mentioned in several early publications. Historian Mildred C. Schoch of the Kent Island Heritage Society has assembled most of the tales. The vault, she reported, has variously been described as a site where Claiborne's settlers were interred until their remains could be returned to England; a burial site belonging to the Chew family; the burial site of a British officer stationed on the island during the War of 1812 who died there, was temporarily interred, and later removed to England; and a Civil War–era burial site in which soldiers were interred (Mildred C. Schoch, *Of History and Houses: A Kent Island Heritage* [Queenstown, Md.: published for the Kent Island Heritage Society, 1982], 85). No record of such burials during the Claiborne occupation has been found. The property upon which the vault was built, however, did once belong to the estate of Samuel Chew, an absentee landlord who was not interred on the island. The War of 1812 story is believed to be a mixture of regional folklore regarding the occupation of Kent Island by forces under Admiral George Cockburn during the War of 1812, the death of Sir Peter Parker at

the Battle of Caulks Field, and the eventual transport of his body back to England, like Nelson after his death at Trafalgar, in a barrel of rum. As the site is mentioned in George Lynn-Laculan Davis, *The Day-Star of American Freedom* (New York: Charles Scribner's Sons, 1855), 44, the Civil War tale was also ruled out.

14. D. K. Creveling, "A Study of an 18th-Century Burial Vault at Darnall's Chance, Prince George's County, Maryland," draft of paper presented at the Mid-Atlantic Archaeological Conference, Ocean City, Maryland, March 1992.

15. Orlando Ridout V to Michael Pohuski, 10 December 1990 (photocopy), DGSC.

Chapter 15: Infrared

1. Michael Pohuski, personal communication; Michael Pohuski, "The Underwater Search for William Claiborne's Seventeenth-Century Settlement in the Upper Chesapeake," in *Underwater Archaeology: Proceedings from the Society for Historical Archaeology Conference, Richmond, Virginia, 1991,* ed. John Broadwater (Society for Historical Archaeology, 1991), 6–9.

2. George Percy, *Observations Gathered out of "A Discource on the Plantations of the Southern Colony in Virginia by the English, 1606,"* ed. David B. Quinn, Jamestown Documents (Charlottesville: University of Virginia, 1967), 89.

3. Kit Wesler, "Towards a Synthetic Approach to the Chesapeake Tidewater: Historic Site Patterning in Temporal Perspective" (Ph.D. dissertation, University of North Carolina, Chapel Hill, 1982), passim.

4. Reginald V. Truitt, "Kent Island: Maryland's Oldest Settlement," in *The Isle of Kent: The 350th Anniversary: A Commemorative History* (1981), 3–9.

5. Mildred C. Schoch, *Of History and Houses: A Kent Island Heritage* (Queenstown, Md.: published for the Kent Island Heritage Society, 1982), 32–33.

6. Fountain John Davidson, personal communication; Bobby Aaron to Michael Pohuski, personal communication.

7. Nicholas F. Nazare, Sr., to Donald G. Shomette, 13 May 1991, DGSC; Nazare to Shomette, 14 August 1991, DGSC.

8. William Baxter, personal communication, notes in DGSC; The *Sun,* 12 December 1991.

9. Paula J. Johnson, ed., *Working the Water: The Commercial Fisheries of Maryland's Patuxent River* (Charlottesville: published for the Calvert Marine Museum by the University Press of Virginia, 1988), 76.

10. Ibid.

11. William Baxter, personal communication, notes in DGSC.

12. For the significance of sponge divers in the discoveries of classical underwater sites in the Mediterranean Sea, see George Bass, *Archaeology Under Water* (New York: Praeger, 1966), and Peter Throckmorton, *The Lost Ships: An Adventure in Undersea Archaeology* (Boston: Little, Brown and Company, 1964).

13. William Baxter, personal communication, notes in DGSC.

14. Ibid.

15. H. Graham Wood to Fred W. Hopkins Jr., personal communication; Charles Lyle to Fred W. Hopkins Jr., personal communication; Fred W. Hopkins Jr. to Michael Pohuski, 26 February 1990 (photocopy), DGSC.

16. John Herbert Claiborne was the leading proponent of Cleborne Hall in Cliburn Parish, Westmoreland, England, as the birthplace of William Claiborne. More recent biographers such as Nathaniel Hale have championed

Crayford, Kent, England, as his place of origin (John Herbert Claiborne, *William Claiborne of Virginia: With Some Account of His Pedigree* [New York and London: G. P. Putnam's Sons, Knickerbocker Press, 1917], 24–42; Nathaniel C. Hale, *The Virginia Venturer: A Historical Biography of William Claiborne, 1600–1677* [Richmond, Va.: Dietz Press, 1953], 4–7). The *Virginia Magazine of History and Biography* 56, no. 4: 438, states that Claiborne's baptism was, indeed, recorded in the Crayford Parish Register on 10 August 1600.

17. Janet Arnison, *A Glimpse of Cliburn Parish* (Penrith, Cumbria: Reed's Limited, 1987), 8. Kirkby Thore is believed to have been the site of the fourth-century Roman garrison of Bravoniacum, which is identified in the famed *Notitia Dignitatum* (Stephen Johnson, *Later Roman Britain* [London: Paladin Grafton Books, 1982], 111).

18. Arnison, 9; Claiborne, 34–35.

19. Dreen Bowness, personal communication.

20. Michael Pohuski, Joseph McNamara, Donald Shomette, and Dr. Fred Hopkins, Application for Permit to Recover Possible 17th Century Barrels from Near Shore Environment on Kent Island, Queen Anne's County, Maryland (photocopy), DGSC; Maritime Archaeology Program Interim Survey Permit, Permit no. 91-IS-1, 19 April 1991 (photocopy), DGSC.

Chapter 16: Baubles, Barrels, and Beads

1. For a comprehensive account of the "bloodsuckers" of the Eastern Shore, see Robert A. Hedeen, *Naturalist on the Nanticoke: The Natural History of a River on Maryland's Eastern Shore* (Centreville, Md.: Tidewater Publishers, 1982).

2. Michael Pohuski, "The Claiborne Project Interim Report: Kent Island Box and Barrel Wells Excavated and Stabilization," 16 October 1990, DGSC.

3. Henry Miller, personal communication.

4. K. Kidd and M. A. Kidd, "A Classification System for Glass Beads for the Use of Field Archaeologists," *Canadian Historical Sites, Occasional Papers in Archaeology and History no. 1* (Ottawa: National Historical Sites Service, National and Historic Parks Branch, Department of Indian Affairs and Northern Development, 1980); Henry M. Miller, Dennis J. Pogue, and Michael Smolek, "Beads from the 17th Century Chesapeake," in *Proceedings of the 1982 Glass Bead Conference*, Research Record no. 16, ed. Charles H. Hayes III (Rochester: Research Division, Rochester Museum and Science Center, 1983), 127–44; Barry C. Kent, *Susquehanna's Indians*, Anthropological Series no. 6 (Harrisburg: Pennsylvania Historical and Museum Commission, 1989), 211–23; Karlis Karklins to Michael Pohuski, 22 May 1992 (photocopy), DGSC.

5. Karklins to Pohuski, 22 May 1992; Miller et al.

6. Miller et al. suggest that although glass beads were included in the goods to be used in the Indian trade by Claiborne and are evidenced both at Kent Island in 1631 and at Palmers Island in 1637 (a "parcell of blue beads 3 lbs 2 oz"), "it is noteworthy that survey inventories of the Kent Island trading settlement for the years 1632, 1633, and 1634 list no glass beads among the diversity of materials produced for the Indian trade." Indeed, from the archaeological and historical record, glass beads were apparently not a major trade item at all in the Chesapeake during the 1630s (*Archives* 5: 173; Miller et al., 127–28).

7. "The Underwater Search for William Claiborne's Seventeenth-Century Settlement in the Upper Chesapeake," in *Underwater Archaeology: Proceedings from the Society for Historical Archaeology Conference, Richmond, Virginia, 1991,* ed. John Broadwater (Society for Historical Archaeology, 1991), 2–20.

Chapter 17: A Forgotten Alcove of Time

1. Augustine Hermann, *Virginia and Maryland,* 1670 [1673], Geographic and Map Division, Library of Congress, Washington, D.C.
2. Edwin W. Beitzell, *Life on the Potomac River* (Abell, Maryland: privately printed, 1979), 194.
3. Walter Hoxton, *Mapp of the Bay of Chesapeak with the Rivers Potomack, Potapsco, North East, and part of Chester,* 1735, Maryland Historical Society, Baltimore.
4. Anthony Smith, *A New and Accurate Chart of the Bay of Chesapeake, 1776,* Geographic and Map Division, Library of Congress, Washington, D.C.
5. Lord Dunmore to Lord Germain, July 31, 1776, *NDAR* (Washington, D.C.: U.S. Government Printing Office, 1970), V, 1,312–14; "Narrative of Captain Andrew Snape Hamond," *NDAR* (Washington, D.C.: U.S. Government Printing Office, 1972), VI, 172.
6. "Narrative of Captain Andrew Snape Hamond," 172–73; Master's Log of H.M.S. Roebuck, *NDAR,* V, 1,194; Dean Allard, "The Potomac Navy of 1776," *The Virginia Magazine of History and Biography,* vol. 84, no. 4 (October 1976), 422–24.
7. Allard, 425.
8. Purdie's *Virginia Gazette,* 6 September 1776.
9. *Maryland Gazette,* 7 November 1776.
10. Master's Log of H.M.S. *Roebuck,* 1,194.
11. *NDAR,* V, 1,207.
12. Joseph Hawkins to Daniel St. Thomas Jenifer, 26 July 1776, *Red Book,* XV, Maryland Archives.
13. Fielding Lucas, Jr., *Geographical, Statistical, and Historical Map of Maryland,* 1822 [1823], William T. Snyder Collection; David H. Burr, *Delaware and Mary-Land,* 1833, Huntingfield Collection.
14. Frederick Tilp, *This Was Potomac River* (Alexandria, Va.: privately printed, 1978), 195; Colonel Sir Henry James, *Richmond,* 1864, in Edward C. Papenfuse and Joseph M. Coale III, *The Hammond Harwood House Atlas of Historical Maps of Maryland, 1608–1908* (Baltimore and London: The Johns Hopkins University Press, 1982), 83.
15. *Port Tobacco Times and Charles County Advertiser,* 5 March 1851.
16. Beitzell, *Life on the Potomac River,* 90.
17. *In the Anacostia Watershed,* vol. VI, no. 1 (Winter 1993), 3.
18. William H. Massman, "A Potomac River Shad Fishery, 1814–1824," (photocopy), CMM.
19. Ibid.
20. Nan Netherton, Donald Sweig, Janice Artemal, Patricia Hicklin, Patrick Reed, *Fairfax County, Virginia: A History* (Fairfax, Va.: Fairfax County Board of Supervisors, 1978), 262.
21. *In the Anacostia Watershed,* 3; Alice J. Lippson, Michael S. Haire, A. Frederick Holland, Fred Jacobs, Jorgen Jemsen, R. Lynn Moran-Johnson, Tibor T.

Notes

Polgar, William A. Richkus, *Environmental Atlas of the Potomac Estuary* (Baltimore, 1978), 202–4.

22. J. J. Young and W. Hesselbach, *Map of Northern Virginia and Vicinity of Washington*, Compiled in Topographical Engineers Office at Division Headquarters of General Irwin McDowell, Arlington, 1862, Geographic and Map Division, Library of Congress, Washington, D.C.

23. Mary Alice Wills, *The Confederate Blockade of Washington, D.C., 1861–1862* (Parson, W.Va.: McClain Printing Company, 1975), 47, 84.

24. Carleton Jones, "Mining a New Treasure Trove of Civil War Relics," *The Sun Magazine*, January 27, 1980, 7.

25. *Port Tobacco Times and Charles County Advertiser*, 1 September 1871.

26. Beitzell, *Life on the Potomac River*, 285; Tilp, *This Was Potomac River*, 21.

27. Tilp, *This Was Potomac River*, 21.

28. Ibid., 21–22.

29. Burgess and Wood, *Steamboats out of Baltimore*, 106.

30. Tilp, *This Was Potomac River*, 253, 265.

31. Ibid., 265; Frederick Tilp, personal communication.

Chapter 18: A Bridge of Wooden Ships

1. Burgess, *This Was Chesapeake Bay*, 165; William J. Williams, *The Wilson Administration and the Shipbuilding Crisis of 1917: Steel Ships and Wooden Steamers* (Lewiston/Queenston/Lampeter: Edwin Mellen Press, 1992), 109.

2. Carlos DeZafra, "Revival of Wooden Shipbuilding as a War Industry," *Transactions of the Society of Naval Architects and Marine Engineers*, vol. XXVI, 1918, 33–34.

3. "Our Unexampled Ship-building Activities," *The Literary Digest*, vol. LIII (12 August 1916), 388–89; William Joe Webb, "The United States Wooden Steamship Program During World War I," *The American Neptune*, October 1975, 275.

4. Williams, 28.

5. Ibid., 90; U.S. Shipping Board, *Certificate of Incorporation and By-Laws of the United States Shipping Board Emergency Fleet Corporation* (Washington, D.C.: Government Printing Office, 1917), 3–14.

6. *New York Times*, 31 January 1917; Williams, 57–58.

7. Edward Nash Hurley, *The Bridge to France* (Philadelphia: J.B. Lippincott Company, 1927), 53; U.S. Congress, House, *Hearings before Select Committee on United States Shipping Board Operations*, 66th Cong., 2d and 3d sess., 1920–21, 3,188, cited hereafter as U.S. Congress, *Hearings*, 1920–21; Webb, 277.

8. H. Cole Estep, *How Wooden Ships Are Built: A Practical Treatise on Modern American Wooden Ship Construction with a Supplement on Laying Off Wooden Vessels* (Cleveland, Ohio: The Penton Publishing Company, 1918), 2, 7.

9. Williams, 75–80.

10. Williams, 76; U.S. Congress, *Hearings*, 1920–21, 3,188.

11. Williams, 113, *Chicago Tribune*, 26 May 26 1917; *New York Times*, 27 May 1917.

12. Williams, 128, 176–79; Woodrow Wilson to John Denman, July 24, 1917, Box 43, George Goethals Papers, Library of Congress; Woodrow Wilson to George Goethals, July 24, 1917, Box 43, George Goethals Papers, Library of Congress.

13. *New York Times*, 25 July 1917.

14. Burgess, *This Was Chesapeake Bay*, 165; Theodore E. Ferris, *Yellow Pine Ship: Specifications for the Construction of a Standard Wood Steamship, Hull Only, for the*

Notes

United States Shipping Board Emergency Fleet Corporation (Washington, D.C.: Government Printing Office, 1917), 7–9; *New York Times*, 6 April 1917.

15. William T. Donnelly, "Wooden Ships and the Submarine Menace," *International Marine Engineering*, June 1917, 251.

16. *New York Times*, 6 April 1917. This concept was first suggested by Frank L. Sprague, an electrical engineer and member of the Naval Consulting Board, noting that "Five boats of 3,000 tons require about five times as many torpedoes to sink as one boat of 15,000 tons." Williams, 66.

17. Hurley, 53; Webb, 280.

18. Webb, 279.

19. Theodore E. Ferris, "Standard Wooden Steamships for United States Shipping Board Emergency Fleet," *International Marine Engineering*, July 1917, 294.

20. Ibid.

21. Webb, 279.

22. "Hough Type Wooden Steamship," *International Marine Engineering*, September 1917, 280–81.

23. Ferris, *Yellow Pine Ship*, 7–9; United States Shipping Board, *Second Annual Report* (Washington, D.C.: Government Printing Office, 1918), 139–40; Webb, 280.

24. Burgess, *This Was Chesapeake Bay*, 165; U.S. Congress, Senate Committee on Commerce, *Cost of Ship Construction, Letter from the Acting Chairman of the United States Shipping Board Transmitting in Response to a Senate Resolution of November 21, 1918, Information Relative to Existing Contracts for Ship Construction, the Cost of Such Construction, in Both Private and Government Shipyards*, 65th Cong., 3d sess., 1919, S. Doc. 315, 6, hereafter cited as Senate, *Cost of Ship Construction*.

25. Ibid.; Webb, 280–81.

26. Burgess, *This Was Chesapeake Bay*, 166.

27. "Ship Timber Wanted," *International Marine Engineering*, October 1917, 468.

28. *New York Times*, 20 December 1917; U.S. Congress, Senate Committee on Commerce, *Hearings Directing the Committee to Investigate All Matters Connected with the Building of Merchant Vessels under the Direction of the United States Shipping Board Emergency Fleet Corporation and Report Its Findings to the Senate, Together with Its Recommendations Thereon*, 65th Cong., 2d sess., 1918, 311–12, hereafter cited as Senate Hearings, *Building of Merchant Vessels*; Webb, 280.

29. *New York Times*, 28 December 1917; Senate, *Cost of Ship Construction*, 5–6; Senate Hearings, *Building of Merchant Vessels*, 574–75; Webb, 281.

30. Senate, *Cost of Ship Construction*, 9; John Lyman, "Wooden Freighters of World War I," *The Marine Digest*, 29 December 1945.

31. *New York Times*, 18 and 19 March 1918.

32. Ibid., 19 March 1918.

33. Ibid.

34. Ibid.; "The Foundation Company-Shipbuilder," *International Marine Engineering*, July 1918, 389, 394; Senate, *Cost of Ship Construction*, 6–7.

35. Senate, *Cost of Ship Construction*, 36.

36. Burgess, *This Was Chesapeake Bay*, 167.

37. Garnett Arnold, personal communication. The events that transpired at the Missouri Bridge shipyard at Quantico and the personal experiences and adventures of Garnett Arnold were related to the author as Arnold approached his hundredth birthday, one of the last surviving shipwrights of the World War I wooden steamship era. His accounts were recorded by the author

during an interview conducted at the St. Clement's Island–Potomac River Museum on November 30, 1993. Arnold died in 1995 at the age of 102. A Potomac River dory, the last of its type, which he built in his early years was entered into the museum collection and has been fully restored.

38. *New York Times*, 11 and 24 November and 18 December 1917; U.S. Congress, *Hearings*, 1920–21, 5,116; Webb, 281; U.S. Congress, *Congressional Record*, 65th Cong., 2d sess., 56, 2,601.

39. S.M. Evans, *A Discussion of Construction Affecting Ship Production Together With an Estimate of Ship Deliveries (Steel and Wood), April to December 1918* (Washington, D.C.: Government Printing Office, 1918), 47–49; Webb, 282.

40. Webb, 282–83.

41. *The Daily World* (Aberdeen, Washington), 26 January 1975.

42. *The Daily World*, 26 January 1975.

43. *The Aberdeen* (photocopy), enclosed in Harold Huycke to Fred W. Hopkins Jr., 30 March 1994, DGSC.

44. *New York Times*, 25 October and 5 November 1918; U.S. Shipping Board, *Third Annual Report* (Washington, D.C.: Government Printing Office, 1919), 80–81; Senate, *Cost of Ship Construction*, 7–9.

45. Record Group 32, U.S. Shipping Board Emergency Fleet Corporation, Alphabetical List of All Types That Are Now or Have Ever Been Under the Ownership or Control of the United States Shipping Board, Washington, 1924, NARS, cited hereafter as "List of Vessels"; "The Wood Emergency Fleet," *International Marine Engineering*, February 1919, 65; Senate, *Cost of Ship Construction*, 8; Webb, 283.

46. Burgess, *This Was Chesapeake Bay*, 166.

47. *New York Times*, 22 November 1918; Senate, *Cost of Ship Construction*, 8–12; Webb, 284; Burgess, *This Was Chesapeake Bay*, 166.

48. "Reports Splendid Record in Trial," *Shipbuilders Bulletin*, vol. 1, no. 5 (10 April 1919), 8.

49. *New York Times*, 4 February 1919 and 26 March 1919; U.S. Shipping Board, *Fifth Annual Report* (Washington, D.C.: Government Printing Office, 1921), 64; Webb, 284.

50. "The Wooden Emergency Fleet," *International Marine Engineering*, February 1919, 65.

51. Ibid.; Webb, 284.

52. U.S. Shipping Board, *Fourth Annual Report*, 53–55; Webb, 285; "Two More Ships For Recruiting Service," *Shipbuilders Bulletin*, vol. 1, no. 4 (25 March 1919), 8.

53. Darrell H. Smith and Paul V. Betters, *The United States Shipping Board: Its History, Activities and Organization* (Washington, D.C.: The Brookings Institution, 1931), 55–56; U.S. Congress, House, *Report of the Select Committee of Inquiry into Operations, Policies, and Affairs of the United States Shipping Board and Emergency Fleet Corporation*, 69th Cong., 1st sess., 1925, H. Rept. 2, 10–11; U.S. Congress, Senate, *Government Owned Ships, Letter from the United States Shipping Board in Response to a Resolution of the Senate, Dated October 14, 1919, Submitting Reply as to the Number of Ships Sold, Offers to Purchase, and the Policy of the Board in Disposing of Ships*, 66th Cong., 1st sess., 1919, S. Doc. 146, 14; Webb, 285–86.

54. U.S. Congress, Senate, Committee on Commerce, *Report of the United States Shipping Board, Letter from the Chairman of the Shipping Board Transmitting in Response to a Senate Resolution of December 27, 1920, A Report Covering the*

Notes

Transactions of the United States Shipping Board and the Emergency Fleet Corporation from Its Inception to February 28, 1921, 67th Cong., 1st sess., 1921, S. Doc. 38, 18; House Hearings, *Select Committee on United States Shipping Board Operations,* 513–35.

55. Burgess, *This Was Chesapeake Bay,* 166–67.
56. The proceedings of the fleet sale offers may be followed through *The New York Times* and *Washington Post* in the many announcements and stories regarding the sales, between 1920 and 1922.
57. U.S. Shipping Board, *Seventh Annual Report* (Washington, D.C.: Government Printing Office, 1927), 147; Record Group 32, U.S. Shipping Board General File, 605–1–921, NARS.
58. "List of Vessels"; Webb, 287.

Chapter 19: Widewater

1. U.S. Shipping Board, *Seventh Annual Report,* 147, 151, 247.
2. William F. Humphrey to Ralph V. Sollit, 14 June 1923, Office of Chief of Engineers, Civil Works, Record of the Chief of Engineers, Record Group 77, 1923–1942, Potomac River, (7245–7249), hereafter cited as OCE, Serials 81–140, Box 1401, Folder 7175, Part I, Rivers and Harbor File, NARS.
3. Ibid.
4. See Serial 1–45, Box 1400, Part I, Folder 6495, OCE, for documentation on the closure of the Alexandria Shipbuilding Corporation yard at Alexandria, Virginia.
5. Tilp, *This Was Potomac River,* 313, 322; Beitzell, *Life on the Potomac River,* 194–95.
6. Humphrey to Sollit, 14 June 1923.
7. *Alexandria Gazette,* 18 April 1923.
8. Ibid.
9. E. G. Huefe to Commanding General Marine Barracks, Quantico, Virginia, 18 April 1923, Box 1401, Folder 7175, Part I, OCE; ibid., M. C. Tyler to Commanding General, Marine Barracks, Quantico, Virginia, 19 April 1923; ibid., W. E. McCaughtry to Commanding General, Marine Barracks, Quantico, Virginia, 25 April 1923; ibid., E. W. Fales to District Engineer, Washington, D.C., 25 April 1923.
10. Ibid.
11. Ibid.
12. Ibid.
13. Ibid.
14. Ibid.; H. E. Whitaker to Chief of Engineers, 20 April 1923, Box 1401, Folder 7175, Part I, OCE.
15. Whitaker to Chief of Engineers, 20 April 1923.
16. Ibid.
17. Ibid., M. C. Tyler to Chief of Engineers, 28 April 1923, Box 1401, Folder 7175, Part I, OCE.
18. Ibid., Lansing H. Beach to Secretary of War, 24 May 1923, Box 1401, Folder 7175, Part I, OCE.
19. Beach to Secretary of War, 24 May 1923.
20. William F. Humphrey to Ralph V. Sollit, 14 June 1923, Box 1401, Folder 7175, Part I, OCE; H. E. Whitaker to District Engineer's Office, U.S. Engineer's Office, Washington, D.C., June 19, 1923, Box 1401, Folder 7175, Part I, OCE.

21. Humphrey to Sollit, 14 June 1923.

22. Ibid.

23. Ibid.

24. Whitaker to District Engineer's Office, 19 June 1923, Box 1401, Folder 7175, Part I, OCE.

25. Memorandum for File: F. B. Dowling, 20 June 1923, Box 1401, Folder 7175, Part I, OCE.

26. J. A. O'Connor to Chief of Engineers, 13 July 1923, Box 1401, Folder 7175, Part I, OCE.

27. Ibid.

28. Ibid.

29. Lansing H. Beach to Secretary of War, 26 July 1923; Ibid., Memorandum: (Potomac River). Subject: Anchorage Ground in Potomac River off Widewater, Virginia, Box 1401, Folder 7175, Part I, OCE.

30. William J. Bacon to William B. Pistole, 1 October 1923, Box 1401, Folder 7175, Part I, OCE.

31. W. A. Snow to Chief of Engineers, 9 October 1923, Box 1401, Folder 7175, Part I, OCE.

32. Ibid.

33. Ibid.

34. Ibid.

35. Alvin T. Embrey to Herbert Hoover, 29 September 1923, Box 1401, Folder 7175, Part I, OCE.

36. McDonald Lee to Chief of Engineers, 4 October 1923, Box 1401, Folder 7175, Part I, OCE.

37. Snow to Chief of Engineers, 9 October 1923.

38. Ibid.

39. Ibid.

40. Henry Taylor to McDonald Lee, 16 October 1923, Box 1401, Folder 7175, Part I, OCE.

41. J. A. O'Connor to Alvin T. Embrey, 16 October 1923, Box 1401, Folder 7175, Part I, OCE.

42. J. A. O'Connor to Chief of Engineers, 12 January 1923, Box 1401, Folder 7175, Part I, OCE.

43. J. A. O'Connor to Chief of Engineers, 26 May 1924, Box 1401, Folder 7175, Part I, OCE.

44. Ibid.

45. Lansing H. Beach to Secretary of War, 19 December 1923, Box 1401, Folder 7175, Part I, OCE; J. A. O'Connor to Chief of Engineers, 8 May 1925, Box 1401, Folder 7175, Part I, OCE; Anchorage Ground in Potomac River off Widewater Virginia and Rules and Regulations Thereto, 19 December 1923, Box 1401, Folder 7175, Part I, OCE.

46. J. A. O'Connor to Chief of Engineers, 8 May 1925.

Chapter 20: A Horde of Squealing Rats

1. J. A. O'Connor to Chief of Engineers, 29 May 1924, Box 1401, Folder 7175, Part I, OCE.

2. Charles County Court, Liber WHA 73, Folio 538; Liber WHA 42, Folio 65, 3 May 1924.

Notes

3. J. A. O'Connor to Chief of Engineers, 29 May 1924.

4. Major General Commandant of Marines to Chief of Engineers, 20 May 1924, Box 1401, Folder 7175, Part I, OCE.

5. Acting Secretary of War to Major General Commandant of Marines, June 1924, Box 1401, Folder 7175, Part I, OCE.

6. R. Walton Moore to Lansing H. Beach, 21 May 1924, Box 1401, Folder 7175, Part I, OCE.

7. J. A. O'Connor to Chief of Engineers, 26 May 1924, Box 1401, Folder 7175, Part I, OCE.

8. J. A. O'Connor to Chief of Engineers, 14 May 1924, Box 1401, Folder 7175, Part I, OCE.

9. Lansing H. Beach to R. Walton Moore, 10 June 1924, Box 1401, Folder 7175, Part I, OCE.

10. Lytle Brown to William F. Humphrey, 21 July 1931, Box 1401, Folder 7175, Part I, OCE.

11. J. A. O'Connor to Chief of Engineers, 6 August 1924, Box 1401, Folder 7175, Part I, OCE.

12. J. A. O'Connor to Chief of Engineers, 8 May 1925, Box 1401, Folder 7175, Part I, OCE; William J. Bacon to William B. Pistole, 1 October 1925, Box 1401, Folder 7175, Part I, OCE.

13. Cross Reference Memorandum to O.E. Weller, 26 April 1928, Box 1401, Folder 7175, Part I, OCE.

14. J. A. O'Connor to Chief of Engineers, 8 May 1925, Box 1401, Folder 7175, Part I, OCE.

15. Ibid.; Permit to Ground, Burn and Dispose of Five Hulks in Potomac River at Mallows Bay or Sandy Point, Md. Application by Western Marine Salvage Co., March 25, 1924 [plan], Box 1401, Folder 7175, Part I, OCE. The later utilization of *Botsford* as a barracks ship is suggested by her presence on the 1929 Army Engineers plan of Mallows Bay and the shipwrecks therein which are identified as having been released (burned) or awaiting reduction. *Botsford* and *Obak* are noted as lying at Sandy Point, but neither is listed in the reduction list.

16. J. A. O'Connor to Chief of Engineers, 8 May 1925.

17. William F. Humphrey to Harry Taylor, 25 April 1925, Box 1401, Folder 7175, Part I, OCE.

18. J. A. O'Connor to Chief of Engineers, 13 July 1925, Box 1401, Folder 7175, Part III, OCE.

19. *Harry Steinbraker v. Lorenzo D. Crouse*, No. 46, October Term, 1935, Charles County Court, La Plata, Maryland, 456; W.D. Luplow to Chief of Engineers, 8 May 1937, Box 1402, Folder 7245, Part II, OCE.

20. W.D. Luplow to Chief of Engineers, 8 May 1937, Box 1402, Folder 7245, Part II, OCE.

21. *Washington Post*, 8 November 1925.

22. J. A. O'Connor to Western Marine and Salvage Company, 14 June 1926, Box 401, Folder 7175, Part III, OCE.

23. Tilp, *This Was Potomac River*, 32.

24. Potomac River at Mallows Bay Survey of Grounding Area, August 11, 1929 (blueprint), Headquarters, U.S. Army Corps of Engineers, Fifth District, Baltimore, Maryland.

25. Ibid.

26. *Steinbraker v. Crouse*, 455, 456, 461.
27. William F. Humphrey to Douglas MacArthur, 18 June 1931, Box 1401, Folder 7175, Part II, OCE; *Steinbraker v. Crouse*, 455.
28. Humphrey to MacArthur, 18 June 1931.
29. Ibid.
30. Lytle Brown to William F. Humphrey, 1 July 1931, Box 1401, Folder 7175, Part II, OCE.
31. Ibid.
32. William F. Humphrey to Lytle Brown, 23 July 1931, Box 1401, Folder 7175, Part II, OCE.
33. Lytle Brown to William F. Humphrey, 31 July 1931, Box 1401, Folder 7175, Part II, OCE.
34. Lytle Brown to William F. Humphrey, 1 August 1931, Box 1401, Folder 7175, Part II, OCE.
35. Tilp, *This Was Potomac River*, 265.
36. *Steinbraker v. Crouse*, 456–57; W. D. Luplow to Chief of Engineers, 8 May 1937, Box 1402, Folder 7245, Part II, OCE.
37. Charles County Court, Liber WHA 56, Folio 306. *Steinbraker v. Crouse* incorrectly cites the date as November 30. *Steinbraker v. Crouse*, 456, 457, 459.
38. *Steinbraker v. Crouse*, 457.

Chapter 21: Fastened His Eyes on These Hulls

1. *Steinbraker v. Crouse*, 455–56, 459, 460–61.
2. Ibid.; J. Read Bailey to Stephen W. Gambrill, 6 July 1934, Box 1401, Folder 7175, Part II, OCE.
3. *Steinbraker v. Crouse*, 461.
4. Garnett Arnold, personal communication.
5. J. Read Bailey to Stephen W. Gambrill, 6 July 1934.
6. G. B. Pillsbury to Stephen W. Gambrill, 16 July 1934, Box 1401, Folder 7175, Part II, OCE.
7. *Steinbraker v. Crouse*, 454; Charles County Court, Liber 60, Folio 204, 22 December 1934.
8. Ibid.
9. W. D. Luplow to Chief of Engineers, 8 May 1937, Box 1401, Folder 7175, Part II, OCE; Tilp, *This Was Potomac River*, 44, 88. According to a popular story published in Tilp, 294, 308, *Ida S. Dow* would later serve as a temporary residence for prostitutes who provided their services to salvors. Tilp reports that the vices of the salvors were indeed well served during the Prohibition era when no fewer than twenty-wix whiskey stills were reported aboard the hulks in the bay. He also reported that as late as 1976, Treasury agents raided a whiskey still on one of the abandoned steamers. I have been unable to document the veracity of these claims.
10. Paul C. Morris, *American Sailing Coasters of the North Atlantic* (Chardon, Ohio: Bloch and Osborn Publishing Company, 1973), 135; Tilp, *This Was Potomac River*, 88.
11. *Steinbraker v. Crouse*, 453–54.
12. Ibid., 454.
13. Ibid., 455.
14. Ibid., 455–60.

Notes

15. Ibid., 460.
16. Ibid.
17. Ibid., 460–61.
18. Ibid., 461.
19. Ibid., 462.
20. Ibid., 461–62.
21. Ibid., 458.
22. See *Stewart v. May*, 119 Md. 10, 19, 1 85A. 957; *Canton Co. v. Balto. & O. R. Co.*, 99 Md. 202, 218, 57A. 637; *Russell v. Zimmerman*, 121 Md. 328, 334, 88A. 337; *Grief v. Leas*, 156 Md. 284, 300, 144A. 231; 45 C.J., 538, 540; *Sollers v. Sollers*, 77 Md. 148, 151, 26A. 188, as cited in *Steinbraker v. Crouse*.
23. *Steinbraker v. Crouse*, 459.
24. Ibid.
25. See *Russell v. Stratton*, 201 Pa. 277, 278, 50A. 975; *Fidelity-Phila. Trust Co. v. Lehigh Valley Coal Co.*, 294 Pa. 47, 143A. 474, 479, as cited in *Steinbraker v. Crouse*.
26. *Steinbraker v. Crouse*, 462–63.
27. Ibid.
28. Charles County Court, Liber 59, Folio 512; Frederick Tilp, *The Chesapeake Bay of Yore: Mainly about the Rowing and Sailing Craft* (Alexandria, Va.: privately published, 1982), 56. A comprehensive examination of the Fred Tilp Collection at CMM failed to locate any data regarding the five purported "arks" at Mallows Bay. Indeed, the only reference to the bay at this point in time appeared in the log of the Sea Scout catboats *Bob Cat* and *Wildcat*, with an entry made while passing the bay on June 28, 1936: "Pass 4 master IDA S. DOW in Mallows Bay. The wrecks seem pretty well stripped." Log of *Bob Cat* and *Wildcat*, June 28, 1936, Sea Scout File, Fred Tilp Collection, CMM.
29. C. D. Rittenhouse to P. C. Dour, 19 May 1937, Box 1402, Folder 7245, Part II, OCE.
30. W. D. Luplow to Chief of Engineers, 8 May 1937.
31. Ibid.
32. Ibid.
33. Ibid.
34. Ibid.
35. Ibid.
36. Ibid. Despite Rittenhouse's threats, the salvors would continue to use dynamite. On 6 July 1938, more than a year after the engineer's warning, Tilp would write in the log of the Sea Scout catboat *Bobcat* during a visit to Mallows Bay: "Into Mallow—very little traffic, but the boys are still dynamiting the old hulls—All scrap iron and whatever looked like scrap is gone to 'Japan to invade China.'" Log of *Bobcat*, 6 July 1938, Sea Scout File, Fred Tilp Collection, CMM.
37. W. D. Luplow to Chief of Engineers, 8 May 1937. The navy's response to the invasion of its waters in Chopawamsic by the derelict(s) was reported in the press some years later and indicates how the problem was ultimately dealt with after the long delays by the army engineers. "The navy was outraged and demanded that something be done about the stray ships. When no one claimed the vessels, the navy ordered their anchor chains out and had them towed to the Maryland shore and secured there for good at a safe distance from the Quantico airfield." Baltimore *Sun*, 10 June 1943.

38. Bullock to Chief of Engineers, 26 May 1937, Box 1401, Folder 7175, Part II, OCE.

39. E. M. Markham to Chief of Engineers, 27 May 1937, Box 1401, Folder 7175, Part II, OCE.

40. W. D. Luplow to Division Engineer, South Atlantic Division, 28 May 1938 [1937], Box 1401, Folder 7175, Part II, OCE.

41. Ibid.

42. Advice of Allotment, 6 June 1937, Advice No. C-2378, Box 1401, Folder 7175, Part II, OCE; Charles County Court, Liber 73, Folio 538; Liber 73, Folio 537.

Chapter 22: These Strange Islands

1. File 179, Box 916, Record Group 179, War Production Board, Salvage Program, July-December 1942, Military Reference Branch, NARS.

2. Minutes of the Metals Reserve Company, 1940–1945, vol. 14, 357–59, 21 October 1942, Records of the Reconstruction Finance Corporation (37 vols.), Record Group 234, Civil Reference Branch, NARS.

3. Ibid.

4. Baltimore *Sun,* 10 July 1943.

5. Charles County Court, Liber 77, Folio 463, 31 December 1942.

6. Baltimore *Sun,* 10 July 1943.

7. Ibid.

8. Minutes of the Metals Reserve Company, vol. 33, 156–57.

9. Ibid., vol. 31, 123–25, 10 March 1944.

10. Ibid., vol. 33, 659–60, 22 May 1944.

11. *Dictionary of American Fighting Ships,* 8 vols., (Washington, D.C.: United States Government Printing Office, 1970), V, 102.

12. Ibid.; Minutes of the Metals Reserve Company, vol. 35, 317, 22 September 1944.

13. Minutes of the Metals Reserve Company, vol. 35, 317, 22 September 1944.

14. *Washington Star,* 2 February 1948.

15. Charles County Court, Liber 113, Folio 283, 20 August 1954.

16. U.S. Congress, House of Representatives, *Report No. 91-1761, Protecting America's Estuaries: The Potomac,* 91st Cong., 2d sess., 1970, 7–8, hereafter cited as House, *Protecting America's Estuaries.*

17. Ibid., 8.

18. Ibid.; Charles County Court, Liber 166, Folio 164, 31 October 1963.

19. House, *Protecting America's Estuaries,* 8.

20. Ibid.

21. Ibid.

22. Ibid., 8–9.

23. *Evening Sun,* 10 February 1967.

24. House, *Protecting America's Estuaries,* 8–9.

25. Ibid.

26. Ibid.

27. Ibid.

28. Ibid.

29. Ibid., 9.

30. Ibid.

31. Ibid.

32. Ibid.
33. Ibid.
34. Ibid., 8–9.
35. Ibid., 10.
36. Ibid.
37. Ibid.
38. Ibid.
39. Ibid., 10–11.
40. Ibid., 11.
41. Ibid.
42. Ibid., 6.
43. Ibid.
44. Ibid.
45. Ibid., 6–7.
46. Ibid., 11.
47. Ibid.
48. James W. Peck to John D. Costello, 24 June 1981, U.S. Army Corps of Engineers file copy, Fifth District, Baltimore, Maryland; Fact Sheet. Derelict Hulks at Mallows Bay, Charles County, Maryland, MAINQUIST, NABOPN/23663, 16 November 1982. U.S. Army Corps of Engineers file copy, Fifth District, Baltimore, Maryland.
49. Ibid.
50. Ibid.

Chapter 23: Telltale Signs

1. Mallows Bay Ghost Fleet: Project Abstract, 28 December 1993 (photocopy), DGSC.
2. Preliminary notes for the Mallows Bay Project Design, 14 December 1992, DGSC.
3. The significant documentation effort by Hopkins has been collected in photocopy form and annotated by the author in the Mallows Bay Project File, DGSC.
4. Site No. 74, Survey Notes, Mallows Bay Project File, DGSC. All site data noted hereafter in the chapter are contained in Field Notes, Mallows Bay Project, DGSC.

Chapter 24: Buried Boats

All site data noted herein are from Field Notes and Survey Record, Mallows Bay Project, DGSC.

Chapter 25: This Is One Evil Place

1. Listing of the Shipyards Represented at Mallow's Bay from the Corps of Engineers, August 11, 1929, Survey of the Grounding Area. Compiled by Fred Hopkins, July 26, 1993, DGSC.
2. Preliminary Sites List, June 1993, Mallows Bay Project File, DGSC.
3. Field Log, 17 July 1993, Mallows Bay Project File, DGSC.
4. Ibid., 12 July 1993.
5. Ibid.; "Potomac River at Mallows Bay Survey of Grounding Area August 11, 1929" (blueprint), Headquarters, U.S. Army Corps of Engineers, Fifth Dis-

trict, Baltimore, Maryland; Listing of the Shipyards Represented at Mallow's Bay; *Merchant Vessels of the United States*, 1919.

6. Thomas C. Gillmer to Professor Fred Hopkins, 13 August 1993 (photocopy), DGSC.

7. "Potomac River Burned Hulls at Mallows Bay, Md.," in Memorandum: Burned Hulls, Mallows Bay, Potomac River, Md., Report to Mr. P.C. Dorr by G.D. Rittenhouse, 19 May 1937, Box 1402, Folder 7245, Part II, OCE. *Kasota* was listed as No. 150 on "Potomac River at Mallows Bay Survey of Grounding Area August 11, 1929."

8. Harry Jones, personal communication.

9. Fred Hopkins to Donald G. Shomette, 2 December 1992, DGSC.

10. Richard V. Elliott, *Last of the Steamboats: The Saga of the Wilson Line* (Cambridge, Md.: Tidewater Publishers, 1970), 143–45; Hopkins to Shomette, 2 December 1992.

11. Fred W. Hopkins Jr. to Donald G. Shomette, 23 January 1993 and 9 September 1993, DGSC.

12. Fred W. Hopkins Jr. to Donald G. Shomette, 2 February 1993, DGSC.

13. Fred W. Hopkins Jr. to Donald G. Shomette, 21 April 1993, DGSC.

14. See Alice J. Lippson, Michael S. Haire, A. Frederick Holland, Fred Jacobs, Jorgen Jensen, R. Lynn Morgan-Johnson, Tibor T. Polgar, and William A. Richkus, *Environmental Atlas of the Potomac Estuary* (prepared for the Power Plant Siting Program, Maryland Department of Natural Resources, 1979) for a comprehensive environmental overview of the Potomac drainage area.

15. Lippson, et al., 20–23.

16. The sediments lost in the sector between Mattawoman Creek and the Chesapeake rate as the lowest levels of loss on the entire river. The highest yield, 682 tons per square mile, is between an area beginning five miles north of Little Falls and ending at the outlet of Mattawoman Creek. Lippson, et al., 59.

17. Ibid., 48–53.

18. Ibid., 86–92.

19. Ibid., 74–83, 132–33, 143.

20. Jean B. Lee, *The Price of Nationhood: The American Revolution in Charles County* (New York and London: W.W. Norton & Company, 1994), 32; Lippson, et al., 184–99.

Chapter 26: Blowout Redux

1. Tilp, *This Was Potomac River*, 306.

2. See Howard I. Chapelle, *American Small Sailing Craft: Their Design, Development, and Construction* (New York: W.W. Norton & Company, Inc., 1951), 104–33, for the most comprehensive overview of sharpie development and design.

3. Tilp, *This Was Potomac River*, 31–32.

Index

Index

Index

155-56; marine transgressions against archaeological resources in, 157-58, 159; box and barrel well traditions adopted, 168; burial vault types common to, 168; impact of pollution on clams of, 180; rise of clamming industry on, 180-81; environmental changes off Kent Island, 183; trading bead types prevalent on, 196; mentioned, 6, 9, 15, 16, 17, 18, 23, 25, 27, 40, 43, 57, 58, 62, 80, 103, 105, 205, 223, 232, 262, 334

Claiborne, William, origins of, 104; as surveyor with Virginia Company, 105; departure for Virginia, 105; survey work in Virginia, 106; service in Indian war, 106; establishes plantation at Accomac, 106; lays out new town of Jamestown, 106; establishes plantation at Kecoughtan, 106; transports servants from England, 107; appointed to Governor's Council, 107; appointed Virginia secretary of state, 107; first commission to explore Chesapeake Bay, 107-8; visits Accomac, 108; first sighting of Kent Island, 108; second commission to explore Chesapeake, 109; determines to make Palmer's Island a trading base, 110; lobbies Privy Council against Lord Baltimore, 112; conducts affairs in England, 112-13; enlists Reverend James, 112; forms partnership with Cloberry and others, 113, 115; loss of confidence in Governor Harvey, 113; company formed to erect a plantation, 113; contracts with Winthrop for corn, 114; accepts secretary of Scotland's trading license, 114-15; sails for America, 116; lands settlers on Kent Island, 117; learns of disastrous fire at Kent Island, 117; shipwrecked, 118; captured by Indians, 118; relations with Harvey, 118-19; as commander and justice of the peace of Kent Island Hundred, 119; encounters with Fleet, 119-20; trades with Potomac Indian villages, 120; supervises improvements at Kent Is-

land, 120, 121; as the most proficient trader in the Chesapeake, 120; good relations with natives, 121; receives first resupply from Cloberry, 121; opposes Maryland Charter, 123; petitions to keep Kent Island under Virginia's jurisdiction, 124; Baltimore challenges authority over Kent Island, 124; Calvert's ultimatum to, 125-26; enlarges settlement on Kent Island, 126; occupies Popeley's Island, 126; erects settlement at Craney Creek, 126; increases shipbuilding, 126; charged with inciting Maryland natives against St. Mary's, 127; arrest of, 127; attacks against, 127; forced to barter in Virginia, 127; erects plantation at Crayford, 128; strengthens Kent Island's defenses, 128; difficulties with Wicomesse and Choptank Indians, 128; Cloberry's petition in behalf of, 129; king orders cessation of Maryland hostilities against, 129; replaced as secretary of state, 129-30; king's commission ignored by Marylanders, 130; retaliates against Maryland for capture of *Long Tayle*, 130-31; supported by West administration, 132; right to Kent Island recognized, 132; birth of son, 132; Cloberry assails record keeping by, 134; recalled to England, 134; first meeting with Evelin, 135; excluded from Council of Virginia, 135; establishes trading post at Palmer's Island, 135-36; erects fort on Palmer's Island, 136; last efforts at accommodation with Evelin, 136; departs for England to address problems of Kent Island, 136; supporters resist allegiance to Maryland, 137; home and fort captured by Calvert, 138; Palmer's Island trading base destroyed, 139; Calvert confiscates property of, 139; charged with piracy and murder, 140; petitions the king, 140; sued for libel by Cloberry, 140; countersues Cloberry, 141; returns to the Chesapeake for depositions, 141; petitions Calvert for return of property, 141; returns to England a third time, 141; appointed treasurer of Virginia, 141; fourth return to England, 141; appointed general and chief commander of Virginia, 141; campaigns against Opechancanough, 141; returns to Kent Island to incite rebellion, 142; Calvert gathers intelligence on, 142; declared enemy of Maryland, 143; conspires with Ingle on invasion of Maryland, 143; seizes Brent's plantation, 144; fails to secure support for invasion of Maryland, 144; corresponds with Governor Stone, 145; appointed commissioner for the Chesapeake, 146; reappointed secretary of state of Virginia, 145; ascendancy over Maryland, 146; submits last claim on Kent Island, 146; Virginia Assembly supports claim to Kent Island, 146; "1593" potsherd a possible link to settlement of, 149; Pohuski begins research on, 150; clues to location of home, 151; destruction of house belonging to, 152; Bozman's and Davis's views regarding, 152; traditional settlement site of, 152; Thom-Steiner claims regarding, 153; Berkeley's claims regarding, 153; Hale's

Index

Claiborne, William (*continued*)
biography of, 154; first evidence of settlement found, 160; wells dug by contemporaries of at Jamestown, 163; settlement site on Tanners Point disputed, 126; family records stolen, 187; mentioned, 150, 151, 165, 173, 177, 178, 186, 187, 188, 196, 197, 200
Claiborne, William, Jr., 133
Claiborne Project, field reconnaissance begins, 147-51, 159-60; first discovery of, 159; investigations of burial vault, 166-68; aerial infrared photography survey, 169-70; discovery of gravestone breakwater, 172-73; discoveries of bulkhead from a collapsed church, 173; discovery of shipwreck, 173; investigations at Tanners Creek, 175-76; artifact collections examined, 176, 182; shovel testing of spoil piles, 176; folk tales regarding Claiborne settlement, 177; importance of watermen's knowledge, 177-80; assisted by Baxter, 181, 182-83; use of satellite positioning system, 182; ground truthing targets, 183; inundation hypothesis supported, 183; clam dredger proposed for trenching, 184; fundraising for, 184-85; underwater investigations begin, 185; the Long Point brick site, 186; research trip to England, 186-88; excavation permit approved, 188; excavation project begins, 189; coffer dam erected for, 189-90; excavation of Well No. 2, 190-93; discovery of Indian trading beads, 191; pumping well dry, 192; excavation of Well No. 3, 193, 195; findings, 195-96; beads compared, 196-97; findings presented to Society for Historical Archaeology and Maryland Historical Trust, 197; mentioned, 292
Claremont, Va., 232, 233
Clark, Val, 224
Chapman, George, 210
Clarke, Robert A., 209
Cleborne, Capt. C. J., 187
Cleborne, Edmund, 104
Cleborne, Grace, 104
Cleborne Hall, 104, 186, 187
Cleburn, Gen. Patrick Renayne, 187
Cleborne, Adm. Christopher James, 187
Cleveland, Pres. Grover, 236
Cliburn, Eng., 186
Cliburn Mills, 188
Clifton, Va., 236
Cloberry, William, partnership with Claiborne, 112-13; to secure royal patent for trading venture, 113; fails to secure royal patent, 114; secures commission from secretary of Scotland, 115; pledges to press for patent, 121; abandonment of Claiborne, 125; vows to combat Baltimore, 128; petitions the king, 129; orders Claiborne's return, 134; secures control of Cloberry and Company, 134; sends Evelin to replace Claiborne, 134; complains to king about Kent Island invasion, 140; relations with Claiborne degenerate, 140; opens law suit against Claiborne, 140; mentioned, 117, 119, 127
Cloberry and Company, 113, 114, 115, 117, 121, 125, 128, 134, 135, 338

Cloberry and Moorhead, 134, 136, 137, 138
Coal Landing, Va., 244
Coan River, Va., 331
Cockpit Point, Va., 203
Cole, Michael, 48, 49, 52
Colmony, Abraham, 4
Colton Point, Md., 290
Commercial Transportation Company of Trenton, 6, 8-9, 11
Committee on Public Information, 220
Confederate Army, 4, 9, 11, 211
Connecticut, 334
Constantine, 121
Continental Congress, 92
Conway, Capt. Robert, 207, 208, 132
Cook, William G., 8
Cook's Point, Md., 35
Cooke, Dr. Jay, 19
Cooke's Ferry, 211, 301
Cornwaleys, Capt. Thomas, 130, 131, 132, 135, 137, 138, 139
Costello, Rear Adm. John D., 286
Council of National Defense, 216
Council of Virginia, 115, 126, 128, 131, 140
Countess of Pembroke, 105
Coursey, James, 180
Cove Creek, Md., 153
Cowes, Eng., 105, 125
Cox, J. W., 263
Cox, Capt. Jerry, 75
Coxe, William, 118
Cralle, Capt. A. K., 12-14, 15-16
Craney Creek, Md., 126, 128, 149, 175, 177-78
Craney Fort, 128
Crayford, Eng., 104
Crayford, Md., 126, 129, 134, 138, 139, 143, 177
Cresswell, Nicholas, 322
Creveling, Donald, 168
Crilly, Capt. J. T., 9
Cronin, Dr. Eugene L., 284
Crosby, H. I., 222
Cross Road, Va., 212
Crouse, Lorenzo D., 259, 262, 263
Crownsville, Md., 338
Cummins, Edward, 142, 144
Curtis, Capt. Edmund, 145
Curtis Creek, Md., 275

Darnall's Chance, 168
Datasonics Corporation, 77, 79, 80, 82
Datcher, Rudy, 329
Daugherty type steamship, 219, 307
David, James L., 263
Davidson, Fountain John, 178-79, 186
Davis, George, 152, 154
Dawson, William, 131
Deale, Eng., 115
Deep Sea Systems International, 48, 68
Delabarr, John, 113, 121, 125, 134
Delaware, 4, 5, 139, 177, 274, 316
Delaware and Raritan Canal, 4, 6, 8
Delaware Bay and River, 4, 6, 11, 25, 116, 130, 210, 232
Delaware State Museum, 332

Index

Index

Index

129; Harvey instructed to assist settlement of, 129; Harvey ignores royal orders regarding, 129; Claiborne's expansion of settlement on, 130; Maryland trade goods sent to, 130; pinnace defeated at Battle of the Pocomoke, 131; Maryland instructed to cease violence against, 132; Claiborne's right to reconfirmed, 132; Cloberry unhappy over management of, 134; Evelin sent to take charge of, 134; Evelin assumes authority over, 137; Evelin depletes corn supplies of, 137; Calvert appoints Evelin commander of Kent, 137; resists Evelin's authority, 137; Calvert's failed invasion of, 137; Calvert's first successful invasion of, 138; local leaders captured, 138; stripped by invaders, 138; Calvert's second successful invasion of, 139; Claiborne contests for in court, 140; Baltimore to cease actions against, 140; Virginia declares island belongs to Maryland, 140; Claiborne petitions for return of, 141; Thompson commands at, 142; Plowden's claims on, 142; Claiborne incites revolt on, 142; Calvert gathers intelligence regarding, 142-43; Claiborne seizes Brent estate on, 144; Claiborne seeks support of residents to capture Calvert, 144; Knight's destruction of, 144; Vaughn appointed commander of, 144; revolts against Maryland, 144; final destruction of settlements on, 144; Claiborne's last efforts to secure, 145-46; oldest ceramic sherd in America discovered at, 149; owners of Kent Fort on, 152; Steiner's description of, 152-53; impact of urban development on, 153; first sighted by Claiborne, 154; Hale's visit to, 154; Isaac's works on, 154; Pohuski begins study of, 154; U.S. Coast and Geodetic survey of, 155; impact of erosion on, 157; critical areas study of, 158; archaeological discoveries resulting from blowout, 160-61; aerial survey of, 169-71; gravestone breakwater at, 172; shipwreck site discovered at, 172; shell midden discovered on, 175; archaeological exploration of, 175; claims regarding first settlement site in Maryland, 177-78; inundated structures near, 178-79; arrival of Roger Baxter at, 180; knowledge of watermen about, 180-82; clammers as information sources, 181; Baxter leads researchers to archaeological sites, 182; Skove site as oldest European site on, 196; burial site discovered on, 197; beads associated with first settlement found, 200; mentioned; 151, 165, 166, 168, 333
Kent Island Heritage Society, 177, 185
Kent Island Hundred, 119, 121, 122, 125, 159
Kent Point, Md., plantation noted on Hermann map, 154; archaeological potentials of, 165; aerial photography of, 179, 172; infrared reveals features near, 172; gravestone breakwater at, 172; underwater investigations near, 186; first evidence of European settlement at, 196; mentioned, 103, 151, 152, 155, 186
Kidd, K., 196
Kidd, M. A., 196

King Charles I, 107, 113, 119, 123, 125, 129, 135, 140, 141
King Charles II, 112, 146, 153
King George I, 180
King James I, 107
Kinny, Larry, 66
Kiptopeke, Va., 232, 315
Kirkby Thore, Eng., 187
Kirwan, Jacob, 12
Kirwan, John H., 12
Kiser, John, 55, 63-66, 72, 79, 80-81, 82, 84, 88, 90, 93, 147, 148, 151, 189
Kiskyack, Va., 119
Knight, Lt. Peter, 144
Koester, Henry, 247
Kristof, Emory, 44-45, 46-47 49-50, 54 55, 58, 59, 81, 92, 94, 96

La Plata, Md., 249, 260, 278 282
Labadie, Patrick, 48
Lake, Ocean and Navigating Company, 219, 307
Lake Erie, 45
Lake Superior, 45, 46, 49, 52
Langley, Samuel Pierpont, 236
Lasker, Albert, 234
Lawson, James, 208
Lazaretto Point Light, 13
Lee, McDonald, 244-45
Lee, Robert E., 10
Lee, W. B., 243, 268, 269
Legg, J. Frank, 153
Lenihan, Daniel, 47, 48, 49, 51
Levin, Jake, 268
Lewger, John, 138, 139
Lincoln, Pres. Abraham, 3, 8
Linton, Samuel C., 279
Little, J. Rodney, 87-88, 95, 97-98, 99, 291, 338
Little Creek, Va., 315
Liverpool, Eng., 215
Liverpool Creek Cove, shipwrecks in, 328-37; exploration of begins, 329; 1994 survey work in, 332-35; blowout in, 332-33; last shipwreck discovered in, 335; survey of composite wreck in, 335-36; mentioned, 205, 336-37
Liverpool Point, Md., fortified, 203; first identified by name, 206; Clark-Barnard ownership of, 209; fisheries station on, 209; connected by road to Port Tobacco, 211; Union troops on, 211; steamboat wharf on, 211; Monroe's sturgeon fishing station on, 211; demise of caviar processing operation at, 253; mapped by army engineers, 253; aerial survey of planned, 291; eagles observed at, 324; survey of Liverpool Point Transect, 327-38; *Mermentau* aground at, 337; mentioned, 205, 212, 297, 321
London, Eng., 113, 114, 121, 125, 134, 142
Londontown, Md., 158
Long Island, N.Y., 142, 232
Long Island Sound, 334
Long Point, Md., as possible site of Kent Fort, 154; archaeological features near, 170; discovery of underwater site near, 186; aid for investigations sought, 200; mentioned, 153, 186

borne challenges Baltimore's patent, 145; capitulates to agents of the Commonwealth, 145; Stone appointed governor of, 145; bipartisan government in, 145; Baltimore restored to authority over, 146; Claiborne's last efforts to secure Kent Island from, 146; Claiborne Project begins in, 147; establishment history of challenged, 177; clamming industry in, 180; findings of Claiborne Project presented, 197; lacks interest in Chamberlin's discovery of melted beads, 200; militia defends Mallows Bay area, 207; militia criticized, 208; fisheries legislation, 210; Confederate invasion of feared, 211; wooden steamship construction in, 223; WM&SC seeks land in, 247; court rules on abandonments in, 264; to share cost of hulk removals from Mallows Bay, 282; Department of Natural Resources correspondence on Mallows Bay, 282; refuses to support hulk removals from Mallows Bay, 283, 285; mentioned, 3, 4, 5, 9, 11, 17, 23, 24, 29, 44, 54, 72, 86, 90, 92, 95, 96, 97, 126, 140, 142, 147, 148, 150, 152, 154, 158, 168, 181, 189, 203, 204, 206, 208, 209, 212, 223, 226, 236, 244, 246, 249, 252, 260, 262, 271, 275, 278, 290, 291, 299, 314

Maryland Advisory Committees on Archaeology, 49, 100, 292

Maryland Department of Agriculture, 297

Maryland Department of Natural Resources, 29, 182

Maryland General Assembly, 11, 99, 135, 270

Maryland Geological Survey, 27, 30, 31, 32, 44, 49, 54, 57, 67, 75, 86, 91, 95, 97, 98, 166

Maryland Hall of Records, 154

Maryland Historical Society, 153, 154, 184

Maryland Historical Trust, 31, 34, 87, 95, 99, 147, 150, 185, 186, 188, 193, 197, 199-200, 291, 317

Maryland House of Delegates, 279; Appropriations Committee, 100

Maryland Maritime Archaeology Program, 100

Maryland National Capital Park and Planning Commission, 168, 299, 306, 323

Maryland Point, Md., 206, 267, 283

Maryland Provincial Congress, 92

Maryland Shipbuilding Company, 223, 308

Maryland State Senate, 96, 100

Maryland Steamboat Company, 12

Maryland Water Resources Act, 31

Mason, Wayne, 164, 165

Massachusetts, 58, 114, 315

Matapeake, Md., 169, 182

Matapeake Indians, 108, 116, 118, 175

Mathews, Samuel, 111, 131

Mathias Point, Va., 210

Mattapany, Md., 130

Mattawoman Creek, Md., 203, 277, 299

Mattapex Post Office, 153

McAdoo, William G., 214

McCarthy, Charlie, 68

McClelland type steamship, 219, 293, 307, 335

McConchie, Md., 299

McDonald, John A., 230

McNamara, Joseph, 31, 35, 40-41, 63, 65, 66, 72, 142, 147, 149, 150, 151, 159, 161, 164, 161, 166

Metals Reserve Company, 271, 273, 274, 275

Mexico, 275

Meyer, Eugene, Jr., 232

Michigan, 46, 274

Miller, Edward M., 33, 34, 57-58

Miller, Dr. Henry, 196

Mississippi River, 164

Missouri Valley Bridge and Iron Construction Company, 223, 224, 225, 226

Mitchell, John, 304, 306, 319

Mobile, Ala., 230

Mobile Shipbuilding Company, 230

Mohawk Indians, 196

Moll, Herman, 154

Monoponson Indians, 116

Monoponson Island, 108. *See also* Kent Island

Monroe, Capt. Morgan L., 211-12, 253; 332

Moore, Don, 46

Moore, Rep. R. Walton, 248

Moorehead, Keith, 46, 47, 49, 66, 93, 94, 98

Moorhead, David, 134

Moreland, Rick, 306, 317, 319

Morgan, Frank O., 273

Morgan, G. H., 268

Morgan, Mildred, 273

Morgan, Theodore, 63, 66

Morris Island, S.C., 3

Mosley, Joseph, 322

Moss Point, Md., 204

Mount Vernon and Marshall Hall Steamboat Company, 212

Mountney, Alexander, 128

Mudd, F. DeSales, 278, 282, 283

Mudd & Mudd, 278

Mullins, Craig, 35

Murdock, Grace, 270

Murdock, Hugh, 270

Murphy, Larry, 86

Nanjemoy, Md., 249, 299

Nanjemoy Creek, Md., 206, 211

Nashville, Tenn., 58

Nassawadex Creek, Va., 164

National Archives, 91

National Geographic Society (magazine), 44, 45, 46, 51, 54, 55, 57, 58, 59, 66, 67, 91, 92, 96, 203, 299, 304

National Museum of History, 183

National Oceanic and Atmospheric Administration, 27, 28, 33, 34, 44, 57, 64, 65, 66, 67, 300

National Park Service, 26, 45, 46, 47, 49, 53, 86

National Register of Historic Places, 54

Nautical Archaeological Associates, Incorporated (NAA), 18, 19, 24, 27, 32, 35, 55, 59, 72

Naval Research Laboratory, 34-35

Naval Ship Research and Development Center, 33

Naval Surface Weapons Test Center, 66

Neve, Richard, 164

New England, 46, 107, 113, 115, 117, 120, 180, 214, 223, 233

Index

Index

Index

Index

Index

Index

shown to governor of Maryland, 97; report employed to secure support for conservation laboratory, 100; damage to cited in congressional lobby effort, 100; cited by Senator Bradley, 100; mentioned, 59, 70, 71, 72, 91, 92

USS *Nokomis* (patrol boat), 330, 335, 331. *See also* USS *Bodkin, Burke, Nokomis II*

Nokomis II. See USS *Bodkin, Burke, Nokomis*

North Bend (wooden steamship), 221, 253, 307

Obak (composite steamship), 230, 250, 293, 300, 307, 335

Okiya (wooden steamship), 238, 249, 256

Option (dive boat), 40, 55

Owatama (wooden steamship), 308

USS *Owl* (tug), 237

Pacific (steam tug), 14, 15

Peter W. Anderson (ocean survey vessel), 34, 35

Potomac (steamboat), 212

Quemakoning (wooden steamship), 335, 336

Quidnic (wooden steamship), 238, 249, 256

Ranger III (ferryboat), 46

Reformation (privateer ship), 143

Revenge (ship), 128, 129

Roanoke (steamboat), 16

HMS *Roebuck* (frigate), 206, 207, 208

Rude (hydrographic research ship), 27

S. R. Spaulding (steamboat), 9

St. Helen (pinnace), 131

St. Margaret (pinnace), 131, 132

St. Nicholas (steamboat), 12

Sarah and Elizabeth (ship), 134, 135

Saris (wooden steamship), 251

Scourge (schooner), 45, 46, 47

Shenandoah (tug), 238

Sonic Boom (dive boat), 71-72, 77, 80, 81, 82, 88, 90, 92, 93, 94, 95, 98

Speagle (ship), 143

Start (shallop), 128

Susquehanna (steamboat), 12

Talcott (dredge boat), 267

Thomas (ship), 136

Thomas A. Morgan (steamboat), 11

Thomas Kelso (steamboat), 12

Thunderhorse (dive boat), 147, 148, 151, 159

Titanic (ocean liner), 45, 53

Transil (steamboat), 15

Tuwetanka (wooden steamship), 335, 336

Utoka (wooden steamship), 231

Vigilante (workboat), 180

Virginia Lee. See Accomac

Voyageur II, 49

W. S. Childs (sturgeon skiff), 253

Warwick (ship), 199

Wasco (wooden steamship), 238, 241

Wonatabe (wooden steamship), 251, 308

Yakima (wooden steamship), 268

Virginia, at outset of Civil War, 3; prospects offered for colonial settlement in, 105; Claiborne's mission as surveyor in, 105; Opechancanough's uprising in, 106; Wyatt becomes first royal governor of, 107; Yeardley becomes governor of, 107; Yeardley gives Claiborne permission to explore, 108;

Potts authorizes Claiborne to trade in, 109; George Calvert's visit to, 111-12; Heath seeks territory of, 112; Claiborne's familiarity with Indian trade in, 112; Claiborne seeks to extend authority of to Kent Island, 113; Cloberry fails to secure patent in, 114; Martiau represents Kent Island in General Assembly, 119; Kent becomes a Virginia Hundred, 119; opposes Maryland charter, 124; to assist Lord Baltimore's colonists, 126; sovereignty over Kent Island upheld by Council, 126, 128; Claiborne barters with Indians in goods from, 127; Harvey fails to support sovereignty of over Kent Island, 129; Harvey ousted from, 131-32; West appointed governor of, 132; controls entrance to the Chesapeake, 132; Harvey reinstated as governor of, 135; declares Kent Island belongs to Maryland, 140; Indian uprising in, 141; Claiborne appointed general and chief commander of, 141; Berkeley favors sovereignty of over Kent Island, 142; Calvert flees to, 143; Parliament orders obedience to Commonwealth, 145; Bennett becomes governor of, 145; in Claiborne's last claim on Kent Island, 146; Dunmore's raid on, 207; fisheries legislation in, 210; smuggling in Civil War, 211; wooden steamship construction in, 223; Prohibition in, 225; Emergency Fleet moored in, 232; recommendations to sink Emergency Fleet off of, 242; fisheries commissioner intervenes in Widewater hulk burnings, 243-44; Representative Moore protests hulk burnings at Widewater, 248; wrecks inspected by army engineers, 267; service of *Accomac* in, 314; mentioned, 3, 8, 9, 10, 81, 104, 105, 113, 116, 118, 123, 124, 135, 144, 145, 154, 164, 188, 204, 205, 206, 209, 210, 211, 212, 225, 226, 233, 234, 235, 236, 237, 243, 246, 260, 262, 273, 283, 314, 335

Virginia Capes, 103, 119, 125, 128

Virginia Company of London, 105, 106, 107, 110, 112

Virginia Convention, 3

Virginia Ferry Company, 314

Virginia Shipbuilding Corporation, 235, 236

Volkmer, Eldon, 18, 19, 55, 68, 75

Vrana, Ken, 48, 49

Wade, Zachariah, 205

Walker, John, 138

War Finance Corporation, 232

War of 1812, 6, 45, 91, 203

War Production Board, 271, 174

Ward type steamship. *See* Grays Harbor type steamship

Warehouse Creek, Md., 169, 176

Warren, Lt. Radcliffe, 130, 131

Washington, 227, 231

Washington, D.C., 28, 68, 92, 103, 173, 205, 220, 224, 225, 235, 244, 254, 256, 259, 263, 268, 276, 281, 284, 299

Washington, George, 206

Washington Monument, Baltimore, 13

Wasserman, Mark, 99, 100

Index